Florida A&M University, Tallahassee
Florida Atlantic University, Boca Raton
Florida Gulf Coast University, Ft. Myers
Florida International University, Miami
Florida State University, Tallahassee
University of Central Florida, Orlando
University of Florida, Gainesville
University of North Florida, Jacksonville
University of South Florida, Tampa
University of West Florida, Pensacola

Gender and the Chivalric Community in Malory's *Morte d'Arthur*

Dorsey Armstrong

University Press of Florida
Gainesville · Tallahassee · Tampa · Boca Raton
Pensacola · Orlando · Miami · Jacksonville · Ft. Myers

08   07   06   05   04   03   6   5   4   3   2   1

Library of Congress Cataloging-in-Publication Data
Armstrong, Dorsey, 1970–
Gender and the chivalric community in Malory's Morte
d'Arthur/Dorsey Armstrong
p. cm.
Includes bibiographical references and index.
ISBN 0-8130-2686-5 (alk. paper)
1. Malory, Thomas, Sir, 15th cent. Morte d'Arthur.
2. Malory, Thomas, Sir, 15th cent.—Political and social views.
3. Literature and society—England—history—To 1500.
4. Arthurian romances—History and criticism. 5. Romances,
English—History and criticism. 6. Knights and knighthood in
literature. 7. Community in literature. 8. Sex roles in literature.
9. Chivalry in literature. I. Title.
PR2045.A76   2003
823'.2—dc22   2003061694

The University Press of Florida is the scholarly publishing
agency for the State University System of Florida, comprising
Florida A&M University, Florida Atlantic University, Florida
Gulf Coast University, Florida International University, Florida
State University, University of Central Florida, University of
Florida, University of North Florida, University of South
Florida, and University of West Florida.

University Press of Florida
15 Northwest 15th Street
Gainesville, FL 32611–2079
http://www.upf.com

Contents

Acknowledgments

I would like to thank the following people for their help in making this book a reality:

First and foremost, thanks go to David Aers whose support and encouragement are the foundation upon which this project is built. He and Sarah Beckwith enthusiastically offered constructive advice and criticism from the very beginning, providing much appreciated guidance and intellectual stimulation. Monica Green and Reynolds Price also were conscientious and supportive readers of this project in the early stages, and I thank them for their thoughtful critiques. Seth Lerer went far beyond the call of duty as an undergraduate advisor, remaining a mentor and friend throughout my graduate school days and beyond; I am grateful for his insight and suggestions. Karen Cherewatuk and Laurie Finke were generous readers in the later stages of my work, and their suggestions and advice strengthened, sharpened, and improved my argument. Amy Gorelick at the University Press of Florida helped guide this book to publication; I deeply appreciate her hard work, support, and friendship.

Friends and colleagues have helped make the long process of writing enjoyable, and I would like to thank the following for their unflagging enthusiasm and good cheer: Dee Abrahamse, Jeremy Adams, Libby Azevedo, Glenn Bach, Jean Blacker, Elyse Blankley, Susan Carlile, Tim Caron, Kate Crassons, Tyler Dilts, Maureen Ettinger, Frank Fata, Bill Fitzhenry, John Flaa and Amy Mendoza Flaa, Jo Goyne, Suzanne Greenberg, Liz Griff and John Hilgart, Chris Grooms, Mimi Hotchkiss, Cliff Jones and Erin Sullivan, Lloyd Kermode, Eileen Klink, Lezlie Knox, Beth Lau, Paulino Lim, Katie Little, Rebekah Long, Jessica Moen, Michael Murphy, Julie Paulson, Doris Pintscher, Joe Potts, Sharon Robinson, Marty Shichtman, Christopher Snyder, Martine Van Elk, Fred Wegener, and of course, the incomparable Bonnie Wheeler.

I owe a special debt of gratitude to the Circulation and Interlibrary Loan staff at California State University, Long Beach, where much of this book was written. Dian Olsen, Gilbert Parra, Alex Rambo, and Leslie Swigart dealt with my many requests on a daily basis for several months and always managed to be cheerful about it.

Some parts of this book have previously appeared elsewhere, and I would like to thank those who have given their kind permission to reprint that material here. Portions of chapter 1 have been published as "Gender and the Chivalric Community: The Pentecostal Oath in Malory's 'Tale of King Arthur,'" *Bibliographical Bulletin of the International Arthurian Society* 51 (1999): 293–312, and "Malory's Morgause," in *On Arthurian Women: Essays in Honor of Maureen Fries,* edited by Bonnie Wheeler and Fiona Tolhurst (Dallas: Scriptorium Press, 2001), 149–60. A portion of chapter 2 has appeared in substantially different form as "Gender and Fear: Malory's Lancelot and Knightly Identity," in *Arizona Studies in the Middle Ages and the Renaissance, 6: Fear and Its Representations in the Middle Ages and the Renaissance,* edited by Anne Scott and Cynthia Kosso (Turnhout, Belgium: Brepols, 2002), 255–73. Unless otherwise noted, all translations of the French Lancelot-Grail are copyright 1993–1996 from the five-volume *Lancelot-Grail: The Old French Arthurian Vulgate and Post-Vulgate in Translation,* edited by Norris Lacy. Reproduced by permission of Routledge, Inc., part of The Taylor and Francis Group.

I am grateful to my family for their continuous love and support: Charles and Susan Armstrong; Katherine Armstrong and Mark Hochstetler; Chuck Armstrong (the younger); Vivian Yunker; Paul and Jan Schneider; Martye Armstrong; Scott, Lora, and Sara Davis; Molly Whiles and Betsy LaFuze.

Finally, an extra-large thanks to my husband, Ryan Schneider, whose love and patience made everything possible: this is for you.

Introduction

This book examines the function of gender in Sir Thomas Malory's *Morte d'Arthur*, arguing that an understanding of the particular construction of gender in Malory's text is critical to any attempt to engage with its narrative project. Like many other medieval romance texts, the *Morte d'Arthur* focuses on the masculine activity of chivalry—fighting, questing, ruling— while simultaneously revealing the chivalric enterprise as impossible without the presence of the feminine in a subjugated position. However, Malory's text differs from other Arthurian and medieval romance literature in the explicit legislation (as opposed to implicit coding) of chivalric values, most notably in the swearing of the Pentecostal Oath, an event unique to Malory's text. This study examines how the institution of the Oath defines and sharpens specific ideals of masculine and feminine gender identities in the Arthurian community, arguing that a compulsion to fulfill these ideals drives the narrative of the *Morte d'Arthur* forward to its inevitable ending. While I generally agree with scholars who see the *Morte d'Arthur* as, at least in part, a comment on the strife and instability of fifteenth-century England, I feel also that the *Morte* is a text that does much more than simply reflect and engage the anxieties of the author's time by turning nostalgically to a long-distant past for guidance and reassurance. Malory's text examines the very idea of chivalry by setting into motion the knightly enterprise and following it through to its ultimate conclusion.

A sustained, book-length treatment of gender in the *Morte d'Arthur* is long overdue; while the works of other medieval authors—most notably Chaucer—have in recent years been subjected to rigorous and fruitful scrutiny by scholars with an interest in gender and feminist studies,[1] the *Morte d'Arthur* has received comparatively cursory attention in this area. In part, this may be due to what some scholars view as Malory's "de-feminization" of his source material. Terence McCarthy argues that Malory's text is "essentially military" in spirit, and that while "in the French texts we will find long soliloquies and analyses of private feeling . . . their absence from the *Morte Darthur* is of vital importance. . . . the interest in love and amorous reputations is dispensed with by Malory, and the difference is considerable. . . . On the other hand there is always time for combat and war."[2] Similarly, Andrew Lynch (who himself has offered some very fine analyses of gender in Malory), has recently privileged a reading of the text as concerned with martial activities, suggesting that "the role of Malory's women can often be interestingly understood through their implication in the language of knightly combat."[3]

My position is somewhat the inverse of Lynch's: I contend that knightly combat and its language are, in a sense, produced and given meaning by Malory's women, or, to put it more precisely, *by the text's understanding and construction of women.* Critics like McCarthy quite rightly point to Malory's excision—or "stripping away"—of moments in his sources concerned with expressions of emotion and love; yet, such a move—even as it reveals a favoring of the public over the private, a privileging of exterior actions over interior feeling—does not diminish the significance of the issue of gender and construction of the feminine in the text. Indeed, if Catherine LaFarge is correct and in Malory "the feminine is located as both the inner and the utterly outside . . . [and] . . . the masculine and the feminine, the public and the private, [exist] in a new and uneasy tension,"[4] then an analysis of gender in Malory is vital to lay bare the structure and workings of the narrative.

While there has recently been a long-awaited and long-overdue increase of insightful articles that address the issue of gender in Malory,[5] I contend that gender issues "pressure" the *Morte d'Arthur* differently at different moments in the narrative, so that the relationship of gender to the other ideals of chivalry expressed in Malory's text must be studied as a force that develops and changes as the story progresses. Thus, the function of gender in the *Morte d'Arthur* can only be adequately explored in a book that traces in depth the development of gender constraints from the beginning of the "Tale of King Arthur" to the "Day of Destiny" and its aftermath.[6]

One reason the *Morte d'Arthur* merits a sustained study in terms of gender is due to its status as the most comprehensive and sustained medieval treatment of the Arthurian legend by a single author.[7] Starting with the Arthurian prehistory of Uther and Igrayne, Malory traces the progression of the chivalric community from Arthur's ascension to the throne and consolidation of power through to the ultimate destruction of the Round Table and the collapse of the kingdom.[8] Malory by and large successfully maintains a linear temporal progression toward a definitive end point and marshalls his sources to conform to the movement of the narrative. This fact makes Malory's text utterly unique in the canon of medieval Arthurian literature. Although it draws heavily on the French Vulgate and Post-Vulgate Arthurian texts for source material, the *Morte d'Arthur* is more focused and unified than this sprawling collection (now more commonly referred to collectively as the *Lancelot-Graal*), the sections of which were composed by a variety of authors over many years. It is likewise more comprehensive and broad in its scope than the shorter Arthurian romances (such as those of Chrétien de Troyes, Marie de France, and the anonymous *Sir Gawain and the Green Knight*), many of which focus on a single episode, adventure, or event, cut loose and extracted from the larger story of the rise and fall of Arthur's kingdom. It differs also from somewhat longer works that contain several episodes, such as the *Alliterative Morte Arthure*; in the *Morte d'Arthur*, Malory rewrites and incorporates the events of the *Alliterative Morte Arthure* into a narrative that is far larger in its vision of Arthur's reign. Micheau Gonnot's compilation of Arthurian texts for the Duke of Nemours, completed in 1470 (BN MS f.fr 112), is the closest analogue to Malory's text in terms of subject, scope, and period of composition, but Gonnot understands himself as a compiler, assembling the writings of others, while Malory, I believe, sees himself as reworking the same sources used by Gonnot to make something new.[9] In short, there is nothing else like Malory in all of medieval Arthurian literature.

Although unique, it must be acknowledged that the *Morte d'Arthur* is not at all an "original" work in the modern sense. Malory draws on a variety of sources—both French and English—in creating his account of the rise and fall of Arthur's kingdom, and does not hesitate to argue for the "historical veracity" of many episodes by telling the reader on several occasions that he is faithfully conveying information from his sources—"the Freynsh booke makyth mencion" (253.14);[10] "the Freynsshe booke seyth" (1217.12–13)—or that he is unable to relate certain details because he has lost a source text, or his sources are silent on particular matters—"And bycause I have loste the very mater of Shevalere de Chayrot I departe from the tale of sir Launcelot" (1154.12–13). While Malory often closely paraphrases or, on some occasions even almost directly translates his sources into fifteenth-century English (the Roman War and Grail Quest episodes being the two most-cited examples), he also makes important additions and revisions to the source material. What he chooses to omit from his sources seems in some instances more significant than what he chooses to retain, and *where* in the narrative of the *Morte d'Arthur* he chooses to include certain episodes found in his sources is frequently more notable than the fact that he chooses to include those episodes at all.

Much attention has been paid to those moments in Malory for which there is no known source: for example, the Pentecostal Oath appears to be original to Malory, and a clear source for the "Tale of Sir Gareth" has yet to be unearthed.[11] Malory "unlaces" the complex *entrelacement* of the French Vulgate, moving the episode of the "Knight of the Cart" to a much later position in his own text than would be in keeping with the source. He also radically rewrites the ending of another source text—the *Alliterative Morte Arthure*—in telling the story of Arthur's Roman War. While it is right to examine these "original" moments for what they might tell us about Malory's conception of the Arthurian legend, it is wrong to dismiss whole sections—as Eugène Vinaver does the Grail Quest—as being "for all intents and purposes, a mere translation."[12] As McCarthy has put it: "Our critical assessment must cover the 'hoole book,' as Malory called it, must take into account the overall impact of a literary recreation for which he is entirely responsible, however little he invented himself."[13]

Malory has made a "new thing" in his massive opus. Thus, while I will engage with and analyze certain episodes that faithfully follow the source text from which Malory drew them, this does not render these episodes any less significant in terms of the *Morte d'Arthur*'s chivalric narrative project or the question of gender. For example, Morgan le Fay (whom I discuss at greater length in chapter 1) is more or less the same hateful figure in the thirteenth-century *Suite du Merlin* as she is in Malory's account of the early days of Arthur's kingdom; yet, her destructive actions resonate differently when placed in the context of Malory's *Morte d'Arthur*. The Morgan of the French text resists her prescribed gender role just as I claim she does in Malory, but the significance of her actions in Malory has a different effect when considered in light of the overarching plot. The Morgan of the *Suite* does not live in a world where knights swear annually to follow the rules set out in the Pentecostal Oath; the Morgan of the *Suite* does not have quite the long career of mischief-making ahead of her that Malory's Morgan does; and the Morgan of the *Suite* will never make a final appearance in a positive and supporting role to carry her wounded brother away to Avalon to be healed: "A, my dere brothir! Why have ye taryed so longe frome me? Alas, thys wounde on youre hede have caught overmuch colde!" (1240.23–25).[14]

While my discussion and analysis of Malory does take into account the historical circumstances in which the *Morte d'Arthur* was composed and the tradition of Arthurian and romance literature from which it derives, the primary goal of this study is not to "ground" Malory in terms of the social, political, and literary realities and conventions of his day.[15] Although I may engage with and use such analyses on several occasions, I am not attempting to excavate historically "real" gender roles and identities in the present study.[16] I agree that in many ways, Malory's text may be read as a reaction to the turbulent fifteenth century and the so-called Wars of the Roses that so affected English society, particularly the knightly class of which Malory was a member. I would hardly be the first person to note the irony of the fact that it is while imprisoned for most unknightlike behavior—including rape, assaulting an abbot, and cattle-stealing—that Malory composes a massive text seemingly dedicated to the glorification of chivalry and knighthood.[17]

While England had enjoyed considerable success in its campaigns into France in the fourteenth century, by Malory's lifetime[18] England had lost all its holdings in France save Calais, and internally the civil Wars of the Roses had created multiple conflicts that affected all areas and levels of English society.[19] For a variety of reasons, including the massive plague-induced depopulation of the mid-fourteenth century, the rise of vernacular literacy, and the development of a precapitalist market economy—marked not only by trade in items such as wool and cloth among large cities but also by an increase in commodity production among peasant communities—fifteenth-century English society was arguably far less rigidly stratified than its neighbors on the Continent.[20] Traditional medieval concepts of hierarchical class structure and social order were undergoing transformation in this period.[21] A series of events over approximately 150 years had contributed to make Malory's England a time and place of social fluidity. It was a time in which it was possible for the daughter of a minor baron, Elizabeth Woodville, to become queen and thereby ennoble her parents, siblings, and children from a previous marriage; in this period, it was possible also for a common family like the Pastons—through a combination of skill in the legal profession and advantageous marriage—to acquire land and wealth on a scale comparable with their noble neighbors, eventually advancing up the social ladder to knighthood itself.[22]

It would seem no small coincidence that in this period of social mobility and uncertainty, Malory would produce a massive text concerned with the office of knighthood, which was itself suffering from the pressures of the age. As Felicity Riddy has rightly noted: "Nor is it a coincidence that among the many texts contributing to the nobility debate in the late fifteenth and early sixteenth centuries, Malory's should be a romance, and not a treatise, a debate, or even an interlude. The myth of class is now appropriately expressed only in a fiction that seems to play with its own fictionality."[23] Indeed, the *Morte d'Arthur* is a story about knights who themselves engage in perpetual storytelling as a means to define and legitimize the office of knighthood and the chivalric community that supports it. By Malory's lifetime and the period in which he composed the *Morte d'Arthur*—roughly between 1468 and 1470—both the practical and idealized aspects of knighthood had been compromised.[24] This was due in part to the steady development of advances in warfare from the late thirteenth century on—the increased use of archers, guns, and other long-distance artillery—which rendered the armored knight on horseback inessential and obsolete. Yet, there remained in existence a knightly warrior class, and those men who called themselves "knights"[25] often resorted to banditry and thieving as a means of support, or engaged (for profit) in the so-called private wars that so marked aristocratic society during this period.[26] Richard Kaeuper has remarked of the fifteenth century that "one of the greatest threats to the peace of the realm came from the day to day conduct of the knightly classes whose violent self-help was often proudly proclaimed and recognized as a right rather than condemned as a crime."[27] The throne of fifteenth-century England changed hands eight times (rarely peacefully),[28] and the frequency of violent successions necessarily compounded those pressures already attendant on knights and nobles faced with the difficulty of negotiating loyalties within a complex and changing system of loyalty and service.[29]

Malory belonged to this knightly class and was himself one of those men who seemed to have difficulty negotiating loyalties. The author of the *Morte d'Arthur* spent the last years of his life in prison, either for his politics or for what seems to have been general lawlessness. Most certainly, he was one of a group of men who ambushed the Duke of Buckingham—his former patron—on a winter's night in 1450. In all likelihood, his political activities and the charges brought against him were at least partially connected; it seems that Malory had initially been a Yorkist supporter, but by 1468 he appears to have changed sides, and in that year was sent to prison for his role in a Lancastrian plot. Remarkably, it is while imprisoned for such very unknightlike behavior that Malory composes his *Morte d'Arthur*, a text that many read as celebrating the knightly chivalric ethos. Yet, such a reading is overly simplistic, for, as Elizabeth Pochoda has noted, the *Morte d'Arthur* enacts "a peculiar tension between . . . Malory's faith in chivalry as a world-saving ideal . . . and the fact that the book also damns chivalry in no uncertain terms."[30] Indeed, the *Morte d'Arthur* seems to be a text that is *both* nostalgic and cautionary. How it is able to be both at once, and how gender concerns participate in this conflict, is one of the main subjects of this book.

. What I think is most interesting and important about Malory's text (and what other critics have failed to recognize adequately) is that he reacts to the trouble of his day by creating a code of conduct—the Pentecostal Oath. By adding this ritual of explicit oath-taking to the beginning of the story of Arthur's reign, Malory effectively sets a series of chivalric guidelines into action; the rest of the narrative tests those chivalric rules, attempting to see how (and if) they function successfully in a variety of circumstances. One of what might be called the "unintentional side effects" of this code of conduct is the formation of a particular gender ideal. A compulsion to fulfill this ideal drives the narrative toward its inevitable conclusion, and the tensions created by the legislation of chivalric behavior and identity are increasingly exacerbated as the text progresses.

In interrogating the function of gender in Malory, I make use of the work of gender theorists such as Judith Butler, Luce Irigiray, and Eve Sedgwick; however, my analysis is not "theory-driven." Rather, I use the work of these and other critics as tools with which to excavate and better analyze forces and drives that are identifiably present in the text *before* any such approach is applied. In other words, the goal of this book is to analyze how gender functions to produce the movement of the narrative toward its unavoidable tragic ending and to discuss how Malory's version of the Arthurian legend is thereby unique in the canon of medieval Arthurian literature. I am not arguing that Malory deliberately set out to represent a particular ideal of gender relations and identity in the *Morte d'Arthur*. Rather, what I am suggesting is that in representing the idealized noble community of Arthur's court, Malory's narrative unintentionally produces and depends upon a certain model of gender identity that not only creates much of the narrative action but also heightens the significance and impact of many episodes and events drawn from his source material. With this in mind, I would like now to offer an exemplary reading that I think demonstrates my methodology and goals in engaging with how the question of gender informs Malory's depiction of the Arthurian community. An analysis of Malory's Roman War reveals that even in the most masculine of spaces—the battlefield—gender concerns over masculine *and* feminine identities produce, mediate, and give meaning to the events of the narrative.

Malory's Roman War

The account of Arthur's war against the Roman Emperor Lucius (Vinaver's Tale II) is one of the most interesting portions of Malory's *Morte d'Arthur:* while vastly understudied relative to other sections of the text, what critical response it *has* received has been remarkably mixed. Part of what gives the debate over Malory's account of Arthur's continental campaign its shape is that the account exists in two very different forms: that found in the Winchester manuscript, and a much abbreviated version, as printed by William Caxton.[31] The very fact of Caxton's seemingly deliberate and ruthless reduction of the text has long been viewed as an implicit critique of what most scholars agree is a "rough prosification"[32] of Malory's direct source, the Middle English *Alliterative Morte Arthure*, composed in the early part of the fifteenth century.[33]

It has become a commonplace in Malory studies to point out that Malory's adaptation of the *Alliterative Morte Arthure* maintains much of the alliteration found in his source. C. S. Lewis famously noted that Caxton's revision made this tale "more Malorian, more like the best and most typical parts of Malory."[34] McCarthy, who has argued for a reconsideration of Malory's story of Arthur and Lucius as an important element in the *Morte d'Arthur's* overall narrative, notes that Tale II "is not a book with occasional stylistic blemishes; it is, as it were, all blemish."[35] It is due to the "closeness" of Malory's Tale II to its source and its "rough" and "unfinished" quality that several scholars contend that Malory most likely composed this portion of the *Morte d'Arthur* first; it seems to show him in the early stages of his project, not yet fully comfortable as an adapter or translator.

I disagree with such an assessment; I think Malory had a clear idea of his project from beginning to end, and that he saw the Roman War as following directly on the heels of the events that take place in the "Tale of King Arthur." Its deliberate placement in his text—as the second narrative block—is critically important to my argument about how gender works in the *Morte d'Arthur*. However, I choose to engage with this episode first—here in the introduction—because I think it provides the clearest example of how Malory's alterations to his sources produce remarkable effects, especially in terms of gender. It is precisely the fact that Malory has *seemingly* done so little in adapting the *Alliterative Morte Arthure* that makes it a compelling site to stage an exemplary reading of his larger text in terms of gender. Although Malory has made some small but significant changes to the account of the Roman War, the way in which he has *framed* this episode is most important for understanding the different valence that the concerns of gender have in the *Morte d'Arthur*. In effect, a critical analysis of Malory's Roman War—and in particular, the episode of the Mont St. Michel giant contained within it—reveals how and why the issue of gender informs and structures the whole *Morte d'Arthur*.

The ultimate source of the story of Arthur's Roman War is Geoffrey of Monmouth's twelfth-century Latin chronicle, the *Historia Regum Brittaniae*, completed in 1136 or 1138.[36] Less than twenty years after the completion of Geoffrey's text, the *Historia* was translated into French octosyllabic couplets by the "clerc lisant" known as Wace, and in the early thirteenth century, the English priest known to us variously as "Laʒamon," "Lawman," or "Layamon" translated Wace into an "archaicizing" English that seems to hearken back to an Anglo-Saxon past in both its form (the alliterative line, although rhymed couplets are also used) and its sympathies. In the late fourteenth or early fifteenth century, the account of Arthur's continental campaign was adapted and expanded by the anonymous author of the *Alliterative Morte Arthure*.[37]

Malory's *Morte d'Arthur* is quite different from these other texts—not so much in the specific concerns that it represents, but more important, in the *way* it represents those concerns. The distinction of the *Morte d'Arthur* from these other texts lies in its status as a romance—not a chronicle or history.[38] Although Malory's text arguably deploys several other modes—including epic, chronicle, and tragedy—the *Morte d'Arthur*'s predominant mode is romance.[39] The "romance coloring" of Tale II is partially effected through the undeniable generic status of the narratives that frame the "Tale of Arthur and the Emperor Lucius." The "Tale of King Arthur" and the "Noble Tale of Sir Launcelot du Lake" are both reworkings of Old French romances.[40] Although he has preserved many of the important episodes that occur in earlier accounts of Arthur's continental campaign, Malory has changed the tenor and the interpretive mode in which one reads the conflict between Arthur and Lucius. By relocating this event early in Arthur's career, by recasting it as an unmitigated success, and by framing the Roman War with two romances, Malory has greatly changed the significance of this episode. In earlier texts, the Roman War usually stands as both crowning achievement and final catastrophe for Arthur, an event that colors the whole of his reign.[41] In Malory, it stands as the high point of Arthur's career as an individual player on the field of chivalry, and seemingly makes possible the marvelous adventures that will be performed by Arthur's knightly agents in the episodes that follow. Although Malory is working with a long-famous and well-known story, his placement of it within his larger narrative creates a new effect and significance.

Although Malory appears to have had a clear idea of the tragic ending of his text, the consequence of his decision to rewrite the *Alliterative Morte Arthure* and make Arthur's continental campaign an unqualified success cannot be overstated. This campaign comes not long after Arthur's creation of the Round Table order and its Pentecostal Oath and shows chivalric ideals functioning at highest efficiency. It also offers for Malory's readers an alternative fantasy to the reality of fifteenth-century English geography, one in which those lands lost to the French during the Hundred Years War still belong to England, and English dominion expands to include most of continental Europe. Felicity Riddy and Patricia Clare Ingham have both recently discussed how Malory's text (and in particular, the Roman War episode) seem to reflect a general longing in fifteenth-century English society for a golden age—or at the very least, for the days of Henry V's glorious victory at Agincourt.[42] This fantasy of English dominance, as Riddy has so aptly put it, is in Malory's day best expressed in a romance.

In writing the complete story of Arthur's reign but writing it primarily from the romance as opposed to chronicle tradition, Malory's Roman War and the episodes it contains take on a new valence. Each of the earlier texts contain the well-known story of the giant of Mont St. Michel's abduction and/or rape of the Duchess of Brittany embedded within the larger narrative of Arthur's military exploits on the Continent. Although the basic elements of this episode are more or less consistent in all of these texts, Malory's particular treatment of this narreme enacts a construction, understanding, and function of gender and its relationship to communal order that differs substantially from that depicted in the sources and analogues.

The main elements of the episode vary only slightly from text to text and run roughly as follows: Some time after his coronation, ambassadors from Rome arrive at Arthur's court and demand that Britain pay tribute to Rome. After some debate, Arthur decides that instead, he will conquer Rome and incorporate it into his kingdom. Shortly after the arrival of his army on the Continent, Arthur receives word that a giant who has been troubling the people of the land has kidnapped the daughter/niece of his kinsman Hoel and absconded with her to Mont St. Michel. Arthur, usually accompanied by Kay and Bedivere, sets out to avenge this injustice, but arrives too late: the duchess has died, leaving behind her old nursemaid to lament her. Arthur then kills the giant, exacting vengeance for the duchess and freeing his continental subjects from the fiend who has been plaguing them.

In each version of this story—from Geoffrey of Monmouth to Malory—the episode of the giant's abduction and rape of the Duchess of Brittany plays an important role in producing the overall effect of the text, especially in terms of the issues of gender and community. The immediate effect of the encounter with the giant is to depict and explore concerns over boundaries and the integrity of bodies—both individual and political. Arthur's voyage across the channel is a drama in which lands that are identified as foreign are able to be conquered and thus incorporated into his own kingdom; the alien threat from the outside is subdued and remade into that which is inside. The giant represents the utterly outside—the alien and unknown. Never able to be fully translated or incorporated into that which is known, he must be destroyed.

In all of the versions of the Mont St. Michel episode, the abduction of the duchess, her rape, and Arthur's killing of the giant help to define the king as a masculine agent of justice, prefiguring and in some sense validating his victory over the Roman Emperor Lucius. Kathryn Gravdal has famously discussed rape as an important narrative device of many medieval texts, particularly romance texts, noting that "Sexual violence is built into the very premise of Arthurian romance. It is a genre that by its definition must *create* the threat of rape" (emphasis in original).[43] In their compelling comparative discussion of the Mont St. Michel giant in both Wace and Laȝamon, Martin Shichtman and Laurie Finke engage with Gravdal's theory of rape in medieval literature. Situating their reading of these accounts of rape in the sociopolitical climate in which the texts were composed, they argue that the episode of the Mont St. Michel giant "coalesces several anxieties about the maintenance of boundaries during times when they are being redrawn in potentially disturbing ways" and that the enactment of this scene is an attempt "to shore up the boundaries between those born to wealth and those born to poverty, between those trained to fight and those who are not, and, most significantly, between the familiar and the foreign."[44]

Jeffrey Jerome Cohen similarly discusses how the figure of the giant in Middle English literature is traditionally the site of such boundary anxieties, but is also contradictorily the place in which such anxieties are also reassuringly expressed and contained: "Throughout his long history in the England of the Middle Ages, the giant conjoined absolute otherness with reassuring familiarity."[45] Focusing primarily on Geoffrey of Monmouth's account of the Mont St. Michel giant, Cohen argues that concerns of gender, community, and individual masculine identity are brought together in this scene in important ways, noting that "the defeat of the giant is a social fantasy of the triumph of corporeal order (in all of its various meanings) written as a personal drama, a vindication of the tight channeling of multiple somatic drives into a socially beneficial expression of masculinity."[46]

Interestingly, Cohen (in his discussion of Geoffrey), and Finke and Shichtman (in their discussion of Wace and Laȝamon), all borrow the idea of the *point de capiton* from Slavoj Žižek to interrogate the episode of the rape. Finke and Shichtman argue that the giant's rape of Elaine "serves as a nodal point (*point de capiton*) that 'quilts' together networks of ideological relations these histories were designed to produce, while itself producing a certain excess . . . that exceeds the rape's ideological and structural function."[47] Cohen suggests that "the heroic name of Arthur in Geoffrey of Monmouth's text becomes a *point de capiton*, a 'quilting point' where the contradictions that inevitably undergird any subject, any ideology, are temporarily allayed by finding embodiment in a 'rigid' signifier. Arthur is autonomous, his will and his desires are efficacious, but at the same time, his identity is radically contingent on his place in the community. . . . Arthur sutures a set of free-floating and potentially contradictory signifiers (community, hero, monster, empire) into a coherent meaningful narrative."[48]

I find these critics' use of Žižek's theorization of a *point de capiton*—in which "the multitude of 'floating signifiers' . . . is structured into a unified field through the intervention of a certain 'nodal point' . . . which 'quilts' them . . . and fixes their meaning"—significant and instructive.[49] I would like to argue that it is precisely the function of this episode as a "quilting point"—a place in which so many seemingly disparate concerns are brought together in significant relational tension with one another—that makes it an exemplary site to discuss the imbrication of gender with all aspects of Malory's chivalric community. Indeed, it seems that in comparison with these early chronicle accounts and with his immediate source, the *Alliterative Morte Arthure*, Malory's treatment of the episode of the giant of Mont St. Michel "quilts" together the concerns of gender, community, individual identity, and kingship by means of tighter and more elaborate stitching (as it were) than any of the antecedent texts. While Finke and Shichtman point to the episode of the rape as the important "nodal point" in the quilting of concerns of gender and empire, and Cohen sees the figure of Arthur as the *point de capiton*, I would like to suggest that in Malory, it is neither Arthur nor the episode of the giant itself that functions to produce meaning; rather, the figure of Guenevere—absent from all earlier accounts—suddenly appears to bind together the threads that trail off from either end of the Roman War. The figure of the queen stitches the issues of gender, community, power, and rule—those that coalesce in the continental campaign—to the rest of the *Morte d'Arthur*.

It is interesting to note that among all the texts that treat the story of the giant of Mont St. Michel, the greatest changes to this episode are made not by Malory but by the author of the *Alliterative Morte Arthure*. In Geoffrey, Wace, and Laȝamon, Arthur sets out to avenge the abduction of the duchess—here described as either the daughter (Laȝamon) or niece (Geoffrey, Wace) of Arthur's kinsman Hoel—accompanied by Kay and Bedivere. Arthur sends Bedivere ahead to scout out the situation, and it is he who encounters the old woman—the duchess's nursemaid—in these three early versions. Her account of what has happened to her mistress is similar in all of these accounts. In Geoffrey's text the nurse relates that after her abduction but before she is actually violated, the Duchess of Brittany dies:

> serenissima alumpna recepto infra tenerrimum pectus timore dum eam nefandus ille amplecteretur uitam diutuniori luce dignam finuit. Ut igitur illam que erat michi alter spiritus, altera uita, altera dulcedo iocunditatis fedo coitu suo detur pare nequiuit, destanda venere succensus michi inuite . . . uim et uilentiam ingessit.

> [when this foul being took her in his arms, fear flooded her tender breast and so ended a life which was worthy of a longer span. Since he was unable to befoul with his filthy lust this child . . . in the madness of his bestial desire he raped me, against my will.][50]

Wace, following Geoffrey, tells us that

> La pucele volt purgesir
> Mais tendre fu, nel pout suffrir
> Trop fu ahueges, trop fu granz
> Trop laiz, trop gros e trop pesanz
> L'aume li fist del cors partir
> Nel pout Eleine sustenir.
>   (11407–12)

[The giant wanted to have sex with the maiden, but she was so tender she could not endure him. He was too large, much too big, too ugly, too huge and too heavy, so that her soul fled from her body; Elaine could not endure it.][51]

Although Wace suggests that the maiden is perhaps crushed under the weight of the giant, the text is ambiguous enough to suggest that Elaine dies prior to any sexual violation. Laȝamon goes a bit beyond Wace; in his *Brut* the old woman tells Bedivere that

> "Sone swa he hider com swa he þat maide inom
> he wolde mon-radene habben wið pan maidene
> Ælde næfde heo na mare buten fihtene ȝere
> ne mihte þat maiden his mone I-þolien
> anan swa he lai hire mide hire lif heo losede sone."
>   (12931–35)

["As soon as he came here, [the giant] grabbed hold of that virgin / He wanted to have intercourse with the innocent girl / She wasn't any older than a mere fifteen years / And being a virgin she couldn't endure his intimacy / The moment he laid her she lost her life immediately."][52]

Laȝamon's version of the story suggests that the duchess dies *because* of rape, not just from *fear of* rape, although graphic details are not given.

It is the author of the *Alliterative Morte Arthure* who makes of the giant a most horrific monster and who renders this sexual violation in the most unambiguous and disturbing terms. There can be no doubt as to how the duchess meets her end in the *Alliterative Morte Arthure:* "He has forsede hir and fylede, and cho es fay leuede / He slewe hir vnslely and slitt

hir to þe nauyll" (978–79).[53] Not only has the giant killed the duchess with
his grossly exaggerated phallus, but he engages in other socially transgressive and horrifying activities as well: when Arthur comes upon the giant in
the *Alliterative Morte Arthure*, the monster is about to partake of a most
gruesome feast. In earlier texts it is goats or sheep that he is eating, but
here we are told of a "Cowle full cramede of crysmed childyre / Sum as
brede brochede, and bierdez þam tournede" (1051–52). The cannibalism of
the giant is mentioned briefly in Geoffrey's *Historia*—"It made no difference whether they attacked him by sea or by land, for he either sank their
ships with huge rocks or else killed them with a variety of weapons. Those
whom he captured, and they were quite a few, he ate while they were still
half alive"[54]—but explicit mention of this gustatory habit of the giant's
disappears from Wace and Laȝamon; the *Alliterative Morte Arthure* author, however, rewrites the giant's cannibalism to make him not just a
threat to those who attempt to attack the giant but a particularly gruesome
danger for the citizens of the land:

> Here es a teraunt besyde that tourmentez thi pople,
> A grett geaunte of Geen, engenderde of fendez;
> He has fretyn of folke mo than fyfe hondrethe,
> And als fele fawntekyns of freeborne childyre.
> This has bene his sustynaunce all this seuen wyntteres,
> And ȝitt es that sotte noghte sadde, so wele hym it lykez!
> In þe contrée of Constantyne ne kynde has he leuede,
> Withowttyn kydd castells enclosid wyth walles,
> That he ne has clenly dystroyede all the knaue childyre,
> And them caryede to þe cragge and clenly dewortyd!
>   (842–51)

Indeed, in the *Alliterative Morte Arthure*, the giant poses a threat to the
very existence of the community, as his consuming of the freeborn "knaue
childyre" for seven winters running compromises the ability of the community to sustain itself genealogically.[55]

Just as he has amplified the horrific qualities of the giant, the author of
the *Alliterative Morte Arthure* augments Arthur's active participation in
the killing of the giant. Although Arthur deals the giant his death blow in
every version, in the earlier texts it is Bedivere who goes ahead as a scout,
and who first encounters the duchess's nursemaid lamenting her charge's
death. In the *Alliterative Morte Arthure*, Arthur instructs Kay and
Bedivere:

For to byde with theire blonkez and bown no fortheyre;
"For I will seke this seynte by my selfe one,
And mell with this mayster mane þat this monte ȝemez;
And seyn sall ȝe offer, aythyre aftyre oþer
Menskfully at Saynt Mighell, full myghtty with Criste."
    (936–40)

The enhanced threat of the giant in this text is met by a heroic figure who himself has been enhanced, both in terms of his direct participation in the action and the severity of his retribution: this adventure is wholly Arthur's, from beginning to end, and while in earlier versions of this episode the giant is decapitated as a symbol of castration, the *Alliterative Morte Arthure* makes the figurative literal: "Ewyn into inmette the gyaunt he hyttez / Iust to þe genitales and jaggede þam in sondre" (1122–23).

When compared to the *Alliterative Morte Arthure*, we see that Malory has followed the episode faithfully in all but what would seem to be a few minor details. The violation of the duchess is described in similarly graphic terms ("he hath murthered that mylde withoute ony mercy; he forced hir by fylth of hymself, and so aftir slytte hir unto the navyll" [201.3–5]); the giant is about to partake of a comparable feast when Arthur encounters him ("and three damesels turned three brochis, and thereon was twelve chyldir but late borne, and they were broched in maner lyke birdis" [202.11–13]); and Arthur castrates his enemy before dealing the death blow ("but the kynge shuntys a lytyll and rechis hym a dynte hyghe uppon the haunche, and there he swappis his genytrottys in sondir" [203.6–8]).

It might seem, then, that the episode of the giant of Mont St. Michel is most ripe for interpretation in terms of gender as it is represented in the *Alliterative Morte Arthure*, rather than in Malory. The *Alliterative Morte Arthure* seems by far the most interesting text in terms of the revisions and enhancements made to the basic narreme, and the question of violation of boundaries—both corporeal and political—comes to the fore more insistently than in the earlier texts. However, Malory makes two very slight changes to this episode that become hugely important for understanding how gender functions in the *Morte d'Arthur* as a whole. Taken on their own, they may not seem highly significant, but it is these moments original to Malory—when considered in terms of their larger narrative context—that make the *Morte d'Arthur* so interesting in terms of gender.

In all of these earlier texts, the duchess's nursemaid warns Bedivere or Arthur against facing the giant, but in Malory, her speech includes something new:

> "But and thou have brought Arthurs wyff, dame Gwenyvere, he woll be more blyther of hir than thou haddyste geffyn hym halfendele Fraunce. And but yf thou have brought hir, prese hym nat to nyghe. Loke what he hath done unto fyftene kynges: he hath made hym a coote full of precious stonys, and the cordoures thereof is the berdis of fyftene kynges. . . . And for Arthurs wyffe he lodgys hym here, for he hath more tresoure than ever had Arthure or ony of his elderes." (201.10–22)

While several of the earlier versions include mention of the giant's coat of beards, none of them make mention of Queen Guenevere; in Malory, then, the giant poses a threat not only to Arthur's subjects—both in the abduction of their women and the consumption of their boys—but also personally threatens *the king*. Arthur's marriage to Guenevere is the founding relationship of the Arthurian community; with his marriage to her he receives the Round Table and the hundred knights who currently "comprise" it. More important, his marriage to Guenevere identifies him as heteronormative, a fit masculine figure to head a homosocial community of knights. It seems highly significant that on the eve of his military conflict against the Roman Emperor, Arthur goes to meet a grossly exaggerated male enemy in single combat, and does so to avenge the Duchess of Brittany who is at once kin, subject, and woman. Malory's inclusion of the mention of Guenevere at this moment emphasizes that a knight's duty is to defend and avenge the helpless and vulnerable—particularly women— and that such acts are critical to the establishment and maintenance of masculine heteronormative identity in the Arthurian community. This original moment suggests—to a degree that the *Alliterative Morte Arthure* does not—that failure to successfully defend the feminine can have serious consequences for the masculine agents of the community. As I discuss at greater length in chapter 1, the homosocial knightly masculine community depends on the feminine for definition—acts of service to ladies help identify knights as legitimate participants in the Round Table community. As the head of the community, Arthur's heteronormative relationship extends to define his subjects as similarly conforming to sex-derivative ideals of gender identity. When the nursemaid makes mention of the giant's desire for Guenevere, she not only identifies a potential danger to his status as king, but also to his status *as a man;* by extension, this threatens the gender status of Arthur's knightly agents.[56]

Apart from the mention of Guenevere, Malory has made additional revisions to his account of the Roman War; in contrast to his source, Malory frames the account of the continental campaign with references to Guenevere and marriage as well. In the *Alliterative Morte Arthure,* the opening and closing lines firmly identify the poem as a self-contained text: it begins with the conventional literary opening device of the prayer, and ends with a reference to the historical tradition of writing in which it participates:

> Thus endis Kyng Arthure, as auctors alegges
> That was of Ectores blude, the kynge son of Troye
> And of Sir Pryamus the prynce, praysede in erthe
> Fro thythen broghte the Bretons all his bolde eldyrs
> Into Bretayne the Brode, as ȝe Bruytte tellys.
>   (4342–46)

In the opening and closing lines of Malory's account of the episode of the Roman War, we see an important innovation that calls attention to the issue of gender. Malory's version begins thus: "Hyt befelle whan kyng Arthur had wedded quene Gwenyvere and fulfylled the Rounde Table, and so aftir his mervelous knyghtis and he had venquyshed the moste party of his enemyes, that sone aftir com sir Launcelot de Lake unto the courte, and sir Trystramys come that tyme also" (185.1–6). None of the antecedent texts make explicit reference to Arthur's wedding to Guenevere, and although (with the exception of Geoffrey) they do make mention of the Round Table, the explicit connection of the table to Arthur's status as a married man is not made, nor are Lancelot and Tristram named as recent newcomers to the court. The opening of the narrative of "King Arthur and the Emperor Lucius" thus explicitly links Arthur's status as king with his marriage to Guenevere and the support of his knightly agents in a way that the other texts do not. Further, with the exception of John Hardyng's chronicle, Malory's account of Arthur's continental campaign is the only medieval English text in which Arthur is actually crowned emperor and returns home in triumph to a stable and peaceful kingdom. Other accounts have Arthur's throne usurped by Mordred in his absence, and his return to England is the prelude to the final battle in which he receives his death wound. Malory's disconnection of the Roman War from Arthur's death indicates that even at this early stage of the *Morte d'Arthur,* Malory must have had a clear idea of the narrative movement and scope of his text.[57]

Most important for my present argument, however, is not that Malory changes the conclusion of the Roman War from tragedy to triumph, but the manner in which he contrives to get Arthur's army back home to England after the Roman War: "Than the knyghtes and lordis that to the kynge longis called a counsayle uppon a fayre morne and sayde, 'Sir kynge, we beseche the for to here us all. We are undir your lordship well stuffid, blyssed be God, of many thynges; and also we have wyffis weddid. We woll beseche youre good grace to reles us to sporte with oure wyffis, for, worshyp be Cryste, this journey is well overcom'" (246.3–10). When Arthur agrees to return home, Malory tells us further that "Whan quene Gwenyvere herde of his coommynge she mette with hym at London, and so dud all other quenys and noble ladyes" (246.23–25). Malory frames and punctuates Arthur's conflict with Lucius with original moments that call attention to marriage in general and Arthur's marriage to Guenevere in particular. Malory's addition of the references to marriage in the Roman War episode thus serve to "quilt" together the concerns of empire with those of the feminine more emphatically than is the case in Geoffrey, Wace, Laȝamon, or the *Alliterative Morte Arthure.* The person of the queen, not the king, is the "nodal point" where the masculine concerns of warfare and empire intersect with issues of gender and identity. Although not even present during Arthur's conflict with the Mont St. Michel giant, the mention of the queen here creates a coalescence of the public and private, home and away, individual and collective. In Malory's text, the concerns of gender are played out in all these spheres.

Malory's account of the Roman War draws us back repeatedly to an earlier moment in the *Morte d'Arthur*—Arthur's wedding—compelling the reader to recall the important events of what Vinaver has called the "Tale of King Arthur." On the occasion of Arthur's marriage to King Leodegran's daughter, he receives not only his bride and a seemingly large and unwieldy wedding gift in the form of the actual physical Round Table but he also significantly receives the knights who comprise the Round Table, and who are the major source of his authority to rule. As the table itself ultimately belonged to his father Uther, he also receives additional confirmation of his right to sit on the throne.[58] The occasion of the wedding feast is also the occasion for Arthur's institution of the Pentecostal Oath, which dictates, among other things, that knights behave in a certain way toward ladies, and which I discuss at greater length in chapter 1. This reminds Malory's readers that status as a married man is an important characteristic of Arthur, and further, that the occasion of his marriage has been the site for the regulation of knightly behavior, especially toward women. Arthur's triumph on the Continent in Malory seems to proceed from the chain of events set in motion by his marriage. In the *Morte d'Arthur*, the concerns of gender are inextricable from what would at first seem to be the wholly masculine homosocial realm of knighthood, rule, and empire; gender is both constructive and destructive, a centripetal and a centrifugal force, and as such it is critically important to any understanding of the *Morte d'Arthur*.[59]

In each of the texts under discussion the giant represents the monstrous "Other," the threat from the margins that can never be wholly incorporated into the social order. His abduction and rape of the duchess reinforces the cultural definition of femininity depicted within these texts—ladies are helpless, needy, and rape-able—as the Pentecostal Oath in Malory has made clear in its pre- and proscriptive "ladies clause": "allwayes to do ladyes, damesels, jantillwomen and wydowes succour; strengthe hem in hir ryghtes, and never to enforce them, uppon payne of dethe" (120.20–23). The occasion of the duchess's abduction provides a site in which Arthur—and by extension, his companions and the order he represents—may enact his masculine identity through rescue (in this instance of the old woman) and retribution (the killing of the giant). Catherine Batt has articulated the interesting tension that rape produces in Malory in terms of the relation between the swearing of the Pentecostal Oath and the episode of the Mont St. Michel giant:

> If rape in the Pentecostal Oath calls to our notice the internal tensions in the Arthurian social order, the *Morte* also develops a rhetoric for rape as a signal of the anti-social, the threat from the margins, that against which the community defines itself. . . . The gruesome physical details of the Giant's behavior divert attention from what the Pentecostal Oath recognizes as the potential actuality of rape as a threat from within. In this adventure, rape (on the part of the Giant), and not raping (which Arthur's prohibition to his troops reinforces . . .) are central to the definition of Arthur and to his male Christian community.[60]

Although the figure of the giant is emphatically male, his exaggerated maleness in fact sets him apart from the masculine as it is defined in the Arthurian community.[61] Thus, when Arthur confronts the giant and ultimately defeats him, he identifies and makes visible the demarcation of the boundary between heroic and destructive masculinity.

It is significant that the apogee of Arthur's career—his triumph as emperor—comes immediately after his marriage to Guenevere, and that after this success, Arthur largely recedes from the pages of the text as an active player. In Malory, the married knight does little that is noteworthy; indeed, as I discuss in chapters 2 and 3, Gareth's marriage effectively removes him from the knightly playing field, while Lancelot's perpetual state of bachelorhood guarantees that he is continually available to aid damsels in distress and thereby enhance his knightly reputation. Similarly, while Arthur manages to achieve unparalleled greatness on the Continent shortly after his marriage to Guenevere, he too seemingly disappears from the text as all but a figurehead. Once the king has enacted the ultimate "jouparde" of his person, that person must then be protected in order that his continued existence may reflect his glorious achievements back onto those knights who are drawn to his court. The reputation of the court as first established by the king is then maintained by those knightly agents who act as his representatives.

Malory makes one other alteration to this episode that I think is important to understanding the elaborate quilting process that the conflict with the giant enacts. As I have indicated above, it is the author of the *Alliterative Morte Arthure* who enhances the threat the giant poses to Arthur's subjects, rendering him as a cannibal who feasts on young children, and characterizing the giant as a figure of violent lust whose exaggerated phallus literally kills the duchess, here standing in as the emblematic vessel of reproduction. Indeed, the lineal hopes and possibilities of patriarchy reside in the control over the reproductive capacity of the duchess (and by extension, other noble ladies). But while Malory follows the lead of his source in emphasizing the horrific nature of the threat posed by the giant, he departs from his source in his description of the messenger who brings the king the news of the giant's activities. In both Geoffrey and Wace, Arthur hears "tidings" of the giant's activities from an unspecified source; in Laȝamon the messenger is identified as "an hende cniht" (12802); in the *Alliterative Morte Arthure* the knightly messenger has become more specifically "a templere tyte" (841). By contrast, Malory tells us that: "And than come there an husbandeman oute of the contrey and talkyth unto the kyng wondourfull wordys and sayde, 'Sir, here is besyde a grete gyaunte of Gene'" (198.5–7).

The choice of a non-noble messenger is significant, as it emphasizes Arthur's status as protector of the commons, a group of people usually invisible in medieval romance. Unlike the Arthur of the *Alliterative Morte*

Arthure, Malory's Arthur champions the lowest class on the social ladder on the eve of his ascension to that same ladder's highest rung. Just as Malory's added references to Guenevere and marriage serve to repeatedly draw the reader back to the moment of his wedding and the swearing of the Pentecostal Oath, Malory's specific characterization of the messenger as a commoner also directs the reader's attention to other events that take place earlier in the narrative, in the "Tale of King Arthur."

I am referring specifically to Arthur's accession to the throne. Again, Malory follows his source—the *Suite du Merlin*—quite closely, except in what might at first appear to be an insignificant detail. After Arthur draws the sword from the stone, there follows a period of uproar; for the next several months, various and sundry knights try their hand at pulling the same sword out of the stone—a sword that Arthur must repeatedly draw and replace, demonstrating again and again his worthiness to be king to the disbelieving barons. The stalemate is finally broken: "And at the feste of Pentecost alle maner of men assayed to pulle at the swerde that wold assay, but none myghte prevaille but Arthur, and he pulled it oute afore all the lordes and comyns that were there. Wherefore all the comyns cryed at ones: 'We will have Arthur unto our kyng! We wille put hym no more in delay, for we all see that it is Goddes wille that he shalle be our kynge, and who that holdeth ageynst it, we wille slee hym'" (16.7–15). Later, in his first military conflict as king, it is again the commons who help defend him from those knights who challenge Arthur's right to rule: "And thenne the comyns of Carlyon aroos with clubbis and stavys and slewe many knyghtes" (19.22–24). Malory's source contains no such comparable moments of lower-class action in the interest of the king.[62]

Framed externally by accounts of Arthur's reign that are both chronologically sensible and generically romantic, framed internally by Guenevere and marriage and with revisions that amplify the concerns dramatized by the *Alliterative Morte Arthure* and connect this episode to the larger narrative of the *Morte d'Arthur,* the figure of the queen in the Mont St. Michel episode functions as a *point de capiton,* quilting together the concerns of gender, community, identity, and power as no other account does. Although the issue of gender is important in the other antecedent texts, an analysis of Malory's account of the Mont St. Michel giant—and Guenevere's presence there—reveals that in the *Morte d'Arthur,* gender issues are inextricable from the matters of community, justice, and rule.

Gender and the *Morte d'Arthur*

As has perhaps become clear by this point, my position on the composition of the "Tale of King Arthur and the Emperor Lucius" is at odds with that of many scholars who feel that the account of the Roman War was the first portion of the *Morte d'Arthur* that Malory wrote. In its location within the larger narrative and the revisions I have just discussed, Malory's account of Arthur's continental campaign self-consciously announces itself as quite deliberately placed into its specific location within the narrative: it looks back to the events of Arthur's ascension to the throne and marriage and it looks ahead to Arthur's death that will come after years of reigning as both king and emperor. Fully invested with all insular authority possible at the conclusion of the "Tale of King Arthur," Malory deliberately connects Arthur's glorious exploits on the Continent to his marriage—the final act that serves to legitimate and secure his right to rule. Once he achieves the ultimate goal—to be crowned emperor and return home in victory—Malory's Arthur withdraws from the main activity of the text, protecting his royal person and turning the "work" of chivalry over to his knightly agents. If Malory did not write these early tales in the order in which they appear in the *Morte d'Arthur*, then at the very least he had a clear idea of their movement, of the arc of Arthur's career. The "Tale of Arthur and the Emperor Lucius" is crafted with the movement of that narrative firmly in mind. Although I have chosen to analyze the episode of the Roman War first, my analysis demonstrates that the "Tale of King Arthur and the Emperor Lucius" can only be fully understood if one recognizes that it comes after Arthur's wedding and before the narratives of individual knights such as Lancelot, Gareth, and Tristram. Engaging the Roman War out of order—as I have done here—in fact affirms *exactly* where in the narrative order of the *Morte d'Arthur* it belongs.

Eugène Vinaver has famously argued that what Malory composed were in fact eight separate and distinct romances, and although it is true that Vinaver's groupings—into Tales or Books—reflect shifts in focus and content within the *Morte d'Arthur*, it is my contention that the way in which Malory has revised, adapted, and manipulated his sources indicates that he saw each of these episodes as a link in the chain of the narrative, each section moving the reader closer to the collapse of the community and Arthur's death.[63] His deliberate rearrangement of events as he found them in his sources[64]—and in the early pages of the *Morte d'Arthur*, his foreshadowing and explicit mention of moments that occur much later in the text—all suggest that Malory's intent was to compose a coherent narrative that told the story of Arthur's kingdom from its beginning to its end.[65] I am, like R. M. Lumiansky "convinced that Malory wrote a single unified book rather than eight separate 'Tales.'"[66] Although I reject Vinaver's contention that Malory's text is a collection of disparate "works," I agree in general that his divisions do make a kind of sense, and as most readers are familiar with his groupings, I thus use Vinaver's titles for each section within this study as a matter of convenience, even though the briefest of examinations of a facsimile of the Winchester manuscript indicates that these "emphatic" divisions are not supported by the structure of the actual document.[67] Likewise, I choose to refer to Malory's text by its most commonly used title, *Le Morte d'Arthur,* in the interest of clarity, although something like Stephen Knight's title for the work—the *Arthuriad*—actually does a much better job of conveying the sense of unity I think the text exhibits.[68]

Thus, in engaging the question of gender I have chosen to move through the text sequentially, thereby hoping to make plain the progressively degenerative results produced by the model of gender installed as a foundational support of the chivalric community in the early pages of the text. As the *Morte d'Arthur* progresses toward its inevitable conclusion, the conflict of the gender ideal with other chivalric ideals—such as mercy and the prohibition to engage in "wrongefull quarells"—is heightened and exacerbated. The tensions produced by the ideal of gender identity that the Arthurian community assumes as a foundational support in the early pages of the narrative rend the fabric of that community in the closing episodes of the text.

In chapter 1, "Gender and the Chivalric Community: The Rise of Arthur's Kingdom," I argue that the early pages of Malory's *Morte d'Arthur* contain in embryo the conflicts and pressures inherent in the values and ideals of chivalric community. Beginning with an analysis of the significance of the swearing of the Pentecostal Oath, I contend that this early section reveals the recurring tropes that will dominate the text, depicting in microcosm the tensions and concerns that will play out throughout the rest of the narrative. I examine the processes by which the chivalric community is formed, the actions that knights must perform as a means of maintaining the coherence of individual as well as communal identity, and the resistance and potential threats posed to this social order. Significantly, several key episodes in this drama are all emplotted through feminine presence and action—Uther's desire for Igrayne, Arthur's adultery/incest with Morgause, Arthur's marriage to Guenevere, and the threat posed by

Morgan le Fay. A careful reading of what Vinaver designates the "Tale of King Arthur" demonstrates the imbrication of gender with all aspects of a society ordered along the ethos of chivalry and reveals the inevitability of the demise of Arthur's realm; an analysis of the beginning of the text suggestively reveals the form of the conflicts that will produce the end. The chapters that follow trace that degenerative movement toward social collapse.

While chapter 1 broadly defines the ideas of gender, community, and identity that will shape the narrative of the *Morte d'Arthur,* chapter 2, "Chivalric Performance: Malory's Sir Lancelot" focuses on the early adventures of Sir Lancelot, using that paragon of knighthood as a means by which to more closely investigate the chivalric ideals of Malory's Arthurian community. Acclaimed by all for his martial prowess, Lancelot is considered the "floure of al knyghtes" for his skill with the sword as well as his devoted service to ladies—and to Queen Guenevere in particular. If the category of the chivalric may be said to be produced at the intersection of martial prowess and courtesy, then Lancelot is the prime exemplar of the chivalric ethos; an analysis of his character reveals that the one aspect of his reputation is inextricable from the other. To maintain the legitimacy of the homosocial subcommunity of knights within the larger heteronormative chivalric society, Lancelot demonstrates the need to repeatedly reassert and reaffirm his masculine identity through a never-ending performance of knighthood.

That this is true becomes even clearer when Lancelot is compared with the character of his dearest friend, Sir Gareth, and his double, Sir Tristram, the focus of chapter 3, "Forecast and Recall." In the first adventure of his knightly career, Gareth succeeds brilliantly and is rewarded with the hand of the lady Lyones. After his marriage, he all but disappears from the pages of the narrative, returning only so that he may die, unarmed and defenseless, bereft of the masculine markers of knighthood. Tristram also provides an important commentary on Lancelot's career and affirmation of masculine knightly identity, as his relationship to his king, Mark, and queen, Isode, clearly stands as a dark reflection of Lancelot's own relationship to Arthur and Guenevere. The "Book of Sir Trystram de Lyones" provides a new perspective on the question of gender in the *Morte d'Arthur,* as it is here that we move away from Arthur's kingdom and view the order of the Round Table and its ideals from the outside. One of the most neglected portions of Malory's text for this very reason, Tristram's tale is in fact *critically* important to the *Morte d'Arthur,* as it provides a new testing ground for the ideals of chivalry articulated in the "Tale of King Arthur" and performed in the accounts of the Roman War, Lancelot's adventures, and Gareth's quest. In the "Book of Sir Tristram" the definitions of "knighthood," "masculinity," and the boundaries of permissible gender performance are expanded, deepened, and indeed, stretched almost to their breaking points.

While the court serves as the center of activity and social cohesion for most of the *Morte d'Arthur*—as the place from which knights issue seeking adventures that will enhance their reputations, and to which they return to offer a report of their accomplishments for their assembled fellows—this focus shifts during the quest for the Holy Grail. Chapter 4 examines the Grail Quest, in which the cohesion of Arthur's court is shattered and the chivalric ethos as a social ideal is severely undermined and critiqued. Affirmed and for the first time wholly unified by the appearance of the grail at Arthur's court and Galahad's fulfillment of the Siege Perilous, the integrity of the Round Table is ironically and irretrievably destroyed as the fellowship splinters to pursue the very object—the grail—that has for one singular moment unified the chivalric community.

The final chapter, "Lancelot, Guenevere, and the Death of Arthur: The Decline and Fall of the Chivalric Community," examines the aftermath of the Grail Quest when those elements contributing to the ultimate demise of the chivalric enterprise (the relationship of Lancelot and Guenevere, the blood feud between the houses of Gawain and Lancelot, and Mordred's attempted usurpation of the throne) are most clearly revealed. While all these factors contribute to the demise of the Round Table and Arthur's community, they are really only symptoms of the larger problem of gender and chivalric identity. I argue that the gender model upheld as an ideal *produces* Lancelot and Guenevere's relationship, Gawain's thirst for vengeance, and the treasonous Mordred himself. The Arthurian community could only ever destroy itself. In the "ending of the ending"—Malory's account of the deaths of Lancelot and Guenevere—the tone of despair that pervades the concluding scenes of the *Morte d'Arthur* ameliorates into hope. Lancelot and Guenevere enter into religious life, and although their conversions exist in uneasy and complex relation to the secular courtly world they have supposedly rejected, both die in an undeniable aura of sanctity and goodness: the "trew lover[s]" do indeed have a "goode ende." Thus, we are left with a narrative that, even as it condemns the chivalric ideal, looks back upon that ideal with nostalgia, and interestingly, finds the possibility for redemption among its ashes.

1

Gender and the Chivalric Community

The Rise of Arthur's Kingdom

In composing the early sections of the *Morte d'Arthur*, Malory drew primarily from the twelfth- and thirteenth-century French prose romances known as the *Merlin* and the *Suite du Merlin*, part of the Post-Vulgate Lancelot-Grail Cycle (also commonly referred to as the Pseudo-Robert de Boron Prose Cycle). Much of Malory's source is concerned specifically with the story of Merlin—early evidence of his prophetic powers and the well-known episode of Vortigern's tower—and in reducing his source, Malory has dispensed with most of the Merlin material, choosing to focus instead on those events that directly concern Arthur.[1] In so doing, he rewrites the central event of the early days of Arthur's reign: the establishment of the Round Table. Malory moves this to a later point in the narrative and disconnects it from direct association with the Grail Quest, a link upon which the *Suite* insists.[2] This move is in keeping with what seems to be Malory's general intent to de-emphasize the elements of the spiritual and supernatural so central to his source and to present a picture of chivalry that is primarily concerned with setting out rules for adventure, a "secular" chivalry.[3] Through revision, reduction, and the disentanglement of the *entrelacement* that structures his source, Malory presents a (largely) orderly, coherent narrative of the formation of Arthur's Round Table community, tracing its development through a series of episodes that are significantly punctuated by a feminine presence. Beginning with the events surrounding Arthur's conception and birth, the section designated by Eugène Vinaver as the "Tale of King Arthur" describes the process by which Arthur achieves, consolidates, and defends against threats to his rule.

As depicted in these early pages of the narrative, the formation and development of the Arthurian chivalric society in Malory is bounded and mediated by the presence of the feminine: Uther's deceptive seduction of Igrayne, Arthur's unwitting incest (and knowing adultery) with his half-sister Morgause, Arthur's marriage to Guenevere, and his conflict with his other half-sister Morgan le Fay. Significantly inextricable from this feminine presence is an economy of violence. The "Tale of King Arthur" makes explicit the link between masculine violence and the marginal—yet essential—feminine. Again and again, passive femininity and masculine violence intersect, perhaps nowhere quite as significantly as in the swearing of the Pentecostal Oath.

The Pentecostal Oath

In the attempt to better understand Malory's text, much research has focused on those parts of the *Morte d'Arthur* that appear to be purely the creation of Malory—that is, with no corresponding passages in the many French and few English texts from which the author drew. One such moment that appears to be wholly original to Malory occurs near the end of the "Tale of King Arthur." It is the swearing of the Pentecostal Oath, in which King Arthur articulates a code of conduct for the members of his knightly community to follow:

> the kynge stablysshed all the knyghtes and gaff them rychesse and londys; and charged them never to do outerage nothir mourthir, and allwayes to fle treson, and to gyff mercy unto hym that askith mercy, uppon payne of forfiture of their worship and lordship of kynge Arthure for evirmore; and allwayes to do ladyes, damesels, and jantilwomen and wydowes socour: strengthe hem in hir ryghtes, and never to enforce them, upon payne of dethe. Also, that no man take no batayles in a wrongefull quarell for no love ne for no worldis goodis. So unto thys were all knyghtis sworne of the Table Rounde, both olde and younge, and every yere so were they sworne at the hyghe feste of Pentecoste. (120.15–27)

Malory's direct source for these early episodes of Arthur's life and reign contains no such injunction to the knights of the Round Table.[4] In his commentary on the first book of Malory's *Morte d'Arthur*, Vinaver calls special attention to the delineation of knightly duties as articulated by Arthur: "This is perhaps the most complete and authentic record of M[alory]'s conception of chivalry. Elsewhere he expresses it incidentally or indirectly, whereas here for the first and perhaps the last time he states it compendiously, in didactic form."[5] Thus, not surprisingly, critics have long regarded this moment as key to understanding the chivalric project of Malory's narrative. But while most scholars have focused on how the articulation of the Pentecostal Oath seems to reveal Malory's views and reactions to the sociohistorical context in which he composed his massive text, I argue that this moment of oath-taking in fact *creates* the action of the narrative that follows.[6] In other words, I contend that the Pentecostal Oath acts as a "master signifier"[7] throughout the *Morte d'Arthur*. The Oath produces and mediates the movement of the text, functioning as the master trope to which all the actions of the characters refer. This act of chivalric legislation early in the *Morte d'Arthur* sets in motion an ideal of knightly behavior; the rest of the text tests that code in a variety of circumstances, revealing the tensions, shortcomings, and blind spots of the chivalric project.

My position would seem to directly contradict the argument of scholars such as Andrew Lynch, who states that "even Malory's most heartfelt generalisations refer primarily to their local context," and further suggests that "we should not make a few speeches into . . . unbending rules for interpreting the whole narrative. . . . [Malory's] famous axioms are generated in the enthusiasm of the moment."[8] Lynch's assertion is certainly true in the sense that Malory's text is quite evidently full of contradictions. Most famously, the "Month of May" passage has long puzzled scholars in its mention of Guenevere, for whom Malory makes "a lytyll mencion, that whyle she lyved she was a trew lover, and therefor she had a good ende" (1120.11–13), especially when read against Guenevere's final farewell to Lancelot, when she states "Thorow thys same man and me hath all thys warre be wrought. . . . for thorow oure love that we loved togydir is my moste noble lorde slayne" (1252.8–11). That two such diametrically opposed views of what—for lack of a better term—we might call "courtly love" or "*fin amour*" are able to exist in the *Morte d'Arthur* is part of what is interesting and important about this text, which itself seems in large measure to be a "working out" of the tensions of chivalry. In his text, Malory attempts to address and resolve the contradictions of noble life in his own time, imagining a standard of action and behavior that might alleviate and prevent political conflicts such as the Wars of the Roses.

Elizabeth Edwards recently has argued that "Despite the oath, which seems to approximate to written code, or positive law, chivalry in Malory is not the result of following the rules; it is more a matter of generating and regenerating the code."[9] Indeed, as the narrative progresses, we see a constant weighing, evaluation, and application of the values expressed in the Pentecostal Oath. The particular articles of the Oath simply articulate the chivalric ideals *already* in place in the community, functioning at the level of convention, if not law. What Edwards calls the "generating and regenerating" of the code never occurs free of the ideals articulated in the Oath; chivalry in Malory is never made from whole cloth, as it were. Throughout the *Morte d'Arthur* we see a discovery, refinement, and testing of the practical application of the chivalric code, a process that also reveals where the chivalric ideal falls short as a means of ordering the Arthurian community.

In Lynch's view, then, the applicability of the Pentecostal Oath might only be responsibly considered in terms of the earliest episodes of the *Morte d'Arthur*, its "immediate context," and indeed, in this chapter these early episodes and their relationship to the Oath are my primary focus. Yet, throughout Malory—and far beyond the "Tale of King Arthur"—numerous characters explicitly cite the Oath: upon learning that two "perelous knyghtes" have disinherited a noblewoman, Sir Uwayne notes that "they ar to blame, for they do ayenste the hyghe Order of Knyghthode and the oth that they made" (177.10–12); when a damsel asks Lancelot's assistance in defeating a serial rapist, Arthur's greatest knight responds with "What? Is he a theff and a knyght? And a ravyssher of women? He doth shame unto the Order of Knyghthode, and contrary unto his oth" (269.22–24); when Gaheris challenges Uwayne to a joust, the other reminds him that "the first tyme that ever ye were made knyght of the Rounde Table ye sware that ye shuld nat have ado with none of youre felyship wyttyngly . . . ye know me well inow by my shylde . . . and thaughe ye wolde breke youre othe, I woll nat breke myne" (546.26–31); when Sir Bleoberys finds himself at a four-on-one combat disadvantage, he gathers his courage by reminding himself, "I am a knyght of the Table Rounde, and rathir than I sholde shame myne othe and my blode I woll holde my way whatsomever falle thereof" (685.25–27). Again and again, knights in the *Morte d'Arthur* recall the Pentecostal Oath and deliberately choose to act in accordance with its strictures.

As the examples above suggest, it seems unlikely that Malory "forgets" that early in his massive work he has made law out of many of the conventions of chivalric behavior. Quite the contrary: throughout the text Malory has the Oath and its rules firmly in mind. But even if it were the case that Malory's creation of the Pentecostal Oath is something done in a fit of momentary enthusiasm, the *reader* cannot help but be reminded of the Oath and its articles as the text returns again and again to the geographic and temporal site of the initial vow and its renewal: the "hyghe feste of Pentecoste" at Camelot. Indeed, most important adventures begin and end at Arthur's court during Pentecost: "Sir Lancelot . . . bade sir Melyot hyghe hym 'to the courte of my lorde Arthure, for hit drawyth nygh to the feste of Pentecoste'" (282.7–9); "'Sir' seyde sir Plenoryus, 'at the nexte feste of Pentecoste I woll be at kynge Arthurs courte'" (475.24–25); "'My lorde, sir Launcelot,' seyde dame Elayne, 'thys same feste of Pentecoste shall youre sonne and myne, Galahad, be made knyght'" (832.7–9); "At the vigyl of Pentecoste, whan all the felyship of the Table Rownde were com unto Camelot" (853.1–2); "Wherefore all maner of knyghtes demed that sir Lavayn sholde be made knyght of the Table Rounde at the nexte feste of Pentecoste" (1098.19–22); "than at the nexte feste of Pentecoste, gyff there were ony slayne or dede . . . than was there chosyn in hys stede that was ded the moste men of worshyp that were called the Quenys Knyghtes" (1121.23–27).

Malory may certainly contradict himself at various moments in his text, but a close analysis of the development of the *Morte d'Arthur* suggests that the ideals of the Oath serve as a guide to proper behavior *throughout* the narrative; indeed, knights cite them as law up until the final pages. That the law is frequently violated or deliberately disregarded by various knights does not render it any less important in interpreting the actions of the chivalric agents of the community; on the contrary, the vehemence and/or cautiousness with which knights who transgress the Oath offer defenses for their behavior[10] suggests that it is indeed the "master signifier" to which all knightly behavior is referred and through which it is interpreted.

Many scholars have attempted to address the "problem" of the Pentecostal Oath, struggling to articulate why the seemingly straightforward legislation of chivalric values creates so much tension within Malory's romance. Thomas Wright has observed that "the shortcomings of the Arthurian code, and of the society which follows it, are to be found in the code's limitations. It is too inflexible and too static; it cannot embrace enough of the contingencies inherent in the human situation. Indeed, though it may at first inspire order and impose justice, it becomes finally the weakest aspect of Camelot."[11] Indeed, even as the Oath seeks to stabilize and regulate the behaviors and identities of the inhabitants of Malory's text, throughout the text it also functions as a site of contestation, struggle, and resistance. We see several examples of this difficulty throughout the *Morte d'Arthur:* Sir Torre grants a maiden her request for

a gift, which turns out to be the head of a knight who promptly begs for
mercy (112.13–36); Accolon serves his lady, Morgan le Fay, by promising
to battle Arthur to the death, an act that surely violates both the "outerage
nothir mourthir" and "wrongefulle quarell" clauses (142–47); Lancelot is
tricked into disarming and climbing a tree by Sir Phelot's manipulation of
the Oath (282.10–37; 283.1–36). Perhaps most significantly, Lancelot's series of defenses of Guenevere that punctuate the end of the text bring
"soccour" for ladies and the prohibition on wrongful quarrels and treason
into direct conflict. Indeed, in his combat with Meleagant, the mercy clause
further complicates matters when Meleagant yields himself:

> "Moste noble knyghte sir Launcelot, save my lyff! For I yelde
> me unto you, and I requyre you, as ye be a knyght and felow of the
> Table Rounde, sle me nat. . . ." Than sir Lancelot wyst nat what to do
> . . . [and] loked uppon the queene. . . . And anone the quene wagged
> hir hede uppon sir Launcelot, as ho seyth "sle hym. . . ." Than sir
> Launcelot bade hym "Aryse, for shame, and perfourme thys batayle
> with me to the utterance!" (1138.21–31, 1139.1–5).[12]

Lancelot is here caught between two articles of the Pentecostal Oath: if he
grants mercy, he displeases—and more important, perhaps harms the
reputation of—the lady to whom he has attempted to render "soccour"; if
he obeys the request of his lady and slays his opponent, he has disobeyed
the mercy clause. Unable to decide which guideline to follow, Lancelot
chooses to disobey both articles. He has run out of options.

Part of the problem is that the Pentecostal Oath is at once too general
and too specific; its clauses delineate proper knightly behavior—that which
knights should do—and improper activity—that which knights should
avoid—without addressing a possible intersection of the two. It also fails to
satisfactorily address the very real need of members of the Round Table
community to "win worship," a process that generally occurs in combat. It
seems that a knight may "win worship" both by adhering to the Pentecostal Oath's articles and disobeying them, depending on the situation. For
example, King Pellinor (whose adventure on the occasion of Arthur's wedding I discuss at greater length below) refuses to stop and aid a damsel in
distress because "he was so egir in hys queste" (114.16–17); the desire to
win worship through successful completion of the quest here compels
Pellinor to transgress against chivalric values concerning women, with
unfortunate results: the maiden commits suicide. While on his own quest,
the newly knighted Sir Gareth is told by his lady that "as yet thou shalt

nat have holy my love unto the tyme that thou be called one of the numbir of the worthy knyghtes. . . . And therefore go and laboure in worshyp this twelve-monthe" (327.8–10). In the Grail Quest, Lancelot belatedly recognizes that the emphasis he has placed on winning worship has been wrong: "And never dud I batayle all only for Goddis sake, but for to wynne worship and to cause me the bettir to be beloved" (897.19–21).

Although not a Round Table knight himself until late in the text, Sir Tristram generally acquits himself admirably, having several encounters that help illuminate the "problem" of worship. For example, one of Tristram's experiences suggests that worship may be won through taking the side of the weaker party in a combat, regardless of which party is in the right: "Sir, leve your fyghtynge with tho twenty knyghtes, for ye wynne no worship of them, ye be so many and they so feaw. . . . Therefore leve your fyghtynge with them for I, to encrese my worship, I woll ryde unto the twenty knyghtes and helpe them with all my myght and power" (526.29–34, 527.1–2).[13] At the request of his uncle, King Mark, Tristram fights for the "trewage" of Cornwall against Marhalt of Ireland, killing the other knight in the process. When captured by Marhalt's kin and commanded to explain himself Tristram tells the king of Ireland he fought Marhalt to defend Cornwall. The other exclaims: "So God me helpe! . . . I may nat sey but ye dud as a knyght sholde do and as hit was youre parte to do for youre quarell, and to encrece your worshyp as a knyght sholde do" (391.17–20).

As the above examples suggest, the issue of "worship" complicates loyalties—and thus adherence to the articles of the Pentecostal Oath—in that in the world of Arthurian romance, one's enemy may frequently be someone whose actions are worthy of admiration. Arthur's early conflicts in trying to consolidate his realm provide clear evidence of this: in his fight against the eleven kings, Malory tells us that Arthur is "passynge wrothe" (34.31) at the war waged against him. His new allies, King Ban and King Bors, who have greater experience as both kings and knights, gently chide Arthur for his anger: "'A, sir Arthur . . . blame hem nat, for they do as good men ought to do. For be my fayth . . . they ar the beste fyghtynge men and knyghtes of moste prouesse that ever y saw other herde off speke. And tho eleven kyngis ar men of grete worship; and if they were longyng to you, there were no kynge under hevyn that had suche elevyn kyngis nother off suche worship'" (34.32–36, 35.1–2). The comment of Ban and Bors here reveals an important truth about conflict in the chivalric community; throughout the text, there is a recurring episodic sequence, in which two knights fight almost to the death, but then are so impressed with one another that they decide to become allies and fast friends. The line between "evermore love" and "evermore warre" in the *Morte d'Arthur* is a fine one indeed.

P.J.C. Field points out that "Malory gives us a style of dialogue which stresses the similarity of all knights, not the difference between individuals."[14] The similarity among knights permits for this ease of movement across boundaries of alliance and animosity in the text; indeed, single combat demonstrates this likeness, for the two knights face each other as mirror images, legible to one another in their shared status, denoted in Malory both by costume and by language.[15] In the early episodes, King Pellinor and Arthur fight as enemies; later, Pellinor becomes a knight of the Round Table and one of Arthur's allies. This fact of chivalric life explains how it can be that Arthur inters his enemy, King Lot, with all the rights befitting a trusted and noble ally: "But of all the twelve kyngis kynge Arthure lette make the tombe of kynge Lotte passyng rychely, and made hys tombe hymselff" (77.30–32).

Yet, the ease with which enemies morph into allies causes problems within the chivalric social order. In order to win worship, knights quite clearly need plenty of opportunities to demonstrate their prowess, but as more former enemies are absorbed into the Round Table order, authorized foes are harder and harder to come by. In order to legitimately counter with other knights outside the confines of the tournament, Malory's text frequently makes use of the "knight in disguise" ploy—particularly in the massive Tristram section—which permits knights to engage with one another when it might otherwise be legally forbidden.[16]

Malory's conception of knighthood in the *Morte d'Arthur* suggests a departure from the focus of knighthood in the *Suite*, where worries over knightly behavior are primarily expressed as concerns over the *spiritual* well-being of individual knights. Malory's text shifts this emphasis, replacing individual, spiritual concerns with a collective, secular focus. The public, annual ritual of the swearing of the Pentecostal Oath demonstrates this. Elizabeth Pochoda notes that "the code . . . displays a striking concern for the welfare of the realm. . . . The oath which the knights swear to at each feast of the Pentecost is basically a code of public service. At its center are the spiritual virtues of mercy and justice to be sure, but the context of these virtues has been changed. . . . [these are] not acts of private individuals; they are done for the community."[17] This attempt to regulate the whole community by means of a select few produces a series of "blind spots" that appear when the values of the Oath are enforced.

One of the greatest of these "blind spots"—and indeed, the source of much of the violation of its articles—is kin (dis)loyalty, which is nowhere explicitly addressed or regulated. Loyalty to blood often problematically supersedes loyalty to the Round Table order and the ideals expressed in the Pentecostal Oath, while *disloyal* acts on the part of one's own blood relations are often the most destructive, in that they are entirely unexpected and unlooked for. Thus, throughout the text, Morgan le Fay causes problems with her numerous attempts to destroy her brother Arthur, who inexplicably is "the man in the worlde that she hatyth moste" (145.34); Queen Morgause is killed by her own son for betraying the memory of her husband (King Lot), by sleeping with Lamorak, the son of the man (King Pellinor) her sons believe killed their father (612.9–35, 613.1–2); Morgan rescues a knight named Manassen from certain death (and kills his captor) for no reason but that he is her lover Accolon's cousin (152.1–31); a maiden demands that Torre behead a knight—despite his pleas for mercy—in order to avenge the death of her brother (112.13–36); and most famously and tragically, at the end of the text Gawain insists that his uncle Arthur wage war against Lancelot (despite the desire of both the major parties to be reconciled) in retribution for the accidental death of his brothers Gareth and Gaheris (1177 ff.).

One of Lamorak's adventures perhaps best demonstrates the problematic collision of loyalty to kin and to knightly brethren: riding through the forest, Lamorak comes upon two knights "hovyng" under a bush. When asked, the two knights reveal that they are lying in wait to ambush Sir Lancelot, who killed their brother. Curiously, instead of criticizing them for such a dishonorable strategy, Lamorak warns them that "ye take uppon you a grete charge . . . for sir Launcelot ys a noble proved knyght" (485.22–23). Lancelot shows up soon after, he and Lamorak exchange courteous words, and the greatest knight of the Round Table departs. When Lamorak finds the brother knights hiding in the wood, he berates them: "Fye on you! . . . false cowardis! That pité and shame hit ys that ony of you sholde take the hyghe Order of Knyghthode!" (486.1–3). Rather than praising the brothers for deciding *not* to attack a fellow knight in a decidedly dishonorable fashion, Lamorak's response suggests that "good" knights avenge their kin, and do so even when it means violating the wrongful quarrel clause.

The Pentecostal Oath's other critical "blind spot" is in the area of gender identity. Among the articles of the Oath is the so-called ladies clause: "and allwayes to do ladyes, damesels, and jantilwomen and wydowes socour: strengthe hem in hir ryghtes, and never to enforce them, upon payne of dethe." Embedded in the center of the Oath, the position of this particular rule reflects the similar embeddedness of gender in the formation and refinement of identity in Malory's chivalric society, and thus, its imbrication in all aspects of the Arthurian community. An analysis of the forces and values operative in Malory's text reveals that identities of self and community are inextricable both from one another and from the chivalric enterprise. While foregrounding masculine activity, chivalry reveals itself as an impossible project without the presence of the feminine, and indeed, *only* possible when the feminine is present in a subjugated position.[18] The legislation of chivalry through the Pentecostal Oath defines and sharpens the issue of gender so that it resonates throughout Malory's fictional Arthurian society.

Knights in Malory always read women as vulnerable, helpless, and ever in need of the services of a knight—in short, the object through and against which a knight affirms his masculine identity. Even as the Pentecostal Oath offers explicit protection to women in the ladies clause, it also simultaneously and deliberately constructs them as "feminine" in the chivalric sense—helpless, needy, rape-able. The threat of sexual violence—and the need to protect women from it—provides knight after knight with the opportunity to test and prove his prowess and knightly identity.[19] As Kathryn Gravdal notes: "[R]ape (either attempted rape or the defeat of a rapist) constitutes one of the episodic units used in the construction of a romance. Sexual violence is built into the very premise of Arthurian romance. It is a genre that by its definition must *create* the threat of rape" (emphasis in original).[20] While Gravdal's assertion is generally correct, she does not articulate its full implications: in affirming his knightly identity and his right to belong to the heteronormative masculine community of the Arthurian court, a knight not only *needs* a vulnerable, helpless woman, but more specifically, he needs "woman" to *signify* as vulnerable and helpless.

In essence, the Pentecostal Oath effects a disciplinary production of gender in both its particular focus—a structure that locates knights at the center, looking outward at the rest of the society—and in the particular articles it legislates, such as the ladies clause. In his theorization of power systems, Michel Foucault has argued that juridical power systems in fact create the subjects that they supposedly represent;[21] in both form and content, the Oath constructs male and female in terms of a binary that opposes active, aggressive masculinity to passive, helpless femininity. The Oath reinforces, affirms, and sharpens the masculine and feminine subject positions as they exist within the chivalric scheme of compulsory heterosexuality. The instantiation of the Oath creates what Judith Butler has identified as "a false stabilization of gender in the interests of the heterosexual construction and regulation of sexuality within the reproductive domain."[22] The stability of identity supposedly produced by the Oath—the masculine as a free, predatory subject and the feminine as a passive, powerless object—is revealed to be a fiction, in that the masculine subcommunity is utterly and deeply dependent upon the feminine for definition.

Malory's text repeatedly demonstrates that the construction of masculine knightly identity occurs at the intersection of knightly prowess and romantic love. On any foray into the forest of adventure, a knight is sure to encounter other knights—*with whom* he may affirm his masculine sameness through a display of martial capabilities—and a knight is sure also to encounter women—*against whom* he may affirm his masculine difference through courteous behavior. These two types of encounter are crucial to the continual process of establishing and maintaining identity in the Arthurian community. Equally important is that the knight return to the court to relate those adventures he has in the forests of adventure. He in effect performs his gender identity twice: once in the quest, and again in the telling of the quest. The movement between these two places is a critically important aspect of Malory's narrative. Elizabeth Edwards points out that "these two locations represent the centripetal force of the attraction of a centralized court (which we might call civilization) and the centrifugal force of adventure (which usually takes place in a wilderness)."[23]

Laurie A. Finke and Martin B. Shichtman have used similar terms to describe the function of violence in the *Morte d'Arthur*: "Malory's *Morte* represents violence not only as a centripetal force encouraging order, hierarchy, and centralization, but also as a centrifugal force that creates disorder, contention, and sometimes unbearable chaos."[24] The Pentecostal Oath attempts to control violence, to harness it, not to outlaw it altogether; if the Oath forbids a knight from participating in "wrongful quarrels," the implication is that there must exist "rightful" disputes, in which the knight is free to take up his sword and slash away. Likewise, the mercy clause presupposes the existence of a battle in which a defeated knight might ask to yield himself as overcome, while the "soccour" commanded in the ladies clause very often manifests itself in the text as defense of helpless women by means of arms. Adherence to the Oath, then, demands that knights participate in sanctioned forms of violence, and opportunities for such are most often to be found away from the court. Thus, knights return again and again to the wilderness to enact the ideals of knightly masculine identity.

The repetition of these identity-shaping episodic units reveals the performative nature of gendered identities in Malory's romance; that is, the *attributes* of masculinity and femininity that characters display are in fact the very constitution of the particular gender identity they supposedly represent. As Butler has argued, "Gender proves to be performative— that is, constituting the identity it is purported to be. . . . There is no gender identity behind the expressions of gender; that identity is performatively constituted by the very expressions that are said to be its results," and she further contends that "the action of gender requires a performance that is *repeated*" (emphasis in original).[25] Butler's definition of gender—that the signs or marks by which one is categorized "masculine" or "feminine" are not the expression of a preexisting gender identity, but rather, the appearance or repeated performance of these signs or marks *is* gender itself— offers a provocative way into Malory's text. In the *Morte d'Arthur*, knightly masculine identity is both the cause and effect of knightly behavior, while feminine identity is similarly the product and the process of its production.[26]

In the *Morte d'Arthur*, feminine acts of facilitation, enabling, and mediation repeatedly manifest themselves as necessary to the project of the quest, the primary vehicle by which knights construct themselves as particular individuals belonging to a particular community. Throughout the "Tale of King Arthur," but particularly in the "triple-quests" of Torre, Pellinor, and Gawain, and Gawain, Ywain, and Marhalt,[27] the feminine operates as either instigator of quest, mediator of quest, or witness to completion (and thereby validation) of the quest. The ubiquitous and seemingly necessary presence of female characters who ask favors, bestow gifts, intercede for, and pass judgment on knights, points to the importance of the feminine in establishing, shaping, and confirming masculine knightly identity. Geraldine Heng points out that "the feminine materialises in order to be inducted into providing the enabling conditions of the chivalric enterprise: to prop, justify and facilitate the masculine drama of chivalry, the feminine is drawn in, allowed a point of access."[28] Although Heng's observation applies with equal facility to both the *Suite* and

Malory, Malory's positioning of these two episodes and some slight changes emphasize the question of gender in the *Morte d'Arthur* in a way the *Suite* does not.[29]

For both Gawain and Torre, these are the first quests of their knightly careers, but the conduct and relative success of each while on quest is strikingly and significantly different. When in the course of his assigned quest Gawain challenges to a battle the knight who slew his hounds, the latter is quickly overcome and begs mercy. "But sir Gawayne wolde no mercy have" (106.18). Just as Gawain raises his sword to behead the knight, the other's lady emerges from an inner chamber, throws herself across her lover, and is herself accidentally beheaded. Gaheris's words of rebuke to his brother at this moment are telling in that they are almost identical to what will become the mercy clause later on in the Pentecostal Oath: "'Alas,' seyde Gaheris, 'that ys fowle and shamefully done, for that shame shall never frome you. Also, ye sholde gyff mercy unto them that aske mercy, for knyght withoute mercy ys withoute worship'" (106.22–25). In violating *one* of the social values—mercy—Gawain entangles himself in another transgression—violation of the values expressed in the ladies clause of the Pentecostal Oath.

Almost immediately after his accidental beheading of the lady, Gawain and Gaheris find themselves "hard bestad" in a battle with four knights; rescue comes in the form of four "fayre ladyes" who intercede on behalf of Arthur's nephews. When, on the following morning, Gawain is lamenting his wounds, one of the ladies tells him, "Hit ys youre owne defaute . . . for ye have done passynge foule for the sleynge of thys lady" (107.30–32). Even as she condemns him for his actions, the lady continues to work on Gawain's behalf, persuading the four knights to allow him to return to Arthur's court. He does not go freely, however; the lady insists that the body of the dead maiden be draped across his horse, her head hung around his neck. Upon his return to court, Gawain relates the whole of his adventure to the king and queen. While Malory tells us that *both* Arthur and Guenevere are displeased with Gawain's behavior, significantly Guenevere metes out punishment while Arthur remains silent: "and there by ordynaunce of the queene there was sette a queste of ladyes upon sir Gawayne, and they juged hym for ever whyle he lyved to be with all ladyes and to fyght for hir quarels; and ever that he sholde be curteyse, and never to refuse mercy to hym that askith mercy" (108.31–35).

In the early pages of the text, Gawain's adventure and Guenevere's verdict underscore the significance of the feminine in defining masculine identity. In the space of less than a hundred lines, Malory has given his Gawain an unforgettable lesson in the power of the feminine. As the accidentally beheaded gentlewoman signifies the potential vulnerability of ladies, the four women who rescue Gawain and his brother from almost certain death demonstrate the power the feminine may exercise over knights. Guenevere's verdict, that Gawain should "for ever whyle he lyved . . . be with all ladyes and . . . fyght for hir quarels" transforms the literal—the maiden attached to Gawain's horse and person—into the figurative, constructing out of her physical body the general dictum that Gawain must follow for the rest of his life. Malory takes care to remind us how service to ladies has shaped Gawain's reputation, even in death. In the closing pages of the *Morte d'Arthur*, the dead Gawain appears to Arthur in a dream, surrounded by "a numbir of fayre ladyes" (1233.29). Gawain brings to his uncle an important message from beyond the grave, and it is his devotion to the feminine while living that makes his visitation and warning possible: "'Sir,' seyde sir Gawayne, 'all thes be ladyes for whom I have foughten for, whan I was man lyvynge. And all the ar tho that I ded batayle fore in ryghteous quarels, and God hath gyvyn hem that grace at their grete prayer, bycause I ded batayle for them for their ryght, that they shulde brynge me hydder unto you. Thus much hath gyvyn me leve God for to warne you of youre dethe'" (1234.1–7). By learning his lesson about ladies early in the text, Gawain is accorded special grace at the end.

In contrast with Gawain in the early pages of the *Morte d'Arthur*, Torre does a much better job in *his* first quest of negotiating the difficult tensions and hierarchy of values in the Arthurian community, although his experience reinforces the connection between knightly behavior and gender suggested by the Gawain episode. Unlike Gawain, *this* new-made knight readily grants mercy to his opponents when they ask it. In the course of fulfilling his quest—retrieving a brachet taken from Arthur's court—he must fight that knight, Abellus, who took it, and in the midst of their battle a maiden arrives and asks Torre for a gift: "'I beseche the,' seyde the damesell, 'for kynge Arthurs love, gyff me a gyffte, I requyre the, jantyll knyght, as thou arte a jantillman.' 'Now,' seyde sir Torre, 'aske a gyffte and I woll gyff hit you'" (112.16–20). The maiden here behaves according to expectations of the feminine as it operates in Malory's text—always in need of *something* that only a knight can provide. The terms of her request cleverly invoke the reputation and identity of both Arthur's court and Torre himself, linking the two and thereby compelling Torre to behave as a "jantillman" should, a move that affirms his own courteous knightly identity as well as that of the Arthurian court that he represents. Both the maiden and Torre "perform" Arthurian gender relations in this scene—his knightly courtesy a performative reaction to the feminine behavior and language of helplessness and need that the damsel employs.

Much to Torre's chagrin, the lady wants Abellus's head; loath to comply, Torre suggests that she seek other recompense. "'Now,' seyde the damesell, 'I may nat, for he slew myne owne brothir before myne yghen that was a bettir knyght than he'" (112.27–29). Upon hearing this, Abellus immediately drops to his knees and asks Torre for mercy. The damsel here uses the same strategy employed by a variety of female figures throughout the text to obtain their desires. It is a strategy that becomes clearer when considered in light of Luce Irigaray's theory of mimesis, which argues that women may resist the assigned position of femininity through deliberate alignment with it:

> One must assume the feminine role deliberately. Which means already to convert a form of subordination into an affirmation, and thus to begin to thwart it. Whereas a direct feminine challenge to this condition means demanding to speak as a (masculine) "subject," that is, it means to postulate a relation to the intelligible that would maintain sexual indifference. To play with mimesis is thus, for a woman, to try to recover the place of her exploitation . . . without allowing herself to be simply reduced to it.[30]

The damsel in this episode performs as a knight would expect her to, mimicking feminine behavior and thus managing to transcend her categorization as such. Although in a sense she *is* a woman in need of knightly assistance, she capitalizes on her position to effectively make Torre her instrument. Here we can see how the rigid conception of gender categories and the attributes that mark those categories actually create a space in which women may wield some measure of power and influence within the patriarchal social project of chivalry. While the Arthurian community understands and values the catalytic effect the feminine has in encouraging feats of bravery and prowess, it fails to anticipate the use of that catalytic effect for ends other than the glorification of the community and the individual knights who comprise it. In this instance, her brother's death provides the damsel with the impetus to act for her own "selfish" interests, rather than subsuming her personal desire into that of the communal good (that is, a test of knightly ability that would bring renown back to Torre and his community). Given the conflicting values in place, Torre makes the best decision he possibly can and beheads the knight. That Arthur and Guenevere praise him for his behavior further reinforces the fact of the helplessness of a knight when confronted by a lady asking favors; the knightly understanding of women as powerless ironically renders them powerful.

The quest of King Pellinor offers an interesting corollary to the Torre-Abellus episode, as he in fact *does not* accede to the request of a lady, and is condemned and punished for this behavior. Malory tells us that early in the quest "as he rode in a foreyste he saw in a valey a damesell sitte by a well and a wounded knyght in her armys, and kynge Pellynor salewed hir. And whan she was ware of hym, she cryed on lowde and seyde, 'Helpe me, knyght, for Jesuys sake!' But kynge Pellynore wolde nat tarry, he was so egir in hys queste; and ever she cryed an hondred tymes aftir helpe" (114.12–18). As he returns to Camelot at the conclusion of his quest, he passes by the same spot and finds the pair now dead, the maiden a suicide, their bodies partially eaten away by wild animals. When he relates his adventure, the king and queen chastise him severely, not least of all because the maiden, he discovers, was in fact his own daughter. Had Pellinor followed the value system of the code and yielded to the lady's request as is convention—and as the Pentecostal Oath will explicitly instruct him later—not only would he have been behaving as a proper knight, but he would have had the added reward of saving the life of his own daughter. Disobedience of both the letter and spirit of the ladies clause results not only in public rebuke (the disapproval of Arthur and Guenevere), but incurs *personal* loss as well (the suicide of his daughter).

In reworking his source material, Malory significantly chooses to insert the Pentecostal Oath immediately at the conclusion of this first triplequest: "Thus whan the queste was done of the whyght herte the whych folowed sir Gawayne, and the queste of the brachet whych folowed sir Torre, kyng Pellynors son, and the queste of the lady that the knyghte toke away, whych at that tyme folowed kynge Pellynor, than the kynge stablysshed all the knyghtes and gaff them rychesse and londys" (120.11–16). Several scholars have pointed out the significance of the fact that the Oath comes immediately upon the completion of these quests. Thomas Wright, for example, argues that "in its own terms Malory's narrative follows a course from disorder and rebellion to the oath of chivalry, itself a code that grows out of the wedding quests and is proved in the adventures that close the 'Tale of King Arthur.' Such departures from the inherited tradition . . . point unmistakably to Malory's conscious drafting of a new version of Arthurian matter, not to his making a mere facsimile of the *Suite du Merlin*."[31] In the *Suite*, Arthur establishes the Round Table before his wedding; in Malory, Arthur's creation of the Round Table order at this moment links his heteronormativity (affirmed through marriage) to the lessons learned by questing knights.[32]

The Ywain-Gawain-Marhalt triple-quest, which occurs *after* the institution of the Pentecostal Oath, reinforces the values enacted in the Gawain-Torre-Pellinor triple-quest, particularly in terms of ladies. Early on in the quest, the three knights encounter three damsels sitting near a fountain:

> And the eldyst had a garlonde of golde aboute her hede, and she was three score wyntir of age or more, and hir heyre was whyght undir the garlonde. The secunde damselle was of thirty wyntir of age, wyth a cerclet of golde aboute her hede. The thirde damesel was but fiftene yere of age, and a garlande of floures aboute hir hede. . . . "We be here," seyde the damesels, "for this cause: if we may se ony of arraunte knyghtes to tech hem unto strong aventures. And ye be three knyghtes adventures and we be three damesels, and therefore eche one of you must chose one of us; and whan ye have done so, we woll lede you unto three hyghewayes, and there eche of you shall chose a way and his damesell with hym" (162.31–38, 163.1–7).

From its inception, this adventure dramatizes the link between feminine presence and the masculine activity of the quest.[33] At the same time, the experiences on this quest also offer a suggestive warning about the power of feminine influence over knights. Gawain, for example, encounters a knight—Pelleas—who allows himself to be regularly captured, simply so that he may be brought into the presence of his unrequited love, the lady Ettard. Gawain offers to help Pelleas but is himself so besotted with the lady that he fails to do his "trew parte" and seduces the lady himself, breaking his promise and compromising his identity as a knight of worship.

Ywain becomes involved with a different kind of conflict that involves a lady. In a scene that appears to be original to Malory, Ywain fights on behalf of the Lady of the Roche, who has been "desheryted . . . of a barony of londis" by two brother knights, sirs Edward and Hew of the Red Castle. Exclaims Ywain when he learns of the lady's predicament: "Madam . . . they ar to blaime, for they do ayenste the hyghe Order of Knyghthode and the oth that they made. And if it lyke you I woll speke with hem, because I am a knyght of kyng Arthurs, and to entrete them with fayrenesse; and if they woll nat, I shall do batayle with them for Goddis sake and in the defence of your ryght" (177.10–15). This original passage is particularly important in terms of Ywain's citation of the Round Table Oath; as Thomas Wright notes, "[Ywain] remembers the sworn oath of Arthur's court, and his actions are so conditioned by it that they attain a moral relevance for which Malory himself is responsible."[34] Here we see one of the first instances in which the institution of the Oath clearly sharpens the issue of knightly behavior—and in particular, behavior toward ladies—when it is compared to its Oath-less source.

All of the women encountered during knightly adventures seem to act with a clear understanding of the knightly code and their expected role in terms of it. In turn, many of these female characters demonstrate an awareness that, while the code does not address women directly, they are implicated in that it addresses the *issue of women* for knights. Significantly, resistance to categorization as feminine, when it does occur, usually occurs *in the terms of the code,* generally through the act of mimesis. The awareness of the code, in combination with the lack of a parallel code designed to regulate feminine behavior, opens up a space of feminine influence at the very heart of the masculine chivalric enterprise. The feminine is so critical to the construction of knightly identity that to acknowledge the possibility of a feminine appropriation of power—let alone to attempt to combat it—threatens to expose the fiction of gender identity upon which the community is founded. These feminine figures, whether or not their conduct is subsumed within a desire for the common good, are able to use the Pentecostal Oath and its understanding of the feminine as either a defense or a weapon against their socially constructed identities.

Gender, Genealogy, and Gifts: Igrayne, Morgause, and Guenevere

Although it comes near the end of the first portion of Malory's text, the Pentecostal Oath articulates the connection between gender and violence that is present from the very first moments of the "Tale of King Arthur." Malory begins his text with an episode from Arthurian prehistory, and significantly, he opens the *Morte d'Arthur* with a familiar romance theme—the love of a man for an unattainable woman—and immediately pairs this motif with the masculine display of violence intrinsic to chivalric literature: "Hit befel in the dayes of Uther Pendragon, when he was kynge of all Englond and so regned, that there was a myghty duke in Cornewaill

that helde warre ageynst hym long tyme. . . . And so by meanes kynge
Uther send for this duk charging hym to brynge his wyf with hym, for she
was called a fair lady and a passynge wyse, and her name was called
Igrayne" (7.1–7). Malory's source makes no mention of a specific conflict
between Uther and Cornwall; in the *Merlin* "Une foiz prist talant au roi
qu'il semondroit touz ses barons et que por l'amour de lui et por s'onor
amenissient tuit lor femmes et preïssient as autres chevaliers de lor terres
que il amenissient les lor" [the king happened . . . to wish to call his barons
together, and, for the honor and love of him, he wanted them to bring their
wives and noble vassals and knights].[35] From the inception of Malory's
narrative, then, masculine rivalry on the battlefield is explicitly amplified
and extended into rivalry over a woman. Martial and marital issues are
linked in a way that they are not in his source.

In response to Uther's overtures, Malory tells us that Igrayne asks her
husband that they depart from court, for "she was a passyng good woman
and wold not assente unto the kynge" (7.11–13). The duke and his wife
secretly leave the court and return to the castle Tintagel, whereupon the
angry Uther convenes his barons to determine what should be done in the
face of such an insult. They advise the king to "send for the duke and his
wyf by a grete charge: 'and yf he wille not come at your somons, thenne
may ye do your best; and thenne have ye cause to make myghty werre
upon hym'" (7.25–28).

By his actions, Uther acknowledges and reaffirms the codependency
of the ruler-subject relationship and its construction of individual and
communal identity in terms of the chivalric ethos; however, the council's
assertion that Uther is justified in attacking Cornwall tacitly affirms and
supports Uther's dishonorable desire for another man's wife. In response
to this dilemma, the conflict between Uther and Cornwall is directed away
from the true source—the woman Igrayne—and redirected toward concerns over power, rule, and insult. Even though partially obscured, however, the feminine—the helpless, vulnerable Igrayne—is still a key component in the definition of communal identity in this episode. As the
contested object in the quarrel between Cornwall and Uther, Igrayne helps
define the identities of the parties involved as heteronormative.

In the Uther-Igrayne-Cornwall conflict, the concerns of masculine warfare are clearly intertwined with those of heterosexual desire. Further
analysis of this episode also reveals that the chivalric community achieves
definition in terms of a Same/Other binarism. Igrayne becomes the feminine Other against which both groups of men define themselves, and simi-

larly, Cornwall and his allies are constructed as a masculine Other against which the Same of Uther and his men are consolidated. In both of these processes, however, the Other necessarily becomes essential to the construction of the Same, and thus, is not really Other, but in fact *proximate*. Jonathan Dollimore has termed this "transgressive reinscription," arguing that "the proximate is often constructed as the other, and in a process which facilitates displacement. But the proximate is also what enables a tracking-back of the 'other' into the 'same.' I call this transgressive reinscription."[36] Significantly, Dollimore's theorization of proximatization is easily applied to both the female-male dynamic of Uther and Igrayne as well as the male-male relationship between Uther and Cornwall, indicating the similarity of formation of heterosexual and homosocial identities. This similarity necessarily provokes anxieties in the heteronormative chivalric society of the *Morte d'Arthur*. To maintain stable boundaries around these identities—to quell such anxieties—is the source and focus of much of the knightly activity of the text.

As with all knightly encounters that take place in the *Morte d'Arthur*, the Same/Other binarism here quickly becomes destabilized and recast as a Same/Same. We are not told the cause of the long-standing feud between Uther and Cornwall that takes place before the opening of the tale, only that in (seemingly) seeking to end it, Uther sends for his enemy and his enemy's wife. The masculine rivalry that already exists between them then extends from the masculine homosocial sphere into the realm of heterosexual desire in a move that links the two explicitly. Drawing on the work of René Girard, Eve Sedgwick has pointed out that in an erotic triangle such as this "the bond that links the two rivals is as intense and potent as the bond that links either of the rivals to the beloved. . . . the choice of the beloved is determined in the first place, not by the qualities of the beloved, but by the beloved's already being the choice of the person who has been chosen as a rival."[37] Although mutual desire for Igrayne causes the conflict to escalate, Uther's *desire itself* would seem to be a product of his earlier conflict with Cornwall.

And while the king and the duke stand in opposition to each other, seemingly each the Other to the Other's Same, it is their likeness that facilitates the fact of their contention: both men are leaders of chivalric courtly communities with similar values, desires, and gender-identity "templates." When ranged face-to-face on the battlefield, they and their armies are as mirror images, just as two armored knights on horseback reflect back to one another the picture of masculinity each is attempting to establish and maintain as his own.[38] In other words, the *similarities* between Uther and Cornwall create the circumstances that manifest their *differences*. After Cornwall's death, we see a literal reinscription: Uther smoothly reincorporates Cornwall's holdings into his own. Gorlois's lands, his men, and his wife are transferred from the duke to the king with little expended effort. What was once the Other is revealed to be the Same. In essence, conflict in the terms of chivalry is made possible by similarity between the warring parties—a shared chivalric ethos, sensibility, or "language" facilitates military engagement.

Malory tells us repeatedly that Igrayne was a "passyng good woman," and holds her up as a model of proper feminine behavior, reasserting the idealized and absolute dependence of women upon men in the chivalric project. Upon learning that her husband has not only been killed, but also passed away hours before her sexual encounter with Uther in the likeness of Cornwall, Igrayne "mourned pryvely and held hir pees" (9.30); she offers no objection when the nobles of the land decide to wed her to Uther, the man responsible for the death of her husband; when Uther reveals to her his deception and that he is in fact the father of the child she is carrying, Malory tells us that "Thenne the quene made grete joye whan she knewe who was the fader of her child" (10.31–32); and upon the death of Uther, her second husband, Malory relates that as was the case with the passing of her first, "fayre Igrayne made grete sorowe and alle the barons" (12.10). Igrayne stands out as *the* exemplary female in Malory's text, quickly and silently adapting to the needs and wants of the men who fight over and exchange her.

When word comes that Cornwall has been defeated by Uther's forces, Malory tells us that "alle the barons by one assent prayd the kynge of accord betwixe the lady Igrayne and hym" (9.31–32), to which request the king accedes and charges Sir Ulfius to make the arrangements for the wedding. As with the decision to attack Cornwall, the king's subsequent marriage is represented as not only the result of his own *personal* desire, but also as an act that will fulfill some perceived need of the community over which he presides; it is a body of—again, significantly male—nobles who comes to this decision. Just as she became the largely silent object of the erotic triangle of king, duke, and lady, Igrayne is the silent corner once again in the development of a plan to reincorporate Cornwall into Uther's larger kingdom: "'Now wille we doo wel,' said Ulfyus; 'our kyng is a lusty knyght and wyveles, and my lady Igrayne is a passynge fair lady; it were grete joye unto us all and hit myghte please the kynge to make her his quene.' Unto that they were all well accordyd and meved it to the kynge. And anone, lyke a lusty knyghte, he assentid therto with good wille, and so in alle haste they were maryed in a mornynge with grete myrthe and joye" (9.36–39, 10.1–4).

While the king's assent to the will of his people is important to the reestablishment of order, Igrayne's explicit consent is deemed unnecessary for the act of reintegrating her first husband's realm into that of her second. Igrayne is the gift, an object that is exchanged for peace, property, and a means of establishing male homosocial bonds within this patriarchal, kin-based social order. In a striking example of community solidarity, several other important unions are consecrated at the same time that Uther and Igrayne are wed: "And kynge Lott of Lowthean and of Orkenay thenne wedded Margawse . . . and kynge Nentres of the land of Garlot wedded Elayne: al this was done at the request of kynge Uther. And the thyrd syster, Morgan le Fey, was put to scole in a nonnery. . . . And after she was wedded to kynge Uryens of the lond of Gore" (10.5–12). This is the first time that the theme of wedding proliferation occurs in Malory; the text insistently repeats this pattern, each time pointing to the importance of such unions in affirming social bonds and the critical role that women play in this exchange and alliance of power and kinship.

Silently, passively, obediently, women are circulated or "gifted" away— by, to, and for men—serving, in their transfer from one male to another, to reinforce and strengthen the homosocial ties that bind the Arthurian community together. Wedding proliferation supports and reinforces the validity of those institutions; the occurrence of these other marriages at the same time as Uther and Igrayne's sanctions the king's actions. At the same time, King Lot and King Nentres derive for their own unions important significance in that they are connected in a special way with the power and status of King Uther. Each of these marriages affirms and increases the significance of the other, and a double benefit is derived: for the community, which is strengthened through this act of solidarity, and for each of the individuals of this community, who derive for themselves some measure of extra power and influence through their participation in this socially important ritual.

While these appropriate transfers of women among kin groups serve to strengthen the chivalric community, the early pages of Malory's text also depict the potentially destructive power of *inappropriate* feminine exchanges. In particular, the relationship of Queen Morgause and King Arthur—unknowing half-brother and half-sister—produces arguably the most destructive element in the text: the incestuously begotten Mordred. At the end of Malory's work, Mordred seeks to re-create the sin of his parents by attempting to wed Queen Guenevere, both his aunt and his stepmother.[39] His act will provoke the final battle at Salisbury Plain, in which Arthur and his nephew/son mortally wound one another.

A moment from the closing pages of the text suggestively points to the negative impact Morgause and Arthur's illicit relationship has had on the chivalric community. On the field at Dover, Arthur stands over his dying nephew Gawain—also Morgause's son—and laments him with a signifi- cant choice of words: "Alas! sir Gawayne, my syster son, here now thou lyghest, the man in the worlde that I loved moste. And now ys my joy gone! For now, my nevew, sir Gawayne, I woll discover me unto you, that in youre person and in sir Launcelot I moste had my joy and myne affyaunce. And now have I loste my joy of you bothe, wherefore all myne erthely joy ys gone fro me!" (1230.11–17). Malory has altered this speech as he found it in his source, the *Mort Artu*. In the French, Arthur exclaims, "Biax niés, grant domage m'a fet vostre felonnie, car ele m'a tolu vos, que ge amoie seur touz hommes, et Lancelot après" ["Dear nephew, your treachery has done me great harm, because it deprived me both of you, whom I loved more than anyone else, and also of Lancelot"].[40] Arthur's choice of words in the *Morte d'Arthur* is notable; while in both the *Mort Artu* and the English *Stanzaic Morte Arthur*, Arthur refers to Gawain as his "nephew," there is no reference to the mother who bore him. The mo- ment when Arthur laments over the body of his "syster son" both exalts and condemns a system of social order founded upon a kin-based patriar- chal structure in which the bodies of women form the locus of masculine homosocial relationships. When viewed through the lens of Morgause, we see that the idealized patriarchal order of the chivalric community is un- done by its refusal to recognize that the exchange of women on which its structure depends may be threatened by those very objects of transaction, should they resist their particular identity construction as commodities to be exchanged.

Although supposedly one of Uther's allies through marriage to Mor- gause, daughter of Queen Igrayne, Lot is also one of several leaders who refuse to accept Arthur as king. Malory tells us that:

> And thydir com unto hym kynge Lottis wyff of Orkeney in maner of a message, but she was sente thydir to aspye the courte of kynge Arthur, and . . . she was a passynge fayre lady. Wherefore the kynge caste grete love unto hir and desired to ly by her. And so they were

agreed, and he begate uppon hir sir Mordred. And she was syster on
the modirs syde Igrayne unto Arthur. . . . (But all thys tyme kynge
Arthure knew nat that kynge Lottis wyff was his sister.) (41.12–25)[41]

When critics speak of this scene, they focus primarily on *Arthur* and his
actions; Morgause merits little discussion. Most of the critical ink spilled
on the subject is devoted to establishing which is the king's greater sin—
adultery or incest. For example, in an issue of *Arthuriana* devoted to the
topic of "Arthurian Adultery," David Scott Wilson-Okamura focuses on
Malory's source for the "Tale of King Arthur," the *Suite du Merlin*, and
states, "My primary goal is to correct what seems to me an oversight on
the part of the *Suite's* previous critics, who have consistently emphasized
the incestuous aspect of Mordred's conception, neglecting its adulterous
aspect altogether."[42] In the same issue, Beverly Kennedy similarly examines the *king's* sin, arguing that Arthur's act of adultery with Morgause
does not result in any loss of honor for the king because "the woman is
willing and the adulterer is not honor-bound to be loyal to her husband."[43]

Scholars have also looked to the first example of adulterous activity in
Malory and his sources—Uther Pendragon's seduction of Igrayne while
disguised as her husband, the Duke of Cornwall—and sought to draw parallels and connections between the two events. Speaking of Malory's
source text, Victoria Guerin attempts to render the nature of the Arthurian
tragedy down to its core elements: "Uther's adultery with Igerna, and
Arthur's own consequent birth, now become a realization of the biblical
threat of 'visiting the iniquity of the fathers upon the children unto the
third and fourth generation.' Arthur is doomed to repeat, in all innocence,
his father's sin of adultery in a far more serious form and . . . to sow the
seeds of his own downfall."[44] While Arthur's adultery with Morgause
should hardly be referred to as an act committed "in all innocence,"
Guerin's succinct description of the factors that produce the final social
collapse suggests that the ending of the *Morte d'Arthur* has been foretold
from its opening pages and that Arthur and the other characters have in
some sense been nothing more than puppets, seemingly unable to avoid
fulfilling the destiny that Uther's acts of deception and conception have
created.

The sin of incest, then, appears subordinate to that of adultery. Although Mordred had from the time of Geoffrey of Monmouth been por-
trayed as Arthur's enemy, the nephew who attempts to usurp the throne
while the king is away, it is not until the thirteenth century and the com-

position of the earliest sections of the French Vulgate that the story of Mordred includes his incestuous conception.[45] While the incestuous aspect of Arthur's relationship with Morgause effectively renders Mordred a more horrific, inherently evil villain for both medieval and modern audiences, what seems to be of greatest importance here is that Arthur is apparently the author of his own undoing, whether it be the sin of incest or adultery that ultimately brings about the destruction of his realm.[46] While critics have long rightly looked to Arthur's incestuous and adulterous relationship with Morgause as the source of one of the destructive forces that will cause the collapse of the Arthurian community, their focus—on *Arthur's* sin—has been entirely wrong. The chivalric social order is not primarily damaged by the actions of the king in begetting the traitorous Mordred. It is not even Mordred, villainous as he is, who is fully to blame: Morgause's behavior is a much more important force in the undoing of the chivalric community.

We can see the full significance of Morgause's actions through a comparison of her relationship with Arthur to that of Uther and Igrayne. The Uther-Igrayne and Arthur-Morgause episodes follow in many ways a similar pattern; however, each has strikingly different outcomes. While Uther's semi-rape of Igrayne produces the noble Arthur, Arthur's consensual yet adulterous liaison with Morgause results in the evil Mordred. What is to account for these different outcomes? The answer is in the role that the feminine plays in each of these encounters, and how each of these women conform to or resist chivalric ideals of femininity. Igrayne never knowingly consents to the betrayal of her lord, while in the case of Morgause, Lot's wife willingly participates in the cuckolding of her husband: "Wherefore the kynge caste grete love unto hir and desired to ly by her. *And so they were agreed,* and he begate uppon hir sir Mordred" (emphasis mine).[47] Where Malory emphasizes the agreement between Arthur and Lot's wife, the source text does not:

> Moult fist li rois Artus grant joie de la dame et moult le festia et li et ses enfans. Li rois vit la dame de grant biauté plainne, si l'ama durement, et la fist demourer en sa court deus mois entiers. Et tant qu'en chelui terme il gut a li et engenra en li Mordrec, par cui tant grant mal furent puis fait en la terre de Logres et en tout le monde.

> [King Arthur received the lady and her children with rejoicing and feasting. He saw that the lady was beautiful and loved her passion-

ately and kept her at his court for two whole months, until finally he lay with her and begat on her Mordred, by whom such wrongs were later done in Logres and in all the world].[48]

The most significant difference between Arthur's and Mordred's conceptions is not the fact that Mordred is conceived incestuously or adulterously, but rather that Morgause is an *active* player in the adultery—she is not seduced, or deceived as Igrayne is. Rather, she *agrees* to commit the sin of adultery. It is her agreement, her active role in the exchange of her body, that threatens the patriarchal social order of Arthur's kingdom.

The work of Claude Lévi-Strauss has relevance here in understanding the problem posed by Morgause's actions. In his discussion of kinship systems (an important preoccupation of medieval literature, specifically chivalric romance literature), Lévi-Strauss identifies the transfer or exchange of women as the means by which such systems generate broader social structures:

> The total relationship which constitutes marriage is not established between a man and a woman, but between two groups of men, the woman figures only as one of the objects in the exchange, not as one of the partners. . . . This remains true even when the girl's feelings are taken into consideration as, moreover, is usually the case. In acquiescing to the proposed union, she precipitates or allows the exchange to take place, she cannot alter its nature.[49]

Lévi-Strauss further identifies the incest taboo as an important element in the formation of kinship systems, arguing that such a constraint amplifies the possibilities for wide-ranging social relationships and linking of kinship groups: "The prohibition on the sexual use of a daughter or sister compels them to be given in marriage to another man, and at the same time it establishes a right to the daughter or sister of this other man. . . . The woman whom one does not take is, for that very reason, offered up."[50] Gayle Rubin, engaging Lévi-Strauss in her now-classic essay "The Traffic in Women: Notes on the 'Political Economy' of Sex," points out that in the distinction between "gift and giver" in such a system, it is those who are the "givers" who enjoy the benefits of social linkage with one other, and that as "gifts" women cannot derive any benefit from their own circulation: "As long as the relations specify that men exchange women, it is men who are the beneficiaries of the product of such exchanges—social organization."[51] In the *Morte d'Arthur*, the social organization effected by such exchanges depends upon the construction of the feminine as silent, passive, and malleable—a commodity to be exchanged.

Morgause, however, resists commodification. Exchanged by her stepfather, Uther Pendragon, to secure an alliance with King Lot of Orkney, Morgause clearly serves her function as a commodity in the patriarchal chivalric community of the *Morte d'Arthur*, a system in which loyalty is indeed first established by blood and then extended in alliance with other kin groups through a practice of exogamy. Once married, Morgause produces four sons and is therefore removed from the marketplace of patriarchy. In the terms of Luce Irigaray, Morgause becomes "use value": "mothers, reproductive instruments marked with the name of the father and enclosed in his house, must be private property, excluded from exchange."[52] But as Morgause's relationship with Arthur demonstrates, patriarchy can only succeed when those commodities exchanged—women— are stringently controlled as property under the name of the father or husband to whom they "belong" or have been "gifted" and when men acknowledge the right of another man to possess a woman, seeking to obtain access to her only through the proper channels. As Gayle Rubin points out, "kinship systems do not merely exchange women. They exchange sexual access, genealogical statuses, lineage names and ancestors, rights and *people*—men, women, and children—in concrete systems of social relationships."[53] Morgause and Arthur transgress patriarchal systems of social relationships by breaking the incest taboo and committing adultery; but what is of greatest import here is the active role Morgause plays in the exchange of her body.[54]

In agreeing to the relationship with Arthur, Morgause effects a transaction of feminine sexuality that subverts the conventions of patriarchy. No man contracts access to Morgause's body, or exchanges it for power, wealth, or status—Morgause is both gift *and* giver, a stark contrast to her mother. Igrayne resists Uther's overtures as long as she is married to another man; upon Cornwall's death, Igrayne's resistance dissipates, and she silently permits herself to be the object of masculine exchange, thereby strengthening the chivalric social order. Morgause's behavior runs contrary to the greater communal good, and her agreement to commit adultery threatens not only her husband, King Lot, but also her transgression poses a danger to the larger Arthurian community, in that the product of that adultery is Mordred. Although it is Mordred's adulterous and incestuous conception that is repeatedly invoked as one of the primary causes of the destruction of the chivalric community, the questions of adultery and incest are silenced beside the larger question of proper feminine behavior. It is Morgause's *agreement*—as was the case with Igrayne's *resistance*—that is critical to an understanding of the destructive impact of this act on the rest of the community.

Through Morgause, then, Arthur acquires one of his greatest allies—his nephew Gawain—as well as his greatest enemy—his nephew/son Mordred. Significantly, Morgause herself is later destroyed by her own kin, killed by her son Gaheris when he catches her in bed with Sir Lamorak: "So whan sir Gaherys sawe his tyme he cam to there beddis syde all armed, wyth his swerde naked, and suddaynly he gate his modir by the heyre and strake of her hede. Whan sir Lameroke saw the blood daysshe uppon hym all hote . . . wyte you well he was sore abaysshed and dismayed of that dolerous syght" (612.9–15). Although a widow at this point, Morgause has again enacted a double transgression against the patriarchal social order by acting as her own agent in gifting herself to Lamorak and further, by betraying the kin group of her husband and sons: Lamorak is the son of King Pellinor, the man whom Gaheris and his brothers believe slew their own father, King Lot.

Tellingly, Gaheris does not slay Lamorak, although he is naked and unarmed at the time of Gaheris's attack on Morgause: "Alas, why have ye slayne youre modir that bare you? For with more ryght ye shulde have slayne me!" exclaims Lamorak. Gaheris's response—"And now is my modir quytte of the, for she shall never shame her chyldryn" (612.18–35)—points up the hierarchy of transgressions and values around which the ideology of the Arthurian community is ordered. Morgause's transgression, clearly, poses the greater threat to the social order than does Lamorak's. Her refusal to adhere to the structures of kin-loyalty and submit to the sanctioned circulation of women between and among groups of men identifies Morgause (or more appropriately, her transgressive actions) as a danger to the Arthurian community. Indeed, Gaheris's act is an attempt to rescue the threatened social order, but it comes far too late. In stepping outside the prescribed role of the feminine in agreeing to a relationship with Arthur, Morgause has already compromised the foundation of the chivalric community years before her relationship with Lamorak. Morgause's willing participation in the liaison that leads to the conception of Mordred—not the adultery or the unintentional incest—makes of Arthur's nephew/son such a monster, a figure for whom the structure of patriarchy has no place.

Thus, when near the end of the text Arthur stands over the mortally wounded Gawain and offers up a lament for his "syster son," he mourns not only the loss of his nephew and ally but also the collapse of the entire community, a collapse in part precipitated by *another* "syster son," Mordred. In her marriage to King Lot and her subsequent production of sons who become strong allies of their uncle Arthur, Morgause exemplifies how the exchange of women is central to the establishment of relationships and alliances between and among men, and further, how such exchanges and relationships form the foundation of the Arthurian social order. As a willing participant in her adulterous liaison with Arthur, she similarly reveals the tenuous quality of that order.

An examination of another of Arthur's sexual liaisons clarifies the destructive nature of Morgause's actions: "Than in the meanewhyle there com a damesell that was an erlis doughter; hys name was Sanam and hir name was Lyonors. . . . And so she cam thidir for to do omage as other lordis ded after that grete batayle. And kynge Arthure sette hys love gretly on hir, and so ded she uppon hym, and so the kynge had ado with hir and gate on hir a chylde. And hys name was Borre, that was after a good knyght of the Table Rounde" (38.27–34). Lyonors, like Morgause, willingly accedes to the king's overtures. The difference is Lyonors's unmarried state. While fornication is a sin as surely as adultery, the lack of anxiety over this coupling and its offspring, Borre, is due to the fact that genealogy is here not a question. That Arthur is Borre's sire does not compromise the integrity of another man's identity and power as Arthur's parentage of Mordred compromises Lot's stable identity, nor does it pose a threat in terms of claims of inheritance, at least from the position of Lyonors's father. Although as an unmarried woman Lyonors is still considered the property of her father in the terms of patriarchy, her union with Arthur—far from shaming her father, who has only control *over* (and not access to) her sexuality—brings Earl Sanam into closer relationship with the king, and thereby derives for him some benefit.[55] As a *husband* Lot's only profit from Morgause's incest and adultery is shame.

The Uther-Igrayne and Arthur-Morgause episodes demonstrate the intense anxiety surrounding gender identities in the Arthurian chivalric community and the need of the masculine to objectify, marginalize, and construct the feminine as passive and vulnerable, thereby maintaining the stable masculine heterosexual identity essential to the maintenance of patriarchy. Having claimed his rightful throne and successfully defended his right to do so against the eleven dissenting kings, to further consolidate his power and assert his heteronormativity, Arthur next takes a wife: Guenevere, daughter of King Leodegran. This episodic subsection of Malory's first tale—called "Torre and Pellinor" in the Winchester manuscript but referred to by Malory in the explicit as the "Wedding of King Arthur"—begins with Arthur's marriage to Guenevere and establishment of the Round Table and concludes with the articulation of the Pentecostal Oath. Arthur's marriage and the activities surrounding it dramatize the function of the feminine in maintaining the coherence of the chivalric community. In her role as queen, Guenevere does what Louise Fradenburg has described as "lend[ing] sovereign authority to sexual difference and heterosexualiz[ing] sovereignty."[56] As Arthur's wife, Guenevere validates the ideal of a compulsory heterosexuality while simultaneously removing any need for Arthur to perform his adherence to this gender scheme; the fact of the king's marriage effects a continuous performance of his heteronormativity.

In exchange for the increase in status Leodegran receives from the transaction of Guenevere, he sends to Arthur an additional gift: "'That is to me,' seyde kyng Lodegreauns, 'the beste tydynges that ever I herde, that so worthy a kyng of prouesse and noblesse wol wedde my doughter. And as for my londis, I wolde geff hit hym, but he hath londis inow, he nedith none. But I shall sende hym the Table Rounde which Uther, hys fadir, gaff me. And whan hit ys fulle complete there ys an hondred knyghtes and fyfty'" (98.3–11). Leodegran's statement makes explicit the link between control of the feminine and access to power. The cementing of homosocial bonds with Leodegran through the exchange of Guenevere provides Arthur with the agents of his chivalric community: the Round Table knights. Although similar to Uther's privy council, the Round Table subcommunity is more rigidly defined, the actions of its members narrowly pre- and pro-scribed by the articles of the Pentecostal Oath. In adhering to these rules, the Round Table knights also engage in a performance of masculinity that quickly emerges as an essential and endlessly repetitive enterprise designed to maintain the Round Table subcommunity as the center of power.

As I have suggested above, in the *Morte d'Arthur* the primary vehicle by which knights construct themselves as particular masculine individuals belonging to a larger particular community is the quest. Feminine acts of facilitation, enabling, and mediation repeatedly manifest themselves as essential to the project of questing. Upon completion of the quest, knights must offer an account—a verbal performance—of their adventures to Queen Guenevere, whose judgment of their behavior either validates or undermines their knightly masculine identities. While Guenevere is one of those feminine figures who later on destabilizes the social order, for much of the text she demonstrates a positive, explicit, and direct engagement with the shaping of knightly identity in her role as queen. In the triple-quest of Gawain, Torre, and Pellinor, Guenevere acts as judge, rendering verdicts on the actions and behavior of the knights as they return from questing.[57] At this early stage in Malory's *Morte d'Arthur*, Guenevere successfully models proper queenly behavior, arguably complementing, enhancing—and indeed, in some sense compensating for—the silent, passive model afforded by Igrayne.[58] As queen, Guenevere functions differently from those female characters who pierce the masculine fellowship from without to present the opportunity for adventure.[59] The queen differs also from those so-called quest maidens who never enter the court at all, but are instead encountered by knights within the mysterious realm of the forest of adventure.[60]

The queen has a special relationship to the Gawain-Torre-Pellinor triple-quest, as the "mervayle" that precipitates it is seemingly created specifically as entertainment to mark the occasion of her marriage to King Arthur: "Than was feste made redy, and the kynge was wedded at Camelot unto dame Gwenyvere in the chirche of Seynte Stephyns. . . . Merlion wente to all the knyghtes of the Rounde Table and bade hem sitte stylle, 'that none of you remeve, for ye shall se a straunge and a mervailous adventure'" (102.22–27). Immediately thereafter, the "adventure" begins. A hart, a brachet, and a lady come into the hall; the brachet is led away by a knight, and when the lady (also its owner) protests, she too is taken from the hall by another knight. Arthur then summons Gawain, Torre, and King Pellinor and charges each respectively with retrieving the hart, the brachet, and the lady.

In charging each knight with his particular quest, Arthur proclaims before the court that "thes three knyghtes shall do mervayles adventures or they com agayne" (103.23–24). Upon completion of these quests, Gawain, Torre, and Pellinor relate their "mervayles adventures" before the assembled court in a presentation that will become an important aspect of the maintenance of the chivalric community. The reenactment of those adventures encountered away from the court functions as a ritualistic performance, allowing king, knights, and other members of the community access to the experiences of the individual knight. Indeed, this oral performance is essential for validating that knightly individual and his actions; one can see how the Arthurian community depends upon the processes of storytelling—of fiction—for self-definition. Each quest offers to the court *more stories about itself,* a plethora of individual experiences valuable primarily as representative experiences of the community as a whole. The moment of storytelling, of recounting the experience of the quest, permits those who have stayed behind to participate through the expression of praise or condemnation. Through its positive or negative response, the community refines and clarifies the idea of proper knightly behavior.

Guenevere's assigned sphere of influence seems limited to the realm of "feminine concerns," and, significantly, the power afforded her is given on the condition that she exercise it in concert with the dominant masculine concerns of the community. If, as Elizabeth Pochoda claims, "the quest is motivated by the desire to perfect the nature of Arthurian society through chivalry,"[61] and the Arthurian chivalric community depends upon a marginalized feminine presence for enactment and completion, then Guenevere's role as arbiter of justice underscores the paradoxical position—critical yet marginal—of the feminine in the masculine activity of the quest. Significantly, Guenevere here models the ideal of feminine chivalric behavior in that all of her judgments in this episode correspond with Arthur's own desires. Guenevere's ability to speak from a position of authority—even though her verdicts must be understood as reflective of Arthur's own concerns—hints at the *potential* for the feminine to co-opt official influence and power. This moment suggests the possibility that her own judgment could diverge from that of Arthur and more dangerously, that the queen might at some point later in the narrative clearly enunciate a belief or opinion, or give an order, that does not correspond to what Arthur would desire in such a circumstance. The potential of *this* threat, however, is nothing compared to the very real threat posed by Arthur's half-sister, Morgan le Fay.

The Lady Who Is Not One: Morgan le Fay

The heading of this section obviously invokes Luce Irigaray's assertion that women constitute "a sex which is not one";[62] my title for this section indicates my belief that Morgan's position transcends categorization as feminine, as that against which the knights may define their masculinity. According to Irigaray, the feminine within patriarchal culture and discourse is repressed to such a degree that it may return only as man's specularized Other.[63] While the dynamics of Malory's text make clear the necessary presence of a marginalized, subjugated feminine presence for enactment and completion of the chivalric project, Irigaray's model is applicable in the sense that the feminine is so crucial to the construction of knightly identity that it becomes fully subsumed within that constructed identity. In other words, the specularized feminine is what makes and identifies masculinity as such; it cannot be understood as simply that *against which* the masculine defines itself. Interestingly, in its depiction of the feminine, Malory's text seems to shift between modes of representation; at moments, the feminine is constructed as a category against which masculinity may define itself but in the clear dependence of the chivalric project upon a feminine presence, there also occurs a slippage, in which femininity becomes subsumed and undifferentiated within constructions of masculine identity. The masculine absorbs the feminine into its construction and the Same/Other binarism destabilizes into a Same/Same.

The character of Morgan is remarkable for the way that she often resists even the circumscribed definition of the feminine generally deployed by Malory's text; simultaneously and never fully *both* masculine *and* feminine in her actions, Morgan poses the greatest threat to the community's model of gender and social identity. Morgan's absolute rejection of a singular position in favor of a diffuse, heterogeneous identity is all the more fascinating because in her socially constructed position, Morgan is more significantly "of" this community than any other woman we see in the "Tale of King Arthur" and indeed, in the *Morte d'Arthur* as a whole. For while Igrayne, Morgause, and Guenevere are all noble-born and become the wives of kings, none of these women can enjoy and wield power in the way or to the degree that Morgan does, nor do they attempt to. The noble-born sister of a king, Morgan enjoys rights and privileges first on the basis of her kinship with Arthur and then achieves for herself a still greater measure of power as the wife of Arthur's ally, King Uriens, through marriage to whom she becomes a ruling queen in her own right. Neither Igrayne nor Guenevere ever occupies two such positions of power *simultaneously* as Morgan does, and while Morgause's position as wife of King Lot is analogous to Morgan's, *her* husband, unlike Uriens, is Arthur's enemy. Morgan's power and status are exponentially amplified through the multiplicity of relationships and sources—marriage, kinship, witchcraft—from which her power derives.

Morgan signals her potential for future trouble-making from her first mention in the text:

And Lott of Lowthean and of Orkenay thenne wedded Margawse that was Gaweyns moder, and kynge Nentres of the land of Garlot

> wedded Elayne: al this was done at the request of kynge Uther. And
> the thyrd sister, Morgan le Fey was put to scole in a nonnery, and ther
> she lerned so moche that she was a grete clerke of nygromancye. And
> after she was wedded to kynge Uryens of the lond of Gore that was
> syre Ewayns le Blaunche Maynys fader. (10.5–12)

The two institutions designed for control of the feminine in the chivalric
community—marriage and the convent—suggestively seem incapable of
containing Morgan. Indeed, not only does she escape the nunnery, but
while there, this "thyrd sister" of King Arthur manages to appropriate and
adapt the function of the convent to suit her own ends. At the end of the
Morte d'Arthur, Guenevere enters a convent and finds redemption there;
she ends her days as a noble figure of queenship and penitence. Morgan's
character undergoes an inverse experience, exiting the convent a witch
when she entered as merely a noble woman. Her marriage to King Uriens
could be viewed, then, as a second attempt to control her, or as an effort to
redress or undo the damage of the potentially dangerous knowledge she
acquires in the convent. As we will see later, however, the attempt at control fails utterly.

After the initial mention of Morgan early in Malory's first book, she
vanishes almost completely from the narrative—Malory makes only a
brief mention of her as accompanying her mother, Igrayne, to Arthur's
court when the latter is sent for to settle the question of Arthur's bloodline.
She next appears as the guardian of Excalibur and its scabbard, and Malory
offers the reader an ominous portent:

> So aftir for grete truste Arthure betoke the scawberde unto Morgan
> le Fay, hys sister. And she loved another knyght bettir than hir hus-
> bande, kynge Uriens, othir Arthure. And she wolde have had Arthure
> hir brother slayne, and therefor she lete make anothir scawberd for
> Excaliber lyke it by enchauntement, and gaf the scawberd Excaliber
> to her lover. And the knyghtes name was called Accolon, that aftir had
> nere slayne kynge Arthure. (78.28–32, 79.1–3)

Based on what we have seen of kin relations so far in the "Tale of King
Arthur," it would seem that Morgan, as Arthur's sister, would be not only
a logical, but also a *good* choice as guardian for Excalibur and its scabbard.
In the request of the maiden who asks Torre for the head of Abellus as
compensation for her brother's death, in the censure of Pellinor for not
preventing the death of his daughter, and in other similar moments too

numerous to mention, one can see that kinship—with its attendant concerns—overrides all other loyalties in the chivalric community. As I have
noted above, character after character in the *Morte d'Arthur* will ignore or
manipulate the rules of the Pentecostal Oath when attempting to fulfill a
perceived obligation to his or her kin. Given how the issues of kinship and
gender trump the articles of the Pentecostal Oath, it thus seems that
Arthur would be right to expect that no matter what other loyalties she
may have, as his sister and wife of one of his strongest allies Morgan would
be the safest choice as a guardian for Excalibur and its scabbard.

For a time, Morgan manipulates the knightly code for her own ends, as
do other women in the *Morte d'Arthur*, employing the strategy of mimicry as a means of achieving her personal goals. Early in the episode of
"Arthur and Accolon," Morgan extracts a promise from the latter, her reputed lover, that he will do battle for her unto the death. Then, by enchantment, Morgan arranges a meeting between Arthur and Accolon, in which
neither knows the identity of the other. Unaware that the sword and scabbard he bears are fakes, Arthur engages Accolon—to whom Morgan has
given the real Excalibur, along with its scabbard—in battle. Although the
text indicates that Morgan betrays her brother for love of Accolon, the
latter's seeming lack of complicity in the deception—at least in the beginning—indicates clearly that Morgan, and only Morgan, is the force behind
the machinations that have taken place.[64]

As the battle between Arthur and Accolon progresses, Arthur, bereft of
his true sword, is at a serious disadvantage; Accolon even offers him mercy
at one point, but Arthur refuses, although his defeat seems assured.
Nyneve, the "Damesel" of the Lake, arrives to witness the battle and inter-
venes to redress Accolon's advantage: "com the Damesel of the Lake into
the felde . . . and she com thidir for the love of kynge Arthur, for she knew
how Morgan le Fay had ordayned for Arthur shold have bene slayne that
day, and therefore she com to save hys lyff" (142.19–24). By "enchauntemente" Nyneve causes Accolon to drop Excalibur, which Arthur retrieves
and recognizes immediately as his own sword.

This scene enacts the realities of the chivalric project in Malory's text:
the masculine is at the center, constructing and affirming knightly identity
through combat, while the feminine hovers at the margins, seemingly secondary and sublimated to the masculine activity.[65] Yet, it is the marginalized presence of the feminine that in fact *creates* and mediates the masculine activity of chivalry. Although Arthur and Accolon strike the blows,
Nyneve and Morgan are locked in combat just as surely as are king and

knight. This episode makes clear how crucial feminine presence is to masculine performance, revealing that the independent agency and dominance of the masculine is a fiction, a fantasy upon which the Arthurian community is founded.[66]

With Excalibur back in his possession, Arthur quickly regains the upper hand, and offers Accolon mercy, something his promise to Morgan forbids the latter from accepting. "'Now telle me,' seyde Arthure, 'or I woll sle the, of what contrey ye be and of what courte.' 'Sir knyght . . . I am of the ryall courte of kyng Arthure, and my name is Accolon of Gaule.' Than was Arthure more dismayde than he was toforehande, for than he remembirde hym of his sistir Morgan le Fay" (145.17–22). Although Accolon knows of Morgan's plan to destroy Arthur, he seems curiously absent from implication in it as an active participant. Still ignorant of Arthur's identity he tells his opponent:

> "ye shall undirstonde that kynge Arthur ys the man in the worlde that she hatyth moste, because he is moste of worship and of prouesse of ony of hir bloode. Also she loveth me oute of mesure as paramour, and I hir agayne. And if she myght bryng hit aboute to sle Arthure by hir crauftis, she wolde sle hir husbonde kynge Uryence lyghtly. And than had she devysed to have me kynge in this londe and so to reigne, and she to be my queene." (145.33–37, 146.1–3)

Accolon—while indicating that Morgan seems, as his lover, to expect his assistance in her quest to destroy Arthur—gives no corresponding indication that he has helped in any way in the planning or the active work of achieving this goal, nor that he intends to do so in the future. "Hir crauftis" that utilize his knightly prowess make him no more than her instrument. The fact that Morgan deliberately keeps Accolon ignorant of his opponent's identity seems clear evidence that his knowing complicity is something she neither wants, needs, or expects. In this light, Accolon's identification of himself as a loyal knight of Arthur's seems genuine. Even when he speaks of becoming king, Accolon seems devoid of any personal ambition: "had *she* devysed to *have me* kynge" (emphasis mine). Accolon never uses the first person plural "we" when he speaks of Morgan's plot.

Arthur himself seems to agree with this analysis. After revealing his identity to Accolon, the king grants Accolon's immediate request for mercy, explaining:

> "I fele be thy wordis at this tyme thou knewest me nat, but I fele by thy wordis that thou haste agreed to the deth of my persone, and

therefore thou art a traytoure; but I wyte the the lesse for my sistir Morgan le Fay by hir false crauftis made the to agré to hir fals lustes. But I shall be sore avenged uppon hir, that all Crystendom shall speke of hit. God knowyth I have honoured hir and worshipped hir more than all my kyn, and more have I trusted hir than my wyf and all my kyn aftir." (146.16–24)

Arthur's choice of language acknowledges that Morgan has slipped outside the bounds of the chivalric feminine. His outraged cry—"more have I trusted hir than my wyf and all my kyn aftir"—suggests the great threat posed by Morgan, and by extension, all those who refuse to perform the gendered roles the chivalric community has assigned to them. While Morgan manipulates and twists the knightly code and the social values underpinning it to suit her needs, she herself feels little or no subjection to the code. This renders her uniquely free to operate unencumbered by the ideals and values that inform its particular clauses. Arthur did right, in the terms of the values of his society, to trust his sister with Excalibur and its scabbard. Connected to Arthur by blood and married to his ally King Uriens, Morgan logically should support the society, its values, and the chief proponent of those values: Arthur. Yet, Morgan does not behave as a wife, a sister, a queen should; she does not act in accordance with the knightly idea of the feminine—helpless, needy, vulnerable—unless to perform that idea of gender renders her some benefit. She is arguably a "lady" who, in the terms of the chivalric community, is not one.

Arthur's threat of vengeance indicates his recognition that his sister can no longer be contained by, or treated in keeping with, the ladies clause and the values that support it. "But I shall be sore avenged uppon hir, that all Crystendom shall speke of hit." This is not the language with which one speaks of or to ladies in the *Morte d'Arthur*. The discourse of vengeance in romance is rarely, if ever, employed by the masculine in the direction of the feminine, and nowhere else in this first book of Malory's does it approach the force with which we see it applied here. Arthur talks as he would of another knight or king who has challenged his authority; that he should name as potential witnesses "all of Crystendom" speaks of punishment and revenge on the largest scale available to the Arthurian world.

Up until this point, Morgan has been playing by a set of rules that allow her to manipulate the knightly code for her own ends, mimicking and performing the feminine to achieve her goals. When she seeks to end the life of her husband, however, she has no compunction about stepping completely outside the bounds of the code and its conception of possible feminine behavior: she does not attempt to cajole another knight into doing her dirty work, but rather undertakes the murder of her husband herself. "[Morgan] callyd unto hir a mayden of her counseyle and sayde, 'Go fecche me my lordes swerde, for I sawe never bettir tyme to sle hym than now'" (149.1–2). She appropriates the most masculine of objects—the sword—to attain her objective, and compounds the transgression by attempting to kill her husband with his own weapon while he sleeps—dishonorable behavior by any measure in the chivalric community.[67] While arguably an act of masculine mimicry, it is a perverse appropriation of the masculine by the standards of Arthurian society. Morgan not only dispenses with the conventions of femininity in achieving her desire, she rejects also the alternative of assuming the position (with its attendant rules for honorable conduct) of a masculine opponent, fairly met in combat. When her son Ywain catches her in the act, however, she immediately returns to a manipulation of the Arthurian code to save herself, crying mercy and begging forgiveness in a typically feminine performance. Predictably, as a knight of the Arthurian court, Ywain honors the rules regarding mercy and those concerning ladies, and states: "'On this covenaunte . . . I woll forgyff you: so ye woll never be aboute to do such dedis" (159.29–30).

More or less reconciled after their battle, Arthur and Accolon retire to a nearby abbey to recover from their wounds; Arthur survives, Accolon does not, and the king sends the other's dead body to Morgan as a warning: "So whan Accolon was ded he lette sende hym in an horsebere with six knyghtes unto Camelot, and bade 'bere hym unto my systir, Morgan le Fay, and sey that I sende her hym to a present. And telle her I have my swerde Excalyber and the scawberede'" (148.27–32). Upon receiving this news, Morgan hastily departs for the abbey where Arthur lies convalescing. She arrives to find Arthur asleep with a guard positioned outside his door, but "no man durste disobey hir commaundmente" and she enters his room. The king has Excalibur clasped in his sleeping hand, so she steals the scabbard and departs. When Arthur awakes and angrily confronts his men, their response is telling in the terms it invokes: "'Sir,' seyde they all, 'we durst nat disobey *your sistyrs* commaundemente'" (150.34–35; emphasis mine).

Near the end of the "Tale of King Arthur," Morgan encounters a knight named Manessen, bound hand and foot and blindfolded. She queries his captor as to his intentions. The knight explains that he is about to drown

Manessen, whom he claims to have found in a compromising position with his wife. Upon further questioning, Morgan discovers that Manessen is a cousin of Accolon's, at which news Morgan declares: "for the love of hym ye shall be delyverde, and ye shal have youre adversary in the same case that ye were in" (152.16–18). When Manessen has drowned his former captor, he asks Morgan if she has any message she wishes him to relate to King Arthur. "'Telle hym,' seyde she, 'that I rescewed the nat for the love of hym, but for the love of Accolon, and tell hym I feare hym nat whyle I can make me and myne in lyknesse of stonys, and lette hym wete I can do much more whan I se my tyme'" (152.25–28). In her statement, Morgan again appropriates and employs the masculine discourse of the knightly challenge, speaking to Arthur not as a woman or a relative, but as a rival knight. Her devotion to Accolon is a warped reflection of the knightly devotion to the feminine that drives the project of chivalry forward in Malory's text, and her remarkably free movement between gender identities—performing masculinity or femininity when it suits her—reveals the instability of the gender model on which the community depends.

Toward the "Day of Destiny"

The early pages of the *Morte d'Arthur* reveal the patterns that repeat throughout the text, moving the narrative relentlessly toward the inevitable collapse of Arthur's realm. For the knightly homosocial subcommunity, the Pentecostal Oath and the values that undergird it make clear the definitive terms of the chivalric society. The inextricability of the ladies clause from the other articles of the code—its embedded position in the center of the Oath—imbricates gender in the construction and negotiation of individual and communal identity. In their absolute dependence upon a feminine presence that is marginalized and sublimated, the masculine agents of the chivalric community cannot allow or conceive of any resistance to gender categories as constructed by the Arthurian society. The lack of a parallel code of conduct for ladies similar to that articulated in the Pentecostal Oath demonstrates this. Ironically, the very inability to admit to the possibility of female agency permits such agency to exist, and indeed to flourish, at the heart of the masculine chivalric enterprise. Morgan le Fay best embodies the numerous strategies of resistance that the feminine offers in response to its chivalric construction—shifting between feminine mimesis and masculine imitation—and indeed, reveals the instability of the model of gender upon which the knightly identities of self and community depend. The masculine knightly dependence and *insistence* on the powerlessness of women paradoxically renders women powerful.

For much of the "Tale of King Arthur," Arthur himself stands as the representative of proper knightly behavior. Yet, after establishing himself as king and founding the order of the Round Table, Arthur recedes from the main action of the narrative, and Sir Lancelot emerges as the prime exemplar of chivalry. In his role as the "floure of al knyghtes" Lancelot represents the fullest realization of knightly endeavor and masculine identity in the *Morte d'Arthur* while simultaneously demonstrating the weaknesses inherent in the chivalric social order. His performance of knightly masculinity—and perhaps more significantly, the way in which women *are able to compel him to perform*—is the subject of the following chapter.

2

Chivalric Performance

Malory's Sir Lancelot

The chivalric community that Arthur establishes in the "Tale of King Arthur" has as its center of power a male homosocial subcommunity of knights, the members of which must constantly seek to affirm what Martin Shichtman and Laurie Finke have described as "hyper-masculinity"[1] in order to maintain their legitimacy in terms of the heteronormativity, or compulsory heterosexuality, that orders the larger community. The primary vehicle by which this masculinity is asserted is the quest. As I noted in chapter 1, on any foray into the forest of adventure, a knight of the Round Table is sure to encounter other knights *with whom* he may affirm his masculine sameness through a display of martial capabilities, and he is sure also to encounter women *against whom* he may affirm his masculine difference through courteous behavior and service. In effect, Malory's knights participate in a never-ending performance, continuously asserting the hegemony of heteronormativity and the rigid, binary, and asymmetrical conception of sex-derivative gender necessary for the maintenance of this social model.

However, knighthood, it must be admitted, is not the *only* "legitimate masculinity" that exists in Malory's text; the *Morte d'Arthur* features a range of acceptable performances for both genders, but with greater evident variety for the masculine agents of the community. Although absent from much of the main activity of the text after the Roman War, King Arthur is wholly immanent in the narrative, even when his character is not physically present; he performs a masculinity that while seemingly passive, legitimates and makes possible the adventures of his knights. *His* identity performance is very different from that of his knights. Likewise, those ubiquitous vavasours inevitably encountered by knights while out on adventure—themselves usually "retired" knights—opt out of direct masculine performance but facilitate the activity of questing knights through their offers of food, lodging, advice and occasionally, daughters. Hermits, monks, and other religious figures also offer alternative masculine performances in the text.

While it is important to recognize that multiple masculinities exist in the world of the *Morte d'Arthur*, it is even more important to recognize how the various categories of identity labeled "masculine" in Malory's text function in relationship to one another. In his work on gender theory, Robert Connell has argued that "To recognize diversity in masculinities is not enough. We must also recognize the *relations* between the different kinds of masculinity: relations of alliance, dominance, and subordination. These relationships are constructed through practices that exclude and include, that intimidate, exploit, and so on. There is a gender politics within masculinity."[2] As I argue below, knights, kings, vavasours, and even hermits all achieve some measure of reputation and thus, identity, as a result of gendered interactions; significantly, these gendered interactions occur not only with women, but also with *other men*. Lancelot is the greatest knight because he is the most "preux" when compared to his fellows; Arthur is the greatest king because he commands the loyalty of such knights. Figures like Sir Tarquin recognize this; his display of the shields of knights he has bested is an attempt to transfer the reputations of his opponents to himself, to enhance and heighten his own masculinity.

However, as important as these male-male interactions are, it is interactions with women that produce the easiest, clearest means of identity consolidation for knights. And although I on occasion discuss these "alternative" masculinities—particularly that modeled by Galahad—my main focus in this study is on the masculinity of knighthood. Judith Butler's theorization of performativity helps clarify the means by which Malory's text produces gender, and why it is that knights—not kings, vavasours, or hermits—merit the greatest attention in terms of gender identity formation. In her book *Gender Trouble: Feminism and the Subversion of Identity*, Butler uses the example of drag to suggest that gender identity is only and always a performance or imitation of an identity for which there is no original template, arguing that the signs or marks that are normally read as *manifestations* of a person's gender are in fact gender itself.[3] Many readers have interpreted this to mean that gender may be taken on and off at will, that in fact, there is a preexisting "one" who wakes in the morning and chooses which gender he or she will perform that day. In *Bodies That*

Matter: On the Discursive Limits of Sex, Butler elaborates and clarifies her earlier argument, maintaining that gender is not a costume one chooses, but rather that the existence of gender norms actually bring the "one" into being: "Femininity is thus not the product of a choice, but the forcible citation of a norm. . . . Indeed, there is no 'one' who takes on a gender norm. On the contrary, the citation of the gender norm is necessary in order to qualify as a 'one,' to become viable as a 'one,' where subject-formation is dependent on the prior operation of legitimating gender norms."[4]

In the *Morte d'Arthur,* characters are rendered legible in chivalric terms to the extent that they conform to such gender norms. Although kings, retired knights, and, on occasion, religious figures may all perform a kind of masculinity, it is *active* knights who are engaged in the day-to-day work of both defining and defending the Arthurian community, and such activity usually coalesces around the feminine. Figures such as Morgan le Fay, whose behavior constitutes an explicit refusal to "cite" the norm of femininity, challenge the very foundation of the chivalric community. Although Morgan does on occasion act as the feminine is expected, the inconsistency of her performance prevents the possibility of any clear consolidation of gender identity. For as Butler notes, the process by which gender norms produce a performance of masculinity and femininity is *repetitive:* "Performativity is thus not a singular 'act,' for it is always a reiteration of a norm or set of norms, and to the extent that it acquires an act-like status in the present, it conceals or dissimulates the conventions of which it is a repetition."[5] Morgan defies gender categorization in that her identity performance lacks consistent, repetitive citation of the norm of femininity. Knights, on the other hand, continuously and eagerly "cite" the dominant model of masculinity.

The narrative of the *Morte d'Arthur* demonstrates an intense concern with the repetitive performativity of gender in the oft-repeated episodic unit of the quest, the primary activity by which knights assert their masculinity.[6] In Malory's text, participation in knightly adventures functions as a citation of masculine behavior; that this affirmation of gender identity is never a *fait accompli* is attested by the fact that knights must constantly re-perform the activity of questing, repeatedly seeking new reasons to leave the court on chivalric errands. While Arthur might seem a logical focal point for an investigation of the construction of masculine identity in the *Morte d'Arthur,* Lancelot quickly emerges as the more appropriate focus for such an analysis. As I noted above, although the entire social order revolves around Arthur, after the first two "tales" the king is largely absent from the main action of the text; he functions primarily as a facilitator who enables the violent activity of the quest. In this role he maintains the locus that is both beginning and end of knightly adventure, the place from which knights issue forth in the attempt to construct and refine their chivalric identities and to which they return to offer a report of their successes and failures in this enterprise.

Arthur's marriage to Guenevere firmly heterosexualizes him; it is his knights—almost without exception unmarried—who must constantly demonstrate their adherence to the *Morte d'Arthur*'s gender model and foundational scheme of heteronormativity.[7] As the prime exemplar of the chivalric ethos, the "floure of all knyghtes," Lancelot most visibly demonstrates this process of identity construction and maintenance in the *Morte d'Arthur*; he is both the most skillful knight in terms of martial prowess (affirming his masculine "sameness" through combat with other knights) and the most courteous (asserting his masculine "difference" through service and devotion to ladies, particularly Guenevere). An analysis of what Vinaver calls "A Noble Tale of Sir Launcelot du Lake"—the first sustained treatment of the activity of questing in Malory's text[8]—reveals a particular and specific representation of gender dynamics that may best be understood in terms of three interconnected factors that coalesce around the figure of Lancelot.

The first of these factors is Malory's conception of proper knightly chivalric behavior. Legislated in the Pentecostal Oath, this knightly code of conduct is deployed and explored in a variety of circumstances, over an extended period of narrative time; this constrained, repetitive performance of gender identities within a scheme of compulsory heterosexuality emphasizes the necessity of a subjugated feminine presence in the construction of individual and communal chivalric identities. While Malory's text is not remarkable in that it follows the romance pattern of co-opting the feminine to enhance knightly endeavor, the particular social paradigm in which the chivalric activity of the *Morte d'Arthur* takes place—structured in keeping with the expression of chivalric ideals in the Pentecostal Oath[9]—intensifies the knightly dependence upon the feminine. This produces a situation in which the model of gender relations that is critical to the maintenance of the social order is also precisely a model of gender relations that is demonstrably unfeasible.

This particular model of knightly behavior that Malory institutes at the beginning of his work necessarily causes him to alter the second component essential for understanding the unique picture of gender modeled in the *Morte d'Arthur:* his source material. A comparison of Malory's version of events in "A Noble Tale of Sir Launcelot du Lake" with those of his sources reveals a deliberate restructuring, revision, and reduction that places the concerns of gender and heteronormativity firmly at the center of the chivalric enterprise.[10] An analysis of Malory's skillful combining and reworking of his source material demonstrates how the concerns of gender come to the fore more insistently in Malory than in his sources.

An examination of the cultural literary context in which the *Morte d'Arthur* was composed—the third factor important to understanding the specific depiction of gender in Malory's text—further reveals the centrality of heteronormative gender identity to the chivalric project. In the fifteenth century, England experienced a revival of interest in all types of chivalric literature—not just within the fictional genre of romance, but an interest that was also manifested in a proliferation of didactic treatises concerned with proper knightly behavior and "mirrors for princes." Although Malory's text should rightly be understood as part of this revival, the performance of gender in his text differs markedly from that found in other chivalric works composed or translated into English contemporary with the composition of the *Morte d'Arthur.*

The combined and interconnected significance of these three elements—the ideal of knightly behavior expressed in the Pentecostal Oath, Malory's revision of his source material, and the distinction of the *Morte* from other contemporary texts concerned with chivalry—is made strikingly clear in one of Lancelot's adventures in "A Noble Tale of Sir Launcelot du Lake." In the course of his questing adventures, Lancelot encounters a maiden who asks for his assistance: "'Sir,' seyde the damesell, 'here by this way hauntys a knyght that dystressis all ladyes and jantylwomen, and at the leste he robbyth them, other lyeth by hem.' 'What?' seyde sir Launcelot, 'is he a theff and a knyght? And a ravyssher of women? He doth shame unto the Order of Knyghthode, and contrary unto his oth. Hit is pyté that he lyvyth!'" (269.19–26). Lancelot's strident indignation affirms the ideal of knightly behavior toward women articulated in the ladies clause of the Pentecostal Oath. Interestingly, the parallel passage in Malory's source, the Prose *Lancelot,* is a bit different:

"Je vos maing," fait ele, "combatre a .I. chevalier qui ci pres maint en ceste forest, qui sert d'un mauvés mestier dont toz li mondes le devroit blasmer, car il destourne touz cels qui par devant lui passant, pour qu'il am puist venir au dessus."

["I am taking you," she said, "to do combat with a knight who lives nearby in this forest and performs an offensive office that everyone should condemn, for he turns aside all those who pass in front of him so that he can conquer them."][11]

Malory transforms the recreant knight's offensive behavior in the source into a specific attack on ladies; the masculine pronoun "cels" here suggests that in the Prose *Lancelot*, the knight is guilty primarily—or only—of attacking *other knights*. Lancelot's horrified reaction in the *Morte* indicates the paradox that Malory's conception of knighthood employs. In attacking helpless women, this knight in a sense attacks the Malorian institution of knighthood; yet at the same time, such attacks are essential in that they provide the opportunity for other knights to perform their masculine identities through defense of helpless women. Malory's transformation of the scene permits Lancelot, in redressing this wrong through combat, to affirm his masculinity along *both* axes of identity construction—engagement with the masculine and service to the feminine.

The *Morte d'Arthur*'s repetitive and obsessive dependence of the knightly enterprise upon the feminine is not to be found in chivalric works contemporary with Malory; while the feminine is certainly present and occasionally pointed to as a catalyst for proper knightly endeavor, almost all of these other texts take devotion to God as a starting point from which to derive a code of knightly ethics. In Malory's depiction of the Arthurian community, such spiritual devotion is largely absent, eclipsed by the omnipresent concerns of heteronormativity, a concern that necessarily replaces devotion to God with devotion to the feminine.

Defining Chivalry: Malory and the Fifteenth-Century Chivalric Revival

But in especiall hit was prevyd on sir Launcelot de Lake, for in all turnementes, justys, and dedys of armys, both for lyff and deth, he passed all other knyghtes, and at no tyme was he ovircom but yf hit were by treason other inchauntement. So this sir Launcelot encresed so mervaylously in worship and honoure; therefore he is the fyrste knyght that the Freynsh booke makyth mencion of aftir kynge Arthure com frome Rome. Wherefore quene Gwenyvere had hym in grete favoure aboven all other knyghtis, and so he loved the quene agayne aboven all other ladyes dayes of his lyff, and for hir he dud many dedys of armys and saved her frome the fyre thorow his noble chevalry. (253.8–19)

Thus begins "A Noble Tale of Sir Launcelot du Lake." Derek Brewer has rightly observed that in the opening lines of the tale "Malory . . . strikes instantly the two notes that characterize Launcelot: his chivalry and his love for Gwenyvere."[12] While these two qualities are specifically present in Lancelot, Malory's repeated characterization of Lancelot as the "best knyghte of the worlde" invokes military prowess and devotion to the feminine more generally as positively held values of the larger Arthurian community. In the world of this text, the measure of a knight—indeed, of a man—is found in his "chevalry," a word that invokes some combination of martial prowess and courteous behavior toward women.[13] Butler argues that "gender is always a doing, though not a doing by a subject who might be said to pre-exist the deed," or that, in other words, the *doing* in fact brings the subject who *does* into existence.[14] In this context, Lancelot's masculine knightly behavior is thus not a visible manifestation of his inherent masculinity, but rather, it is the repetition of the *behavior itself* that characterizes him as masculine. In Malory's text, the one type of *doing* that brings into being the masculine subject—combat—often proceeds from or is motivated by the other *doing* by which knightly identity may be established—courtesy. This relentless intersection of military prowess and feminine presence results in the production of the category of the chivalric in the *Morte d'Arthur*, and it is Lancelot who is repeatedly invoked as the prime exemplar of those attributes.

"A Noble Tale of Sir Launcelot du Lake" emphatically depicts Lancelot as the particular champion of ladies. He defends, rescues, and serves them repeatedly—acts that establish his identity as the "floure of all knyghtes," the role model for the rest of the Round Table knights. It seems that around every bend in the road, behind every tree, within every castle or village encountered by the hero, there is a maiden who requires of him some service, and that service is almost always situated within a context of knightly violence. And while Lancelot strives constantly to serve all ladies, it is the figure of Guenevere and his devotion to her that produces his constant need to "preve" himself with deeds of physical valor and gentlemanly behavior toward women. In his successful service to ladies and his triumph in combat with other knights, Lancelot models the constitutive acts of chivalric identity formation. However, Lancelot's notable failures in this section also make plain the flaws in this system of identity formation. These problematic episodes that threaten Lancelot's chivalric identity similarly threaten the entire social order that he represents. For example, in addition to praising Lancelot's character in the opening lines of this tale, Malory also calls attention to those things—"treason" and "inchauntement"—that pose the greatest threat to Lancelot himself, and in turn, which endanger the chivalric community. Throughout the *Morte d'Arthur*—and in particular within "A Noble Tale"—the hazards of "treason" and "inchauntement" reveal themselves as key components of the romantic quest even as they simultaneously and contradictorily pose threats to the agents of the quest.

Malory's articulation of knightly values and dangers at the opening of "A Noble Tale" is unique: not only is a similar articulation absent from the Prose *Lancelot*, but Malory's text is also strikingly different from other fifteenth-century chivalric treatises and manuals in the concerns it expresses. The enactment of chivalric ideals and hazards in the *Morte d'Arthur* demonstrates the clear distinction between representations of gender in Malory's work and other texts that were the product of the fifteenth-century chivalric revival in late medieval England. Stephen Knight has rightly noted of fifteenth-century England that: "For various complex reasons, including the loosening of feudal and manorial ties, the increasing pressure on the legal system, and the related development of a money economy and social and geographic mobility, the period was notorious for civil disorder."[15] In the midst of this period of "civil disorder" there was a heightened interest in texts that dealt with the concept of chivalry. I would like briefly to discuss this climate of enthusiastic reception for chivalric treatises, guidebooks, and romances in fifteenth-century England, touching upon the historical events and shifts in thinking that contributed to produce such a climate.

As far back as the end of the thirteenth century, it had become clear that what has been called the "feudal" system[16] in England no longer functioned successfully as a mechanism of social order,[17] a dysfunction that became most clear when it came time to gather forces for war—and the time for war, it seemed for well over a century, was always at hand. Changes in the technical aspects of warfare—the increased importance of archers, gunners, and the like—made the presence and prowess of the individual knight armed with sword and shield less important than had previously been the case, and when Edward III introduced the indenture system for military recruitment, one could say that the decline of the office of knighthood had begun.[18] A variety of factors exacerbated this decline in the so-called practical function of knighthood.

The outbreak of plague in 1348–49 so reduced the population that there were quite simply not enough of the peasantry to sustain the manorial system of social order; this created significant changes in the labor relations of the period.[19] The Statute of Laborers of 1351, which froze wages at preplague levels and severely restricted the mobility of the peasantry, was an attempt to shore up the manorial system, but the Uprising of 1381 made plain that this was not a feasible solution.[20] Wage labor became increasingly important in the process of cultivation on any scale beyond that of a single peasant holding.[21] With the continuing growth of the market system, and especially exports of wool and cloth, the tripartite model that divided society into three orders—nobles, clergy, and laborers—was losing its coherence.

As the old social order changed, the so-called feudal system gave way to a new system of relationships, often described as "bastard feudalism."[22] The chivalric ethos played a significant role in those relationships characterized as feudal or "bastard feudal" and functioned as an important ideological social model as far back as the twelfth century and far beyond the fifteenth; the chivalric ideology was simply understood, co-opted, and utilized differently throughout the medieval period. In Malory's day one response to the civil disorder of the Wars of the Roses and the external pressures of conflict with France seemed to be a corresponding and remarkable growth in the popularity of texts that dealt with chivalry. Indeed, as what might be termed the practical function of knighthood began to disappear in England, a heightened interest in chivalry as a mechanism for social order began to manifest itself among all classes. Among the aristocracy, no doubt, this changing role of chivalric ideology was a function of the anxiety over the threat to their exclusive position in English society, while the upwardly mobile and increasingly literate merchant classes looked to chivalric texts for what Susan Crane has called "scripts for noble behavior," desiring to co-opt whatever aspects of noble identity they possibly could.[23] More generally, the population as a whole sought in these works a means of restoring England's former glory.[24]

The desire to look back with nostalgia is understandable given the political situation in Malory's day. As Patricia Clare Ingham has recently noted, the fifteenth century "is noted for its cultural innovations, if also for its changeabilities: Caxton's press, new technologies of court and monarchy, the development of vernacular prose, of national histories, and the emergence in London of an increasingly diverse population of foreign merchants."[25] Beyond the "innovations" of court and monarchy, the conflict of the Wars of the Roses created uncertainty and confusion in a more pressing and real sense: the English throne changed hands at least six times during Malory's own lifetime, changes all the more significant in that the movement was not just from sovereign to successor, but from an "unfit" ruler (the Lancastrian Henry VI, whose bouts of insanity made declaration of a protector necessary on occasion) to a rival line (the Yorks) and back (largely due to the heroic efforts of Henry's queen, Margaret of Anjou) and back yet again. Lower down the social ladder the peasantry were enjoying an improved quality of life, leaving serfdom behind and becoming free landowners, thereby increasing social pressures.[26]

This civil instability, coupled with the territorial losses of lands to France, created a climate in which the nostalgic mourning of the *Morte d'Arthur* met with a ready and avid audience. Felicity Riddy has recently suggested that "we can see [the *Morte*] as a post-imperial, or even post-colonial, text which speaks with the voices of these 'noble and dyvers gentylmen' of Malory's generation, for whom the loss of the French territories in 1453 had been a personal disaster, and who could not accommodate themselves to the diminished view of their country and of their own role and prospects—both financial and social—that that loss brought with it."[27] It is no coincidence, I think, that the year of the *Morte d'Arthur*'s first printing by William Caxton—1485—is the same year in which the long-running conflict between the houses of York and Lancaster is resolved by their defeat and absorption into the house of Tudor.[28] That Malory's text is just one of many chivalric works enjoying widespread popularity and circulation in the turbulence of fifteenth-century England speaks to a general climate of nostalgia for a chivalric "golden age."[29]

This category of chivalric texts popular in fifteenth-century England includes not only romances such as Malory's *Morte d'Arthur*, but chivalric "guidebooks" and "mirrors for princes," or *speculum principis* that offered specific and practical advice on the office of knighthood and the governance of the realm.[30] Karen Cherewatuk has recently examined the *Morte d'Arthur* in this context of late-medieval chivalric literary production, paying particular attention to chivalric anthologies or "great books." Cherewatuk notes that "[t]he great books share with the *Morte d'Arthur* a complex and syncretic vision of knighthood which undergirds Malory's work and which the author, his audience, and even his editor held in common."[31] As Cherewatuk and others have noted, the chivalric works so popular at the end of the fifteenth century not only "brought together in one volume the myriad lessons of chivalry" but were also read by people on various rungs of the social ladder who saw these texts as "not merely a means of flattering men higher on the social scale . . . [but] a means of self-improvement."[32]

Many of these chivalric texts were translations or adaptations of earlier French texts, and thus, following a pattern extending as far back as the romances of Chrétien de Troyes, English conceptions of chivalry were largely derivative from the French. It is interesting that appropriation of these ideals into a conception of knighthood characterized as suitable (and indeed, essential) to the salvation of the English state seemed to occur with little problem. Many of the thirteenth- and fourteenth-century treatises on knighthood translated into Middle English and given wide distribution in fifteenth-century England based their definitions of chivalric behavior—at least in part—upon *earlier* representations of knighthood depicted in French Arthurian romances, including the *Lancelot do lac,* the Prose *Lancelot, La Mort La Roi Artu,* and *La Queste del Saint Graal.* It seems that each genre, in its model of knightly chivalry, was influenced by the other, and thus, a relatively unified picture of ideal knighthood appears across time, space, and genre. While literary texts such as Malory's are properly placed alongside these more didactic works when examining the phenomenon of what might be termed a "fifteenth-century chivalric revival," the *Morte d'Arthur* stands apart from these texts (and from other romances) in its particular concern with—and representation of—gender.

As the popularity of chivalric texts in the fifteenth century indicates, the concerns of the times were obviously not only explored in the reading of romances such as Malory's, but also addressed in chivalric treatises that exhorted knights to emulate the knightly models of earlier times. For example, in his 1484 translation of the *Libre del ordre de Cauayleria* written by the Majorcan Ramon Lull in the late thirteenth century, William Caxton appends his own stirring exhortation to the end of the text, locating this instructional treatise on proper knightly behavior firmly within an English tradition: "O ye knyghtes of Englond where is the custome and vsage of noble chyualry that was vsed in tho dayes / . . . And some not wel aduysed vse not honest and good rule ageyn alle ordre of knyghthode / leue this / leue it and rede the noble volumes of saynt graal of lancelot / of galaad / of Trystram / of perse forest / of percyual / of gawayn / & many mo / Ther shalle ye see manhode / curtoyse & gentylnesse."[33] Caxton's epilogue suggests the ease with which manuals of knighthood were linked to romantic depictions of knights and the possibility of either genre offering feasible models of behavior to rectify or alleviate the myriad perceived ills plaguing society.

While Malory's *Morte d'Arthur* shares much in common with the picture of knighthood represented by more didactic works of chivalry popular in the late fifteenth century, his text differs from these others in that his narrative offers a *sustained deployment and enactment* of those knightly values; rather than examining the knightly ideal within the confined borders of a single narrative episode, the *Morte d'Arthur* enacts chivalric values over a long span of narrative time, allowing the code of conduct expressed by the Pentecostal Oath to be subjected to a series of tests. In imagining a chivalric society, the *Morte d'Arthur* not only explicitly articulates and performs knightly values and ideals, but also follows their enactment and the constrained performance of knightly and ladylike identity through to their ultimate expressions. This sustained deployment and exploration of the values articulated in the Oath eventually makes clear the structural failings of the knightly code.

A brief examination of the prominent themes of popular chivalric guidebooks distinguishes their conception of chivalry from Malory's. In attempting to situate the *Morte d'Arthur* within this proliferation of chivalric literature at the end of the fifteenth century, I would like to look particularly at the *Livre de chevalrie* of Geoffroi de Charny and Ramon Lull's *Libre del ordre de Cauayleria*, with brief attention paid to the anonymous thirteenth-century poem the *Ordene de chevalrie* as well as Christine de Pizan's *Les Faits d'Armes et de Chevalerie.*[34] An analysis of the conception of knighthood in these texts points to the existence of what might be termed a "crisis of chivalry" that co-existed with the "chivalric revival" of fifteenth-century England.[35]

As I have noted above, one attribute that these texts emphasize that Malory's does not is devotion to God. While the community of the *Morte d'Arthur* measures time in terms of the Church calendar year, there is little that is particularly demonstrative of religious piety or devotion in Malory's text. The holy days of Pentecost, Easter, and Christmas are subsumed within the masculine chivalric project, providing only the occasion for a feast, at which some "mervayle" is sure to appear that will propel the Round Table knights out on a quest which, successfully completed, will bring renown back to Arthur's court and affirm their identities as members of the elite Arthurian society. By contrast, most "manuals of knighthood" circulating in the fifteenth century emphasized devotion to God as the most important component in the making of a true knight. Indeed, Lull, a seneschal poet at the court of James II of Catalonia, had himself undergone a religious experience in 1266 (seeing the body of the crucified Christ in a vision on five successive nights) that prompted him to compose his *Libre* in an attempt to direct knighthood away from any involvement or concern with courtly love and steer this most important of social offices toward devotion to God.[36] Caxton's faithful translation from the French (almost word for word) maintains this emphasis: "Offyce of a knyght is thende and the begynnynge / wherfore began the ordre of chyualrye. . . . The offyce of a knyght is to mayntene and deffende the holy feyth catholyque / by whiche god the fader sente his sone in to the world to take flesshe humayne in the gloryous vyrgyn our lady saynt Mary."[37] If to defend the faith is a knight's most important obligation, Lull's text and Caxton's translation also make plain his obligations to his temporal lord and to the weak and helpless: "Thoffyce of a knyght is to mayntene and deffende wymmen / wydowes and orphanes / and men dyseased and not puyssaunt ne stronge."[38]

It seems clear that Lull based his description of the duties of a knight and his explanation for the symbolism of his knightly accoutrements (sword, shield, et cetera—all of which are imbued with a religious significance) in large measure upon the section of the French Prose *Lancelot* in which the Lady of the Lake explains to a young Lancelot what it means to be a knight:

> "Au commenchement, quant li ordre de chevalerie commencha, fu devisé a chelui qui voloit estre chevaliers et qui le don en avoit par droite election qu'il fust cortois sans vilonie, debonaire sans felonie, piteus envers les souffratex et larges et apparelliés de secoure les besoigneus, pres et apparelliés de confondre les robeors et les ochions, drois jugieres sans amour et sans haine, et sans amour d'aidier au tort por le droit grever, et sans haine de nuire au droit por traire le tort avant." (21a, 11)

> ["In the beginning, when the order of knighthood began, it was required of anyone who wanted to be a knight and was legitimately chosen that he be courteous and not base, gracious and not a scoun-

drel, compassionate toward the afflicted, generous and helpful to the needy, ready and able to foil thieves and murderers, an upright judge unswayed by love or hatred—love that might weigh against the right or hatred that might plead in favor of the wrong."][39]

Like Lull, Malory drew from the Prose *Lancelot* for much of the content of his *Morte d'Arthur,* and the chivalric values described by the Lady of the Lake are, in large measure, both implicitly and explicitly incorporated into Malory's own conception of the office of knighthood; however, both the Lady of the Lake and Lull's *Libre* go on to stress the importance of the office of knighthood in defending the faith:

> "Chevaliers fu establis outreement por Sainte Eglize garandir, car ele ne se doit revanchier par armes ne rendre mal encontre mal; et por che est a che establis li chevaliers qu'il garandisse chelui qui tent la senestre joe, quant ele a estéferue en la destre. Et sachiés que au commenchement, si com tesmoigne l'Escripture, n'estoit nus si hardi qui montast sor cheval, se chevalier ne fust avant, et pot che furent il chevalier clamé." (21a, 11)

> ["Above all, knighthood was established to defend the Holy Church, for the Church cannot take up arms to avenge herself or return harm for harm; and this is why knights were created: to protect the one who turns the other cheek when the first has been hit. Know, too, that in the beginning, according to the Scriptures, no one but knights dared to mount a horse—a *cheval*, as they said—and that is why they were called horsemen, or *chevaliers*."][40]

The *Livre de chevalrie* of mid-fourteenth-century French knight Geoffroi de Charny similarly blends concepts of courtesy, loyalty, and prowess with piety in defining chivalry; like Lull, Charny appears to draw from the Lady of the Lake's sermon on chivalry in the Prose *Lancelot,* as well as from other Arthurian romances, such as the *Lancelot do Lac*. In 1352, King Jean II of France conceived of a new chivalric order, the Company of the Star, initiated in response to Edward III's creation of the Order of the Garter a few months prior. The French king assigned Charny the task of composing instructive chivalric guides (of which he wrote three), the longest being the *Livre*. In composing his tract, Charny, like Lull, was influenced by the anonymous early-thirteenth-century poem, the *Ordene de chevalerie,* which emphasizes devotion to God as the most important attribute of a knight. Claims Charny:

Et pour ce est il que souverainement leurs estaz et leurs vies doivent
estre come pour servir et deservir de touz leurs cuers a Nostre
Seigneur et a la gloriouse Virge Marie de bons confors et des tres
honorables eschapemens que Nostre Sires leur a faiz et fait de jour
[en jour]. (42.87–90)

[Therefore the position and way of life of these men-at-arms should
above all be devoted to serving with all their hearts Our Lord and the
glorious Virgin Mary in return for the good comfort and honorable
escape from death which Our Lord has granted them from day to
day.][41]

Indeed, as many scholars have noted, Charny's text seems to conclude with
a combination prayer and battle cry, vividly representing the link between
religious devotion and chivalry: "Priez a Dieu pour celui qui ce livre fait a.
EXPLICIT CHARNI! CHARNY!" (44.59–60) ["Pray to God for him who
is the author of this book. EXPLICIT CHARNI! CHARNY!"].[42]

When situated in the context of these other works concerning chivalry,
Malory's text—and particularly his "Noble Tale of Sir Launcelot du
Lake"—seems oddly and strikingly devoid of religious sentiment. The
Morte d'Arthur reflects the values expressed in contemporary chivalric
works distortedly, and in Malory's text, the gap left by the lack of devotion
to God is filled in with devotion to the service of ladies. To put it more
accurately: in Malory's text, devotion to God is not merely *replaced* by
devotion to ladies, but rather, *the compulsion to serve ladies precludes devotion to God*. Dedication to the feminine is indeed the primary source of
Lancelot's honor and reputation, and the need to consistently affirm and
balance both a heterosexualized masculinity and homosocial fellowship
leaves little time for other devotions.[43]

Omnipresent female characters who require the services of a knight
crowd the pages of Malory's text. Significantly, however, these feminine
figures often simultaneously present a threat to that community, and they
are able to do so in large measure because the Pentecostal Oath does not
address potential actions of ladies, only knightly reactions in terms of service to them. While the Morte d'Arthur is largely silent on this matter,
these other chivalric works—although primarily religious and spiritual in
orientation—make clear mention of the role that the feminine is expected
to play in constructing or influencing masculine knightly behavior. In the
anonymous Ordene de chevalerie, for example, the new-made knight is
instructed:

Dame ne doit ne damoisele
Pour nule rien fourconsillier;
Mais s'eles ont de lui mestier
Aidier leur doit a son pooir
Se il veut los et pris avoir;
Car femes doit on honourer
Et pour lor drots grans fais porter. (268–74)

[A knight should mislead neither / lady nor maiden for any reason; /
But if they have need of his skill/office / He is to help their cause with
his might / If he wants to have his esteem and praise; / Because one
must honor women / And do great deeds in support of their rights.][44]

The implication here seems to be that knights are to help women when
they have just cause to do so, but not necessarily to obey their every whim,
a sentiment echoed by the quote from Caxton's translation of Lull, cited
above. Christine de Pizan's *Faits d'Armes et de Chevalerie*, a work primarily concerned with the technical specifics of warfare (also translated by
Caxton and printed in England in 1489), makes a similar pronouncement:
"the prynce may iustly yf it please hym to ayde & helpe euery prynce
baron or other hys alye or frende / or any contre or londe yf be he re-
quyred / *in caas that the quarell be iuste* / & in this poynt be comprised of
wimmen, wydowes / orphans / & alle them that may haue necessite" (emphasis mine).[45]

It is significant that most of these texts make explicit mention of the
need to succor *helpless* women; the rather vague wording of the first item
of the ladies clause of the Pentecostal Oath in the *Morte d'Arthur* suggests
that in Malory's Arthurian universe, *all* ladies are helpless and therefore
always in need of the services of a knight: "and allwayes to do ladyes,
damesels, and jantilwomen and wydowes socour" (120.4–5). The nonspe-
cific nature of the word "socour" constrains knights to obey or grant almost any request made by a woman, and suggests also that women are
always in need of "socour." In Malory, the feminine represents the perpetual *opportunity* for positive construction and refinement of the masculine knightly identity. To admit to the possibility that the feminine need
not always be helpless and vulnerable would be to admit to a potential
threat to the idealized stable gender system of the *Morte d'Arthur*. As the
example of Morgan le Fay makes clear, this idealized stability of gender
categories is a fiction, a story that the masculine reassuringly tells itself.
The anxious repetitive performance of knightly masculine identity we see

throughout the text indicates that the knightly subcommunity is aware of the precarious foundation upon which its identity rests. This would seem to explain the interesting fact that a misogynistic patriarchy such as Mal-ory's Arthurian community conceives of the feminine as so benign, easily co-opted by the masculine for the furtherance of its own ends; that the feminine is never *perceived* to be a threat to the hegemony of the mascu-line is in fact the main threat to that very hegemony.

Charny's *Livre* is particularly interesting when considering the role women are given to play in the chivalric enterprise. Again, although a text that emphasizes the importance of religion, "Charny accepts discreet love affairs. There is a sense of balance here. A love can make a warrior more *preux* but he will always be wise to think less about his body and more about his soul and his honor."[46] The lack of parallel codes of conduct for both men and women creates much of the tension surrounding gender relations in the *Morte d'Arthur;* by contrast Charny's text, remarkably, seems to have such a code for women, although not expressly articulated as an oath. Acknowledging that knights may be spurred on to marvelous feats of valor and increased reputation by the love of a woman, Charny claims:

> Et bien doit l'en honorer, servir et tres bien amer icelles tres bonnes dames et autres que je tien toutes a dames, qui ainsi font les bons, et par elles sont faiz chevaliers et les bonnes genz d'armes. Et pour ce toutes bonnes gens d'armes sont tenuz de droit de garder et deffendre l'onnour de toutes dames contre tous ceulx qui voudroient dire ne mesdire ne faire le contraire. (12.15–20)

> [And one should indeed honor, serve, and truly love these noble la-dies and others whom I hold to be ladies who inspire men to great achievement, and it is thanks to such ladies that men become good knights and men-at-arms. Hence all men-at-arms are rightly bound to protect and defend the honor of all ladies against all those who would threaten it by word or deed.][47]

Charny then proceeds to instruct both knight and lady as to how they should behave toward one another:

> Et pour ce est il que l'en doit bien aimer, celer, garder, servir et hon-orer toutes dames et damoiselles par qui sont fait et se font les bons corps des chevaliers et des escuiers et les bonnes gens d'armes, dont tant d'onnour leur vient et leur acroist leur bonne renommee. Et

aussi icelles tres bonnes dames doyvent et sont bien tenues d'amer et
honorer ycelles bonnes gens d'armes qui, pour deservir d'avoir leur
tres bonne amour et leur bonne acueil, se mettent en tant de perilz de
corps comme li mestier d'armes desire, quant pour avenir et attaindre
a celui hault honnour pour lequel haut honnour ilz pensent a deservir
d'avoir l'amour de leurs dames. (20.32–41)

[Therefore men should love secretly, protect, serve, and honor all
those ladies and damsels who inspire knights, men-at-arms, and
squires to undertake worthy deeds that bring them honor and increase their renown. And these noble ladies should, as is their duty,
love and honor these worthy men-at-arms who, in order to deserve
their noble love and their benevolence, expose themselves to so much
physical danger as the vocation of arms requires from those who aim
to reach and achieve that high honor through which they hope to
serve in the love of their ladies.][48]

Charny's conception of gender relations suggests a mutual increase in
honor, reputation, and satisfaction for both knight *and* lady; the lady's encouragement of her knight to commit brave deeds in turn provides her
with the reward of a better, braver, and more noble love interest. Although
not an oath, Charny's exhortation is clearly meant to encourage a certain
kind of behavior on the part of all the parties involved. While in Malory's
text interactions between knights and ladies are primarily the site of the
construction and refinement of *masculine* identity, in Charny's text the
building and enhancement of noble identity is a *mutual* enterprise.

All of these chivalric guides make clear the knight's responsibilities to
women, identifying them generally as among the "helpless" (along with
orphans and weak, ill, or old men), indicating that a knight should aid
women, widows, and maidens when there is a clear need. What these texts
do *not* suggest is that knights should make themselves answerable to all
women at all times; even Charny, whose *Livre* readily acknowledges devotion to a woman may spur a knight on to honorable achievements, makes
clear that a knight's first commitment should be to God and offers behav-
ioral guidelines for women to follow in order to maintain this devotional
balance. While Malory's text makes no such direct comment on the behavior of ladies, the pressure and influence of the feminine in the *Morte
d'Arthur* pervades—and in fact constitutes—masculine knightly identity,
something of which the more didactic treatises on chivalry cannot conceive.

The fifteenth-century English chivalric revival thus provides an illuminating context for understanding the significance of gender in the *Morte d'Arthur*. When deployed in "A Noble Tale of Sir Launcelot du Lake," Malory's chivalric ideal reveals how critical a particular, rigidly defined gender model is to the maintenance of the Arthurian social order, and how the dependence on this model ultimately undermines the foundation of the chivalric community. In the next two sections of this chapter, I explore first the specific means by which individual knightly identity is constructed in terms of the communal chivalric ethos, and second, the weaknesses of this social model made plain in the enactment of its values.

Lancelot in the Forest of Adventure: The "Floure of al Knyghtes"

After Malory's description of Lancelot and Guenevere's relationship that opens "A Noble Tale of Sir Launcelot du Lake," he relates that after returning from the successful campaign in Rome against the Emperor Lucius, "sir Launcelot rested hym longe with play and game; and than he thought hymself to preve in straunge adventures, and bade his nevew, sir Lyonell, for to make hym redy, 'for we muste go seke adventures'" (253.20–23). The desire to "preve" oneself through adventures is a typical theme that recurs in the *Morte* and other romance texts, and in its insistent repetition reveals itself as a critical component in the establishment and maintenance of masculine, knightly identity. In performing the activities of a questing knight, Lancelot in fact "performs himself."[49] Yet, as Butler's theorization of gender argues and as the narrative of Malory's text compellingly demonstrates, it is not a preexisting "self" that performs these activities, but rather, the performance of these activities renders intelligible the "self" who performs them.

The visible mark of gender afforded by armor and the accoutrements of knighthood provide one of the most important components of this "preving." Kathleen Coyne Kelly has discussed the importance of armor in signaling gender identity, pointing out that knightly armor "both exaggerates and obscures the lineaments of the male body enclosed within it."[50] An analysis of the double-function of armor as that which both conceals and reveals offers a way in to understanding masculine gender identity and the male homosocial relationships so important to Malory's narrative. Lancelot and his nephew appropriately set off on their adventure "mounted on their horses, armed at all ryghtes" (253.23–24), swords and shields at the ready; in the *Morte d'Arthur* these accessories identify a man as both a member of a knightly community and as a particular individual (recognizable by the symbol on his shield) of that community. A knight's name similarly plays a crucial role in establishing and maintaining masculine identity. The signifier with its two components—the masculine and aristocratic designation "sir" followed by the particular knight's name—establishes both his communal and individual identity in the same way that armor and shield do. "Sir" represents the elite community of which the knight is a member, while the name that comes after the title is his mark of individual difference and distinction within that community. Without the larger identifying mark of the community the knight's individual name loses its strength and force; yet, the powerful agency and status afforded by the mark of the larger order to which a knight belongs depends, in turn, upon the *particular* identities of the knights who *comprise* that community. In the Arthurian chivalric society, to lack armor and shield is to lack a stable masculine identity—in effect, *to lose one's name,* and thus, one's place within the collective.

Lancelot, while out on adventure, will manipulate—and be manipulated by—the significance and understanding of the knightly name. For while naming is meant to provide both stability and differentiation in Arthurian society, the category of identity based on the particular individual name of each knight is susceptible to appropriation and potential abuse. While the knight's armor and the designation "sir" both reinforce one another as signs of membership in an elite knightly community and are relatively stable as signifying marks, in contrast, both the shield and the *particular* name are transportable commodities, easily withheld or appropriated and manipulated. Sometimes this is done playfully, or with good intentions, but occasionally this knightly identifier is manipulated for malicious reasons. I would like to suggest that the representation and consolidation of masculine knightly identity in the *Morte d'Arthur* amounts to a sort of *masquerade,* a performance of gender identity that at moments approaches the carnivalesque. Such a performance, as it seeks to establish a clear gender hierarchy in relationship to that which is defined as feminine within a scheme of compulsory heterosexuality, also simultaneously and paradoxically licenses and permits an enactment of the masculine/feminine binary within the bounds of the male homosocial knightly community.

Masquerade, as it is usually understood in feminist, gender, and psychoanalytic theory, is a term applied to women, suggesting that "womanliness" (whatever that may be) is only ever a mask worn by women in an attempt to conform to masculine expectations of femininity. Joan Riviere's 1929 study was the first to clearly articulate the impossibility of distinguishing the idea of masquerade—occasionally characterized as an "exaggeration" of those attributes and qualities assigned the cultural value of "feminine"—from any sort of pregiven, inherent womanly identity: "The reader may now ask how I define womanliness or where I draw the line between genuine womanliness and the 'masquerade.' My suggestion is not, however, that there is any such difference; whether radical or superficial, they are the same thing."[51] Expressed in such terms, the idea of masquerade thus resonates with the Butlerian suggestion that gender attributes "are not expressive but performative . . . effectively constitut[ing] the identity they are said to express or reveal," and with Irigaray's theorization of mimesis, in which women resist their construction of femininity through deliberate alignment with (and perhaps exaggeration of) the pre- and proscribed position of the feminine.[52] Indeed, Irigaray argues that

> the masquerade has to be understood as what women do in order to recuperate some element of desire. . . . In the masquerade, they submit to the dominant economy of desire. . . . What do I mean by masquerade? In particular, what Freud calls "femininity." The belief . . . that it is necessary to *become* a woman, a "normal" one at that, whereas a man is a man from the outset. He has only to effect his being-a-man, whereas a woman has to become a normal woman, that is, has to enter into the *masquerade of femininity* [emphasis in original].[53]

While Irigaray here suggests that "being-a-man" is straightforward when compared to the means by which a woman becomes "normal," an examination of knightly activity in the *Morte d'Arthur* reveals that masculinity is in fact not established "from the outset"; the accoutrements of knighthood—sword, shield, horse, and most important, armor—may be appropriately described as instruments consciously wielded in an anxious attempt to assert/signify/perform masculine identity. Knightly armor affirms identity through an exaggeration of "maleness," simultaneously revealing and concealing the body inside. The visible manifestations of knighthood become a costume, an identity that may be put on, taken off, and transferred almost at will.[54]

We see the value of knightly accessories as indicators of masculine prowess from the opening of "A Noble Tale of Sir Launcelot du Lake." Early in the quest, Lancelot falls asleep under an apple tree, and while thus removed from the action of the narrative, his nephew Sir Lyonell is taken prisoner—along with three other knights—by the evil Sir Tarquin, who makes it a habit to imprison any knights he encounters. After defeating each knight with whom he has "ado," this Sir Tarquin displays, as a mark of his prowess, the shields of all those knights he holds prisoner. Once defeated and imprisoned in Tarquin's keep, Lyonell's mark of individual identity within the knightly community is taken from him, to join the shields of the other knights-prisoner. Tarquin does not destroy the shields of those knights whom he defeats, but rather, he significantly puts them on display in an attempt to appropriate some of that power for himself. If the name and reputation of knights are in a sense inscripted in the particularity of each shield, linking the bearer of the shield with the specific reputation for ability in combat associated with the shield, then Tarquin's defeat of those knights effectively signifies his superiority in terms of physical prowess.

Lancelot makes plain the dependence of knightly identity upon the idea of the name—not just the noble appellation "sir," but the individual, particular name that embodies for others the essence of a specific knight's unique chivalric identity. Awake from his nap, Lancelot encounters a maiden and asks for direction toward some place where he may test his knightly mettle. This forest maiden of adventure tellingly first asks Lancelot his name, and then leads him to Sir Tarquin. After engaging with Tarquin in battle, the latter, exhausted, offers him the opportunity for peaceful accordance betwixt the two of them: "Thou art the byggyst man that ever I mette withall, and the beste-brethed, and as lyke one knyght that I hate abovyn all other knyghtes. So be hit that thou be not he, I woll lyghtly acorde with the" (266.14–17). The knight whom Tarquin loathes above all others is, of course, Lancelot, a fact that Tarquin himself seems to suspect, given the description of his present opponent and comparison of that opponent to Lancelot; that the two happen to be one and the same person seems self-evident.[55]

In this episode, then, Lancelot in fact *appears* to be what he *is*. In the Lacanian understanding of masquerade, the feminine—that which is defined as "being" the Phallus within the symbolic order, and which exists in contrast to the masculine that "has" the Phallus[56]—*appears* as such through a performance that manages to blur the lines between "appearing" and "being," rendering them the same thing. If it is possible to understand knightly behavior in the *Morte d'Arthur* as a performance of gender identity, as I contend, then Lancelot's actions as fully armored and shielded knight—his masculine identity exaggerated from helm to greaves—participates in a kind of masquerade of the masculine. But what happens when Lancelot himself attempts to masquerade as *another knight?* Judith Butler has argued that

> acts, gestures, and desire produce the effect of an internal core or substance, but produce this *on the surface* of the body, through the play of signifying absences that suggest, but never reveal, the organizing principle of identity as cause. Such acts, gestures, enactments, generally construed, are *performative* in the sense that the essence of identity that they otherwise purport to express are *fabrications* manufactured and sustained through corporeal signs and other discursive means.[57]

The accessories that inscribe his body as masculine announce Lancelot's identity as a "hypermasculine" member of the knightly homosocial elite; these accoutrements are also part of his specific and particular identity performance as Lancelot du Lake, "kynge Bannis sone of Benwyk." As the episode with Tarquin suggests, so unique is Lancelot's fighting ability, and so far removed is his chivalric prowess above that of his fellow Round Table knights, he is unable to assume an effective, convincing disguise. While throughout the *Morte d'Arthur* other knights generally successfully assume the identities of one another (or create a false identity) through the simple borrowing or covering of shields, such deceptions do not work (or at least, not for very long) in the case of Lancelot.[58] His unique combination of physical prowess and knightly courtesy is so distinct as to be unmistakable, even when he is clad in the armor of another; he is indeed the über-knight. If onlookers do not immediately leap to the conclusion that the knight in question is in fact Sir Lancelot, comparisons to Lancelot are constantly invoked. When Lancelot assumes the identity of the wounded Sir Kay in the course of his questing activities, the deception is short-lived, but his deliberate decision to appropriate Kay's identity offers a significant comment on the way in which personal identity is a function of the community that gifts it to the individual knight.

In the midst of his many adventures in the forest, Lancelot comes upon three knights, who are pursuing the hapless Sir Kay. "'Truly,' seyde sir Launcelot, 'yondir one knight shall I helpe, for hit were shame for me to see three knyghtes on one, and yf he be there slayne, I am partener of his deth'" (273.12–14). When he has delivered Kay, both knights retire to a nearby hermitage for the evening. In the morning, Lancelot takes the sleeping Kay's armor and shield and sets out on further adventures. In Malory's source, this borrowing is entirely accidental, while in the *Morte d'Arthur* the deliberate appropriation of Kay's armor seems due to a desire on Lancelot's part to further strengthen the society of the Round Table. Lancelot's assumption of Kay's identity and the deeds he does while disguised as his comrade are more than merely a magnanimous gesture toward a fellow knight: in improving the reputation of Sir Kay, Lancelot thereby improves the reputation and standing of the Round Table itself, which then, in a circular fashion, in turn conveys more status and power on the individual knights who make up the population of the community.

Throughout "A Noble Tale of Sir Launcelot du Lake" Lancelot's successes against other knights and his repeated courteous service to ladies consolidate and affirm his heteronormative masculine identity. Indeed, Malory reinforces Lancelot's identity as the "best knyght of the worlde" in terms of the *Morte d'Arthur*'s chivalric value system by altering his sources—as in the example with which I opened this chapter—so that Lancelot's adventures are specifically connected to service to the feminine. One of these adventures involves fighting two giants who stand guard over a castle. They are taken care of quickly, after which success:

> there com afore hym three score of ladyes and damesels, and all kneled unto hym and thanked God and hym of his delyveraunce. "For," they seyde, "the moste party of us have bene here this sevene yere theire presoners, and we have worched all maner of sylke workys for oure mete, and we ar all gret jentylwomen borne. And blyssed be the tyme, knyght, that ever thou were borne, for thou haste done the moste worshyp that ever ded knyght in this worlde." (272.1–9)

In the Prose *Lancelot*, Lancelot rescues quite a different group—in terms of gender, not class—from the giants: "Lors fu la porte del chastel ouverte; si conmancerent a venir dames et damoiseles et chevaliers et dient a Lancelot que bien soit il venuz comme cil qui des or en avant sera lor sires et lor mestres" [Then the castle gate was opened; ladies, maidens, and knights began pouring forth to welcome Lancelot as the one who henceforth would be their lord and master].[59] Malory transforms the courtly community of his source into a homosocial subcommunity of gentlewomen. When Lancelot tells them his name, their collective response is typical of all those who encounter this greatest knight. "'A, sir,' seyde they all, 'well mayste thou be he, for ellys save yourself, as we demed, there myght never knyght have the bettir of thes two jyauntis; for many fayre knyghtes have assayed, and here have ended. And many tymes have we wyshed aftir you, and these two gyauntes dredde never knyghte but you" (272.14–19). That the giants have "dredded" Sir Lancelot speaks to his knightly prowess; that the maidens have "wyshed aftir" Lancelot specifically affirms his reputation as the particular champion of ladies. The juxtaposition of the giants' fear and the maidens' hope signals Lancelot's unique identity among knights. Lancelot's reputation as the true champion of women seems to ensure that ladies will in fact be the main focus of any quest he undertakes. Thus, his reputation reinforces and is reinforced by all his knightly activities; in the process of identity construction that is itself the process of the quest, Lancelot can only become himself.

While Lancelot's series of adventures consolidates his heteronormative masculinity, Kay's status is somewhat less clear; indeed, Lancelot's rescue of Kay from the three knights in many ways recalls his numerous rescues of maidens and ladies from straitened circumstances. It seems particularly significant that after sending the three defeated knights to Guenevere, Lancelot and Kay retire to a hermitage where Malory tells us explicitly that they "were lodged togydyrs in one bed" (274.30–31). By contrast, the Prose *Lancelot* says that "Kex se jut en .I. moult riche lit en la chambre ou Lancelot gisoit" [Kay slept in a splendid bed, in the room with Lancelot].[60] Striking in the lack of manifest anxiety it provokes, this lodging "togydyrs" suggests that within the all male homosocial subcommunity of knights, the heterosexual gender binary is reinscribed in relationships between knights, with those more "preux" and valiant knights occupying a masculine position in opposition to those less martially adept knights who occupy a more subservient, "feminine" role.

This male-male knightly relationship is repeatedly echoed in the *Morte d'Arthur*, and is most frequently represented as a situation in which an older, more experienced knight acts as mentor to a younger knight, who serves his elder with devotion. Not only does Lancelot occupy the dominant position in relationship to Kay, but he also inspires the love and devotion of Sir Gareth, and Sir Lavayne, brother of the Fair Maid of Astolat. Indeed, as the Fair Maid pines away due to her unrequited love for Lancelot, Lavayne explains to their father that "she doth as I do, for sythen I saw first my lorde sir Launcelot I cowde never departe from hym, nother nought I woll, and I may folow hym" (1091.12–15). Stephen Jaeger has recently discussed a similar phenomenon—relationships between noblemen that are described in the terms of romantic or erotic love, but which seem quite clearly not to involve what would be described in modern terms as "homoeroticism." This "charismatic friendship," as Jaeger terms it, served in many instances an ennobling function for one or both of the participants.[61] That, it would seem, is what is happening in this scene: Lancelot, the greatest knight of the Round Table, "ennobles" Kay, his fellow within the community, by sharing his sleeping space with him. While the episode with Kay suggests that such relationships between knights are acceptable *within* the confines of the Round Table order, *without* the elite subcommunity, knights must constantly offer a performance of heterosexual masculinity to the rest of the chivalric society in order to legitimately maintain their central position of power. Hence, when on the following morning Lancelot sets out disguised as Kay, he masquerades not only as the *masculine*, but also as a particular *man*.

Lancelot's disguise, as I have noted, proves particularly ineffective.[62] Every knight Lancelot engages with sees right through the deception: "Yondir knyght is nat sir Kay, for he is far bygger than he" (275.31); "yondir knyght hath slayne sir Kay and hath takyn hys horse and harneyse" (275.32–33); "mesemyth by his person hit is sir Launcelot" (276.2–3); "Methynkyth that knyght is muche bygger than ever was sir Kay" (277.17–18); "Ye may say hit well . . . that he is a man of myght, for I dare ley my hede hit is sir Launcelot: I know hym well by his rydyng" (278.12–14). While quickly recognized as himself—rather than the knight he at first *appears* to be—Lancelot's encounter with Sir Belleus, the knight of the pavilion, confirms the general necessity of armor and other knightly accoutrements as objects of masculine identification for knights. The pavilion scene implies that without armor, not only does one knight risk not recognizing another as his fellow or equal, he risks not recognizing him as a *man*. Feminist theorist Elizabeth Grosz has pointed out that "through clothing and makeup, the body is more or less marked, constituted as an appropriate, or, as the case may be, an inappropriate body for its cultural requirements. It is crucial to note that these different procedures of corporeal inscription do not simply adorn or add to a body that is basically given through biology; they help constitute the very biological organization of the subject."[63] The pavilion demonstrates how visible signs of knightly masculinity effectively "constitute" knights as "biologically organized" males.

The episode begins when Lancelot, tired from a full day of questing, begins to look for a place to spend the night.

> than was he ware in a slade of a pavylon of rede sendele. "Be my feyth," seyde sir Launcelot, "in that pavylon woll I lodge all this nyght." And so he there alyght downe, and tyed his horse to the pavylon, and there he unarmed hym. And there he founde a bed, layde hym therein, and felle on slepe sadly. Than within an owre there com that knyght that ought the pavylon. He wente that his lemman had layne in that bed, and so he leyde hym adowne by sir Launcelot and toke hym in his armys, and began to kysse hym. And whan sir Launcelot felte a rough berde kyssyng hym he sterte oute of the bedde lyghtly, and the othir knyght after hym. (259.22–33)

In Malory's source, Lancelot responds eagerly to the amorous advances of the knight of the pavilion, and it is this other knight who first reacts with violence to the realization that the figure in his embrace is in fact not his wife, but another man.

> Apres ce ne demora gueres que laienz vint .I. chevalier, celui cui li pavillons estoit . . . Il . . . se couche errant delez Lancelot et se trest pres de lui et l'acole et le conmance a baisier, car il cuidoit vraiement que ce fust sa fame. Quant Lancelot sant celui qui einsint le baisoit, si saut sus touz desvez et cuide bien que ce soit dame ou damoisele: si l'aert a .II. braz. Et cil s'aperçoit tantost et cuide que ce soit li lichierres sa fames, si se desvoleppe de lui et aert a .II. braz.

> [Not long afterwards, a knight arrived, to whom the tent belonged. . . . He was quickly undressed and lying beside Lancelot; he snuggled up to him, hugged him, and began to kiss him, because he really thought it was his wife. As soon as Lancelot felt the knight kissing him, he leapt on him all confused, thinking it must be some lady or damsel, and grabbed him with both arms. The knight immediately realized it was a man, thought it was his wife's lover, loosed himself from Lancelot's grasp, and seized him with both arms.][64]

The rest of the scene concludes quickly in the Prose *Lancelot*. The knight of the pavilion, realizing that Lancelot is more than his match in prowess, flees toward the forest with Lancelot in pursuit, both of them still naked: "si le chace tant sanz robe qu'il l'aconsielt, si le fiert par mi la teste de

l'espee si qu'il le fant tout dusqu'es danz et cil chiet morz a terre" [so without stopping to dress he pursued him until he caught up with him and
struck him a blow that split his head to the teeth, and the knight fell down
dead].[65] Malory has reworked his source to maintain the characterization
of Lancelot as a chaste knight, as yet innocent of the act of adultery, removing any hint that Lancelot responds positively to the other knight's ca-
resses.

Without benefit of armor or shield—those marks by which the owner
of the pavilion could "read" Lancelot as a fellow knight—the newly arrived knight interprets the sleeping Lancelot as not just "not a knight" but
"not a man" in both the *Morte d'Arthur* and its source.[66] Tellingly, after
realizing their mistake the two leap from the bed but make no attempt to
verbally clarify the misunderstanding. In the source, the knight of the pavilion snarls: "Certes, lerres, mar me venistes faire honte et mar vos
couchastes avec ma femme en mon pavillon meismes" ["Scoundrel! You'll
be sorry that you've shamed me and slept with my wife in my own
tent!"].[67] Although Lancelot makes no verbal response, he immediately
understands the mistake, and the threat of sexual violence dissipates. By
contrast, in Malory's text the knights do not speak; instead, they reach for
their swords, those most masculine of identifying objects, in an attempt to
redress as strongly and absolutely as possible the mistaken reading of the
other as female. When examined in conjunction with the lodging of Sir
Lancelot and Sir Kay in one bed, an acceptable and nonthreatening act, this
scene highlights the potential problems and tensions of the homosocial
bonding so important to the Arthurian knightly community. Lancelot's
immediate and violent reaction reflects an awareness of the potential danger of homosexual rumor and reputation that overshadows such a community of males, underscoring once again the important role the feminine
plays in terms of male-male interactions that take place *outside* the confines of the Round Table community. Belleus, the knight of the pavilion, is
not a member of the Arthurian male homosocial elite, and the presence of
a lady—either physically, or in the abstract as motivation for proper behavior and questing—alleviates this potential danger, making possible the
maintenance of homosocial bonds while diffusing the threat of homoeroticism and rendering Belleus legible in the terms of the Arthurian knightly
subcommunity.

The real threat for Lancelot on this occasion is *rape*, a threat that holds
the potential to entirely subvert the masculine knightly identity he has
striven so long and hard to establish and maintain—both in terms of his

identity as the *primus inter pares* of the Round Table order as well as his reputation in the wider chivalric social context.[68] I have argued that knights in Malory's text understand the feminine as helpless, vulnerable, and in constant need of protection; indeed, the Pentecostal Oath makes plain that rape specifically threatens the feminine and lists it among the injunctions of the ladies clause: "never to enforce them, uppon payne of dethe" (120.6–7). Interestingly, those *knights* that Lancelot rescues from dire straits—for example, Sir Kay—in a sense may *also* be said to occupy a feminine position when viewed in relationship to Lancelot's clear performance of masculine knightly prowess; Kay, then, while needing to stridently assert his masculine heterosexuality for the community at large, simultaneously and unproblematically takes up the role of the feminine within the male homosocial subcommunity of knights. To become a victim of rape would radically disrupt Lancelot's identity in *both* communities—the larger chivalric Arthurian society and the more elite homosocial knightly fellowship—locating him, by definition, in the role of the feminine. He would become, in other words, the very thing *against which* he has constructed his identity.

Only after Lancelot and Belleus have satisfactorily engaged one another in the masculine ritual of combat—in which the knight of the pavilion is wounded and yields to Sir Lancelot—do they speak: "'Sir,' sayde the knyghte, 'the pavylyon is myne owne. And as this nyght I had assigned my lady to have slepte with hir, and now I am lykly to dye of this wounde.' 'That me repentyth,' seyde sir Launcelot, 'of youre hurte, but I was adrad of treson, for I was late begyled. And therefore com on your way into youre pavylyon, and take youre reste, and as I suppose I shall staunche your bloode'" (260.5–11). The explanation that involves a lady further ameliorates the threat of feminization that combat has countered, and thus firmly restores the boundaries of homosocial interaction. When the lady arrives and is understandably upset to see her lord, Sir Belleus, wounded, he asks her to hold her peace, for "this knyght is a good man and a knyght of aventures" (260.17–18). Within the ideology of chivalry, it is acceptable—and even preferable—to be penetrated by the sword of another knight and die, masculine identity intact, than the (literally) unspeakable alternative.

When the lady learns that this is the famed Sir Lancelot, her reaction is typical of those who encounter this greatest knight: not only did she have an inkling of his identity before it was revealed—"So me thought ever be youre speche, for I have sene you oftyn or this, and I know you bettir than ye wene"—but his reputation for courtesy in conjunction with the ladies clause of the Oath prompts Belleus's lady to request a favor of Lancelot:

> "But now wolde ye promyse me of youre curtesye, for the harmys that ye have done to me and to my lorde, sir Belleus, that whan ye com unto kyng Arthurs courte for to cause hym to be made knyght of the Rounde Table? For he is a passyng good man of armys and a myghty lorde of londys of many oute iles." "Fayre lady," sayde sir Launcelot, "latte hym com unto the courte the next hyghe feste, and loke ye com with hym, and I shall do my power; and he preve hym doughty of his hondis he shall have his desyre." (260.28–37)

The terms of Belleus's lady's request reveal the largely unacknowledged potential for power and constraint that the feminine exercises in Malory's text. The lady invokes first Lancelot's reputation for courtesy and proceeds to name herself and *then* her lord as those who have suffered "harmys." Her request, while at first glance straightforward, cleverly manipulates the values and ideals of both the particular knight and the larger community that he represents so that Lancelot will feel compelled to accede. Although in assuming a suppliant position she fulfills Lancelot's expectations regarding ladies—helpless to act in their own interests and always requiring the services of a knight—it is really she who is in the position of power here, aware that a knight of King Arthur's court would have no other recourse but to agree to such a request. Irigaray's theorization of mimesis— a behavior that deliberately enacts or performs the position of femininity and in so doing resists that very prescribed position—is certainly applicable here.[69] Belleus's lady uses mimesis, offering up a performance of femininity to attain her desire. The fact that the lady—not Belleus— makes this request closes off the possibility of Lancelot's refusal. Round Table knights are as strongly conditioned to yield to ladies' requests as they are to accept masculine, martial challenges. Lancelot's response to the lady similarly demonstrates the values and norms of the community, likewise acknowledging the necessity of a feminine presence in maintaining the masculine chivalric enterprise as the defining project of the community: "and loke ye com with hym." The presence of Belleus's lady at court will help define the suppliant knight not as the potential rapist of Lancelot but as the defender of his lady and thereby an acceptable candidate for Round Table membership.

In revising his source material, Malory creates a complex and sometimes contradictory picture of gender in "A Noble Tale of Sir Launcelot du

Lake." Lancelot's performance of himself as a particular heteronormative knight and member of a male homosocial order demonstrates that the consolidation and affirmation of knightly masculinity is effected through masquerade, an exaggeration that equates "seeming" with "being." At the same time, even as *all* knights of the Round Table participate in this performance of heteronormativity, there appears to be room for other sorts of performances, for knights to take on other gender positions, within the confines of the homosocial subcommunity. Although Lancelot's performance of combat, service to ladies, and the rescue of other knights establishes him as masculine in both these social spheres, to maintain this gender position proves to be a task fraught with difficulty.

Lancelot in the Forest of Adventure: A "Knyght Wyveles"

While knightly accoutrements, participation in combat, and service to ladies all "mark" and maintain knightly identity, almost immediately upon setting out to "seke adventures," Lancelot's experiences demonstrate the inadequacy of these devices for fulfilling their designated purpose within the parameters of acceptable knightly behavior. Although repeatedly performing his masculine heternormativity, his reputed devotion to Guenevere in combination with his persistent status as a "knyght wyveles" render Lancelot vulnerable to attack and critique while in pursuit of identity-affirming adventures.

While Lancelot is asleep under an apple tree and after Sir Lyonell has been taken captive by Sir Tarquin, Malory tells us "Aboute the none there con by hym four queenys of grete astate. . . . And anone as they loked on his face they knew well hit was sir Launcelot, and began to stryve for that knyght, and every of hem seyde they wolde have hym to hir love" (256.19–29). The queens' imitation of masculine behavior subverts and challenges the paradigms of competition, fellowship, and recognition/identity that Malory's text usually models. While the Arthurian universe of Malory's text sanctions the formation of a masculine community devoted to the principles of chivalry and creates a code by which to govern that community, it does not anticipate any parallel feminine version of "felyship," and certainly not a fellowship of *queens*. Although queens in Malory consistently derive their ruling powers from their husbands, in this episode, the masculine is present only in an attendant, subservient role: "there rode four knyghtes aboute hem and bare a cloth of grene sylke on four sperys betwyxte hem and the sonne" (256.20–22). There is no code of conduct—prescriptive or proscriptive—for a fellowship such as this, and the feminine here manifests itself as a dangerous force against which there is no real defense for a knight who has sworn to uphold the articles of the Pentecostal Oath, especially the ladies clause. The potential problem of the feminine that Geoffroi de Charny's text seems to half recognize becomes plain here: in that women are essential to the chivalric project, they should be acknowledged as such and given some sort of guidance as to how they might best fulfill that role.[70]

Although Lancelot's shield is present, the four queens—one of whom is Morgan le Fay—do not recognize him in the terms of this most important knightly accessory. Instead, Malory tells us that "anone as they loked on his face they knew well hit was sir Launcelot, and began to stryve for that knyght, and every of hem seyde they wolde have hym to hir love." To their feminine gaze, a knight is primarily recognizable in the terms of his body, that which is usually both concealed and revealed as masculine, identifiable to other knights by the envelope of armor and the mark on his shield.

E. Ann Kaplan, challenging the idea that in gaze theory men are always looking and women are always looked at, claims that "To own and activate the gaze . . . is to be in the masculine position."[71] The four queens here disrupt the knightly conception of femininity and occupy in this episode a position of dominance, centrality, and power that is usually only generically available to the masculine: they look; Lancelot is looked *at*. Just as Kay and those other knights that Lancelot rescues in the course of his adventures may be said to occupy a feminine position in relationship to a knightly masculine liberator, Lancelot suddenly finds himself in the passive, vulnerable role. An examination of Lancelot's rescue of Kay suggests that within the homosocial masculine subcommunity the heteronormative gender binary of masculine/feminine may be safely reinscribed, with a knight unproblematically taking up one of these gender positions in relationship to another knight as long as he maintains a hypermasculine, continuous performance of knightliness for the benefit of the larger chivalric society. Lancelot's situation here does not permit such a simultaneity of masculine/feminine identification. Rather, captured, enchanted, and imprisoned by four powerful females who are outside the homosocial Round Table order, the helpless Lancelot is feminized, his identification as aggressive/masculine/dominant in *both* spheres of community undermined.

The queens' position doubly threatens the masculine order of the community in that while they occupy a masculine position, they do not interpret or react as men are expected to, refusing to "read" Lancelot's shield as the identifying marker it would be to other knights. Morgan does not—perhaps *cannot*—read the masculine language of the Arthurian community, the symbols of which are the physical accessories of knighthood. Far from simply casting these signs as unintelligible, Morgan, in her recognition of Lancelot's face and appropriation of his shield, deliberately seeks to subvert and rewrite the masculine symbology with which the community describes and defines itself. This ability to penetrate heraldic and genealogical identifications—to read through or beyond them—is part of the danger she poses. Morgan's appropriation of the masculine position is all the more threatening because rather than offering a masculine challenge (such as combat), she operates by "treson" and "inchauntement," those things to which Malory has called specific attention at the opening of "A Noble Tale" as threats to Lancelot. As in the "Tale of King Arthur" she is both simultaneously and never potentially masculine *and* feminine in her actions, and thus, she radically disrupts the model of gender so crucial to the construction of knightly social identity and indeed, to the very foundation of the larger Arthurian community.

In the danger she poses to the masculine chivalric community, Morgan also ironically provides that community with tests which, when successfully passed by the knight in question, serve to strengthen the institution of knighthood. Yet, even though she is usually defeated, knights rarely escape her clutches by the sole means of those instruments and skills acquired through membership in the Round Table community; "outside" help, often in the form of beneficent sorcery, is generally necessary. The masculine agents of the community never adequately deal with Morgan's threat; the knights do not seem to learn anything from these encounters in terms of strategy, should they meet her again.

Once released from his enchanted sleep, the four queens offer Lancelot a choice: choose one of them to be his lover, or else die in Morgan's prison. Although Morgan speaks for the group—"for I am quene Morgan le Fay, quene of the londe of Gore, and here is the quene of North Galys, and the quene of Estlonde, and the quene of the Oute Iles" (257.30–32)—Malory significantly indicates that the offer should be understood as being made simultaneously by all four women, speaking as one:

the four quenys seyde, "thou muste undirstonde thou art oure presonere, and we know the well that thou art sir Launcelot du Lake, kynge Banis sonne. And because that we undirstonde youre worthynesse, that thou art the noblest knyght lyvyng, and also we know well there can no lady have thy love but one, and that is quene Gwenyvere, and now thou shalt lose her love for ever, and she thyne. For hit behovyth the now to chose one of us four . . . that thou wolte have to thy paramour, other ellys to dye in this preson." (257.22–34)

If Morgan as a single, transgressive female was a threat in the "Tale of King Arthur," four such powerful females who come together to form a community of their own is four times as threatening. Although most certainly these women derive their titles and status through marriage, they tellingly reject the mark of that position—the name of the husband (or father)—and choose to identify themselves in terms of geography. This method of self-identification is striking when compared and contrasted with the terms in which they identify Lancelot: he is "kynge Banis sonne." Such a description—and the omission of the customary secondary geographical identifier "of Benwick"—locates him firmly within the patriarchal order, and places the four queens just as firmly—and deliberately— outside of it.

This contrast in modes of identification and their signification resonates all the more strongly when compared with Malory's source. In the Prose *Lancelot*, the queens never recognize the sleeping knight as Lancelot, and they desire him not because of his reputation as a knight or as Guenevere's lover, but simply because he is handsome: "Par Dieu, dame, vos poez bien dire que onques mais ne veistes si bel tousel" ["By God, ladies, you can certainly agree you've never seen a more handsome young man!"].[72] In this episode of the *Morte d'Arthur* the four queens appropriate and distort masculine behaviors of courtship, occupying the position of agressor to Lancelot's passive feminine position as the object of amorous interest. This imitation of masculine behavior in a sense complements Irigaray's model of feminine mimesis. Many of the quest maidens encountered by Lancelot throughout his tale resist the position of the feminine through a performance of that very feminine identity, by imitating that which knights think they are, and eliding the differences between "appearing" and "being." Morgan le Fay and the "felyship" of queens attempt to resist their gendered identities by appropriating the behavior of the masculine, that which they *are not*. That both these models of resistance are present in Malory's text—and that both are to some degree effective in opposing the prescribed position of the feminine—indicates that the model of gender upon which the Arthurian chivalric community constructs identity is one that perceives masculine and feminine to be stable and defined categories, while simultaneously revealing that this perception is incorrect.

While in both the *Morte d'Arthur* and Malory's source the episode with the four queens demonstrates the potential for disruption of the heteronormative gender categories that order the chivalric society, Malory's revisions of and additions to this tale depict masculine knighthood as constantly threatened or challenged by that which in fact produces it: in this case, Lancelot's devotion to Guenevere. The queens' demand that Lancelot choose one of them reminds the reader, yet again, of Lancelot's illicit relationship with Queen Guenevere.[73] In emphasizing the role that Guenevere plays in the construction of Lancelot's knightly identity, Malory also interestingly suppresses any explicit evidence of adultery.[74] Throughout "A Noble Tale of Sir Launcelot du Lake," female figures like the four queens constantly confront Lancelot with the accusation of his adulterous affair with Guenevere. Significantly, Malory's inclusion of these moments of accusation permits Lancelot to respond by affirming both the chaste nature of his love for the queen and the positive role that his devotion for her has in refining his knightly identity, thereby supporting the community of which he is a member. Says Lancelot to his captors: "And as for my lady, dame Gwenyvere, were I at my lyberte as I was, I wolde prove hit on youres that she is the trewest lady unto hir lorde lyvynge" (258.4–6).

We see this concern over Lancelot's status as the champion of the queen articulated in the conversation—original to Malory—between Lancelot and the forest maiden who has led him to the "aventure" of Sir Tarquin. After praising his skill in combat and thanking him for his help, the maiden then criticizes him for the very thing that has contributed to his status as the "floure of al knyghtes": "But one thyng, sir knyght, methynkes ye lak, ye that ar a knyght wyveles, that ye woll nat love som mayden other jantylwoman. . . . But hit is noysed that ye love quene Gwenyvere, and that she hath ordeyned by enchauntemente that ye shall never love none other but hir" (270.18–24). Evading the accusation of a love affair with Guenevere, Lancelot claims that if he were to take a wife, he would have to "couche with hir and leve armys and turnamentis, batellyes, and adventures. And as for to sey to take my pleasaunce with peramours, that woll I refuse" (270.30–33). If we take Lancelot's assertion to be an honest one (and at this point in the narrative, such would seem to be the case), then Guenevere is an appropriate object of devotion for him: distant and unattainable, she will not distract him from his knightly en-

deavors; yet, as the highest ranking lady of the land, it is only fitting that
the greatest knight should seek out adventures in order to win her favor.[75]
Indeed, as Geraldine Heng has suggested, Lancelot's character is so wholly
the product of feminine interests and desires—particularly those of
Guenevere—that his character is "located within a world of feminine purpose without which a Lancelot as we know him would be unimaginable;
seen thus, Lancelot's desire, then, is the desire not *for* the feminine, but *of*
the feminine."[76]

In this sense, while Malory portrays Lancelot's devotion to Guenevere
as constitutive of masculine knightly identity, close scrutiny reveals that
the idealized relationship modeled by Lancelot and Guenevere is also vulnerable, open to critique and threat. The simultaneous constructive and
destructive nature of the knight-lady relationship calls into question the
stability of the entire Arthurian social order as it questions the possibility
of sustaining the Lancelot-Guenevere relationship as both devoted and
chaste. Malory seems to have gone to great pains to characterize the
Lancelot-Guenevere relationship as free from adulterous activity at this
point, but as Felicity Riddy has pointed out, although "the opening para-
graph of the book seems almost willfully bent on establishing a Lancelot
who is not the lover of Arthur's wife . . . [his] other identity, displaced from
the centre, nags at the tale: on three occasions Lancelot is accused by other
women of loving Guinevere."[77] Thus, Malory's source material—even revised, rewritten, redacted—haunts his own text, pressuring Malory's new
conception of knightly identity with the concerns of the old.

Lancelot's response to the maiden evokes Chrétien de Troyes's "Erec et
Enide." In Chrétien's version of the story, the valorous knight Erec loses
interest in the office of knighthood after his marriage to the beautiful
Enide: "Erec was so in love with her that he cared no more for arms, nor did
he go to tournaments. . . . he wanted to enjoy his wife's company, and he
made her his lady and his mistress. He turned all his attention to embrac-
ing and kissing her; he pursued no other delight. . . . the nobles said that it
was a great shame and sorrow that a lord such as he once was no longer
wished to bear arms."[78] This is clearly what Lancelot fears and the justifi-
cation for his answer to the maiden's criticism. Janet Jesmok has suggested
that in the maiden's criticism that Lancelot is a "knyght wyveles," Malory
attempts to characterize the greatest knight as misled in the reasons he
offers for his bachelor status, claiming that "the love affairs of Gareth and
Pelleas, both of which end in marriage, enhance their chivalry and Arthur's

society"; if Lancelot were to follow this model, according to Jesmok, his marriage, too, would enhance the Arthurian community.[79]

However, while the events leading up to the marriages of Gareth and Pelleas follow the pattern of the questing knight and positively reinforce the idea of knightly devotion to the feminine and the role that female characters play in the constitution of knightly identity, both Pelleas and Gareth largely disappear from the progression of the larger narrative after their marriages. When they do appear again, it is usually as helpless, imprisoned, or vulnerable—they occupy a state that looks remarkably like that in which women are expected to be found, providing an opportunity for other knights to demonstrate their abilities and reinforce their reputations through rescue and the like. Indeed, Gareth's most unknightlike final appearance—weaponless and vulnerable in the path of Lancelot's sword—is also the occasion of his destruction.[80] Lancelot, then, seems right to worry that taking a wife would mean the end of his career. Put another way, Lancelot's response to the maiden's criticism is to argue that he will not be able to serve any and all ladies if he is married to just one whose presence will curtail his ability to pursue adventures. Willing to risk his life to succor a damsel in distress, Lancelot cannot risk marriage because of the potential consequences to his knightly career.

Yet, while fulfilling the needs of ladies and damsels in distress has been the making of Lancelot, near the end of "A Noble Tale of Sir Launcelot du Lake," the "floure of al knyghtes" has two encounters that demonstrate how the requests and desires of ladies may also be his unmaking. As we have seen, the forests of adventure are seemingly brimming with damsels in need of the services of a knight, and knights seem only to be able to "read" these women as needy and incapable of deception. Thus, knights never readily perceive or anticipate the occasional malicious female who seeks to harm or destroy a knight. Arthur's knights have no mechanism or means by which they may recognize or effectively deal with such a danger. Such malevolent women echo, to a lesser degree, the hazard that Morgan le Fay poses to the community, and while the individual episodes are usually (but not always) resolved satisfactorily in favor of the knight, the very fact of their repeated occurrence bodes ill for the continued prosperity and existence of Arthur's kingdom.

Although supposedly still riding through the forest in Kay's armor, Lancelot is recognized by the sister of Sir Melyot of Logres, who approaches him and asks for help:

"Well be ye founde, my lorde. And now I requyre you of your knyghthode helpe my brother that is sore wounded and never styntyth bledyng. . . . and there is a lady, a sorseres, that dwellyth in a castel here bysyde, and this day she tolde me my brothers woundys sholde never be hole tyll I coude fynde a knyght wolde go into the Chapel Perelus, and there he sholde fynde a swerde and a blody cloth. . . . and that swerde sholde hele my brother, with that his woundis were serched with the swerde and the cloth." (279.15–26)

Lancelot, of course, agrees and sets off for the Chapel Perilous, where he duly recovers the sword and the cloth. As he is departing the sorceress Hallewes approaches and admonishes him: "Sir Launcelot, leve that swerde behynde the, other thou wolt dye for hit" (280.35–36). Here we come upon an interesting problem for a sworn knight of the Round Table: what to do when asked by two ladies to perform conflicting acts? It seems that his earlier promise to the sister of Sir Melyot constrains him to refuse the command from *this* damsel, even though to disobey might result in his death. As it turns out, Lancelot's refusal is the proper course of action, as Hallewes reveals that "and thou dyddyste leve that swerde quene Gwenyvere sholde thou never se" (281.1–2). Hallewes then asks Lancelot for a kiss, which he refuses on the basis of a prior oath taken and commitment made to another, Queen Guenevere:[81]

"Well, sir" seyde she, "and thou haddyst kyssed me thy lyff dayes had be done. And now, alas," she seyde,"I have loste all my laboure, for I ordeyned this chapell for thy sake. . . . I have loved the this seven yere, but there may no woman have thy love but quene Gwenyver; and sytthen I myght nat rejoyse the nother thy body on lyve, I had kepte no more joy in this worlde but to have thy body ded. Than wolde I have bawmed hit and sered hit, and so to have kepte hit my lyve dayes; and dayley I sholde have clypped the and kyssed the, to the dispyte of quene Gwenyvere." (281.7–20)

In effect, Lancelot's prior commitments to Guenevere and Melyot's sister save him. The larger implications of this scene are chilling: what if he had encountered Hallewes before meeting Melyot's sister, and acquiesced to her requests as he would seem bound to do? In this instance, Lancelot does not successfully "preve" himself through either adherence to the Pentecostal Oath, a display of his martial prowess, or exceptionally courteous behavior—he is just lucky. Yet, at this moment in the *Morte d'Arthur*, arguably, it is not just luck, but intention. Malory has ordered his text in such a way so that at this stage, he only hints at the potential problem of conflicting demands and loyalties that later will threaten the community; Malory builds gradually to the tragic denouement that will ultimately be the result of these conflicting obligations and tensions that he here suggestively depicts. As Andrew Lynch has pointed out, Lancelot's seeming "luck" in this instance is a product of the "story's wish to demonstrate Lancelot's consummate knightly identity . . . necessitat[ing] that the action he takes is right."[82]

The significance of the episode of the Chapel Perilous in terms of the representation of Lancelot's character and identity within the *Morte d'Arthur*—and the broader implications this has for understanding chivalric knighthood more generally—is emphasized in Malory's reworking of this scene, which he found not in the French Prose *Lancelot*, but in the thirteenth-century *Perlesvaus*. In Malory's source, two women confront Lancelot—one an evil enchantress who wishes to kill him, and the other a maiden madly in love with him.[83] In combining the two women into one, Malory renders Hallewes's double request—that Lancelot leave the sword and render her a kiss—a more explicit link between Lancelot's martial prowess and his loyalty to the queen.[84] As Elizabeth Edwards points out, this episode is just one of many that reveal that "A Noble Tale" is "a particularly haunted text, crowded with ghostly subtexts. . . . It is a tale organised by an anxiety about the duplicity and hostility of women and the establishment of chivalric male identity."[85] While anxiety structures this tale, it does not yet undermine the Arthurian community as a whole.

Crucial to sustaining this connection between Lancelot's prowess and his love for Guenevere are those accessories of knighthood—sword, shield, armor—that I earlier suggested knights use to participate in a "masquerade" of masculinity, a performance of knighthood. Such accoutrements symbolically differentiate the manly knight from the lady he serves, whose femininity is frequently marked by an *exposure* of flesh, opposing the signification of masculinity effected through an *enclosure* of the body in armor.[86] An episode that appears to be original to Malory further underscores the importance of armor in defining masculine identity.[87] Lancelot comes upon a falcon, caught in a tree by its tether, and the presumptive owner emerges from the castle as Lancelot passes by. She recognizes him immediately, as do most of the women he encounters, and makes her appeal, echoing in formulaic fashion the requests of Sir Belleus's lady, Sir

Melyot's sister, and the forest maiden who criticizes his bachelor status: "A, Launcelot, Launcelot! as thow arte floure of all knyghtes, helpe me to gete me my hauke; for and my hauke be loste my lorde wolde destroy me, for I kepte the hauke and she slypped from me. And yf my lorde my husbande wete hit, he is so hasty that he wyll sle me" (282.22–26). Her request draws upon all the elements of Arthurian knighthood—and Lancelot's specific, singular, knighthood—that will facilitate acquiescence. Lancelot's renown as the "floure of al knyghtes" and his reputation as the particular protector of ladies is invoked when the woman characterizes herself as the potential helpless victim of her husband, who supposedly is "so hasty that he wyll sle me."

Lancelot's response significantly pairs a subtly implied reluctance to comply with an acknowledgment of what dutiful knightly behavior would be. It also acknowledges the lady's proper use of the terms and conventions that may exact such behavior, suggesting that on some level, Lancelot is aware of the potential of the feminine to pose a threat in that his oath of knighthood compels him to acquiesce to her demands. "Welle, fayre lady, syn that ye know my name and requyre me of knyghthode to helpe, I woll do what I may to gete youre hauke; and yet God knowyth I am an evyll clymber, and the tre is passynge hyghe, and fewe bowys to help me withall" (282.30–33). Lancelot then disarms, the better to climb the tree, and once he returns the falcon to the lady, discovers he has been betrayed.

> therewithall com oute sir Phelot oute of the grevys suddeynly, that was hir husbonde, all armed and with his naked swerde in his honde and sayde, "A knyght, sir Launcelot, now I have founde the as I wolde," he stondyng at the boole of the tre to sle hym. "A, lady!" seyde sir Launcelot, "why have ye betrayed me?" "She hath done," seyde sir Phelot, "but as I commaunded hir, therefore is none othir boote but thyne oure is com that thou muste dye." (283.4–13)

As in the episode of the pavilion, the removal of Lancelot's armor immediately exposes him to danger, and a possible loss of identity should Phelot defeat him—not just the loss of his particular identity as the "floure of all knyghtes," but in more general terms, his identity as a man. Caught in the tree *sans* both weapon and armor Lancelot anticipates his own defeat— "Alas ... that ever a knyght sholde dey wepynles!" he mourns. His expression of concern is significant in its emphasis; while the possibility of death certainly alarms him, the prospect of dying without his sword, the strongest mark of his masculine identity, is more troubling. Death fixes the reputation, freezes it, and the manner of a knight's death in effect gives the shape, the final reading, to the totality of his achievements that have heretofore constituted that identity. As the episode of the pavilion so clearly demonstrates, sword and armor are essential for signifying knightly masculinity; here Lancelot is without either, and seems well aware that to perish in such circumstances would undermine and destabilize the knightly masculine identity he has worked so hard to establish. If he must be defeated, it would be preferable to do so with his body enclosed in the armor that signifies his masculinity. Being the great Sir Lancelot, he makes do with a tree branch, and successfully defeats Phelot.

While numerous instances such as these demonstrate how the absence of a code of conduct for ladies opens up a space of feminine power and influence at the heart of the chivalric enterprise, in this scene duplicity on the part of a fellow knight is the real danger. Phelot's wife is only the instrument—not the instigator—of the plot to destroy Lancelot. As a knight fully committed to the knightly ideal delineated by the Pentecostal Oath, Lancelot is unprepared for conflict with another knight that is anything but direct. Indeed, the final "forest adventure" in which Lancelot participates underscores the existence of this weakness in the foundation of the Arthurian community.

Lancelot encounters a knight chasing his wife with drawn sword, jealous of her devotion to her cousin, and naturally seeks to intervene at the lady's request: "I requyre the of trewe knyghthode, kepe me and save me, for whatsomever he sey he woll sle me, for he is withoute mercy." Lancelot quickly seems to have the situation well in hand: "Sir," seyde the knyght, "in your sight I woll be ruled as ye woll have me" (284.35, 285.1–5). As they ride along, the lady between them, the lady's husband, Pedivere, distracts Lancelot. While he is looking away "suddeynly [Pedivere] swapped of the ladyes hede. And whan sir Launcelot had aspyed hym what he had done, he seyde and so called hym: 'Traytoure, thou haste shamed me for evir!' And therewithall he felle to the erthe and gryped sir Launcelot by the thyghes and cryed mercy. 'Fye on thy,' seyde sir Launcelot, 'thou shamefull knyght! Thou mayste have no mercy: therefore aryse and fyghte with me!'" (285.12–21). Not only has this knight shamed Sir Lancelot, tarnishing his reputation as the particular protector of women, but also he further confounds Arthur's greatest knight by refusing a direct challenge to combat. This knight doesn't play by the rules of masculine behavior, and the rigidity of the knightly ideology reveals itself here as its greatest weakness: for the values of the Pentecostal Oath to succeed as the guiding law of the kingdom, the articles of the Oath must be recognized as the norm, the frame or context within which actions, behaviors, and attitudes are judged and responded to accordingly. As Brewer has rightly observed of this scene, "this is not a flaw in Lancelot's character but an indication that Malory recognizes the vulnerability of his nobility. When the knight tricked him he thought no treason."[88] Edwards has echoed Brewer, noting that by the end of "A Noble Tale" we see that "the external world fails, increasingly, to conform to the chivalric ideal which Lancelot wishes to impose on it."[89]

Temporarily at a loss when his challenge is refused, Lancelot quickly comes up with an alternative punishment. He settles on this judgment not because as sentencer Lancelot feels it serves justice, but because as the sentenced, the lady's husband accepts the conditions. "'Well,' seyde sir Launcelot, 'take this lady and the hede and bere it upon the: and here shalt thou swere uppon my swerde to bere hit allwayes uppon thy bak and never to reste tyll thou com to my lady, quene Gwenyver'" (285.29–32). Here the simple refusal of his opponent to behave appropriately in accordance with chivalric ideology overturns Lancelot's rightful position as arbiter of justice. In Lancelot's consternation, bewilderment, and failure to satisfactorily perform his knightly duties at this moment, Malory's text reveals that the problems and conflicts that plague Lancelot, the knightly role model and representative of the Arthurian community, are similarly problematic in terms of the chivalric society as a whole. This problem becomes clearer and more pressing as the *Morte d'Arthur* progresses toward its conclusion.

As Malory notes in the opening of "A Noble Tale of Sir Launcelot du Lake," Lancelot repeatedly demonstrates himself as the greatest of knights, "for in all turnementes, justys, and dedys of armys, both for lyff and deth, he passed all other knyghtes, and at no tyme was he ovircom but yf hit were by treason other inchauntement" (253.9–11). By the conclusion of the tale, the threats posed by "treason" and "inchauntement" have been rendered more than clear and their dangers largely avoided or resolved. Yet, this avoidance seems only temporary, and the resolutions are largely unsatisfactory. Malory's text offers no indication that the Arthurian community and its individual knights have learned anything productive from these experiences, or will be better able to combat these hazards the next time they are encountered. The source of conflict that ultimately results in the destruction of the Arthurian community is in fact the constitutive ideals, values, and behaviors upon which the Arthurian community is built and defined. Thus, knights are helpless to combat or resist those forces that threaten to rend the fabric of the chivalric society, because to do so would effectively unmake knightly identity, annihilating the only means of "knowing" oneself and others that the text offers.[90]

In this respect Malory's text stands apart from the large body of chivalric literature so popular in late-fifteenth-century England. Unlike chivalric treatises that contained guidelines for proper knightly behavior, or other romances that depict an ideal world of knightly devotion, prowess, and clearly defined gender roles, Malory's *Morte d'Arthur* deploys the values and behavior expressed by these other works on a scale that demonstrates the inevitable degenerative progression of the chivalric community toward its end. Gender is just one of the pressure points that Malory's text as a whole—and the early adventures of Lancelot, in particular—identifies as a source of potential conflict, demonstrating how the idealized knightly devotion to ladies of which chivalric tracts speak may become twisted and warped.

So far, I have focused primarily on Arthur and Lancelot as representatives of masculinity and community within the *Morte d'Arthur*, but there are a range of other masculinities and alternative communities depicted in Malory's text. In particular, the "self-contained" Gareth offers a striking contrast when studied against the massive (and massively understudied) "Tristram" section. The "Tristram" depicts the Arthurian community as viewed from the outside, problematizing the idealized concepts of masculinity and femininity deployed with the institution of the Pentecostal Oath that are played out to satisfactory conclusion in the "Gareth." The "Tristram" also offers an alternative to Arthur and his community in the "dark double" of King Mark and his reign in Cornwall. Although often neglected in discussions of Malory, these two portions of the *Morte d'Arthur* offer a critical elaboration and expansion of the function of gender in the text, especially when viewed together.

Forecast and Recall

Gareth and Tristram

It may strike some as odd that I choose to discuss the "Tale of Sir Gareth of Orkeney" and the "Book of Sir Tristram de Lyones" together in a single chapter, especially as these two narrative sections of the *Morte d'Arthur* easily make up almost half its bulk. They are also the two sections of the text that seem most different in terms of narrative structure: where the "Gareth" moves forward in a more or less linear fashion, the "Tristram" wanders, rambles, and loops back on itself; where the "Gareth" maintains its focus on its namesake character, the "Tristram" leaves the title figure for long periods of time to follow the adventures of other knights; and while the "Gareth" is the most easily "detached" from the main matter of the *Morte d'Arthur*, the most "self-contained" of the tales, much of the significance of the "Tristram" lies in its myriad connections to people, ideals, and events that take place both before and after this narrative block. Different as they may seem from each other on the surface, I discuss them together because in terms of gender, these two sections perform a similar function: they refine and develop the ideal of courtly gender identity established as a foundation of the Arthurian community.

Established in the "Tale of King Arthur" and given its fullest articulation *in the person of the king* in the "Tale of Arthur and the Emperor Lucius," the gender ideal expressed in the Pentecostal Oath is next enacted and explored in the adventures of Lancelot, the greatest of all Arthur's knights. As we have seen, even the "floure of chevalry" has difficulty negotiating the demands of the code. In this middle portion of Malory's text, it is time for the "average" knight to have an opportunity to follow the guidelines of the code. On the other side of the "Tristram" the Grail Quest begins, and another singular knight—Lancelot's unique son Galahad—will test the spiritual limits of knighthood, after which the Arthurian community begins its inevitable final downward spiral to destruction. But it is here in the middle—in the "Gareth" and the "Tristram"—that we see some of the most interesting and varied knightly performances of the entire text. The treatment of knighthood in this middle portion of the *Morte d'Arthur* more fully develops and amplifies themes and ideals that are presented earlier and which become increasingly important as the narrative moves toward its conclusion. The shortcomings of chivalry—feminine power, kinship rivalry, and the desire to achieve worship, to name just three—recur so insistently in the middle portion of the text as to make the inherent contradictions of the chivalric project inescapable.

Malory's "Tale of Sir Gareth" and "Book of Sir Tristram" are remarkable in that, compared to the rest of the *Morte d'Arthur*, they have received little critical attention. The "Gareth" has attracted scant scholarly analysis (save concerning the question of sources) perhaps due to the clarity and simplicity of its story line;[1] Gareth moves through the countryside on his quest, encountering knight after knight, each increasingly more famous and skilled than the one before. He succeeds in winning his lady, marries, and all but disappears from the *Morte d'Arthur* until the concluding scenes.[2] By contrast, the "Tristram" has been relatively neglected due to its sheer size and seeming unmanageability. Indeed, it has become almost a commonplace in Malory studies to lament the neglect of the "Tristram" and to argue for its rehabilitation and restoration as a critical component of the narrative scheme of the *Morte d'Arthur*.[3]

Many critics have demonstrated that Malory went to great pains to create narrative links between the "Tristram" and the rest of the *Morte d'Arthur*,[4] suggesting that Malory saw this narrative unit as an important part of the larger story of the rise and fall of Arthur's kingdom.[5] In particular, the "Tale of King Arthur" seems to be filled with moments that have been reworked to elevate Tristram's status compared to other knights, or even to include him in scenes from which he is absent in the sources.[6] As Maureen Fries notes, "While earlier sections contain hints of a moral collapse to come . . . it is in the *Book of Sir Tristram de Lyones* that Arthurian society is first pictured as abandoning in large numbers the tenets of the oath still hypocritically renewed every Pentecost."[7] Thus, the "Tristram" prepares the reader for the clash of loves and loyalties that will precipitate the final social collapse as the text winds down to its inevitable conclusion; the middle third of the *Morte d'Arthur* supplies the reader with *reasons* for the final conflict that would only be hinted at or dimly suggested if Malory had not included the *Tristan* material in his text.[8]

A close examination of Malory's "Book of Sir Tristram" not only reveals the importance of this section to the logic of the *Morte d'Arthur* as a whole but also—and of even more importance—explores, develops, questions, and problematizes the issue of gender more insistently and significantly than any other portion of the *Morte d'Arthur*. Its representation of gender interactions as frustrated and frustrating is all the more significant in that the "Tristram" follows hard on the heels of the "Gareth," with its seemingly uncomplicated representation of the knightly activities of winning and wooing. The two tales tell startlingly divergent stories of knighthood. And although, as I have noted above, the "Gareth" and the "Tristram" are strikingly different in terms of overall narrative structure, the main narrative events of each—most notably single combat—seem to happen again and again with only minor variations.[9] The "Gareth" provides an image of knighthood that the "Tristram" reflects back as a broken mirror might—jagged, interrupted, unconnected.

The "Gareth" prepares us for the coming division among the sons of Lot, as Gareth receives the order of knighthood from Lancelot, and from that point chooses to side with Arthur's greatest knight even if it means opposing his own kin. The implications of Gareth's choice are made clear in the "Tristram," when we see the blood-feud between the houses of Pellinor and Lot burst through the constraints of knightly loyalty, civility, and courtesy that have just barely kept it in check. In one of the more disturbing moments of the "Tristram" the reader learns that King Pellinor's son Sir Lamorak has been killed (offstage, as it were) by Sir Gawain and his brothers—the children of Lot: "And at [Sir Lamorak's] departynge there mette hym sir Gawayne and his bretherne, and wyth grete payne they slewe hym felously, unto all good knyghtes grete damage!" (688.6–10). Although kin loyalty seems to triumph over the ideal of honorable knightly behavior expressed in the Pentecostal Oath, Sir Gareth notably refuses to participate in this act of retribution with his brothers, stating: "For well I undirstonde the vengeaunce of my brethirne, sir Gawayne, sir Aggravayne, sir Gaherys, and sir Mordred. But as for me . . . I meddyl nat of their maters, and therefor there is none that lovyth me of them. And for cause that I undirstonde they be murtherers of good knyghtes I lefte there company, and wolde God I had bene besyde sir Gawayne whan that most noble knyght sir Lamorake was slayne!" (699.1–9). The problem is not that one kind of loyalty (to blood) triumphs over another (to fellow knight), but rather that *both* loyalties function with equal force.

The "Tristram" also prepares us for other coming events: it marks the reappearance of the malevolent figure of Morgan le Fay, who here proves a greater challenge to individual and communal knightly identity than she did in her early appearances. Morgan now directs her evil action not only toward individual knights and the person of her brother the king, but also and more ominously, toward the Arthurian community at large: she sends to Arthur's court a drinking horn out of which only a chaste woman may drink without spilling (429ff.); Morgan also forces Tristram to bear a shield representing the adulterous Lancelot-Guenevere relationship into a tournament (554ff.). Although Sir Lamorak redirects the horn to Mark's court and Tristram refuses to explain the significance of the shield to Arthur, Morgan's threat to the social order has increased; she executes her attacks upon communal stability within the spheres of the public and the social— the court, the tournament—whereas previously she was most usually encountered by individual knights in the enchanted ground of the forest. The heart of the *Morte d'Arthur* shows us chivalry at its heights as well as its depths. Narratives of extremes and contrasts, the "Gareth" and "Tristram" bring the opposing ends of the spectrums of honor, prowess, and nobility into contact with one another.

Part of what is so frustrating about this middle portion of the *Morte d'Arthur* is also what is most important about it: in the endless series of events and situations that repeat, reemphasize, and reflect one another, Malory has found room to incorporate a variety of characters and attitudes absent from other portions of the narrative. Like variations on a theme, the repeated encounters of individual knights with one another in this section emphasize the *general* likeness of the masculine agents of the community while affording Malory the first real opportunity to demonstrate specific, *individual* differences among those figures. For example, although the triple-quest of Gawain, Torre, and Pellinor in the "Tale of King Arthur" first explicitly suggested the possibility of different degrees of knightly success, these sections considerably expand the spectrum of knightly honor, reputation, and prowess. The definition of knighthood is here broad enough to include not only the expected figures of Lancelot, Gawain, and Tristram, but also those nontraditional knights, such as the Saracen Palomides, the ever-grumpy Kay, the saintly Galahad, the "japer" Sir Dinadan, and that "thorough rotter"[10] Sir Breunis Saunz Pitié.

As this quick description suggests, this middle portion of the *Morte d'Arthur* is so complex, varied, and multilayered that one could easily write a whole book on the function of gender in the adventures and events recounted here. I have elected to focus on two aspects that I feel best articu-

late the important function of gender within this narrative unit and the
Morte d'Arthur as a whole: the repeatedly enacted episode(s) of the Fair
Unknown and the problematization of knightly identity as depicted in two
moments of cross-dressing.

Repetition and Reflection: The Fair Unknown

As I have already suggested, the "Tristram" includes several episodes that
demonstrate a remarkable pattern of similarities, allusions, and con-
gruences—both to earlier moments recounted in the *Morte d'Arthur* and
to other events that take place within the narrative bounds of the "Tristram" itself. The most obvious example of this similarity between characters is exemplified by those two "floures" of chivalry, Lancelot and Tristram.[11] Much critical attention has been paid to the *likeness* of Tristram
and Lancelot, and while their similarity (and the emphatic insistence repeatedly placed on it) is certainly important, the character of Tristram differs from Arthur's greatest knight in that he acts as one of the principal
players in the narreme of the Fair Unknown. Although Malory tells us
that Lancelot had to go through a period in which he was unknown to the
knightly community and needed to prove his right to join the ranks of the
Round Table—"evyn suche one was sir Launcelot whan he cam fyrst into
this courte, and full fewe of us knew from whens he cam" (459.31–33)—
we never actually *see* Lancelot's initial assertion of knightly prowess; he
leaps, as it were, into the main narrative of the *Morte d'Arthur* fully
formed and in the prime of knighthood. By contrast, the story of Tristram
opens with his birth and perilous childhood: his mother dies in childbirth
and his father remarries a woman who attempts to have him killed. Surviving these early trials, Tristram becomes the only knight willing to do
battle on behalf of his uncle King Mark, who has been ordered by the King
of Ireland to pay truage that Cornwall owes to Ireland. When Mark refuses, the Irish king sends his son, Marhalt, to fight a Cornish champion.[12]
After receiving his father's blessing, Tristram comes to the Cornish court
to meet the challenge. When pressed by King Mark, he identifies himself
only as having been sent "frome kynge Melyodas that wedded your systir,
and a jantylman, wete you well, I am" (378.28–29). Although fairly
quickly forced to reveal his identity to his uncle (due to Marhalt's refusal
to fight anyone less than the son of a king), Mark significantly grants Tristram the honor of knighthood and the challenge of Marhalt *before* he
knows that the "passyngly well made" young man is his nephew.

While Tristram's time as a Fair Unknown is brief, his participation in this narreme cannot help but remind the reader of the most memorable example of a Fair Unknown in Malory, Sir Gareth of Orkney.[13] As happens repeatedly within the boundaries of its narrative, the "Tristram" draws the reader back to earlier events in the *Morte d'Arthur* and then reiterates, reinforces, and revises their main thematic elements with variations that serve as a kind of commentary. Like Tristram, Gareth is the nephew of a king, and he comes to court in disguise to prove himself through the "prowess of hands" rather than relying on his blood relationship with the monarch as an avenue to knighthood. Gareth's story begins at the feast of Pentecost, a time when Arthur traditionally refrains from eating until "som mervayle" has occurred. On this particular occasion, that occurrence is the arrival of young man, "the fayrest that ever they all sawe" (293.29), who enters the great hall and asks for three gifts: "And they shall nat be unresenablé asked but that ye may worshypfully graunte hem me. . . . And the fyrste donne and gyffte I woll aske now, and the tothir two gyfftes I woll aske this day twelve-monthe, wheresomever ye holde your hyghe feste" (294.6–11). The first gift that the unknown knight requests is to be supplied room and board until the time of his asking for the other two gifts. Arthur encourages him to ask for more, but the young man refuses, and is thus sent to the kitchens, where he lives for a year in drudgery. He is constantly mocked by the ever-troublesome Sir Kay, who christens him with the sarcastic sobriquet "Beawmaynes," or "Fair Hands"—an unlikely name for kitchen knave.

Gareth's calculated deception of the court creates the circumstances that will allow him to establish a knightly reputation free from any hint of preference or partiality due to his kinship with the king. By obscuring his bloodline, a hero in disguise may better prove his inherent aristocracy, affirming his rightful place within the chivalric society through completion of challenges or tasks that only the most noble of men could possibly accomplish.[14] By deliberately choosing a position on the margin of the courtly community, Gareth elects to prove his worth by working his way up the chivalric social ladder from an "entry-level" position. His success is all the more notable in that his knightly career at Arthur's court begins from a position of prejudice rather than preference.[15] And as is usually the case within Malory's text, the establishment of his knightly reputation is effected through desire for—and thus service to—a woman. The story of Gareth takes the gender model first enacted in the "Tale of King Arthur" and later amplified in "A Noble Tale of Sir Launcelot du Lake" and confirms how the compulsion to fulfill ideals of gender identity produces the action of the narrative. Just as Lancelot's adventures had clarified the ideals of gender identity first demonstrated in the "Tale of King Arthur" by emphatically demonstrating the critical position that the subjugated feminine occupies in the formation and maintenance of knightly identity, Gareth's tale adds an important corollary to the rules of Arthurian gender performance.[16]

Again and again Malory's text demonstrates that opportunities for knightly career-building swirl around the locus of women's bodies, needs, and desires, clustering most thickly around single ladies. Although married ladies occasionally need the assistance of a Round Table knight, it is *single* ladies who provide the greatest opportunity for deeds of valor. In the patriarchal society of Malory's Arthurian community, noble wives are appropriately most often rescued and defended by their husbands, whereas single ladies in distress not only provide a questing knight with the chance to perform an act of rescue or service, but they also afford that knight an opportunity to repeat such actions through the establishment of an attachment, or what we might term a "love relationship." As the knight seeks to win the ultimate favor—the lady's hand in marriage—he is spurred to perform greater and more impressive feats of valor, thereby further enhancing and consolidating his chivalric reputation and that of the community he represents. In converting the desirable single woman into his wife, however, the knight effectively undermines his career by removing any impetus to perform noble deeds of martial prowess. A wife must be protected and defended; a single woman must be *won*. In the *Morte d'Arthur*, the elective activities of winning and wooing demand and inspire more glorious and impressive acts from knights than do the compulsory duties of protection and defense.

No other episode in Malory so sharply demonstrates the power and importance of the single woman in constructing knightly identity than the "Tale of Sir Gareth of Orkeney." The Gareth episode depicts in its entirety the inception, development, and effective conclusion of a knightly career. More clearly here than anywhere else in Malory, we see the powerful influence exerted by an unmarried noblewoman on the actions of a knight, and the way in which the fulfillment of the knight's desire for the available lady—achieved through a repetitive and continuous performance of knightly prowess and skill—effectively brings both the performance and his knightly career to an end.

At the end of Beawmaynes's/Gareth's year in the kitchens, a young maiden named Lyonet comes to Arthur's court to request assistance: "'Sir' she seyde, 'I have a lady of grete worshyp to my sustir, and she is beseged with a tirraunte, that she may nat oute of hir castell. And bycause here ar called the noblyst knyghtes of the worlde, I com to you for succoure'" (296.20–23). At this moment, Gareth steps forward and asks to be granted his two remaining requests. His first request is to be given the task of assisting the damsel, the second to be knighted by Sir Lancelot, the great-est knight of the realm. Arthur grants both wishes, and, much to the aston-ishment of the court, Gareth (still known to all as Beawmaynes, the kitchen knave) suddenly appears before the court in a fine suit of armor, takes his leave, and sets off on an equally fine horse. While Gareth may be happy with his assignment, Lyonet is none too pleased: "'Fy on the,' seyde the damesell, 'shall I have none but one that is your kychyn knave?' Than she wexed angry and anone she toke hir horse" (297.21–23). Gareth fol-lows after her, as does the rest of the court, to see what will transpire. Before he has gotten properly on his way, Kay challenges Gareth, and in the ensuing conflict Gareth handily defeats him, taking the other knight's shield and spear as trophies. Afterwards, Lancelot offers a more courteous challenge, at the end of which he suggests that they call a draw. Gareth eagerly asks Lancelot, "'Hope ye so that I may ony whyle stonde a proved knyght?' 'Do as ye have done to me' seyde sir Launcelot, 'and I shall be your warraunte'" (299.15–18). Lancelot then conveys the order of knight-hood upon Gareth.

Thus, Gareth begins his adventure as a Fair Unknown—and his knightly career—auspiciously. He proves his prowess to the assembled court in defeating Sir Kay, and he confirms that victory by admirably ac-quitting himself in what might be termed "polite combat" with the great-est knight of the realm; so impressed is Lancelot, he not only affirms that Gareth is worthy of knighthood, but also agrees to confer that honor upon him with his own hand. Although Gareth has proven himself a worthy knight in the eyes of Arthur's court, in the eyes of Lyonet he is still a "bawdy kychyn knave." As his tale progresses, so does his knightly reputa-tion as he successfully meets challenger after challenger. Lyonet withholds her approval of Gareth as a champion and knight longer than anyone else, vituperatively insisting that he is not worthy to be her escort or to engage in combat with other knights. When he is successful in any contest of knightly ability, she bemoans the fact that ever a mere "kychyn knave" defeated a knight. As Andrew Lynch has pointed out, "[Lyonet's] instincts are sound. It would be unacceptable for a kitchen knave to fight, let alone defeat, knights. 'The Tale of Sir Gareth' toys with the idea of true valour in a churl, in order to deny it."[17]

Throughout the tale, Lyonet mocks, berates, and scorns Gareth, refusing to acknowledge his clear display of innate nobility even though Gareth conducts himself as befitting a knight of the court of King Arthur: rescuing other noble knights in distress, defeating miscreant knights who seek to do harm to himself or to Lyonet, and perhaps most remarkably, enduring the constant jibes of his reluctant companion with grace and courtesy. For example: "'What art thou but a luske, and a turner of brochis, and a ladyllwasher?' 'Damesell,' seyde sir Beawmaynes, 'sey to me what ye woll, yet woll I nat go fro you whatsomever ye sey, for I have undirtake to kynge Arthure for to encheve your adventure, and so shall I fynyssh hit to the ende, other ellys I shall dye therefore'" (300.13–19). And later: "'Alas,' she seyde, 'that ever suche a kychyn payge sholde have the fortune to destroy such two knyghtes. . . .' 'Damesell . . . ye may sey what ye woll, but whomsomever I have ado withall, I truste to God to serve hym or I and he departe, and therefore I recke nat what ye sey, so that I may wynne your lady'" (302.12–22). Despite her constant harassment—or indeed, *because* of it—Gareth works hard to adhere to the highest standard of knightly behavior. Although he has won the admiration of his own court and the respect of knights from other communities, Lyonet refuses to recognize his innate nobility. If anything, she redoubles her criticism of her companion as he defeats knight after knight, and tellingly, her criticism matters much more to Gareth than the approval or admiration he receives from any other quarter. As Gareth's own words indicate, his ultimate goal is to "wynne" her, and thus, he cannot be satisfied with his achievements until she *is won*. As an unmarried and thus potentially available woman, Lyonet plays a far more important role in creating and shaping Gareth's knightly identity and reputation than do those knights with whom he engages in direct conflict, for she is the catalyst that creates the opportunities for such conflicts.

The moment following Gareth's defeat of the Green Knight aptly demonstrates that Lyonet is the most powerful force in the transformation of Beawmaynes the kitchen knave into Sir Gareth, the Round Table knight: "'All is in vayne,' seyde Bewmaynes, 'for thou shalt dye but yf this damesell that cam with me pray me to save thy lyff. . . .' 'Lat be,' seyde the damesell, 'thou bawdy kychyn knave! Sle hym nat, for and thou do thou shalt repente hit.' 'Damesell," seyde Bewmaynes, "your charge is to me a plesure, and at youre commaundemente his lyff shall be saved, and ellis nat'" (306.12–36). Granted his life, the grateful Green Knight pledges homage to Gareth, and expresses puzzlement at Lyonet's verbal abuse of so obviously noble an escort.[18] Moments later, an almost identical scene is played out with the Red Knight: once again, Gareth defeats his opponent, and once again, he asks Lyonet to choose whether the other knight should live or die. After having his life spared, the Red Knight also marvels that "allwayes this damesell seyde many foule wordys unto Bewmaynes" (310.16–17).

Gareth himself finally gives a clear explanation for his patient endurance of Lyonet's abuse:

> "Damesell . . . ye ar uncurteyse so to rebuke me as ye do, for mesemyth I have done you good servyse, and ever ye thretyn me I shall be betyn wyth knyghtes that we mete but ever for all your boste they all lye in the duste or in the myre. And therefore y pray you, rebuke me no more, and whan ye se me betyn or yoldyn as recreaunte, than may you bydde me go from you shamfully, but erste, I let you wete, I woll nat departe from you; for than I were worse than a foole and I wolde departe from you all the whyle that I wynne worshyp." (310.34–36, 311.1–7)

Her criticism and scorn compel Gareth to challenge yet bigger and stronger knights.[19] Every time he successfully counters her disdain with victory in a contest of knightly ability, he enhances and solidifies his reputation; soon, Gareth becomes famous as the valorous knight accompanied by a verbally abusive maiden. Yet, had Lyonet changed her opinion of him after his first victory and acknowledged his martial ability, he might not have met each knightly challenge with such eagerness. Gareth does not rest until he has the approval of his chosen lady; the withholding of that approval makes him a better knight. At long last, Lyonet offers praise for Gareth's behavior, and the terms of her approbation are significant, as is Gareth's response:

> "Mervayle have I," seyde the damesell, "what maner a man ye be, for hit may never be other but that ye be com of jantyll bloode, for so fowle and shamfully dud never woman revyle a knyght as I have done you, and ever curteysly ye have suffyrde me, and that com never but of jantyll bloode." "Damesell," seyde Bewmaynes, "a knyght may lytyll do that may nat suffir a jantyllwoman, for whatsomever ye seyde unto me I toke none hede to your wordys, for

the more ye seyde the more ye angred me, and my wretthe I wre-
kid uppon them that I had ado withall. . . . the mysseyyng that ye
mysseyde me in my batayle furthered me much and caused me
to thynke to shew and preve myselffe at the ende." (312.29–36,
313.1–6)

Only after she has expressed her approval of his knightly conduct does
Gareth share with Lyonet the secret of his lineage and the fact of his
knighting at the hands of Sir Lancelot. The news of his identity pleases
Lyonet, as it further confirms that Gareth's knightly actions arise from an
appropriately noble source.

Once she has given her approval of his actions, however, Lyonet loses
the influence she was previously able to wield over Gareth's career. That
power is immediately and seamlessly transferred to Lyonet's imprisoned
sister, Lyones. While in an immediate sense Gareth's adventure has been
the result of Lyonet's request for assistance, the ultimate catalyst for his
knightly career is the maiden who is *truly* in distress. Lyones is not only
unmarried, but the object of desire of another knight whose advances she
has long resisted, finally barricading herself in her castle. In the chivalric
patriarchal society, her value thus automatically increases due to her apparent desirability, but ultimately, as a single noblewoman in the
Arthurian community, she is truly valuable in terms of how she can benefit those knights who seek to possess her. Gareth has derived all the benefit he can from his relationship with Lyonet; once she is no longer useful
in helping him consolidate and maintain his masculine knightly reputation, Gareth looks for another woman to fulfill that role, to help him further enhance his already admirable heteronormative chivalric identity.

As Gareth arrives on the battlefield to fulfill the obligation he under-
took back in Arthur's court, he asks to have the woman for whom he fights
pointed out. After seeing her from afar, he remarks "I aske no better
quarrell than now for to do batayle, for truly she shall be my lady and for
hir woll I fyght" (321.28–29). When Lyones's attacker, the Red Knight of
the Rede Landes,[20] claims her for his own lady, Gareth rebukes him, and
further claims that "I love hir and woll rescow hir, othir ellys to dye therefore" (322.8–9). Although he has never seen her up close or spoken with
her, the fact of her availability as a potential wife and the extreme quality
of her distress provoke Gareth to proclamations of love and devotion. If his
patient endurance and service to Lyonet are born out of a sense of duty and
obligation to a damsel in need, the more desperate need of Lyones leads

him to declare himself her lover, and one singularly devoted to her. This particular challenge—more than any other he has encountered on the long road leading up to it—affords Gareth the opportunity not only to enhance his own reputation but also to win for himself the devotion of an available lady clearly deemed desirable by the standards of the community.

When Gareth and the Red Knight engage in battle over the lady Lyones, it is, appropriately, the most difficult contest of his knightly career thus far: the battle rages for an entire day. Every time Gareth tires, Malory tells us, his recollection of the desperate situation of his newly proclaimed lady-love helps him find renewed strength and energy with which to continue the fight. Lyonet herself plays on this: "A sir Bewmaynes! Where is thy corrayge becom? Alas! my lady my sistir beholdyth the, and she shrekis and wepys so that hit makyth myne herte hevy" (324.12–14). Not surprisingly, Gareth redoubles his efforts and finally defeats the Red Knight, who asks for mercy. Gareth hesitates to grant the request, as the Red Knight has "shamfully" been responsible for the deaths of many other "good knyghtes" and, in Gareth's estimation, deserves to die. When the Red Knight asks for a chance to explain himself, the excuse he offers is the only one that could possibly save his life: all of his "shamfull" actions were done at the request of his former lady. Upon learning this, Gareth grants him his life: "But insomuche all that he dud was at a ladyes requeste I blame hym the lesse" (325.24–25). In his act of mercy, Gareth recognizes that for a knight, the request of a lady constitutes a command that cannot be disobeyed.

Although Gareth has proven his martial capabilities in combat against Kay, Lancelot, and the variety of other knights encountered in his quest, although he has proven his courtesy by graciously defending Lyonet and enduring her verbal abuse, and although he has even proven his right to love and defend the desirable Lyones by defeating the powerful Red Knight, he has not yet won the right to truly call her his lady. When he turns from his victory on the battlefield to regard Lyones at her window, instead of immediately granting him her love, she calls out: "Go thy way, sir Bewmaynes, for as yet thou shalt nat have holy my love unto the tyme that thou be called one of the numbir of the worthy knyghtes. And therefore go and laboure in worshyp this twelvemonthe, and than ye shall hyre newe tydyngs" (327.7–11). As a consolation, she promises to be true to Gareth while he is gone and to love him until her death, but she withholds the possibility of marriage—the ultimate prize—until he has affirmed his status as a knight worthy to be her husband. She thus provokes him to achieve still greater heights of glory and nobility, to spread the news of his valorous reputation still further. Lyones uses this delay to try to discover his lineage; for although Gareth *seems* to be a man of noble birth, she cannot possibly consider marriage to him until she knows for certain: "for tyll that I know what is his ryght name and of what kyndrede he is commyn shall I never be myrry at my herte" (328.17–19). Once she learns his lineage, she suspends the twelve-month assignment, and "than they trouthe-plyght other to love and never to fayle whyle their lyff lastyth" (332.35–36). Their marriage is postponed, however, until Gareth—in a new disguise, so that none might know him—returns to Arthur's court where he performs admirably in a tournament in which all the greatest knights of the Round Table compete. His career has thus come full circle, and he returns in triumph to the court where he began his knightly adventures as a kitchen knave.

Once unmasked and saluted, acknowledged and lauded by his fellow knights, Gareth and Lyones are married at the feast of Michaelmas. In honor of the event, another tournament is held, but this time, significantly, Malory tells us that "the kynge wolde nat suffir sir Gareth to juste, because of his new bryde; for, as the Freynsh boke seyth, that dame Lyonesse desyred of the kynge that none that were wedded sholde juste at that feste" (362.22–26). There could not be a stronger piece of evidence to suggest that the office of knighthood and the state of matrimony cannot successfully coexist in the chivalric community. With his marriage, Gareth has achieved the prize toward which all his efforts as a knight have been directed; his reward for exemplary behavior as a knight, however, also ironically ends his chivalric career. Once married, he all but disappears from Malory's text.

Although Tristram's actions as a Fair Unknown do not initially intersect with the concerns of gender, the early events of his career cannot help but remind the reader of Gareth. Gareth's tale emphatically demonstrates the important role that the feminine plays in constructing and maintaining knightly identity in the *Morte d'Arthur*, while simultaneously revealing the ironic fact that when a knight finally achieves the ultimate "prize"— marriage to his beloved—the actions and reputation that have helped him to achieve this "reward" suddenly become the undoing of that same identity that has made such a reward possible. Tristram's status as devoted to a single lady would seem to be compromised by his *marriage blanche* to Isode White Hands, but in one sense this could be viewed as a strategy for concealing his relationship with Queen Isode, and thus permitting their relationship to continue; in similar fashion, Lancelot makes a great show of serving any lady who asks for help as a means of directing attention away from his relationship with Guenevere. As Lancelot says to the queen: "And wyte you well, madam, the boldenesse of you and me woll brynge us to shame and sclaundir. . . . And that is the cause I take uppon me more for to do for damesels and maydyns than ever y ded toforne, that men sholde undirstonde my joy and my delite ys my plesure to have ado for damesels and maydyns" (1046.25–31). Similarly, although Tristram's relationship with Sir Segwarides's wife would seem to complicate the fact of his single-ness of devotion to Isode, it in fact reinforces the lesson demonstrated by the rise and steep fall of Gareth's career—Tristram sets his sights on a married lady early on in his career in order to enhance his reputation as a knight of valorous deeds without having to worry that eventually he will have to marry her and forego knightly activity.

The early events of Tristram's career not only recall Gareth's story, but more insistently call our attention to two other narrative episodes in the "Book of Sir Tristram": the adventures of "La Cote Male Tayle" and "Alexander le Orphelin." Indeed, at the beginning of Gareth's tale, Lancelot's admonishment to Kay after he has bequeathed the nickname "Beawmaynes" to Gareth directs the reader's attention ahead to the "Tristram" section (confusingly, the events of which seem to occur in the chronological *past*). Lancelot reminds Kay that "so ye gaff the good knyght Brunor, sir Dynadans brothir, a name, and ye called hym La Cote Male Tayle, and that turned you to anger aftirwarde" (295.15–18). The "Book of Sir Tristram de Lyones" thus explicitly links a series of knights and their adventures—both within the "Tristram" itself and elsewhere in the *Morte d'Arthur*—to one another. The stories of Tristram, Lancelot, Gareth, La Cote Male Tayle, and Alexander the Orphan all recall various aspects of the others, particularly in terms of gender and the formation of individual and communal identities. This multiplicity of parallel, overlapping, and amplifying episodes converge in the "Tristram" section like a palimpsest, rendering the ideals of gender and knighthood present in the *Morte d'Arthur* with greater depth and detail than any single one of these narrative strands could convey on its own.

The story of La Cote Male Tayle echoes Gareth's, particularly in many of its early details; just as Kay mocks Gareth, calling him "Beawmaynes" so too does the grouchy seneschal offer a repeat performance, conferring upon the young man the moniker "La Cote Male Tayle" on account of the ill-fitting and bloodstained coat that he wears. Like Gareth, La Cote is not yet a knight, and when opportunity presents itself in the form of a quest maiden who arrives at court seeking a champion, La Cote asks for the chance to prove himself. The quest maiden scorns the help of one such as La Cote and sets off alone, compelling the young knight to chase after her in order to have his chance to "preve" himself in "straunge aventures." Not only does this maiden heap scorn upon La Cote as Lyonet did to Gareth, but her very name signals her nature: she is the "damesell Maledysaunte." Indeed, it seems that she has been stealing from Lyonet's playbook, as it were. For example, after early encounters with Arthur's fool, Dagonet, and the knights Bleoberys and Palomides, the damesell says:

> "What doste thou here in my felyship? For thou canste nat sytte no knyght nother wythstonde hym one buffette but yf hit were sir Dago-net." "A, fayre damesell, I am nat the worse to take a falle of sir Pa-lomydes. And yett grete dysworshyp have I none, for nother sir Bleoberys nother yett sir Palomydes woll not fyght with me on foote." "As for that . . . wete you welle they have disdayne and scorne to alyght of their horsis to fyght with suche a lewde knyght as thou arte." (463.21–30)

As in Gareth's case, other knights who encounter the pair chide the maiden for her treatment of La Cote. Even Sir Mordred criticizes her verbal assaults, telling her "ye ar gretly to blame so to rebuke hym, for I warne you playnly he is a good knyght, and I doute nat but he shall preve a noble man" (466.10–13). Lancelot offers the strongest critique of Maledy-saunte's actions, indicating that he will only accompany the pair "so that ye wyll nat rebuke thys knyght sir La Cote Male Tayle no more, for he ys a good knyght, and I doute nat but he shall preve a noble man" (471.11–14). As was the case with Lyonet's constant criticism of Gareth, we learn that Maledysaunte had only her companion's best interests at heart: "I rebuked hym never for non hate that I hated hym, but for grete love that I had to hym, for ever I supposed that he had bene to yonge and to tendur of ayge to take uppon hym thys aventure" (471.17–20). Her criticism has, of course, inspired La Cote to perform marvelous feats of prowess, and in the end of his narrative, he takes the damsel—newly renamed "the lady Byeau-Vyvante"—as a wife, and does so using his true name, "Breune le Noyre." It is as if the names that they have employed up until this point have been critical components of the gender performance in which each has been engaged; once married and safely heterosexualized, these names must be discarded for others that demonstrate that this pair have left the playing field of identity construction.

Alexander is not a true Fair Unknown—he obscures his identity for only a brief period during his questing activities—but his adventures are so similar to those of La Cote that one cannot help but think of them in tandem; indeed, it would seem that the later episode is intended to recall the earlier. As Donald Hoffman points out: "due in part to the mere misfortune of succession, [Alexander] seems to be imitating La Cote imitating Gareth."[21] Both La Cote and Alexander are charged with avenging the deaths of their fathers, and given articles of clothing—stained with the blood of the father—to remind them of their duty. And like much in the "Tristram," Alexander's story has the added significance of reminding the reader —even if explicit comparison is lacking—of Sir Tristram himself and his plight: Alexander, like Tristram, is a nephew of King Mark; also like Tristram, Mark considers Alexander his enemy. This young knight is identified as "l'orphelain" because Mark has murdered Alexander's father, who also happens to be Mark's brother. Like La Cote, Alexander enters the world of knighthood to embark upon a quest to avenge his father, and also like La Cote, he tests and tempers his prowess through encounters with the feminine. In Alexander's case, however, the feminine is represented primarily by Morgan le Fay, who reappears in the "Tristram" after a long absence from the Morte d'Arthur. As might be expected, Morgan mostly hinders—rather than helps—Alexander's knightly development and progress. Alexander's narrative provides an important corollary to La Cote's, compellingly demonstrating how the feminine not only helps construct and maintain knightly identities, but also poses the greatest threat to them.

After being wounded in a contest of arms arranged by a damsel of Morgan's, Alexander finds himself completely beholden to Arthur's half-sister for his well-being. Morgan uses Alexander's incapacity and his need to somehow perform his knightly heteronormativity as a means to hold him captive:

Than Morgan le Fay com to sir Alysaundir and axed hym yf he wolde fayne be hole. "Madame, who wolde be syke and hy myght be hole?" "Well," seyde Morgan, "than shall ye promyse me by youre knyghthode that this twelve-monthe and a day ye shall nat passe the compace of this castell, and ye shall lyghtly be hole." "I assent me," seyde

sir Alysaundir. And there he made hir a promyse and was sone hole.
And whan sir Alysaundir was hole, he repented hym of his othe,
for he myght nat be revenged uppon kynge Marke. (642.34–36,
643.1–7)

Since a knight who cannot fight is essentially a contradiction in terms,
Alexander is compelled to make whatever bargain necessary to restore his
health and thus make it possible for him to return to the realm of the quest
and the tournament. Wounded as he is, the only portion of his knightly
identity still available to Alexander is that of courtesy and service—particularly to ladies—which Morgan quickly invokes. Morgan has returned
to the text in the same role she occupied in the "Tale of King Arthur";
inexplicably hostile to Arthur's realm and to knighthood, she compromises knightly identity by invoking and manipulating those attributes
that give it definition.

When Alexander learns that Morgan desires to keep him as her lover,
he responds with the unexpectedly graphic: "I had levir kut away my
hangers than I wolde do her ony suche pleasure!" (643.24–25). Although
Alexander's violent response appears to be a direct translation from Malory's source, it takes on a greater significance in Malory than in the French
Prose *Tristan*.[22] In the "Tale of King Arthur," Morgan attempts to cause
Arthur's death by using her feminine wiles to manipulate Accolon; in "A
Noble Tale of Sir Launcelot du Lake," she and her three companion queens
similarly demand that Lancelot chose one of them as a paramour or else
remain their prisoner. Alexander's violent response to her desire recognizes the escalation of the threat she poses, especially when considered in
light of her previous behavior in the narrative. Morgan manipulates the
knightly understanding of ladies and uses the powers of enchantment to
achieve her ends, and every time she does so, she paradoxically moves further and further away from the realm of the feminine as Malory's text
understands it. Alexander's declaration that he will "kut away my hangers" speaks not only to his distaste for the advances of a woman who is
opposed to the Arthurian project of chivalry, but also suggests that Morgan has crossed a boundary and is no longer a "real" woman in the terms
of the knightly understanding of such: sex with her would not *be* heterosexual or heteronormative, due to her emphatic denial of her gendered
position, and thus, Alexander is willing to emasculate himself physically to
avoid the symbolic emasculation and heteronormative transgression that
sex with Morgan would create.

Freed from his obligation to Morgan by the clever machinations of another damsel, Alexander redresses the emasculation he experiences as a prisoner of his oath by going to the opposite extreme. Immediately after escaping from Morgan's clutches, Alexander participates in a tournament of arms, giving so impressive a performance that he inspires love in one of the observers. La Beal Alys leaps from her seat and grabs Alexander's mount by the bridle, demanding:

> "Fayre knyght! Of thy knyghthode, shew my thy vysayge." "That dare I well," seyde sir Alysaundir, "shew my vysayge." And than he put of his helme, and whan she sawe his vysage she seyde, "A, swete Fadir Jesu! The I muste love, and never other." "Than shewe me youre vysayge," seyde he. And anone she unwympeled her, and whan he sawe her he seyde, "A, Lorde Jesu! Here have I founde my love and my lady! And therefore, fayre lady, I promyse you to be youre knyght, and none other that beryth the lyff." (645.20–29)

Alexander's performance in the tournament temporarily restores gender relations to their natural order—so spectacular is his demonstration of martial skill in the masculine arena of combat that it quite rightly inspires immediate and complete love on the part of the most desirable lady watching. And La Beal Alys is most definitely the most desirable woman present, as we learn in a moment original to Malory that she is "of the bloode of kynge Ban, that was fadir unto sir Launcelot" (646.26–27). Alexander's immediate reciprocal response to her declaration of love indicates his reincorporation into the heteronormative economy of the knightly community. His next adventure, however, almost completely undoes that reassimilation.

So completely has Alexander committed himself in love for La Beal Alys, that he seems guilty of that knightly danger that causes Lancelot to remain a "knyght wyveles": "Ryght so cam the false knyght sir Mordred and sawe sir Alysaundir was so afonned uppon his lady, and therewithall he toke hys horse by the brydyll and lad hym here and there, and had haste to have lad hym out of that place and to have shamed hym" (647.7–11). When it becomes clear that Alexander is in danger of serious compromise to his identity as a knight of prowess—indeed, in his reverie he has become helpless and passive, a position usually occupied by the feminine—the damsel who helped him to escape from Morgan again comes to his rescue. She resorts to extreme measures, appropriating masculine behavior to counter the emasculated, feminized, position that Alexander seems suddenly and paradoxically to occupy as a result of his love for La Beal Alys: "she lete arme her and sette a shylde uppon her shuldir. And therewith she amownted uppon his horse and gate a naked swerde in hir honde, and she threste unto Alysaundir with all hir myght, and she gaff hym suche a buffet that hym thought the fyre flowe oute of his yghen" (647.13–18). Awakened from his trance, Alexander quickly returns to his senses and his identity as a knight of Cornwall, and Malory tells us that he and La Beal Alys "wente into their contrey of Benoy and lyved there in grete joy. . . . And by Alis he gate a chylde that hyght Bellengerus le Beuse. . . . And he revenged his fadirs deth, for this false kynge Marke slew both sir Trystram and sir Alysaundir falsely and felonsly" (648.2–10).

Although Malory never explicitly tells us if Alexander and Alys are formally married, the fact that they have a child together and that Alys "wolde never go from hym" (648.1–2) indicates that their relationship functions, for all intents and purposes, as at least a *de facto* marriage. As Gareth's example has demonstrated, marriage is the goal toward which knights seem to strive in an on-going process of identity construction; achieving the goal, however, paradoxically undoes the very reputation that such striving has created.[23] As in Gareth's tale, the "marriage" of Alexander and Alys effectively brings his career to an end. Alexander does not avenge the death of his father, Malory tells us; that must be left up to Alexander's son. Instead, Alexander is treacherously murdered by King Mark, as was his own father. Arguably just as tragic as his death is the fact that his relationship with Alys seems to have knocked him not only "off course" in terms of his quest for vengeance, but also *literally* "off course" in terms of his physical journey: "And hit happed so that sir Alysaundir had never grace ne fortune to com to kynge Arthurs courte. . . . And grete dole was made for hym" (648.11–15). Alexander never avenges his father, never becomes a Round Table knight, it seems, because he has been distracted by the pleasures of his lady, La Beal Alys.

Thus, the examples of Sir Gareth, La Cote Male Tayle, and Alexander the Orphan all demonstrate convincingly the double-edged sword that is the feminine in the *Morte d'Arthur*. Critical to the formation and maintenance of masculine knightly identity, the feminine also has the power to undo the very identities it is instrumental in constructing and supporting. Marriage may destroy knightly reputations, but the courtship that precedes matrimony is somewhat paradoxically the strongest support of masculine chivalric identity.

Clothing, Gender, and Knighthood

The events of the "Tristram" call attention to the function of gender not only in terms of the *particular* event or episode, but more important, by deliberately alluding to and recalling other "gender significant" moments that precede and follow in the *Morte d'Arthur*. In the Fair Unknown analogues I've discussed above, the story of Tristram's early exploits link him to La Cote Male Tayle, Alexander the Orphan, and perhaps must suggestively, to the story of Gareth. Gareth's tale, in its coherent "self-containedness" offers in microcosm a view of the ideal progression of a knight—from untried newcomer to proven warrior to rewarded husband—from the beginning to the (effective) end of a knightly career. In doing so, Gareth's tale clarifies, emphasizes, and elaborates the performative nature of knighthood. In the words of Judith Butler, "gender is always a doing, though not a doing by a subject who might be said to preexist the deed."[24] The figures of Gareth, Tristram, Lancelot, La Cote Male Tayle, and Alexander come into intelligibility—as particular knights *and as men*—through their repeated actions in the sphere of knightly adventure. Butler's theorization that "gender is . . . a kind of becoming or activity . . . that . . . ought not to be conceived as a noun or a substantial thing or a static cultural marker, but rather as an incessant and repeated action of some sort" neatly lends itself to the formation of knightly reputation in Malory.[25]

Gareth must repeatedly prove himself to Lyonet *and* Lyones, even when he has satisfactorily demonstrated his right to bear arms in his encounters with other knights and his fitness to marry a noble lady through his defeat of the Red Knight of the Red Lands. Likewise, La Cote Male Tayle and Alexander the Orphan achieve status and reputation after a lengthy series of trials involving repeated demonstrations of prowess of arms and service to ladies, repeatedly citing the norm of masculine behavior. Tristram himself mirrors these stories of individual knights' acquisition of name, status, and gender on a larger scale: his story serves as the theme that binds much of the middle portion of the *Morte d'Arthur* together, as he progresses from Fair Unknown who offers to serve Cornwall, to the greatest of Cornish knights, to member of the Round Table. If the narratives of Gareth, La Cote, and Alexander are notable in their "detachability" from the *Morte d'Arthur*, then Tristram's adventures are notable for just the opposite reason. Absent from his own tale for much of the time, Tristram's frequent appearances and reappearances weave together the themes that run throughout the "Book of Sir Tristram de Lyones." Tristram's story is the unifying element of this most massive and unwieldy portion of Malory's text, and it connects this section to the rest of the *Morte d'Arthur*.

In my discussion of Lancelot's character and development in chapter 2, I focused considerable attention on the physical accessories of knighthood—shield, sword, horse, and most important, armor. Armor, as Kathleen Coyne Kelly and others have noted, is remarkable for the way it simultaneously conceals the body inside while announcing that that body is gendered male.[26] Lancelot's experience in the pavilion of Sir Belleus compellingly demonstrates how his unarmed body leaves itself "open to a different interpretation, as it were."[27] Out of his armor and in the soft bed of the pavilion, Belleus interprets the sleeping Lancelot as not only "not a knight" but also as "not a man," a misunderstanding that Lancelot significantly redresses through a violent display of masculine knightly prowess. Gareth's story reiterates the importance of armor. The court is astonished when the kitchen knave Beawmaynes takes his leave of Arthur bedecked in all the accoutrements of knighthood: "And with that there com one to Bewmaynes and tolde hym his horse and armour was com for hym, and a dwarff had brought hym all thyng that neded hym in the rycheste wyse. Thereat the court had muche mervayle from whens com all that gere" (297.24–28).

Although Gareth's story seems at first to suggest that knightly standing may be achieved through displays of martial capability—almost as if the Round Table were some kind of meritocracy—his story, like all Fair Unknown narremes, reinforces the idea of the inherent nobility of blood. His lineage—son of King Lot and Queen Morgause, nephew to King Arthur—is obscured so that his actions may be judged "knightly" without any taint of preference or advantage; when his bloodline is revealed near the end of his story, it only confirms what his actions and success while adventuring have already made clear: Gareth can only be a member of the noble elite. Although only an aside, the importance of Gareth's possession of a coat of armor before he sets out on his quest cannot be overstated. It signals to the court that he is a fit candidate for knighthood generally and this adventure in particular.

While armor is one of the key defining attributes of the right to belong to the order of knighthood in Malory, the "Tristram" section expands the definition and significance of noble knightly garb. Suggestively linked as they are to Gareth in so many other ways, the figures of La Cote Male

Tayle and Alexander the Orphan decisively echo each other in their apparel. Indeed, Malory begins his account of La Cote Male Tayle with an unusual focus on his appearance:

> To the courte of kynge Arthure there com a yonge man bygly made, and he was rychely beseyne, and he desyred to be made a knyght of the kynge. But his overgarmente sate overthwartely, howbehit hit was ryche cloth of golde. "What is youre name?" seyde kynge Arthure. "Sir, my name is Brewnor le Noyre, and within shorte space ye shall know that I am comyn of goode kynne." "Hit may well be," seyde sir Kay the Senesciall, "but in mokkynge ye shall be called 'La Cote Male Tayle,' that is as muche to sey, 'The Evyll-Shapyn Cote.'" "Hit is a grete thynge that thou askyste," seyde the kynge. "But for what cause weryst thou that ryche cote?" "Hit is for som cause, sir. . . . I had a fadir, a noble knyght, and as he rode an-huntyng uppon a day hit happed hym to ley hym downe to slepe, and there cam a knyght that had bene longe his enemy. And whan he saw he was faste on slepe he all to-hew hym, and thys same cote had my fadir on that tyme. And that makyth this coote to sytte so evyll uppon me, for the strokes be on hit as I founde hit, and never shall hit be amended for me. Thus to have my fadyres deth in remembraunce I were this coote tyll I be revenged. And because ye ar called the moste nobelyst kynge of the worlde, I com to you to make me a knyght." (459.4–27)

Significantly, Arthur avoids giving a direct answer to Brewnor's request for knighthood, noting only "Hit is a grete thynge that thou askyste." That he immediately follows his evasive response with an inquiry about the coat signals his apprehension about Brewnor's fitness to be a knight—although the coat is admittedly "ryche," its torn and bloody state indicates that the body that wears this garment may not be a proper candidate for knighthood. It is notable that Malory's first description of Brewnor looks past the coat to the body it encases. Although his physical body, like Gareth's, suggests that he may be a member of the knightly class, the clothing on that body seems to offer an opposite interpretation. The first descriptive notice we receive is of how La Cote is "bygly made" and "rychely beseyne," phrases that suggest his innate nobility. The "evyll-shapyn" coat that covers this body presents a problem, in that, for all its "rychness," its torn and tattered condition indicates something different than La Cote's "bygness" and "rychness"; the signals conflict.

The work of Judith Butler and Marjorie Garber here provides a productive means for engaging with the function of clothing in the *Morte d'Arthur*. In her theorization of cross-dressing and drag, Butler argues that not only are bodies in some sense "marked" as conforming to masculine or feminine genders through clothing, but that in fact, the body itself is rendered intelligible by the "cultural inscription" that clothing produces: "This marking is the result of a diffuse and active structuring of the social field. This signifying practice effects a social space for and of the body within certain regulatory grids of intelligibility."[28] In Malory, such "grids of intelligibility" signal class and gender through both the physical body and the clothing that covers it. As Garber has pointed out in her groundbreaking study of cross-dressing: "vestimentary codes, clothing as a system of signification, speak in a number of registers: class, gender, sexuality, erotic style. Part of the problem—and part of the pleasure and danger of decoding—is in determining which set of referents is in play in each scenario. For decoding itself is an erotics—in fact, one of the most powerful we know."[29]

From our first encounter with La Cote, the reader is invited to try and decode the signals that crowd the signifying field of his body. If armor properly clothes bodies that are masculine, "byg" and "ryche," then it might seem as if a torn coat should properly clothe a body that is *not* fit for knighthood. La Cote himself seems to recognize the mixed signals sent by his body and his clothing when he hastily assures Arthur that he is "comyn of goode kynne." La Cote's explanation for his wearing of such a torn and bloodied piece of clothing successfully transfers the symbology usually conveyed by armor and shield to that of his misshapen garment. A knight's armor and shield with coat of arms announces both his genealogical right to belong to the order of knighthood and his individual reputation. La Cote's garment literally demonstrates his blood affiliation; his familial relations are signified not by a symbol on a shield, but by the actual blood of the actual father.

Impressed with his dedication to honor and vengeance, Arthur agrees to grant Brewnor knighthood, but importantly, Brewnor does not actually receive this honor until he has proven himself worthy through his actions—not until his deeds confirm both his words and his body. Arthur and his knights leave the court to go hunting, leaving Brewnor behind with the queen and her retinue of knights. "By a suddeyne adventure" a lion enters the court, striking terror into all those present; the majority of the queen's knights flee, and it is left to Brewnor to kill the lion, which he does most calmly and effectively. Hearing the story upon his return,

Arthur exclaims, "Uppon payne of myne hede, he shall preve a noble man and feythfull and trewe of his promyse!" (460.27–28). Without further delay, Arthur makes him a knight. After his formal investiture, Sir Brewnor turns to the king and says: "Now, sir . . . I requyre you and all the knyghtes of the courte that ye calle me none other name but La Cote Male Tayle" (460.30–32). It was as "La Cote Male Tayle" and not "Brewnor" that the young man of noble lineage performed his first "knight-worthy" act, and thus, he chooses to build his reputation on this foundation. Indeed, when the Damesell Maledysaunte comes to court bearing a shield of adventure, La Cote proudly accepts this quest and deliberately identifies himself by his new name. "'Well may thou be callyd so,' seyde the damesell, 'the knyght wyth the evyll-shapyn coote! But and thou be so hardy to take on the to beare that shylde and to folowe me, wete thou well thy skynne shall be as well hewyn as thy cote'" (462.7–11). In her response to La Cote, the maiden acknowledges (and properly so) how unfit this young man appears to be to take on this task.

In Brewnor's decision to be known as "La Cote" he deliberately casts himself in a position of disadvantage, just as Gareth does in agreeing to serve as a kitchen knave for a year. As Beawmaynes and La Cote work their respective ways toward "becoming" Gareth and Brewnor, the huge gap that stands between the origin and conclusion of their knightly careers signifies the importance of establishing reputation in Malory's Arthurian community. Although Malory tells us that after his marriage to the Damesell Maledysaunte, La Cote "preved a passyng noble knyght and a myghty, and many worshipfull dedys he ded aftir in hys lyff" (476.16–19), tellingly, we see none of those adventures. Amazingly, the achievement of his first goal—to avenge the death of his father—occurs "offstage," noted seemingly in passing in the final line of La Cote's story: "and also as the Freynshe booke makith mencion, sir La Cote Male Tayle revenged the deth of hys fadir" (476.23–24). Although vengeance precipitates La Cote's movement into the realm of the recognizable subject in Malory's world, the *Morte d'Arthur* emphasizes the process, the citation of the norm of masculinity that La Cote's actions enact, rather than the culmination of that process. In fact, the triumph of La Cote seems to lie in his admirable impression on and subsequent marriage to the Damesell Maledysaunte. It is as if, once married, La Cote's triumph over his father's murderer is comparatively unimportant; if still an unmarried knight at the time of his act of vengeance, then such an act might have been the crowning achievement of his masculine performance of heteronormativity.

It might seem that in my analyses of Gareth and La Cote Male Tayle I am "trying to have it both ways"—suggesting that in the one instance marriage effectively ends a knightly career (Gareth) and in the other, marriage so firmly establishes a knightly identity that success in the original quest becomes a foregone conclusion (La Cote Male Tayle). I think both interpretations are correct. What is most interesting and important is how both these narratives emphasize the process of knightly becoming, a process put on display yet again in the narrative of Alexander the Orphan.

Alexander's story participates in the "doubling" effect of the "Tristram," as his adventures repeat, in a different key, those of La Cote Male Tayle, and in a sense, the adventures of both these knights reflect and repeat the story of Gareth. Alexander, like La Cote, seeks to avenge the death of his father, murdered by his uncle, his father's brother, King Mark of Cornwall. Like La Cote, Alexander bears evidence of his family bloodline in a literal sense—he wears "his fadirs dublet and his shurte with the blody markes" (635.12). His story departs from the details of La Cote's in that he does not receive the right to wear these items until the day he is made knight; La Cote comes to Arthur's court wearing the mark of his father's treasonous death and points to his need to avenge his father as the reason he should be made knight. In the case of Alexander, the sequence of events is inverted, and his knighthood occasions the bestowal of this bloody coat of arms and thus, simultaneously sets in motion his quest. In both instances, knightly performance brings the seemingly unknightly clothing—and by extension, each knight's identity—into the "grid of intelligibility" of the community.

I have dwelt for some time on the significance of the clothing worn by La Cote Male Tayle and Alexander the Orphan because it seems to me that the "Tristram" section offers an expanded and more complex vision of how apparel constructs identity than we see elsewhere in Malory. The narratives of La Cote and Alexander suggest that clothing in the *Morte d'Arthur* participates in the formation of identity just as actions do, calling attention to the performative aspect of garments in such a way as to enhance the signification of armor as discussed in chapter 2. If La Cote's and Alexander's narratives expand the significance of apparel, then the episode of the "Tournament at Surluse" pushes the significatory boundaries of clothing to the breaking point. Apart from the examples of La Cote and Alexander, the "Tristram" plays with the link between outward appearance and inward identity in that it includes two moments of cross-dressing, an event that happens nowhere else in the text. Although women appropriate

the typical accessories of knighthood and masculinity in isolated mo-
ments—Morgan attempts to kill Uriens with his own sword, the queen of
Ireland attempts to kill Tristram, the lady huntress accidentally shoots
Lancelot in the buttocks, a damsel takes up sword and shield to restore
Alexander to his senses—these episodes generally occur away from the
public spaces of the community; witnesses are few. In the "Tristram," the
Morte d'Arthur gives the reader two moments of *masculine* cross-dressing that are as notable for their singularity as they are for the space in
which they each occur—the public realms of tournament and great hall.

As Dhira Mahoney has noted, the "Tale of Sir Tristram" "resounds with
the joy of fighting."[30] Indeed, battles large and small crowd the pages of
this tale, so that the "resounding" joy of fighting becomes an almost over-
whelming din. Tournaments, jousts, fights undertaken while questing,
single combat—around every bend in the road there seems to be a knight
waiting with sword drawn or lance at the ready to take on all comers.
Scholars such as Mahoney have pointed out the unusual number of tournaments in the "Tristram" when compared to the rest of the *Morte
d'Arthur*. In terms of gender, the most significant tournament in this tale
is the "Tournament at Surluse." At the end of the several days of
celebratory jousting and "encountering" that mark this particular event,
there are two occurrences of knights dressing "in drag" as women. One
knight does so deliberately, to effect a sort of practical joke, while the other
is clothed in a dress against his will, as the butt of that same joke. An analysis of the different responses to these two moments of knights-in-drag and
the particular space in which each of these episodes occur further emphasizes and clarifies the Arthurian community's understanding of masculine
identity formation. The episode in question occurs on the last day of the
tournament and is worth quoting at some length:

> Sir Dynadan departed and toke his horse, and mette with many
> knyghtes and ded passyngly well. And as he was departed, sir Laun-
> celot disgysed hymselff and put uppon his armour a maydyns gar-
> ment freysshly attyred. Than sir Launcelot made sir Galyhodyn to
> lede hym thorow the raunge, and all men had wondir what damesell
> was that. And so as sir Dynadan cam into the raunge, sir Launcelot,
> that was in the damesels aray, gate sir Galyhodyns spear and ran unto
> sir Dynadan. . . . But whan sir Dynadan saw a maner of a damesell,
> he dradde perellys lest hit sholde be sir Launcelot disgysed. But sir
> Launcelot cam on hym so faste that he smote sir Dynadan over his

horse croupe. And anone grete coystrons gate sir Dynadan, and into the foreyse there besyde, and there they dispoyled hym unto his sherte and put uppon hym a womans garmente and so brought hym into fylde; and so they blew unto lodgyng, and every knyght wente and unarmed them. And than was sir Dynadan brought in amonge them all, and whan quene Gwenyver saw sir Dynadan ibrought in so amonge them all, than she lowghe, that she fell downe; so ded all that there was. "Well," seyde sir Dynadan, "sir Launcelot, thou arte so false that I can never beware of thee." Than by all the assente they gaff sir Launcelot the pryce. (669.15–36, 670.1–5)

A careful reading of this moment reveals that it is much more than an episode of comic relief in an otherwise mostly violent and bloody narrative. While most of the acts of knightly identity formation that I have discussed thus far involve individual knights who encounter challenges, adventures, or ladies while out questing, the context of the tournament here sharpens the import of the spectacle played out. And spectacle it is; the tournament is a site not only for activities that establish, consolidate, and maintain knightly identity, but also dramatizes those activities for an audience of witnesses. A knight returning from a quest is required to narrate his adventures before the assembled court so that his actions may be approved or condemned and "official" communal judgment may be passed. The space of the tournament creates an odd effect, in that the knightly activities usually only verbally recounted for the court are here *performed* for the noble audience. The tournament offers a representation of gender that complicates gaze theory, in which men look and women are *looked at*. Here, men perform, and an audience made up primarily of women watch. As Alexander's example suggests, the performance itself appears staged, designed to produce the same results as knightly questing. La Beal Alys immediately falls in love with Alexander after witnessing his tournament performance. Her reaction—and his acceptance and return of her love—consolidate Alexander's position within the heteronormative, homosocial, order of knighthood.

That the first instance of masculine cross-dressing is both deliberate *and* takes place within the tournament field is significant; Garber has pointed out (as have any number of Shakespeare scholars) that cross-dressing that occurs as theater, as spectacle, is "safe" drag. Both performer and audience share in the knowledge that the masculine body in women's clothing is not "really" cross-dressing; the "performance" is just that.[31]

Like the Shakespearean stage, the medieval tournament field should be understood as theater—as a space of self-aware performativity—particularly in the context of Malory's England.

Several historians of medieval chivalry have noted the transformation the tournament underwent from its earliest incarnation to its late medieval form. While in the thirteenth century the tournament held "real risks of fatal injury,"[32] by Malory's day a series of adjustments, regulations, and advances in equipment had made the tournament a relatively low-risk activity, although serious injury and death to participants did, on some occasions, still occur.[33] As Maurice Keen has noted of fifteenth-century tournaments: "Steadily, these sports were becoming more and more divorced from the central activity with which they were originally associated: real fighting in real war."[34] So distinct had the activities of warfare and tourneying become that by Malory's day, knights used different equipment for each.[35] The tournament not only became more about entertainment and less about training for war but also, in the organization of these spectacles for an eager audience, organizers and participants drew more and more from romance literature for inspiration, and in particular, from Arthurian romance literature.[36] Thus, although Malory borrows the "Tournament at Surluse"—and its two moments of knightly cross-dressing—from the much earlier French Prose *Tristan*, the theatricality of the tournament as depicted in the *Morte d'Arthur* is in some ways very close to the reality of tourneying in Malory's day. As Benson notes: "the grand tournaments in the *Morte d'Arthur* reflect the customs of Malory's own time, and the more elaborate they are the more closely they resemble real tournaments."[37]

That the theatrical aspect of medieval tournaments was perhaps at its highest during Malory's lifetime and the period in which he composed the *Morte d'Arthur* helps to give us a context for understanding the significance of the "Surluse." As I argued in the introduction to this book, the *Morte d'Arthur*'s representation of gender differs significantly from that found in Malory's sources; the larger narrative context (and in this case, the realities of the fifteenth-century tournament) cause even moments lifted directly from the Prose *Tristan* to signify and resonate differently—especially in terms of gender—than they might in the source text. The "Tournament at Surluse" stands at the heart of the "Book of Sir Tristram de Lyones," which itself is at the center of the *Morte d'Arthur*. Although this episode contains the only two moments of masculine cross-dressing in the whole of Malory's text, cross-dressing was in fact—and somewhat surprisingly—a regular part of medieval tournaments in Malory's day.[38] This episode would have been both striking and familiar to a fifteenth-century reader—striking in that it is the only occurrence of knightly cross-dressing in the text, familiar in that such cross-dressing regularly occurred in the "real world" of the late medieval tournament.

At the moment when Lancelot enters the lists with "a maydyns garment" over his armor, the reader cannot help but recall the earlier moment in which Lancelot was accidentally mistaken for a woman by Sir Belleus, the knight of the pavilion. That *this* moment of gender confusion results in amusement and entertainment for the assembled audience is partially due to the fact that there *is* an audience. Away from the court, abed in a pavilion in the woods, such a misunderstanding/misrepresentation would not be humorous. Outside the theatrical space of the tournament field, any moment in which a masculine agent of the community "performs" or represents himself as feminine—as other than what he is—would be considered dangerous and transgressive. As Ad Putter has argued: "The tournament defuses the transvestite's subversive potential not only because of the *a priori* assurance that all its active participants are male anyway . . . but also because it encodes cross-dressing as 'play.'"[39] Thus, Lancelot's assumption of the "socially coherent" markers of femininity in order to play a joke on Sir Dinadan works as a joke precisely to the extent that tournament spectators see through the dress to the armor underneath it. Significantly, it is not that the audience sees through the dress to a masculine body, but rather, to the clothing/apparel that codes that body as masculine. The theatrical circumstance of this moment helps the audience to properly interpret the dual coding of Lancelot's body: encased in armor, which is then covered by a dress. The context of the tournament, in conjunction with the relative proximity of each sartorial marker to Lancelot's physical form, signal that his masculinity is "real," his femininity is "play." What this moment also suggests, however, is the fragility of gender identity in the Arthurian community. As Butler has rightly argued, "in imitating gender, drag implicitly reveals the imitative structure of gender itself—as well as its contingency."[40] As an imitation of knightly activity, the tournament suggests something similar about knighthood and gender identity in Malory.

Part of what makes this joke so funny is not only that Lancelot dresses as a maiden but also that he "smote sir Dynadan over his horse croupe." If Dinadan were truly defeated by a female knight, his humiliation—and that of the patriarchal community he represents as a tournament participant—would far outweigh any humor. That the spectators know that the "damsel" who defeats Dinadan is really Lancelot brings the ratio of humiliation to humor back into equilibrium; the community laughs at the ultimate masculine knightly humiliation—defeat by the feminine—without it actually happening. Lancelot's "play" as a damsel thus actually supports the sex-derivative heteronormativity of the Arthurian community. In Putter's words: "Behind the transvestite joke thus lies a deep conservatism, for *getting* it requires our acceptance of the incompatibility of the two sexes, just as *taking* it demands the audience's profession of this fact in the form of laughter."[41]

Guenevere's reaction to the aftermath of the Lancelot-Dinadan confrontation demonstrates the importance of laughter in signaling that such cross-dressing is "play." After being knocked "over his horse croupe," Lancelot arranges for some "grete coystrons" to take Dinadan into the forest, where they "dispoyled hym unto his sherte and put uppon hym a womans garmente and so brought hym into fylde; and so they blew unto lodgyng." Dinadan's status as a cross-dressed knight differs from Lancelot's in that his "womans garmente" is not superimposed over a suit of armor; Malory significantly tells us that the "coystrons" who drag him into the forest undress him all the way down to his "sherte," so that when Dinadan reappears in a dress, he lacks the most obvious signal of knightly masculinity—the suit of armor—that made Lancelot's joke such a roaring success. And although first brought to the "field," a context that identifies knights in drag as only "playing," we do not see a reaction to Dinadan until later, when he is brought into the hall before the assembled tournament participants. In such a space—away from the unambiguously masculine locale of the joust and lacking his armor—the cross-dressed Dinadan represents much more insistently than Lancelot's similar performance the tenuous contingency of gender construction.

Guenevere's response to Dinadan's appearance in the hall at first might seem extreme: "whan quene Gwenyver saw sir Dynadan ibrought in so amonge them all, than she lowghe, that she fell downe; so ded all that there was." Guenevere rarely displays much in the way of a sense of humor in the *Morte d'Arthur*, and this moment of such uncontrolled laughter on the part of a character usually prone to petty temper tantrums brings the reader up short. Why does she laugh so hard here that she "fell downe"? In his analysis of this scene, Ad Putter has used Freud's theorization of the joke—that laughter results when energy used to "maintain defensive inhibitions" is no longer necessary—to explain Guenevere's response at this moment: "The laughter of relief works in this way: liberated from the mental strain of fearing the worst, 'psychical energy' finds an outlet in laughter, the intensity of which is proportionate to the anxiety that previously consumed this energy."[42] I agree in general with Putter's analysis of this scene and with his basic argument that Guenevere's laughter at this moment derives from an initial anxiety about Dinadan in drag. But in contrast to Putter, I see her hilarity at this moment not as reflecting the dissipation of gender anxiety, but rather, functioning as a strategy to diffuse such anxiety.

Notably, Malory makes no explicit mention of laughter—uncontrolled or otherwise—during the first stage of Lancelot's prank on Dinadan. In a dress worn over armor and appearing before an audience that expects all the "players" in the tournament to be male, Lancelot's performance is self-evidently funny; the laughter from the spectators would seem to be a foregone conclusion. Dinadan's circumstances, by contrast, are not nearly as "obviously" funny—he lacks armor to offset the gender coding of the dress, and he appears in the mixed-gendered space of the court. He offers a greater potential threat to the heteronormativity of the community than does Lancelot; thus, Guenevere's exaggerated reaction functions to alleviate the potential threat his figure poses. Her laughter signals that Dinadan's performance at this moment is "play"; the fact that she laughs so hard she falls down implies that the potential threat of a knight-in-drag, encountered outside the "safe" space of the tilt-yard, warrants an extreme reaction. Significantly, Malory tells us that after the queen laughs and falls down, "so ded all that there was." As queen and woman, Guenevere models the proper reaction to Dinadan in drag, and the rest of the court quickly follows suit: if everyone present "gets" the joke, then the possible threat to masculinity posed by a knight in a dress is thoroughly alleviated.

This moment in the "Book of Sir Tristram de Lyones" is all the more significant in that Malory seems to have made some slight but significant changes in adapting his source material. Although both Lancelot and Dinadan participate in cross-dressing in the Prose *Tristan*—Lancelot willingly, Dinadan against his will—Malory alters the tenor of this scene by altering the character of Dinadan. While maintaining many of the distinguishing aspects of Dinadan he presumably found in his sources, Malory has softened Dinadan's character, smoothing out the rough edges while leaving what is essential about his character intact.[43] Dinadan is unique among the brotherhood of Round Table knights: he loves no lady; he often fights reluctantly (or refuses to fight when challenged); he loves to play practical jokes; and as Helen Cooper has pointed out, he is one of the few knights who relates to other knights outside the constraints and issues of kinship.[44] Judged by his peers as "a good knyght" even though he refuses to serve a lady, or indeed, even to fight for one when directly asked, Dinadan's character increases the pressure on the already strained social model of the Arthurian community by offering an alternative to the ideal of knighthood operating from the beginning of the *Morte d'Arthur*. Good knights love and protect ladies, bad knights attack and rape them. Dinadan seems to exist somewhere in between these two extremes, as the following conversation with Isode suggests:

> "Madame," seyde sir Dynadan, "I mervayle at sir Trystram and mo other suche lovers. What aylyth them to be so madde and so asoted uppon women?" "Why," seyde La Beall Isode, "ar ye a knyght and ar no lovear? For sothe, hit is grete shame to you, where fore ye may nat be called a good knyght by reson but yf ye make a quarrell for a lady." "God defende me!" seyde sir Dynadan, "for the joy of love is to shorte, and the sorow thereof is duras over longe. . . ." "Now I pray you, for my love," seyde La Beall Isode, "wyll ye fyght for me wyth three knyghtes that doth me grete wronge? And insomuche as ye bene a knyght of kynge Arthurs, I requyre you to do batayle for me. . . ." "I shall sey you ye be as fayre a lady as evir I sawe ony, and much fayrer than is my lady quene Gwenyver, but wyte you well, at one worde, I woll nat fyght for you wyth three knyghtes, Jesu me defende!" Than Isode lowghe, and had good game at hym. (693.26–35, 694.1–19)

Isode's initial response to Dinadan clarifies the problem he presents in terms of the knightly ideal in the *Morte d'Arthur*; but the fact that his refusal to fight for Isode when asked provokes only laughter and "good game" further suggests that Dinadan represents a positive alternative to the standard "knights who serve ladies" paradigm. When we compare Malory's Dinadan to that of the Prose *Tristan*, we see that he is a much more likeable character overall, a fact that further underscores the idea that Malory attempts here to present a positive alternative to the ideal of knightliness heretofore modeled by the *Morte d'Arthur*.[45]

That Malory has "softened" Dinadan thus suggests that he seeks to expand the definition of positive knighthood already established by earlier moments in the text. By altering the Dinadan of his source text so that his positive knightly qualities outweigh his negative attributes, Malory makes it impossible for Dinadan to be easily discounted or ignored. That Malory also makes a point of mentioning Dinadan's death at the hands of the Orkney brothers seems to indicate he recognizes that this attempt at expanding the parameters of knighthood cannot be successful:

> Than rode sir Dynadan unto sir Mordred and unto sir Aggravayne.
> ... Whan they undirstode that hit was sir Dynadan they were more
> wrothe than they were before, for they hated hym oute of mesure.
> ... For sir Dynadan had suche a custom that he loved all good
> knyghtes that were valyaunte, and he hated all tho that were destroy-
> ers of good knyghtes. ... And aftir, in the queste of the Sankgreall,
> cowardly and felonsly [Aggravayne and sir Mordred] slew sir Dyna-
> dan, whyche was a grete dammage, for he was a grete bourder and a
> passynge good knyght. (614.19–36, 615.1–8)

Recent critical debates surrounding Dinadan question whether this most unusual of knights affirms or critiques knighthood; I contend that he does both.[46] In his role as the "bourder" and "japer" who refuses to participate in a love relationship, Dinadan offers a new possibility for knightly identity than that which we have hitherto seen in the *Morte d'Arthur*. Lancelot, Tristram, Gareth, La Cote Male Tayle, and Alexander—to name just the most obvious examples—all demonstrate how repetitive acts of service to ladies involving a display of martial skills form and consolidate knightly identity. In his very existence, the character of Dinadan seems to ask if there might not be another possibility. Dinadan is important not only for his status as comic, nonlover, reluctant fighter, and individual free from the constraints of kin loyalty, but also and more important, for his participation in the episode of cross-dressing in which Lancelot also takes a part. In all his aspects and actions, Malory's Dinadan presents a problem to the social order that is only seemingly solved with his death.

Toward Chivalry's Truest Test

In the "Tale of Sir Gareth of Orkeney" and the "Book of Sir Tristram de Lyones," Malory expands his definition of knighthood, effectively testing the limits of the possibilities for knightly behavior in the secular chivalric world. In this portion of the *Morte d'Arthur*, the figures of Gareth, Galahad, Palomides, Breunis Saunz Pitié and Dinadan all stretch and occasionally critique the definition of knighthood. Although at other moments in the *Morte d'Arthur* we encounter "bad" knights—Sir Tarquin perhaps being the clearest example—no mal-intentioned knight returns so often and so emphatically to the text as does Sir Breunis. Knights such as Tarquin play an important role in the *Morte d'Arthur*, in that they provide necessary challenges for knights to overcome and thereby establish, enhance, or maintain reputation; Breunis is unusual in that he is neither killed nor incorporated into the order of the Round Table, as is usually the case with defeated knights. He returns again and again to confound and challenge the *Morte d'Arthur*'s ideal of knighthood. As D. Thomas Hanks notes, "the listing of Breunys's misdeeds could stretch on for some time. . . . He represents the ideology of the armed man, but he is not knightly in terms of Arthur's Pentecost Oath. . . . He is, in fact, a thorough rotter."[47] Breunis's repeated appearances expand the possibilities for knighthood, as does Sir Palomides, who offers our first sustained view of a non-Christian knight in the *Morte d'Arthur*, although when we encounter him in the text he is already always on his way to baptism. If Palomides is the noble Saracen, then Galahad represents a complement to his character; Lancelot's son is always already on his way to being the most successful Grail Quest knight, and in the predominantly secular coloring of the "Book of Sir Tristram de Lyones," he stands out as a unique representative of Christian knighthood. It is no accident, I think, that Malory places the quest for the Holy Grail after the tale of Sir Tristram. This juxtaposition shows him deliberately moving once again into a new context in which to test the ideals of the Pentecostal Oath. It is also a significant move that he chooses to dispense with the third book of the Prose *Tristran* when he decides to recount the Grail Quest, using the more spiritually oriented *Queste del Saint Graal* as his source.

After expanding the ideals and possibilities of knighthood in the "Gareth" and the "Tristram," Malory significantly constricts the definition of knightly success in the "Tale of the Sankgreal." In this most spiritually oriented of Malory's narrative threads, knightly devotion to God reveals itself as problematic in terms of the chivalric project of the Arthurian community and inextricable from the constructive values of gender and kinship that pervade the text. In the "Tale of the Sankgreal" the Arthurian community's idealized gender scheme and the issues that pressure that ideal—kinship, winning worship, knightly loyalty—clash with each other and with spirituality as nowhere else in the text. If the "Gareth" and the "Tristram" provide the *Morte d'Arthur* its heart, the "Sankgreal" provides the text its hinge; the quest for the Holy Grail marks a turning point in Malory's text, and after its conclusion, nothing can ever be the same again. It is to the "Sankgreal" that I now turn my attention.

Gender, Kinship, and Community

The Quest for the Holy Grail

In his commentary on Malory's "Tale of the Sankgreal," Eugène Vinaver offered his now-famous assertion that

> Malory's *Tale of the Sankgreall* is the least original of his works. Apart from omissions and minor alterations, it is to all intents and purposes a translation of the French *Queste del Saint Graal*, the fourth branch of the thirteenth-century Arthurian Prose Cycle. . . . His attitude may be described . . . as that of a man to whom the quest of the Grail was primarily an *Arthurian* adventure and who regarded the intrusion of the Grail upon Arthur's kingdom not as a means of contrasting earthly and divine chivalry and condemning the former, but as an opportunity offered to the knights of the Round Table to achieve still greater glory in *this* world [emphasis in original].[1]

While true that in comparison with his manipulation of his other source texts Malory's account of the quest for the Holy Grail follows the French *Queste del Saint Graal* with remarkable fidelity, this does not mean that we should understand this narrative portion of the *Morte d'Arthur* as "for all intents and purposes" merely a translation.[2] The "omissions and minor alterations" of which Vinaver speaks so dismissively are in fact highly significant, a significance that Vinaver cannot see in part because of his assertion that what Malory composed was not a "hoole book" but eight separate and self-contained romances. Vinaver completely ignores the question of narrative context so critical to understanding the function of the Grail Quest for Malory's Arthurian chivalric community.[3] Taking issue with Vinaver's assertion regarding the Grail Quest, Charles Moorman has more accurately pointed out that "Malory took great pains to connect the Grail adventure with the rest of his story . . . attempt[ing] in his 'Tale of the

Sankgreall' to present the Grail quest as an integral part of his own particular version of Arthurian history."[4] More recently, scholars have concurred with Moorman's assessment that Malory's treatment of his source
material merits sustained critical attention in terms of the overarching
narrative movement of the *Morte d'Arthur*.[5] Indeed, the Grail Quest maps
the limits and boundaries of Arthurian chivalry and marks a turning point
in the movement of Malory's narrative—a pivotal moment that reveals
the inevitable decline and degeneration of the Arthurian chivalric community from which there is no return.[6]

The major alteration Malory makes in adapting the French *Queste del
Saint Graal* for inclusion in the *Morte d'Arthur* is his quite literal "reduction" of his source: the "Tale of the Sankgreal" is only one-third as long as
the French *Queste*. Malory effects this reduction primarily through the
excision of dialogue, particularly lengthy theological discourses offered by
hermits as explanations and explications of the dreams and visions of
knights. Although Vinaver and others have seen this reduction as an attempt to secularize the story of the quest for the Holy Grail,[7] Malory's
excisions function primarily to strip away matter extraneous to his main
focus; although not interested in theology *per se*, Malory is most definitely
interested in exploring the functional limits of a knightly code of conduct.
The Grail Quest offers him an opportunity to explore how that code functions in the spiritual realm. The resulting narrative offers a high-relief
depiction of the conflict and tensions inherent in the constitutive social
ideology articulated in the Pentecostal Oath.[8] The "Tale of the Sankgreal,"
with its emphasis on the spiritual, is one in a series of contexts that provide
a testing ground for the chivalric ideal upon which Arthur's community is
founded.

In representing the Grail Quest as a test for the chivalric community,
Malory has altered not only the length of his source material, but has also
shifted the tone. The French *Queste* depicts Lancelot's attempt to achieve
the grail as a failure, whereas Malory's "Tale of the Sankgreal" offers the
reader an alternative reading, one in which Lancelot's experiences while in
pursuit of the grail may be construed as a semisuccess. Malory's revision of
his source material and his amelioration of Lancelot's Grail Quest performance should be understood in the context of fifteenth-century English
religious culture. Indeed, Elizabeth Edwards points out that "much of the
evidence that supports Malory as reflective of fifteenth-century piety
chiefly involves the view that Lancelot has accomplished something on
Malory's quest that he has not accomplished in the source."[9] Similarly,

Felicity Riddy has argued that fifteenth-century English spirituality "was being profoundly affected by a revaluation of the *vita activa* and thus of the idea of commitment to a life led, as Lancelot's is, among one's fellows."[10] The writings of fourteenth-century mystics such as Richard Rolle, Walter Hilton, and the author of the *Cloud of Unknowing*—writings that emphasized the necessity and validity of the active life, and indeed argued that such a life alone might lead to salvation—were increasingly widely read by fifteenth-century lay people. While Malory's Grail Quest maintains the distinction between "earthly" and "heavenly" chivalry found in his source, the treatment of the characters of Lancelot and Galahad in the "Tale of the Sankgreal" offers a more complicated and nuanced depiction of the difference and distinction between these two types of knightly behavior than does the French *Queste*. Malory certainly treats the distinction hierarchically—with the contemplative, spiritual life represented by Galahad depicted as superior to the more typical, active knightly life embodied by Lancelot—but the latter is not condemned in light of the former. Malory's revision of the French text casts the relationship of the flawed knight exemplar Lancelot and his innocent, holy son Galahad in a more positive light.[11]

While the "Tale of the Sankgreal" largely preserves the structural integrity of the quest paradigm that the *Morte d'Arthur* has hitherto deployed, the code of conduct that previously prevailed is largely useless to the knights on a spiritual errand such as this. Malory's Grail Quest critiques the ideal of knighthood upon which the chivalric society is predicated, problematizing the heteronormative gender scheme that renders masculine knightly identity intelligible to the Arthurian community. For example, although some maidens are encountered by the Grail Quest knights in their pursuit of the sacred vessel—most notably Perceval's sister[12]—the typical character of the mediating quest maiden is strikingly absent from the grail narrative; indeed, the place of the feminine has been taken by a series of holy figures—hermits, good men, the occasional anchoress, and disembodied voices—whose conditions of chastity and virginity resist the mark of gender and call into question both the heterosexual and homosocial desires that function as productive aspects of communal and individual identity.

In this chapter, I explore how the "Tale of the Sankgreal" offers a critique of the Arthurian community through its revelation of the importance of kinship and its radical revision of chivalric gender relations. In its treatment of kin relations, knightly identity, and feminine presence, the

"Tale of the Sankgreal" amplifies the tensions sketched out in the earlier tales of the *Morte d'Arthur* while suggestively delineating the shape of the tragedy to come. Strikingly different in tone and emphasis than any other of Malory's tales, in its "unlikeness" the "Tale of the Sankgreal" serves as the hinge, the turning point around which the narrative of the *Morte d'Arthur* as a whole revolves. The pursuit of the grail by Arthur's knights makes undeniably plain the inability of the Arthurian chivalric ideology to maintain itself.

Kinship and Codes: Lancelot and Galahad in an "Unsyker" World

> "Now, fayre nevew," seyde the kynge unto sir Gawayne, "assay ye for my love." "Sir," he seyde, "sauff youre good grace, I shall nat do that." "Sir," seyde the kynge, "assay to take the swerde for my love and at my commaundemente." "Sir, youre commaundemente I woll obey." And therewith he toke the swerde by the handyls, but he myght not stirre hit. "I thank you," seyde the kynge. "My lorde sir Gawayne," seyde sir Launcelot, "now wete you well thys swerde shall touche you so sore that ye wolde nat ye had sette youre honde thereto for the best castell of thys realme." "Sir," he seyde, "I myght not withstey myne unclis wyll." (857.1–14)

The moment when King Arthur asks Gawain to "assay to take the swerde" may seem a curious place to begin an examination of Malory's "Tale of the Sankgreal," yet the events surrounding this "mervayle" resonate throughout this portion of the *Morte d'Arthur* and beyond, revealing the preeminence of kinship concerns. These concerns impinge upon the structures of community, knighthood, and gender, playing a critical role in the final collapse of Arthur's kingdom. This particular episode comes near the beginning of the "Tale of the Sankgreal," when a squire comes to court with "mervaylous tydynges" of "a grete stone whych I saw fleete abovyn the watir, and therein . . . stykynge a swerde" (856.3–5). When Arthur and his knights investigate they find written on the sword's pommel a warning that only the "beste knyght of the worlde" may carry the sword. Lancelot being the obvious candidate, Arthur offers him the opportunity to take what would seem to be rightfully his. Significantly, however, Lancelot declines, and more significantly, Arthur does not press him, but asks Gawain to "assay." Gawain's refusal, unlike Lancelot's, is not accepted by the king, who then *orders* his nephew to attempt the task. Gawain's subsequent obedience, however, is not to his king—or even to the man who dubbed him a knight—but rather to his *uncle:* "I myght nat withstey myne unclis wyll." It may seem somewhat surprising that the invocation of the kin relationship—not the ruler-subject relationship—compels Gawain to attempt the removal of the sword, despite his having been clearly warned that any failed attempt to extract the sword will result in his receiving such a wound that "he shall not be longe hole afftir" (856.24–25).[13]

The parallel moment in the *Queste del Saint Graal* lacks this emphasis on kinship: when the Lancelot of the *Queste* rebukes Gawain after his failure—"or sacheiz que ceste espee vos touchera encore de si pres que vos ne la voldriez avoir baillée por un chastel" ["be forewarned that this sword will touch you so closely one day that you'll give anything, even a castle, not to have touched it today"][14]—the other responds: "je n'en poi mes; se je en deusse orendroit morir, si le feisse je por la volenté *mon seignor* accomplir" ["What else could I have done? . . . I would have obeyed *our lord's* command even if it meant dying"] (emphasis mine).[15] Although both texts make clear the blood relationship between Arthur and Gawain, Malory alters his source to emphasize the authoritative position held by the elder kinsman at this moment. He makes several such alterations to his source, as Sandra Ness Ihle has noted in her comparative study of the "Tale of the Sankgreal" and the French *Queste:* "Malory emphasizes brotherhood, familial and knightly, in contrast to the *Queste*, in which all earthly ties fade the nearer one approaches perfection."[16]

While this shift in emphasis may at first seem to be, in Vinaver's terms, a "minor alteration," Malory's revision of this moment—slight as it is—resonates throughout the episodes that both precede and follow this scene. We have seen familial loyalty lead to blood feud and conflict earlier in the text, particularly in the "Tale of King Arthur," but the kinship bond here becomes more emphatically constraining and potentially dangerous. For though aware that his attempt to withdraw the sword will put him in mortal peril—and indeed, even though he expresses to his uncle his desire to abstain from the contest—Gawain appears helpless in the face of a direct command from Arthur, his uncle and his king. Malory's suggestion here and elsewhere that familial allegiance potentially overrides all other chivalric concerns foreshadows the final act of kin loyalty in the *Morte d'Arthur*, when, in a reversal of the circumstances here, Arthur will be constrained to do battle against Lancelot even though he expresses a desire to be reconciled with his greatest knight. Enraged that Lancelot has (accidentally) killed his brothers and Arthur's nephews Gareth and Gaheris,

Gawain will not be satisfied with any recompense other than Lancelot's death. Faced with his kinsman's unswerving demand for vengeance, Arthur is compelled to treat Lancelot as an enemy; his loyalty to his nephew precludes any peaceful resolution to the conflict with the man formerly hailed as the greatest knight of Arthur's realm.

This emphasis on kin obedience and loyalty would, of course, have had particular resonance for Malory and his contemporaries who experienced that familial conflict commonly referred to as the Wars of the Roses. A. L. Morton was one of the first critics to suggest that "the more carefully one reads *Le Morte Darthur* the more one is struck by the part played by the two great rival groups in Arthur's court—the kindred and faction of Gawain and the kindred and faction of Lancelot. This was something which Malory, who had lived through and participated in the Wars of the Roses, the outcome of just such a feud, was particularly fitted to appreciate."[17] Edward Donald Kennedy has argued that Malory's treatment of kin relations is partially a reaction to the marriage of Edward IV, who married Elizabeth Woodville in 1464 against the advice of his kinsmen; the king's actions produced an angry response from his family, most notably the Earl of Warwick: "Edward's marriage probably affected [Malory] directly. . . . Malory . . . would have been a follower of Warwick and would have been likely to turn against Edward when the earl did."[18] While I do not at all mean to suggest that Malory was writing a political allegory, I feel that the heightened emphasis on kinship and loyalty in Malory's account of the Grail Quest is best understood when placed in the context of fifteenth-century England.

The scene with the sword in the stone thus foreshadows the role that familial allegiance will play in the ultimate destruction of the Arthurian community; however, the treatment of kinship that we see in the "Tale of the Sankgreal" extends far beyond the mere suggestion of compulsion and harm. The relationship between Lancelot and his son, Galahad, represents the matter of family loyalty as a complex force operating within the chivalric ideology. Like devotion to the feminine, allegiance to blood simultaneously supports and threatens the social order. In Lancelot's bloodline is to be found both the failure and the success of the quest for the Holy Grail; his position as a secular knight, committed to the performance of good works but unable to comprehend the spiritual terrain of the Grail Quest prepares the way for the saintly Galahad, who, although technically a knight, manages to avoid by and large the worldly taint of chivalry and knighthood.

The Grail Quest is unlike any other undertaken by the members of the Round Table, and in the multiple knightly failures that take place in this narrative the *Morte d'Arthur* offers the strongest criticism we have seen thus far of the code of conduct by which the chivalric community defines and orders itself. Yet, somewhat contradictorily, the appearance of the grail within the court at Camelot—and the ability of the knights to even *partici- pate* in the quest, even though they might fail—must be understood on some level as a sign of approval of the Round Table community; indeed, in its first magical and mysterious appearance within the court, the grail is accompanied by thunder and a beam of light, and "Than began every knyght to beholde other, and eyther saw other, by their semyng, fayrer than ever there were before" (865.21–23). In the French *Queste*, a similar visual enhancement occurs, but the emphasis is more on the *source* of the enhancement, not the positive reflection of the light on Arthur's knights; those present "fussent enluminé de la grace dou Saint Esperit"[19] ["were illuminated by the sweet grace of the Holy Spirit"]. In the French, the knights express a desire to "savoir la verité del Saint Graal"[20] ["to know the truth of the Holy Grail"], while in Malory, Gawain characterizes the quest as a desire to look upon the physical object of the grail: "never shall I returne unto the courte agayne tylle I have sene hit more opynly than hit hath been showed here" (866.10–11).[21] In his adaptation, Malory shifts the focus of the quest from a pursuit of understanding to a hunt for the physi- cal object of the grail; Gawain's articulation of his desire to see the grail more clearly reflects the general inability of the knights to understand the spiritual nature of this quest.

Lancelot is the link that allows these knights (oriented in terms of the secular and the literal) to seek the grail—that which is spiritual and mys- tical. While many critics have argued that Lancelot in the "Tale of the Sankgreal" is an inherently *unstable* figure,[22] I contend that the opposite is true; what appears at first to be instability (as demonstrated by Lancelot's failures, misunderstandings, and "backsliding" into sin and error) over the course of the Grail Quest, is in fact a delicate, deliberate, and necessary balancing act in which Lancelot's superiority as a courteous man of arms is consistently offset by his lack of spiritual understanding. Lancelot is in- deed "unstable" in terms of the Christian traditions in which "instability" is equated with a lack of spiritual understanding: throughout the "Tale of the Sankgreal" Lancelot persistently misreads, misinterprets, and misbe- haves due to his inability to comprehend the spiritual landscape that sud- denly confronts him.[23] Yet, his spiritual instability is in fact due to his stability of character; he fails in the Grail Quest because he continues to follow the code of behavior that has brought him such renown.

The juxtaposition between Lancelot's spiritual instability and his secular, knightly stability provides a "link" between the realms of the secular and the spiritual. Lancelot's status as the best knight of the Arthurian society makes the Grail Quest—or more accurately, the participation of the Round Table in the Grail Quest—possible, even though Lancelot himself cannot achieve the grail. His consistency of character and behavior— which for the most part serves him so well in the realm of secular, chivalric activity, and to which he largely adheres even in the changed circumstances of the Grail Quest—is insufficient for the spiritual demands such a sacred enterprise entails. It is not Lancelot who is "unsyker" or "unstable," but rather, the world around him has changed, and his actions in trying to adapt to these changed circumstances may seem at first to indicate instability. In fact, through his struggle he maintains his important position and function in terms of the Grail Quest, occupying a sort of middle ground. While he himself cannot succeed, he also does not wholly fail in that he makes possible the eventual completion of the quest: the grail is finally achieved through his son, Galahad.[24]

Lancelot's important position as a link between the secular world of the court and his most Christian son is made clear from the outset of the "Tale of the Sankgreal," when a "fayre jantillwoman" comes to Camelot and requests that Lancelot accompany her "hereby into a foreste." She asks nothing of the king but Lancelot's location—indeed her attitude toward Arthur seems almost dismissive, dispensing with all but the most cursory niceties and coming right to the point of her errand: "At the vigyl of Pentecoste . . . ryght so entrid into the halle a full fayre jantillwoman on horsebacke that had rydden full faste, for hir horse was all beswette. Than she there alyght and com before the kynge and salewed hym, and he seyde, 'Damesell, God you blysse!' 'Sir,' seyde she, 'for Goddis sake telle me where ys sir Launcelot'" (853.1–10). The lady has come on behalf of Galahad, whom Lancelot—tricked into believing he was in bed with Queen Guenevere—had conceived on King Pelles's daughter Elaine many years before. Galahad has long resided with a group of nuns in an abbey in the forest, and now desires to be made a knight and enter—at least for a time—the secular world of the court. After Lancelot arrives at the abbey, a group of twelve nuns bring Galahad before his father (who is unaware that this is his son) saying "we brynge you hyre thys chylde the whycch we have norysshed, and we pray you to make hym knyght, for of a more worthyer mannes honde may he nat resceyve the Order of Kynghthode" (854.14–17).

As both Galahad's father and the "best knyghte of the worlde," Lancelot is the only one capable of bridging the gap, of bringing Galahad from the sacred space of the abbey to the secular space of the court. Although himself impure—due to his desire for Guenevere and his fornication with Elaine—as Galahad's father Lancelot is also in part the source of Galahad's purity, the link in the lineage of Joseph of Arimathea of which Galahad is the ultimate result: "for sir Launcelot ys com but of the eyghth degre frome oure Lorde Jesu Cryst, and thys sir Galahad ys th[e] nyneth degre frome our Lorde Jesu Cryst. Therefore I dare sey they be the grettist jantillmen of the worlde" (865.9–12). Lancelot's position as both secular knight exemplar and father to/investor of Galahad legitimizes the latter in the secular world of the Round Table; in turn, Lancelot's dubbing of his son as knight in a sacred space, outside of the court, insures that Galahad remains as untainted as possible by secular concerns while still participating in the membership of a primarily secular order.

Although now a knight, Galahad refuses the invitation to return with Lancelot, choosing instead to make his first appearance at court alone. That Galahad's investiture occurs outside the court serves to characterize his arrival at Camelot as that of a man coming to join his peers in fellowship; he need never assume the inferior position of a supplicant, desiring the favor of knighthood, as it has already been conferred on him. By arriving singularly, rather than in a company, Galahad also foreshadows the nature of the quest for the Holy Grail, which will be a campaign that demands for its successful completion the rejection of fellowship and community—those things that have defined the activity of questing up to this point. Instead, this quest requires isolation and solitude, the better to facilitate introspection of one's soul.

Having created his son knight, Lancelot returns to the Round Table and prepares the way for Galahad's arrival. While the rest of the fellowship can only marvel at the gold letters that have magically appeared on the Siege Perilous—"FOUR HONDRED WYNTIR AND FOUR AND FYFFTY ACOMPLYVYSSHED AFTIR THE PASSION OF OURE LORDE JESU CRYST OUGHTE THYS SYEGE TO BE FULFYLLED"—it is Lancelot, recently returned from the sacred space of the community of nuns, who interprets the import of these words: "'Hit semyth me,' seyd sir Launcelot, 'that thys syge oughte to be fulfylled thys same day, for thys ys the Pentecoste after the four hondred and four and fyffty yere. And if hit wolde please all partyes, I wolde none of thes lettirs were sene thys day tyll that he be com that ought to enchyve thys adventure'" (855.12–24). Of greatest significance in this episode is not the meaning of the words that foreshadow Galahad's arrival, but rather, Lancelot's concern that the letters be covered. The desire that "none of thes lettirs were sene" registers a sense of discomfort on Lancelot's part with the very presence of a "mervayle" of such a spiritual nature within the court, and by extension, a discomfort with Galahad's inevitable presence there; the desire to cover the letters stems perhaps from a desire to shield them (and in like fashion, Galahad) from the secular, "active" knightly life. The act of covering the letters and the discomfort it bespeaks suggest as well that Galahad will pose a threat to the unity of the homosocial knightly subcommunity; even before his arrival, his empty seat functions as a break in the circular unity of the Round Table.[25] Just as the empty seat indicates disunity before Galahad's arrival, so will it similarly signify after his departure; Galahad occupies the Siege Perilous for only the briefest of moments, and it is within that moment only that the Round Table may be called complete, all its chairs filled in an unbroken, unified circle of brotherhood.

Indeed, Arthur himself senses the difference of this quest and laments the dissolution of his fellowship, recognizing that it may not be only temporary. Up until this point, the activity of questing has followed a familiar pattern: a single knight (sometimes in the company of one or two of his fellows) departs from the court to seek adventures in which to "preve" himself; once he has completed his quest, the knight returns to the court to relate his tale of adventure before an audience of king and fellows-in-arms, thus to be judged and hopefully have his masculine knightly identity validated and legitimated. This quest is different in that all the members of the Round Table are compelled to depart en masse, and some knights may not return: "'Now,' seyde the kynge, 'I am sure at this quest of the Sankegreall shall all ye of the Rownde Table departe, and nevyr shall I se you agayne holé togydirs, therefore ones shall I se you togydir in the medow, all holé togydirs! Therefore I woll se you all holé togydir in the medow of Camelot, to juste and to tourney, that aftir youre dethe men may speke of hit that such good knygtes were here, such a day, holé togydirs'" (864.5–12).

Arthur decides to stage a final group demonstration of chivalry—a tournament—as a sort of farewell to, and celebratory memorial of, secular knighthood. The knights will joust and the ladies will witness the competition in what amounts to a theatricalization of the chivalric, an event that stages the values of the community as spectacle. It is in a sense a memorial to the Arthurian community at its apogee. Galahad's arrival completes the Round Table; his occupancy of the Siege Perilous creates an unbroken circle of unity. At the same time, the Arthurian society as a whole receives its highest mark of commendation and validation through the appearance of the grail and the call for knights to undertake to seek it. As Jill Mann notes, "the appearance of the grail at the evening supper consecrates the completion of the Round Table, the eradication of its one remaining gap, but it also initiates the quest that will scatter the fellowship."[26] And as the knights scatter in their pursuit of the grail, their adventures do not bring renown back to the community, as is the case on a typical quest, but serve rather to undermine the very idea of the knightly community.

The Grail Quest repeatedly juxtaposes typical knightly behavior—such as that displayed at the tournament—with the spiritual chivalry necessary for successful completion of this particular quest. The emphatic contrast between these two types of knighthood—and indeed, the repeated demonstration of the inadequacy of secular chivalry—quickly transforms the Grail from a symbol of honor to one of shame for the Arthurian community. The hypermasculinity so appropriate to questing in the pre-grail world of adventure is inappropriate here. The Grail Quest explicitly condemns knightly violence and feminine presence—those two elements that intersect to produce the category of the chivalric in the *Morte d'Arthur*. Nacien the hermit articulates the difference and distinction of this particular adventure from other questing enterprises when he announces that the custom of bringing along ladies and gentlewomen on quest is inappropriate in these changed circumstances: "none in thys queste lede lady nother jantillwoman with hym, for hit ys nat to do in so hyghe a servyse as they laboure in" (869.1–2). Subjugated feminine presence, so central to other knightly quests, is largely displaced here: the sacred nature of the grail allows it to function as motivation for the quest, as mediating force, and as its own witness, or validation, at the conclusion of the quest, occupying in this particular endeavor those spaces usually inhabited by ladies.

Galahad, the most successful Grail Quest knight, is also the most Christian and the most chaste. While his achievement of the grail confers a mark of honor back upon the community of which he is so briefly a member, his success also ironically threatens the Arthurian order. Galahad's unblemished virginity confronts and rejects the chivalric emphasis on service to the feminine. Unknightlike in the sense that he has no use for *courtoisie*,

Galahad also stands apart from the other members of the Round Table in that his acts of violence are kept to a minimum.[27] He defeats the seven wicked brothers standing guard over the Castle of Maidens without killing a one, dubious "success" by the usual standards of knightly conduct; a day later Gawain, Gareth, and Ywain slay those same wicked brothers, for which act they are rebuked by a hermit. In chastising Gawain a hermit explicitly links Galahad's success with his virginity: "Sir Galahad ys a mayde and synned never, and that ys the cause he shall enchyve where he goth that ye nor none suche shall never attayne. . . . For sertes, had ye nat bene so wycked as ye ar, never had the seven brethirne by slayne by you and youre two felowys: for sir Galahad hymself bete hem all seven the day toforne, but hys lyvyng ys such that he shall sle no man slyghtly" (891.33–36, 892.1–6).

This praise of Galahad and criticism of Gawain extends to implicate Lancelot, as the hermit's explanatory speech strongly critiques the forces that have driven the action of the *Morte d'Arthur* forward to this point. As the father of Galahad, Lancelot is clearly no virgin, and while Malory has altered his source material to defer until the end of his text any explicit acknowledgment of an adulterous affair between Lancelot and Guenevere, Arthur's greatest knight is still guilty of loving the queen—with his heart and mind if not his body. This illicit love in combination with the new emphasis on virginity and chastity in the spiritual terrain of the grail narrative precludes Lancelot's successful participation in the quest. His midquest confession to a conveniently met hermit makes this plain:

> And than he tolde there the good man all hys lyff, and how he had loved a quene unmesurably and oute of mesure longe. "And all my grete dedis of armys that I have done for the moste party was for the quenys sake, and for hir sake wolde I do batayle were hit ryght other wronge. And never dud I batayle all only for Goddis sake, but for to wynne worship and to cause me the bettir to be beloved and litill or nought I thanked never God of hit." (897.15–22)

The source of his sin lies in what he has done *for the love of the queen*, not what he has done *in loving the queen*; in other words, it is the typical activity of chivalry—tournaments, jousts, battles—that is condemned here. As a model for knightly inspiration and action, Lancelot's love for and devotion to Guenevere makes success in the Grail Quest impossible for those knights of the Round Table who seek to emulate the man who is called by all "the floure of al knyghtes." Indeed, in his confession Lancelot reveals the flip-side of the coin of chivalrous courtesy: not only may ladies spur knights on to perform honorable and valorous deeds, but devotion to a lady may also corrupt a knight, causing him to perform dishonorable acts in order to please her.

Thus, what may seem at moments to be "instability" in the figure of Lancelot is in fact the attempt of this greatest knight to negotiate between the realms of the secular and spiritual. As part of that negotiation, he undertakes penance to atone for his sin in loving queen Guenevere in hopes that this may permit him to participate in the mysteries of the grail. It is this attempt to change and adapt that has provoked the characterization of Lancelot as "unstable," an assessment most critics have made on the basis of a speech by Nacien the hermit: "[Launcelot] hath takyn upon hym to forsake synne. And nere were that he ys nat stable, but by hys thoughte he ys lyckly to turne agayne, he sholde be nexte to encheve hit sauff sir Galahad, hys sonne; but God knowith hys thought and hys unstablenesse. And yett shall he dye ryght an holy man, and no doute he hath no felow of none erthly synfull man lyvyng" (948.23–29).[28] Here, Nacien's assertion that Lancelot "ys nat stable" clearly describes Lancelot's lack of spiritual understanding, and the likelihood that he will backslide into sin and error. Lancelot's seeming "instability" in this narrative originates in his attempt to forsake the code of secular chivalry for a spiritual chivalric ethos—in other words, to deny his true nature as the best "erthly" knight. That identity—the "floure of al erthly knyghtes"—in fact never changes, try as Lancelot might to overcome it. He can never be other than the greatest knight of martial skill and prowess, devoted to the wife of his king; this "stability" of identity compromises even honest remorse.

We see Lancelot's struggle to negotiate this new terrain—and clear evidence that he can only be Lancelot, the greatest of "synful" knights—in the tournament of white and black knights. Seeing that the black knights are sorely overmatched, "than thought sir Launcelot for to helpe there the wayker party in incresyng of hys shevalry" (931.24–25). This decision, an anchoress later reveals, was incorrect because

> "that turnamente . . . was but a tokenynge of oure Lorde. . . . the erthely knyghtes . . . they which were clothed all in blake . . . betokenyth the synnes whereof they be nat confessed. And they with the coverynge of whyght betokenyth virginité. . . . And whan thou behelde the synners overcom thou enclyned to that party for bob-

baunce and pryde of the worlde, and all that muste be leffte. . . . for in thys queste thou shalt have many felowis and thy bettirs, for thou arte so feble of evyll truste and good beleve." (933.14–32, 934.1–3)

As Ihle notes, in the secular, pre–Grail Quest world of the Round Table, Lancelot's decision to help the weaker party "would have been magnanimous. Here, then, is clear evidence of Lancelot's inability to deal with a world whose rules have changed and where events are not just themselves but represent moral truths as well."[29] In effect, Lancelot is guilty of "reading" the episode literally, not comprehending the spirit of the visual text: that the tournament was in fact "a tokenynge of oure Lorde."

Although rebuked here by an anchoress and later by hermits, holy men, recluses, and the occasional disembodied voice, the criticisms of his behavior primarily emphasize Lancelot's superior position. As the best knight of the Round Table, Lancelot is held to a stricter set of standards than are the other knights on quest; his fellows do not receive nearly the same amount or degree of censure that Lancelot does.[30] As Stephen Atkinson has rightly put it: "Lancelot's worldly chivalry [is] both the cause or context of his sin and . . . evidence of God's special favor which now entails new demands."[31] As the most important representative of his community, Lancelot's position parallels in microcosm the situation of the larger society he represents: although a mark of special favor for the Arthurian court, the Grail Quest simultaneously criticizes the values and ideals that have defined the chivalric community. Lancelot is the nexus where courtly activity and spirituality are brought into contact; his status as flawed knight exemplar is essential for the realization of the Grail Quest, and the fact of his existence as both "best" and "flawed" makes the Grail Quest possible *both* for Galahad and for the Round Table. The Grail Quest narrative repeatedly emphasizes his contradictory and conflicted status: after Galahad pulls the sword from the floating stone—the same sword that Lancelot declined to claim as his own—a damsel arrives at court to alert Lancelot to the fact that he is no longer the "best knyght of the worlde," but qualifies this assertion with "that were ye, and ar yet, of ony *synfull* man of the worlde" (863.30–31; emphasis mine); later a hermit exhorts him to "thanke God more than ony knyght lyvynge, for He hath caused you to have more *worldly* worship than ony knyght that ys now lyvynge" (896.29–31; emphasis mine); the good man who explicates one of Lancelot's visions echoes the hermit's words reminding Lancelot he "ought to thanke God more than ony othir man lyvyng, for of *a synner erthely* thou hast no pere as in knyghthode nother shall have" (930.14–16; emphasis mine); an anchoress tells him that "of all *erthly* knyghtes I have moste pité of the, for I know well thou haste nat thy pere of ony *erthly synfull* man" (934.21–23; emphasis mine).

Although Galahad surpasses his father on the spiritual scale, Lancelot remains the best that earthly, secular knighthood has to offer, and indeed, it seems clear that he must maintain this position if the Grail Quest is to succeed at all. If he were able to emulate his son's conduct in the Grail Quest, it would further remove Lancelot—already distinctly set apart from his fellow knights by virtue of his prowess in chivalric terms—from the fellowship of the Round Table, effectively severing the link between the spiritual and secular realms and making successful completion of the Grail Quest nearly impossible for the remaining knights. Galahad is bound to the secular, knightly realm only through Lancelot's dual role as his kinsman and source of his knighthood. For the Grail Quest to continue to exist as a campaign of the Round Table (and thus, as any sort of validation of the Arthurian community), Lancelot must maintain his position just on the edge of the spiritual world, able to peer into the next realm—even able to point the way there—but himself unable to make the crossing.

Throughout the "Tale of the Sankgreal" Lancelot continually finds himself occupying such a liminal space, trapped between the spiritual and the secular. Early on in the quest he comes upon a chapel within which he sees "a fayre awter full rychely arayde with clothe of clene sylke. . . . and whan sir Launcelot saw thys . . . he had grete wylle for to entir the chapell, but he coude fynde no place where he might entir" (893.34–36, 894.1–3). Immediately after his unsuccessful attempt to enter into this sacred space, Lancelot finds himself in the presence of the grail but unable to participate in the miracle that occurs—the healing of a sick knight—as he is trapped in a state of consciousness which Malory significantly describes as "half wakynge and half slepynge." Those in the company of the sick knight spy Lancelot, asleep on his shield before the cross of the impenetrable chapel, and comment that his exclusion from full participation in the miracle must be due to his sinful behavior: "'But I mervayle of thys slepyng knyght that he had no power to awake when thys holy vessell was brought hydir.' 'I dare well sey,' seyde the squyre, 'that he dwellith in som dedly synne whereof he was never confessed.' 'Be my fayth,' seyde the knyght, 'whatsomever he be, he ys unhappy. For as I deme he ys of the felyship of the Rounde Table whych ys entird in the queste of the Sankgreall'" (895.7–14). His high earthly status allows him to experience in a limited fashion the miracles of the grail, but full participation is never permitted. So close and yet so far, his limited experience emphasizes his exemplary yet sinful nature much more effectively than would complete exclusion from the Grail miracles.

The strongest confirmation of Lancelot's status as a liminal figure comes at the Castle of Corbenic, when he finds himself before the door of the grail chamber. Finding that he cannot open the door through force, Lancelot offers up a prayer: "Fayre swete Fadir, Jesu Cryste! If ever I dud thynge that plesed The, Lorde, for Thy pité ne have me nat in dispite for my synnes done beforetyme, and that Thou shew me somthynge of that I seke" (1015.11–14). His prayer is granted and the door opened, but as he prepares to enter the chamber, a voice calls him back: "'Sir Launcelot, flee and entir nat, for thou ought nat to do hit! For and if thou entir thou shalt forthynke hit'" (1015.20–22). Although instructed to "flee," the fulfillment of the command does not seem to require his actual departure from the castle; his movement away from the door is adequate.[32]

While sufficiently holy and righteous to have his prayer to see "somethynge" of what he seeks immediately answered, his lack of "prowess" in the realm of the spiritual is reasserted—as it was in the episode of the black and white knights—when Lancelot again misreads the miraculous events he is permitted to witness:

> Before the holy vessell he saw a good man clothed as a pryste . . . and hit semed to sir Launcelot that above the prystis hondys were three men. . . . and so he lyffte hym up ryght hyghe and hit semed to shew so to the peple. And than sir Launcelot mervayled nat a litill, for hym thought the pryste was so gretely charged of the vygoure that hym semed that he sholde falle to the erth. And whan he saw none aboute hym that wolde helpe hym, than cam he to the dore a grete pace and seyde, "Fayre Fadir, Jesu Cryste, ne take hit for no synne if I helpe the good man whych hath grete nede of helpe" (1015.28–35, 1016.1–7).

When he disobeys the command to "flee and entir nat," even though his motives are altruistic, it is inevitable that he will be punished for such a flagrant transgression of a direct order. However, the twenty-four–day coma that is the result of his disobedience—one day for every year of his life as a sinful man—is in fact not really a punishment at all, but rather a reward of sorts. When he at last awakes, he demands to know "Why have ye awaked me? For I was more at ease than I am now" (1017.6–7), indicating that the state of unconsciousness was far from unpleasant. Such "discipline," in its gentleness, then, seems to include an implicit acknowledgment that Lancelot in fact had no choice but to cross the threshold; his behavior is a function of his role as the fulcrum between the spiritual and secular realms, and it is a role he cannot step out of. Once roused from his mysterious sleep, the people of Corbenic inform him that "the queste of the Sankgreall ys encheved now ryght in you, and never shall ye se of Sankgreall more than ye have sene" (1017.30, 1018.1–2).

Grateful for the grace he has been shown, Lancelot returns to Camelot. Three other Round Table knights, however, are more successful; Bors and Perceval join Galahad in celestial knighthood, but Lancelot's son stands apart from his two fellows. While Bors and Perceval are perfectly *respectable* in terms of the secular world of chivalry, they are largely unremarkable as hypermasculine specimens of knighthood—their success in the quest for the grail is due to their chastity, a quality not generally high up on the list of desirable knightly attributes in the *Morte d'Arthur*. Significantly, Galahad, the most chaste of the three, achieves the greatest success, while Bors (he who "trespassed but onys in hys virginité") will be the only one to return to the secular, knightly world of the court.

The actual experience of the grail is strangely empty in both the *Queste* and the *Morte d'Arthur*. A holy man commands that Galahad come forward to an altar at the castle of Corbenic "and thou shalt se that thou hast much desired to se" (1034.19–20). Galahad complies, but what he sees is apparently indescribable and can only be approached or rendered indirectly, in terms of the young knight's reaction: "And than he began to tremble ryght harde when the dedly fleysh began to beholde the spirituall thynges. Than he helde up his hondis towarde hevyn and seyde, 'Lorde, I thanke The, for now I se that that hath be my desire many a day. Now, my Blyssed Lorde, I wold nat lyve in this wrecched worlde no lenger, if hit myght please The, Lorde'" (1034.21–27). In the final miracle, we see why knights like Gawain, who expressed a desire to "see more openly" the physical object of the grail, are doomed to fail in the quest; the experience cannot be described or objectified, it is intangible, linguistically incomprehensible, perhaps invisible to worldly eyes like Gawain's.

Before his soul departs to heaven, Galahad asks Bors to take a message to his father: "My fayre lorde, salew me unto my lorde sir Launcelot, my fadir, and as sone as ye se hym bydde hym remember of this worlde unstable" (1035.10–12). In the French *Queste* Galahad simply asks to be remembered to his father: "Boorz, saluez moi monseignor Lancelot mon pere si tost come vos le verroiz" ["Bors, give my greetings to Sir Lancelot, my father, when you see him"].[33] The "worlde" that Galahad refers to in the *Morte d'Arthur* and which Bors later mentions to Lancelot—"Also, sir Launcelot, sir Galahad prayde you to remembir of thys unsyker worlde" (1036.27–29)—does not, ultimately seem to be one distinctly secular or spiritual; rather, the actions of secular, chivalrous knights in pursuit of the sacred object of the grail create this "worlde." In this space, the spiritual and secular, usually so distinctly separate, intersect, producing instability or "unsykerness." Although perhaps at first Lancelot seems to be a prime example of instability and error, he is in fact the balanced center of the "Tale of the Sankgreal," providing access to the Grail Quest for the fellow-ship of the Round Table *and* for his son. Galahad desires the office of knighthood only insofar as it provides him access to the Grail Quest and, accordingly, has no use for the Round Table—or the secular world in general—once the quest has ended. As the Grail Quest ends, so too does Lancelot's need to continue in the role of a mediating force, poised between two realms. With Galahad's death, Lancelot's link with the spiritual world is all but severed, and upon his return to the *communitas* of the Round Table, he reassumes his status as the greatest of all "erthly" men.

Yet, although completed, the impact of the Grail Quest on the knightly community reverberates throughout the closing pages of the text; the Arthurian society has been irrevocably altered by the experience. The critique of chivalry continually enacted by the quest—the revelation of the inflexibility and tensions inherent in the code of conduct articulated by the Pentecostal Oath—makes clear that the Round Table order is in decline, unable to sustain itself for much longer. In his brief presence among Arthur's knights, Galahad demonstrates what "true" knighthood is, and reveals that it can only exist as a temporary state. His kinship with Lancelot emphasizes how close the Round Table is to achieving this perfection, as well as the impossibility of achieving such a state—a divide both infinitesimally small yet infinitely vast.

Virginity and Genealogy: Galahad and Perceval's Sister

Virginity and kinship. These, as Martin Shichtman has pointed out, would seem to be the twin obsessions of the "Tale of the Sankgreal," embodied in the figure of Galahad.[34] More recently, Karen Cherewatuk has emphasized the inherently contradictory effect produced by the idealization and valuation of these two obsessions: "While advocating chastity at a surface level, the *Sankgreal* also promotes fathering sons as natural and even redemptive."[35] Galahad derives his special status in equal parts from his virginity and his bloodline, while Lancelot both partially fails *and* partially succeeds in the Grail Quest due to his position as Galahad's father. Without Lancelot, the Grail Quest would not even be possible.

The Grail Quest marks the unique Galahad's equally unique and brief presence among the Round Table knights, but as my discussion above demonstrates, Galahad is not often the main focus of scholarly criticism on the "Tale of the Sankgreal," even though he and he alone fully achieves the grail. Mary Hynes-Berry has observed that "Galahad is the supreme example of how a perfect knight is the perfect Christian. But he exists on a plane inaccessible to most of us," and further that "Galahad . . . is out of our empathic range."[36] Likewise, Donald Hoffman notes that "Galahad is not an imitable model . . . [he is] a unique chivalric messiah, like whom no other knight can choose to be."[37] In his perfection, his effortless virginity and knightly prowess, Galahad—to put it bluntly—is somewhat of a bore.[38] He is analytically useful primarily as a critique of Arthurian chivalric values. However, that critique is represented not only in the bland successes of Galahad, but also and more interestingly in the colorful failures and shortcomings of the other knights on the quest, particularly those of his father, Sir Lancelot.[39] Thus, the figure of Galahad himself has received comparatively little critical treatment, with the bulk of scholarly attention focused on Lancelot, who occupies a primary position in the pages of Malory's narrative before, during, and after the Grail Quest—unlike his son who comes late and leaves early.

I contend that the very blandness of Galahad, the flat surface of his character, offers a challenge to the heteronormative gender dynamic of the chivalric community, dislocating the masculine-feminine binary so central to the knightly enterprise. In his virginity, he silences the intertwined claims of gender, kinship, and genealogy, even as he simultaneously and paradoxically is the fullest realization of those very ideals, bringing them to the forefront of the narrative. The descendant of Joseph of Arimathea "in the nynth degré," he is the crowning product of his family's bloodline, and in his perfect chastity, he is also the cause of its failure.[40] As a virgin, Galahad is a blank, in effect, an empty space that resists full inscription with the masculine mark of gender. Although as a knight with armor, shield, and sword, Galahad is rendered masculine in the symbology of chivalry, his complete and utter detachment from all things feminine simultaneously challenges the superficial mark of gender that such knightly accoutrements impose on his body. His commitment to celibacy, and the way in which Galahad refrains also from establishing any strong homosocial bonds (except with his father or other chaste knights), renders him in effect without gender as it is understood in chivalric terms.

As a spiritual preoccupation or mark of identification, virginity in the medieval period was most frequently associated with women, especially from the eleventh century on.[41] As a condition of sainthood, virginity was seemingly de rigueur for women, while not nearly as critical to the beatification of men.[42] While I cannot here give a full account of the development of an ideology of virginity throughout the medieval period,[43] I feel that the special circumstance of Galahad's virginity cannot be fully appreciated without at least a general understanding of his atypical status as not only knight and virgin, but more important, as knight, virgin, *and* romance hero. As we have seen throughout the *Morte d'Arthur*, chastity is occasionally found in the person of a knight, but generally only when the knight is far advanced in his years, long finished with his knightly activities. Those "good men," vavasours, and hermits who offer help to knights out questing have given up the active life for the contemplative only after long careers in which they have satisfactorily performed their knightly masculinity. Galahad challenges this pattern by embodying both knightly prowess and spiritual asceticism in the very first quest of his career, and further, by succeeding where all others fail. Indeed, Barbara Newman, in arguing that the "talismanic quality of the virgin—imaged in the precious balm, the golden bowl, and ubiquitous allusions to the 'seal of maidenhood'—pertained only to the female body," qualifies this statement by pointing out that "a rare exception is the romance hero Galahad, whose success in the Grail quest depends on his perfect virginity."[44] While indeed unique, Galahad does not owe his special identity as an heroic knightly virgin to any alterations or revisions made by Malory in adapting the *Queste;* his status as such is merely emphasized and enhanced by the context in which Malory places his account of the Grail Quest, "breffly drawn out of Freynsh."

If Galahad's character stands out in the narrative of the French *Queste,* a text concerned only with a singular spiritual endeavor, then he cuts an even more disruptive figure when transported into the center of Malory's massive Arthurian opus, a text in which knightly questing is usually a strident heteronormative performance of masculine identity. Somewhat contradictorily, Malory's faithfulness to the Galaad of the French *Queste* in part contributes to the jarring effect Galahad has on the knightly community in the *Morte d'Arthur:* given that there were certainly other narrative versions of the Grail Quest available to him, Malory's decision to reject the more secular Grail Quest of the Prose *Tristan* (to which he surely had access) and use the more *celestial* and *spirituel* French *Queste* heightens the contra-distinction between the grail hero and the other knights who people the *Morte d'Arthur*. Galahad's "ostentatious, aggressive virginity"[45] resonates throughout the "Tale of the Sankgreal," insistently problematizing the ideal of knightly service to ladies. While in earlier quests, the ubiquitous forest maidens often functioned to lead knights on to new adventures wherein they might prove their knightly prowess, in the "Tale of the Sankgreal" the forest maiden no longer shows the way to adventure, but herself provides a very different kind of test than that which we have hitherto seen in Malory's text.[46] An examination of the experiences of Bors and Perceval makes this clear.

In the course of his adventures, Perceval encounters a "jantillwoman of grete beauté" who asks him for his help; in exchange, she will give him information concerning the Red Knight, the man that Perceval most wants to confront. Thus far, the "jantillwoman" functions much as a typical quest maiden, leading Perceval on to knightly adventures through which he may assert and confirm his masculine identity. The favor she asks of him in recompense also seems fairly typical. She claims to be a "jantillwoman disheryte," and in requesting Perceval's help carefully follows the formula we have seen employed by other damsels in distress: "And for that I know that ye ar a good knyght I beseche you to helpe me, and for ye be a felowe of the Rounde Table, wherefore ye ought nat to fayle no jantillwoman which ys disherite and she besought you of helpe" (917.26–29).[47] After agreeing to help her, the lady then shows her appreciation by preparing a bed for Perceval, and plying him with food and drink—the "strengyst wyne that ever he dranke" (918.8). Thus satiated and addled, he begins to think her "the fayryst creature that ever he saw" (918.11), and she manages to extract a promise that he will be her "trew servaunte" if she agrees to sleep with him. Just in time, Perceval's gaze falls upon the cross-shaped pommel of his sword, and he instinctively makes the sign of the cross on his forehead. "And therewith the pavylon turned up-so-downe and than hit chonged unto a smooke and a blak clowde" (918.34, 919.1). Abashed and ashamed, Perceval draws his sword and wounds himself in the thigh, crying "A, good Lord, take thys in recompensacion of that I have myssedone ayenste The, Lorde!" (919.16–17).

In this episode, the woman herself is the adventure itself, and not just the means to it. Perceval emerges victorious but wounded, just as he might in a battle with another knight, and unlike other battles that are fought on behalf of ladies or fellows in arms, Perceval himself is both the fighter and the prize for which he fights: "How nyghe I was loste, and to have lost that I sholde never have gotyn agayne, that was my virginité, for that may never be recoverde aftir hit ys onys loste" (919.19–22). That he inflicts a wound on his thigh—a symbol of castration—reveals his understanding of the spiritual terrain on which this quest plays out.[48]

Virginity is valuable because it is vulnerable. Unlike knightly reputation, which can be lost and then won again through acts of valor, virginity once gone can never be restored. Thus, "adventure" on the Grail Quest is not so much a struggle against external threats and forces as it is a battle to maintain one's purity against temptation and the weakness of the flesh. The main opponent in this struggle, Perceval discovers, is in fact the devil himself. Having narrowly escaped from the fiendish woman of the pavilion, Perceval tells a good man that "well I wote the fynde sente hir hydir to shame me" (920.1–2), to which the good man responds: "A good knyght . . . thou arte a foole, for that jantillwoman was the mayster fyende of helle" (920.3–4).

Bors, the other successful Grail Quest knight, has a similar experience with "the fayryst lady that ever he saw, and more rycher beseyne than ever was quene Guenyver" (964.26–27). She makes plain her desire to be Bors's paramour, at which he is "ryght evyll at ease, but in no wyse wolde he breke his chastité" (965.7–8). At his resistance, the lady then invokes the courtly language of knightly service. He refuses her at every turn, even when she claims that she will die if he does not become her lover, and—even worse—that Lancelot, the greatest knight of Arthur's realm and Bors's cousin, will also die if Bors does not submit to her desire. When it becomes clear that he will not accede to the request of one woman, the lady gathers around her twelve other gentlewomen at the top of a battlement: "A, sir Bors, jantill knyght! Have mercy on us all, and suffir my lady to have hir wyll; and if ye do nat, we muste suffir dethe with oure lady for to falle downe of this hyghe towre. And if ye suffir us thus to dye for so litill a thynge all ladys and jantillwomen woll sey you dishonoure" (965.30–34). It is a mark of Bors's distinction as a successful Grail Quest knight that he is able to resist such a clear invocation of the knightly code of conduct to which he has sworn allegiance. The value system of this quest has clearly shifted so that virginity and chastity are the main concerns; thus, those knights—such as Perceval, Bors, and Galahad—who are concerned above all with preserving their chastity are the most successful. As the ladies fall from the tower, Bors, like Perceval before him, crosses him-

self, and the entire scene disappears. Also like Perceval, he has escaped from
the devil. While in earlier quests in the *Morte d'Arthur* knights often succeeded *because* of their devotion to a particular lady, in the "Tale of the
Sankgreal," knights must succeed *in spite of* the feminine.[49]

That the preservation of virginity is the highest order of business on
this particular quest is further underscored by a dilemma encountered by
the same Sir Bors. He comes upon his brother, Sir Lyonell, who is the prisoner of two other knights. Yet, before he can make a move to rescue
Lyonell, he sees on "the other syde of hym" a lady about to be ravished by
a miscreant knight. Like the fiends disguised as women, this lady invokes
his knightly oath, asking "for kynge Arthures sake, which I suppose made
the knyght, that thou helpe me and suffir me nat to be shamed of this
knyght" (961.10–12). In earlier episodes of the *Morte d'Arthur*, the
courtly language of supplication has been appropriated by ladies whose
desires are not always altruistic, and knights, compelled to comply due to
their sworn adherence to the Pentecostal Oath, more often than not have
found themselves in danger. While the she-fiends, like those other malevolent ladies, attempt to coerce knights to perform deeds contrary to a sanctified code of chastity, in the "Tale of the Sankgreal" these demands are
revealed to have little force. Maintaining virginity and chastity is para-
mount, and thus, renders the devilish ladies' requests impotent.

In other words, Bors decides to help the lady not because she has used
the proper formula in pleading for deliverance from her attacker, but
rather because she has identified her virginity as that which is threatened.
Faced with saving his brother or saving the maidenhead of the lady before
him, Bors opts for the latter option in a speech that strikingly echoes
Perceval's lament for his almost-lost virginity: "For if I latte my brothir be
in adventure he muste be slayne, and that wold I nat for all the erthe; and
if I helpe nat the mayde she ys shamed, and shall lose hir virginité which
she shall never gete agayne" (961.14–17).[50] That Bors makes the right
choice in helping the maiden is confirmed when she tells him "and I had
lost my maydynhode fyve hondred men sholde have dyed therefore"
(962.7–9).

Family ties, so important to this particular quest, are simultaneously
revealed to be subordinate to the concerns of virginity and indeed, in this
particular instance, a threat to chastity itself.[51] When Bors asks the identity
of the knight who was about to rape her, the maiden replies, "By my fayth,
he ys my cosyne" (962.11).[52] The ugly spectacle of incest that here clouds
the ideal of kinship recurs later in the Grail Quest, when Galahad, Bors,

and Perceval *ensemble* slay three wicked knights. At first repentant for having killed, they are told by a priest that in fact they have done a very good deed: "Here was a lorde erle. . . . And he had three sonnys, good knyghtes of armys, and a doughter, the fayrist jantillwoman that men knew. So tho three knyghtes loved their syster so sore that they brente in love. And so they lay by her, magré her hede. And for she cryed to hir fadir they slew her, and toke their fadir and put hym in preson and wounded hym nye to the deth" (997.28–35). As in other instances in the "Tale of the Sankgreal," this passage both supports and undermines the Arthurian chivalric ethos, offering praise with one hand and conferring blame with the other. The sons are described first as "good knyghtes of armys," a characterization that reflects their technical prowess, an important attribute of any good knight. However, they violate several of the rules of the Pentecostal Oath, specifically "allwayes to do ladyes, damesels, and jantilwomen . . . sucour . . . and never to enforce them, uppon payne of dethe."

Significantly, these knights violate the unwritten foundational support of patriarchy: the incest taboo. As I argued in chapter 1, the incest taboo (as described by Claude Lévi-Strauss) is a constitutive element of the chivalric social structure depicted in Malory's *Morte d'Arthur:* "The prohibition on the sexual use of a daughter or sister compels them to be given in marriage to another man, and at the same time it establishes a right to the daughter or sister of this other man. . . . The woman whom one does not take is, for that very reason, offered up."[53] This system establishes links between men by a process in which women are "gifted" away in exchange for power, status, and wealth—what Luce Irigaray calls the "hom(m)osexual monopoly."[54] Here, we see the inappropriate application of heterosexual desire and the threat that it poses to the same social order that produces and promotes that desire as a communal support. Even though Galahad, Bors, and Perceval punish these transgressors, this episode still suggestively criticizes the institution of knighthood, as their high degree of knightly prowess allows the wicked brothers to escape punishment for so long.

Through the person of Galahad, the quest for the Holy Grail reveals the potential problems inherent in the heteronormative gender paradigm and the heterosexual desire it promotes—desire that functions both as a means to, and evidence of, conformity to this gender scheme. Judith Butler has theorized that the "person" comes into being by conforming to the "gendered norms of cultural intelligibility," and further that "'[i]ntelligible' genders are those which in some sense institute and maintain relations of coherence and continuity among sex, gender, sexual practice, and *desire*" (emphasis mine).[55] In this context, then, Galahad's virginity offers a serious challenge to the matrix of intelligibility operating in the Arthurian chivalric community. For while Bors and Perceval are also chaste knights, evidence of their desire codes them as heterosexually masculinized. As Butler notes, "desire reflects or expresses gender, and . . . gender reflects or expresses desire."[56] Although both Bors and Perceval overcome the temptation to compromise their chastity, significantly *they are tempted.* Galahad, by contrast, does not suffer from temptation at all; he has no desire, save that for the grail. In the explication of Gawain's vision of the hundred and fifty bulls, a hermit explains that the three white bulls represent Galahad, Perceval, and Bors: "The too whyght betokenythe sir Galahad and sir Percivale, for they be maydens and clene withoute spotte, and the thirde, that had a spotte, signifieth sir Bors de Gaynes, which trespassed but onyes in hys virginité" (946.21–25). Bors's trespass suggests strongly masculine heterosexualized desire now sublimated to chastity, and although a "clene" virgin, Perceval similarly demonstrates his masculine gender identity and conformity to the compulsory heterosexuality of the chivalric community in his desire for the maiden of the pavilion, which he only at the last minute resists.

Galahad is never tempted by the feminine while in pursuit of the grail, and of even more significance, there is no evidence that he is ever *desired by* the feminine. He is unique among the heroic characters of Malory's text. As a knight, he is an agent of the Arthurian society and the chivalric ethos upon which that community is founded, yet, even Galahad's activities as a knight are contradictory: he rejects the violence and ideals of fellowship so intrinsic to the Round Table order while still managing to exceed all of its members in pursuit of the grail. He is, in a sense, "almost a knight" in the terms of Arthur's court. And if, as I have argued above, the consolidation of masculine gender identity is a continual and never-ending process for knights of the Round Table subcommunity, then Galahad and his success pose a further challenge to the foundational ideology of that society in that his time among its members is so brief. He leaps, Athena-like, from the spiritual realm of the convent into the secular realm of the quest, where he immediately assumes the highest rank and status without needing to establish or affirm his identity through the process of adventuring.[57] He challenges the heteronormative gender paradigm not only through lack of both desire and desirability, but also by making impossible any sort of homosocial identification with other knights. Butler points out that "Coherently heterosexualized deflections require that identifications be effected on the basis of similarly sexed bodies and that desire be deflected across the sexual divide to members of the opposite sex."[58] As the unique, messianic knight, Galahad forecloses the possibility of identification with other knights in the same way that his virginity—and more important, absence of sexualized desire—renders him almost unintelligible in the cultural symbology of chivalry.

I say "almost unintelligible" because he does, in many ways, demonstrate an at least superficial adherence to the norms of knightly behavior: he wears the trappings of knighthood, engages in the activity of combat, and on one notable occasion, he does do the bidding of a lady. That lady is Perceval's sister, who first appears in the guise of a stereotypical quest maiden in need of Galahad's services: "'Sir Galahad,' seyde she, 'I woll that ye arme you and lyght uppon thys horse and sew me, for I shall shew you within thys three dayes the hyghest adventure that ever ony knyght saw'" (983.1–4). Galahad complies, and she leads him to a ship where he is reunited with Bors and Perceval. On board the ship, Galahad and Perceval's sister participate in an exchange that at first seems to be an enactment and affirmation of the idealized heteronormative gender scheme of chivalry, but which actually challenges the idealized compulsory heterosexuality of the community through a kind of mimesis. Like Galahad, Perceval's sister is a virgin, both physically *and* spiritually. Perceval's virginity, while physically intact, is spiritually inferior to Galahad's in that Perceval has experienced heterosexualized *desire;* his sister is a "true" virgin, Galahad's equal in terms of chastity, in that she has not. This is made plain on board the ship, wherein the three knights and the maiden find a sword, scabbard, and girdle, this last in a state of advanced decay. According to magical lettering on the sword, the girdle may only be replaced by "THE HONDIS OF A MAYDE, AND THAT SHE BE A KYNGIS DOUGHTER AND A QUENYS. AND SHE MUST BE A MAYDE ALL THE DAYES OF HIR LYFF, BOTH IN WYLL AND IN WORKE" (988.1–4). Perceval's sister does indeed replace the girdle—with one that she has fashioned out of her own hair.[59] In their mutual "aggressive virginity" Galahad and Perceval's sister displace the courtly model of heteronormative masculine and feminine relations through an ironic enactment of that very relationship. Theirs is a gender performance that is emptied of all meaning by the fact that their chastity resists the gender categories of masculine and feminine, even as they each in a sense take up those positions in relationship to one another.

After Perceval's sister has explained the meaning and significance of the sword and scabbard and produced the new girdle fashioned from her hair,

Galahad takes up the sword: "And then he gryped about hit with his fyngirs a grete dele, and than she gurte hym aboute the myddyll with the swerde" (995.25–26). Martin Shichtman has offered a compelling reading of this scene as a moment of consummation, in which Galahad's "grypping" of the phallic sword and Perceval's sister's sacrifice of her hair stand in for the physical, fleshly consummation more typical of romance.[60] In contrast to my reading of this scene, Shichtman argues that Perceval's sister's virginity does not compromise her gendered identity: "Her role is always gendered, always filled with sexual tension."[61] Although I agree with Shichtman that this moment should be read as a scene of sexual consummation, the particular register in which this exchange takes place paradoxically empties this moment of heteronormative gender identification by seeming to perform it. In their quasi-mystical chastity these two figures challenge the literal knight-lady relationship upon which the chivalric project depends. After this symbolic exchange, they engage in a significant exchange of words: "'Now recke I nat though I dye, for now I holde me one of the best blyssed maydyns of the worlde, whych hath made the worthyest knyght of the worlde.' 'Damesell,' seyde sir Galahad, 'ye have done so muche that I shall be your knyght all the dayes of my lyff'" (995.27–31). Such proclamations and promises are typical of knights and ladies in the *Morte d'Arthur*. In this instance, however, the deaths to which each looks forward are imminent. When they occur, the heteronormative gender roles that both Galahad and Perceval's sister here momentarily seem to perform are radically upended; in their deaths, they each take up gender positions in direct opposition to those they enact in the sword and girdle scene.

Upon leaving the ship, a knight accosts the three knights and the maiden and inquires as to the virginity of Perceval's sister. When he discovers that she is indeed a "clene mayde," he asserts that she must "yelde us the custom of thys castell . . . what mayde passith hereby, sholde hylde thys dyshe full of bloode of hir ryght arme" (1000.26–31). The purpose of the custom, he reveals, is to attempt to cure the lady who lives therein, whose undefined "malodye" may only be healed by the blood of a noble virgin. Upon hearing this, Perceval's sister quickly offers up her arm over the protestations of her knightly companions.[62] In healing the lady, Perceval's sister bleeds to death, performing what Donald Hoffman has identified as an act of *imitatio Christi*; she "most radically imitates the pattern of the best of men, which is dramatically neglected by the rest of Malory's vast array of male models."[63] On the occasion of her death,

Perceval's sister not only seems to effect an act of *imitatio Christi*, but she also significantly appropriates the masculine position as it has been represented throughout the *Morte d'Arthur*. Just as a Round Table knight might engage in combat to protect a lady, Perceval's sister engages in a type of test, or combat, to save the lady of the castle; in the course of that battle, she receives a wound from which she dies. For a knight to die in the service of a lady "fixes" his reputation as legitimately heterosexualized; that Perceval's sister here dies in the service of a lady—indeed, while three knights look on—necessarily questions the acts and symbols by which the heteronormative chivalric ideology is defined.

By contrast and/or similarly, Galahad's death is most unknightlike, and therefore, unmasculine in the terms of the community. Of all the Round Table knights, Galahad alone escapes being wounded; in a sense, he therefore lacks the marks or signs by which he becomes intelligible to other knights as one who legitimately belongs within the homosocial subcommunity of the Round Table—he does not "read" as a man. As Kathleen Coyne Kelly points out, "Galahad represents an unassailable masculinity that is forever out of reach on Malory's knightly scale of perfection. Ideally masculine in his bodily integrity, Galahad . . . is also ideally feminine in his virginity."[64] Indeed, Galahad dies a most unknightly death: his end comes not amidst the clash of swords and at the hands of a single enemy met in combat; rather, he departs alone and in silent prayer. "And therewith he kneled downe tofore the table, and made hys prayers. And so suddenly departed hys soule to Jesu Cryste, and a grete multitude of angels bare hit up into hevyn in the syght of hys two felowis" (1035.13–16).

Hoffman has argued that Galahad's character, in his resistance to the feminine, attempts to "resolve the dilemma of masculinity" enacted throughout the pages of Malory's text. Succinctly articulating the different *kinds* of masculinity available to knights in the *Morte d'Arthur*, Hoffman contends that while Galahad's is a unique, original response, it, like other performances of masculinity, fails:

> The longing Lancelot, the married Gareth, and the adulterous Tristram all present models of masculinity compromised by the desire for a woman, a desire that becomes equally problematic whether the woman is present (Gareth) or absent (Lancelot) or both (Tristram). Galahad, the chastest of chaste knights, attempts to resolve the problem by avoiding women altogether. But Galahad's supposed solution through lack proves to be as ineffectual as Tristram's resolution

through excess, and finally resolves neither the problem of woman nor the problem of desire.[65]

Hoffman rightly identifies Galahad's character as performing a new strategy of masculinity, and suggests that the most successful performance of masculinity is finally given by Lancelot, who after the Grail Quest recognizes "the validity of the [chaste] model and his inability to achieve it."[66] Even if he recognizes the inadequacy or impossibility of these potential masculine performances, Lancelot is unable to offer an alternative performance; at the end of the text, long after the Grail Quest has concluded and the kingdom has collapsed, Arthur's greatest knight and the small "remnaunte" of Round Table knights that remain continue to cling to the norms of masculinity earlier modeled by figures such as Gareth, Tristram, and of course, Lancelot.

With the conclusion of the Grail Quest, the remnant of Arthur's knights return to Camelot and attempt to restore the social order that the pursuit of the Holy Grail has disrupted. It is a project doomed to failure, for the Grail Quest has made glaringly plain the contradictions and failures inherent in the chivalric code by which Arthur's kingdom is ordered; once revealed, these shortcomings can never be fully concealed again. As Butler points out, in a scheme of heteronormativity "one is one's gender to the extent that one is not the other gender, a formulation that presupposes and enforces the restriction of gender within that binary pair."[67] The figure of Galahad reveals the idealization of that binary configuration in Malory's text to be a fiction; neither masculine nor feminine, Galahad "exists outside the homosocial bond, and, in fact, prevents the homosocial from becoming fully realized."[68] Paired with Perceval's sister, he offers a strident critique of Arthurian heteronormativity and predicts its ultimate downfall. In the last pages of the *Morte d'Arthur*, the members of the knightly community attempt to undo the damage done to the community by Galahad's brief presence among them. Ironically, in their efforts to preserve the chivalric ethos as a social ideal, they only hasten its demise.

Lancelot, Guenevere, and the Death of Arthur

The Decline and Fall of the Chivalric Community

The quest for the Holy Grail is a watershed moment for the Arthurian chivalric society. On the eve of the quest, the Round Table is for the first and last time whole, unified and unbroken when Galahad takes his place in the Siege Perilous. In the quest itself, however, that unity is irrevocably shattered, as the desire for the grail that has made the community whole ironically breaks apart the fellowship of knights when they set out in pursuit of it. The critique of Arthurian society enacted by the Grail Quest renders clear the cracks and fissures in the foundation of the chivalric community, the tensions and conflicts inherent in the knightly ideology upon which the existence and activity of Arthurian society are predicated. Once revealed, these faults and shortcomings can never be silenced, covered up, or satisfactorily healed, and as the Grail Quest ends, so does the ending of the *Morte d'Arthur* itself begin.

In the episodes that follow the "Tale of the Sankgreal"—what Vinaver terms the "Book of Sir Launcelot and Queen Guinevere" and the "Most Piteous Tale of the Morte Arthur Saunz Guerdon"—the Arthurian community continues the slide toward collapse initiated by the Grail Quest, a progressive and inexorable degeneration that cannot be slowed or stopped. Nowhere else in Malory's text is the clear link between all the component parts of the *Morte d'Arthur* more compellingly enacted than in the progression of the final pages.[1] This narrative of social collapse begins on the first page after the Grail Quest, when Malory tells us that

> So aftir the queste of the Sankgreall was fulfylled and all knyghtes that were leffte on lyve were com home agayne unto the Table Rounde . . . than there was grete joy in the courte, and enespeciall kynge Arthure and quene Gwenyvere made grete joy of the remenaunte that were com home. . . . Than, as the booke seyth, sir

> Launcelot began to resorte unto quene Gwenivere agayne, and for-
> gate the promyse and the perfeccion that he made in the queste . . .
> and so they loved togydirs more hotter than they ded toforehande,
> and had many such prevy draughtis togydir that many in the courte
> spake of hit, and in especiall sir Aggravayne, sir Gawaynes brothir, for
> he was ever opynne-mowthed (1045.1–21).

This passage identifies all the elements of the final collapse of the
Arthurian order: the fractured nature of the Round Table fellowship, seriously weakened in that only a "remenaunte" return to court from the
Grail Quest; the relationship between Lancelot and Guenevere, once a
source of support for the community, now the site of much suspicion and
gossip; and the issue of kinship, here demonstrated by the "opynne-
mowthed"-ness of Arthur's nephew Aggravain, whose hostility toward
Lancelot stems at least in part from his belief that as the son of Arthur's
sister, he should be entitled to greater status and favor than Lancelot, a
foreigner unrelated to the king.

These three elements—disunity within the homosocial subcommunity
of knights, Lancelot's love for Guenevere, and kinship—will intersect and
intertwine to produce the final battle in which Arthur meets his end and
the order of the realm is undone. Formerly functional as supports of the
chivalric social order, at the end of the text homosociality, heteronormative
desire, and kinship come into conflict with one another. In this chapter I
trace the destructive force of these elements through an examination of
Lancelot's acts of service to Guenevere, Arthur's conflict with his nephew/
son, Mordred, and Guenevere and Lancelot's final redemption as religious
figures. When examined in conjunction with one another, these three episodic units of the conclusion of the *Morte d'Arthur* offer a complex picture
of the Arthurian social order; it becomes clear that the Arthurian community is destroyed through forces of its own making, but the agents of that
destruction are, interestingly, redeemed at least in part through their adherence to this courtly social mode.

Lancelot and Guenevere: Loyalty and Justice

At the end of the *Morte d'Arthur*, Lancelot rescues Guenevere from the
stake for the third and final time, killing several of his former fellows in
the process. Tragically, he also accidentally strikes down Sir Gareth,
nephew to the king and arguably the knight that Lancelot loves best in the

world. When Arthur is told the news, his reaction indicates his awareness that the community over which he rules will now be divided against itself, with no possibility of reconciliation: "Alas, that ever I bare crowne uppon my hede! For now have I loste the fayrest felyshyp of noble knyghtes that ever hylde Crysten kynge togydirs. Alas, my good knyghtes be slayne and gone away fro me, that now within thys two dayes I have loste nygh forty knyghtes, and also the noble felyshyp of sir Launcelot and hys blood, for now I may nevermore holde hem togydirs with my worship. Now, alas, that ever thys warre began!" (1183.7–14). Arthur is mourning the fracture of the Round Table, the order that ironically meets its demise due to the very thing which it has stridently promoted as a means to legitimize itself: knightly devotion to the feminine, or what in other circumstances might be termed "courtly love" or "*fin amour*."[2] The courtly relationship, as modeled by Lancelot's relationship to Guenevere, provides a ready-made script wherein knights and ladies perform their gender identities. If one concurs with Butler's argument that "gender proves to be performative— that is, constituting the identity it is purported to be,"[3] then the knight-lady relationship in Malory clearly produces as a social support a structure wherein such identities may be performed according to a script of courtliness. Maureen Fries has noted that the courtly *fin amour* system, with its scripts for gendered behavior, functions successfully as a communal support as long as it is deployed with "moderation,"[4] something which Lancelot and Guenevere, however, are clearly unable to do.

At issue here is not *fin amour*, or courtliness, but *adultery*. The idea of *fin amour* seems perfectly able to be absorbed into the ideal of Christian marriage, as the examples of Gareth and Pelleas suggest; that it is not possible for Lancelot and Guenevere's relationship to culminate in such a marriage is partially what produces much of the final conflict of the *Morte d'Arthur*. Lancelot's rescue of Guenevere from the fire is as inevitable as the fact that in so doing, he will strike down many of his close friends. That the courtly ideal has been intended all along as a means to advance masculine interests with little regard to, or at the expense of, the feminine, is made plain in Arthur's lament after Lancelot has rescued the queen: "And now more I am soryar for my good knyghtes losse than for the losse of my fayre quene; for quenys I myght have inow, but such a felyship of good knyghtes shall never be togydirs in no company" (1184.1–5).[5] That this ideal should ultimately and inevitably destroy the order it was intended to support is made clear through an analysis of Lancelot and Guenevere's relationship at the end of Malory's text.

In the final pages of the *Morte d'Arthur*, Malory effectively rewrites his sources to problematize the dependence of the feminine on the masculine for protection and defense. At the same time, he critiques the parallel dependence of the masculine upon the feminine for identity definition. The relationship of Lancelot and Guenevere reflects the deterioration of the model of gender relations operating in Malory's text: the feminine has shifted from being a catalytic impetus in the making of masculine and social identity to acting as a destructive force that threatens to destroy the entire chivalric community. We see the escalating bonds of constraint in which Lancelot, Guenevere—and indeed, Arthur himself—find themselves as citizens of a society that values physical prowess above reason and logic in settling disputes and answering accusations of wrongdoing. The particular case of Lancelot and Guenevere highlights the untenable nature of a system whereby "truth" is determined in combat and knightly devotion to one's lady is valued so highly.

In the concluding episodes of Malory's text, the transformation of the relationship of Lancelot and Guenevere that has been gradually effected over the course of the *Morte d'Arthur*—its shift from a positive to negative factor in the health of the chivalric community—is represented in miniature in the episodes of "The Poisoned Apple," the "Knight of the Cart," and "Slander and Strife." In each of these episodes, the concerns of gender and the justice system come into contact with one another, a contact that emphasizes the structural contradictions and disintegration of chivalric ideology. Three times Lancelot saves Guenevere from being "brent," and each time, the socially divisive impact of his act of rescue increases.[6]

In the first episode, "The Poisoned Apple," Lancelot's actions as Guenevere's champion are characterized as completely proper and correct as she is indeed innocent of the charge laid against her. Their relationship here in many ways represents the early chaste and honorable stage of their devotion. Malory has altered this story as he found it in his sources (the section of the French Vulgate Cycle entitled *La Mort le Roi Artu* and the fourteenth-century English *Stanzaic Morte Arthur*), extricating it from its *entrelacement* with "The Fair Maid of Astolat."[7] Although Malory regularly unwove interlaced source narratives in creating his *Morte d'Arthur*, the impact of such a disentanglement here is particularly striking, in that it creates the effect of dramatic progression toward an unavoidable conclusion in a way that his sources do not.

While the text makes clear that Lancelot has forsaken the vows he made

while on the Grail Quest concerning his relationship with Guenevere—
"sir Launcelot began to resort unto quene Gwenivere agayne and forgate
the promyse and the perfeccion that he made in the queste" (1045.10–
12)—this episode also demonstrates Lancelot's continued attempt to negotiate a balance of some sort between standards of behavior, as he did in the
quest for the Holy Grail, precariously negotiating a space between the
secular and the spiritual in his desire to achieve glory for both Guenevere
and for God. In this instance, he attempts to maintain a similar balance in
a courtly, secular context, resuming his relationship with Guenevere but
also acting on behalf of numerous other ladies who request his services:
"So hit befelle that sir Launcelot had many resortis of ladyes and damesels
which dayly resorted unto hym that besoughte hym to be their champion.
In all such maters of ryght sir Launcelot applyed hym dayly to do for the
plesure of our Lorde Jesu Cryst, and ever as much as he myght he with-
drew hym fro the company of quene Gwenyvere for to eschew the
sclawndir and noyse. Wherefore the quene waxed wrothe with sir Launcelot" (1045.22–29). Lancelot's actions here run contrary to the chivalric
ideal of a knight pledging himself to serve a single lady; his attempt to
sustain these multiple devotions finally brings these service activities into
conflict with one another. Sensible as his behavior may seem in light of the
suspicions of the members of the court and Sir Aggravain's "opynne-
mowthed"-ness, his actions nonetheless incur Guenevere's wrath, and she
jealously rebukes Lancelot for the attention he pays to other women. Even
though Lancelot proffers reasonable excuses for his behavior, the queen
banishes him from the court. In Malory's source, Lancelot's acceptance of
the sleeve of the Fair Maid of Astolat causes Guenevere's anger; in disen-
tangling the *entrelacement*, Malory needed to devise a new reason for
Guenevere's displeasure, and in his revision he focuses more attention on
Lancelot's devotion to the feminine.

   In "A Noble Tale of Sir Launcelot du Lake," Lancelot has a reputation as
the particular champion of maidens, damsels, and gentlewomen, a reputation that seems to ensure that the majority of his adventures, indeed, involve service to ladies. His acts of valor serve to confirm and enhance the
reputation that he already has—in other words, Lancelot only becomes
more himself. In "A Noble Tale," Lancelot's identity as the protector of all
women exists in easy relationship to his other identity as the devoted
champion of the queen; in fact, his desire to accrue honor for Guenevere—
and for himself in Guenevere's eyes—compels him to depart from the
court to "preve" himself in "straunge adventures," adventures that gener-

ally involve damsels in distress. As Geraldine Heng points out, "Lancelot is
the most effective agent in the text for the transliteration of female will
and desire because the logic of serving a particular lady translates poly-
semously for him into dedication to a feminine principle, affirmed in the
enormous variety of requests successfully made of him by women."[8]
While Heng's assessment may be true of the Lancelot we see in the early
pages of the narrative, by the end of Malory's text, Lancelot's twin devotions to ladies in general and Guenevere in particular can no longer peace-
ably coexist.

As a counter to Lancelot's very public displays of service to ladies,
Guenevere determines to stage a demonstration of her affection for the
other knights of the Round Table: "So the quene lete make a pryvy dynere
in London unto the knyghtes of the Rownde Table, and all was for to shew
outwarde that she had as grete joy in all other knyghtes of the Rounde
Table as she had in sir Launcelot" (1048.12–15). At the dinner, the unregu-
lated issue of kinship again reveals its destructive potential. Included
among the four-and-twenty knights invited to dine with the queen is a
certain sir Pyonell, whose kinsman Lamorak has been killed by Sir
Gawain.[9] Sir Pyonell attempts to extract vengeance for his kinsman's
death by poisoning an apple, knowing that Gawain is partial to fruit. By a
"myssefortune" a knight called Sir Patryse eats the poisoned apple meant
for Gawain and dies immediately. After this occurrence all the knights
present at the dinner—and most significantly Sir Mador de la Porte,
cousin to the dead knight—"had a grete suspeccion unto the quene
bycause she lete make that dyner" (1049.31–32) and "Mador stood stylle
before the kynge and appeled the quene of treson. (For the custom was
such at that tyme that all maner of shamefull deth was called treson)"
(1050.1–3).[10]

Arthur is understandably upset by the turn of events, and Malory has
altered his source yet again by having the king state his belief that his
queen is innocent of the charge against her: "'Fayre lordys,' seyd kynge
Arthure, 'me repentith of thys trouble, but the case ys so I may nat have
ado in thys mater, for I muste be a ryghtfull juge. And that repentith me
that I may nat do batayle for my wyff, for, as I deme, thys dede com never
by her'" (1050.4–8). By contrast, in the French source, *La Mort le Roi Artu*,
Arthur makes no comments on his wife's guilt or innocence, but rather
allots her "reasonable" time to find a champion to take up her cause:
"'Sire,' fet la reine, 'porroie ge trouver autre conseill en vos?' 'Dame,' fet li
rois, 'nenil; car ge ne feroie tort ne por vos ne por autre'" ["My lord," said

the queen "might I find other support/defense in you?" "My lady," said the king, "no; because I cannot make defense for you or any other"].[11] Arthur's assertion of Guenevere's innocence in the *Morte d'Arthur*, accompanied by his statement that he must abstain from taking up arms on her behalf, suggests a faith in trial-by-arms as a means of discerning truth. That Arthur does not fight for Guenevere due to his need to be a "ryghtful juge" indicates an attempt on the part of the king to portray chivalric judgment as fair and just, not determined by mere physical strength and skill. "Jugement," rather than martial prowess, suggestively stands as that which will determine the outcome of Guenevere's trial. As the narrative draws toward its conclusion, the slight distinction between force and justice here maintained erodes, and the two become one and the same for the members of the chivalric community.

The trial-by-arms that Malory here depicts was an accepted form of deciding legal disputes in the Court of Chivalry,[12] which, after the Statute of Treasons of 1352, was defined as a proper venue for settling serious criminal charges brought by one noble against another.[13] While statutes enacted in 1384 and 1389 had sought to limit the scope of the cases tried in the Court of Chivalry, it remained the proper arena for settling disputes of arms, war, and treason.[14] By the fifteenth century, trial by combat was almost nonexistent, although the possibility of deciding issues by arms remained as an option into the modern period.[15] Within the aristocratic world of Arthur's chivalric society, there seems to be no recourse to the common-law trial, which had become the usual and preferred means of deciding disputes by Malory's day.[16]

The moment when Guenevere is compelled to seek a champion because her husband may not have "ado" in the matter resonates for a number of reasons. First, it casts a different light upon the relationship of Lancelot and Guenevere. No longer can it be viewed as a relationship merely born out of mutual admiration and chivalrous honor. This seemed to be the case earlier when, in the opening of "A Noble Tale of Sir Launcelot du Lake," Malory tells us that Lancelot surpassed all other knights, "*wherefore quene Gwenyvere had hym in grete favoure aboven all other knyghtes, and so he loved the quene agayne aboven all other ladyes*" (253.15–17; emphasis mine). Malory's statement here indicates that their devoted relationship arises logically, given that Lancelot is the greatest knight and Guenevere the highest ranking lady of the land; it is status and prowess that are invoked here, not love or desire. In addition, Arthur's self-proclaimed inability to defend his queen according to custom indicates that

Guenevere, as the wife of the king, *needs* her own champion—distinct from her husband—as there are certain roles, typically filled by a lady's husband or father, from which Arthur must hold himself exempt as sovereign: "I muste be a ryghtfull juge. And that repentith me that I may nat do batayle for my wyff."[17] Significantly, trial by combat is the sole means of settling disputes in the Arthurian chivalric society, an act that women clearly are unable to perform in their own defense; as king, Arthur cannot risk the royal person and defend his wife.

Given these circumstances, it would seem fitting that the highest ranking woman in the land be championed by the greatest knight, and thus Lancelot and Guenevere's relationship—at least in its initial stages—is fully legitimized as necessary. Indeed, when Arthur is compelled to promise Sir Mador that he will have his opportunity fifteen days hence to seek justice, the king immediately questions Guenevere about Lancelot's whereabouts. Arthur himself expects that it would be Lancelot who would act as defender for the queen; the king seems to regard their close relationship as both appropriate and logical. "'Where ys sir Launcelot?' seyde kynge Arthure. 'And he were here he wolde nat grucche to do batayle for you.' 'Sir,' seyde the quene, 'I wote nat where he ys, but hys brother and hys kynessmen deme that he be nat within thys realme'" (1051.11–15). Of necessity, Arthur needs a champion to serve his lady in fulfilling those duties from which he must hold himself excused, and the choice of king and queen both is Sir Lancelot. Indeed, in exasperation Arthur demands of Guenevere: "'What aylith you . . . that ye can nat kepe sir Launcelot uppon youre syde? For wyte you well,' seyde the kynge, 'who that hath sir Launcelot uppon his party hath the moste man of worhship in thys worlde uppon hys syde'" (1051.29–33).

Above and beyond the logical choice of the greatest knight to serve as the queen's champion, Lancelot, we learn, has another compelling reason for acting on Guenevere's behalf. Lancelot recalls a moment that we do not see in the *Morte d'Arthur*—the day that he was knighted—on which occasion he lost his sword. Guenevere found the sword and "lapped" it in her train so that she might return it to Lancelot when he had need of it. If it had not been for Guenevere, Lancelot proclaims, "had I bene shamed amonge all knyghtes. And therefore, my lorde Arthure, I promysed her at that day ever to be her knyght *in ryght other in wronge*" (1058.29–32; emphasis mine).[18] Lancelot's assertion that he is Guenevere's knight "in ryght other in wronge" brings to the surface the problem such loyal relationships can pose when the behavior or cause of one of the parties in the relationship is less than noble. His statement, while specifically calling attention to the problematic nature of his relationship with Guenevere, also more generally characterizes the nature of Arthurian gender relations as potentially threatening to the larger social order.

This first trial of Guenevere provides us with a look at the judicial system as it is supposed to operate in Malory's text, and the implications in terms of gender relations are significant. When the other knights criticize Bors for taking up the queen's cause, he staunchly defends her, asserting that: "for good love she bade us to dyner and nat for no male engyne. And that, I doute nat, shall be preved hereafftir, for howsomevere the game goth, there was treason amonge us" (1054.18–21). In Bors's assertion that *"howsomevere the game goth,* there was treason amonge us" (emphasis mine) lies the suggestion that the judicial mechanism by which guilt or innocence is decided in the chivalric community is imperfect. The implication of such a statement is that, even if Bors fails in combat, such failure should not necessarily be understood as confirmation of the queen's guilt.

The fact that a man's righteousness and honor is regarded as a direct function of his martial prowess suggestively compromises the possibility of an equitable and fair justice system within the chivalric community. The fact that women are almost completely removed from the process of accusation and defense, even when they are one of the parties directly involved in such a case, further undermines the idea that "true" justice might exist within the courtly society. A man at least has recourse to his sword, while a woman, deliberately constructed in the direction, focus, and language of the Pentecostal Oath as passive, submissive, and marginal, has recourse only to her father, husband, or brother.[19] Guenevere's predicament—her lack of a knight to champion her cause—while in one sense specific to her particular situation as wife of the king, also raises the spectre of other women of the community, perhaps without benefit of a husband or male kinsman, who might find themselves accused of a crime and without a means of defense. Although women occasionally and momentarily appropriate swords, the gender paradigm operating in the *Morte d'Arthur* certainly does not allow for the possibility that a woman may take up the sword on her own behalf in trial by combat.[20]

Malory further emphasizes this problem when he tells the reader that this judicial custom is seemingly standard at all levels in the Arthurian community: "so the quene was than put in the conestablis awarde and a grete fyre made aboute an iron stake, that an sir Mador de la Porte had the bettir, she sholde there be brente; for such custom was used in tho dayes;

for favoure, love, nother affinité there sholde be none other but ryghtuous jugemente, as well uppon a kynge as uppon a knyght, and as well uppon a quene as uppon another poure lady" (1055.9–15). In criminal matters, women in the *Morte d'Arthur* are only as innocent as their champions are martially capable. Malory himself, however, in a departure from his source, seems to register his own discomfort with this custom. After Lancelot has duly arrived (in disguise) and defeated Sir Mador de la Porte, Malory adds a passage not found in the *Mort Artu*, in which text Lancelot's defeat of Mador is easily accepted as clear proof of Guenevere's innocence. In the *Morte d'Arthur*, by contrast, Nyneve, the Damsel of the Lake, arrives to proclaim the truth of the episode: "And so whan she herde how the quene was greved for the dethe sir Patryse, than she tolde hit opynly that she was never gylty, and there she disclosed by whom it was done, and named hym sir Pynell, and for what cause he ded hit. There hit was opynly knowyn and disclosed, and so the quene was excused" (1059.15–20).

This alteration indicates an awareness of the problematic questions raised by the Arthurian justice system. While in Malory's time the *Morte d'Arthur* was read by many as a courtesy book that demonstrated proper noble behavior and modeled an ideal society,[21] contradictorily, the main message of the text is that noble rank and noble behavior were inherited qualities, a birthright that could not be learned. From such a perspective, the idea that the rightness of one's quarrel or position could be determined through combat makes sense. Ideally, the truth would manifest itself in the same way that the Fair Unknown repeatedly plays out in Malory's text: through a demonstration of innate ability. Malory's insertion of the Damsel of the Lake's proclamation seems, then, a recognition that the myth of nobility—and the linked idea that "right" could be proved through a display of "might"—had lost some of its luster by the fifteenth century.

Although truly innocent in "The Poisoned Apple," Guenevere is only technically innocent of the charge laid against her in the "Knight of the Cart." Of all Malory's "reductions" and reworkings of his source material, I would argue that this is by far his most important revision, the only place in the *Morte d'Arthur* in which the reader is given unequivocal confirmation that Lancelot and Guenevere are indeed engaged in an adulterous affair. Having its ultimate source in Chrétien de Troyes's *Le Chevalier de la Charette*, it seems most likely that Malory was working with a version of the story as it appears in the French work most often referred to as the Prose *Lancelot*.[22] In his source, the narrative of the "Knight of the Cart" occurs in the section of the text that corresponds to the events of "A Noble

Tale of Sir Launcelot du Lake." Malory's deliberate excision of this episode from the earlier portion of his text seems clearly to be a function of his desire to characterize the relationship of Guenevere and Lancelot as devoted yet chaste in the early stages, progressing gradually toward adultery and treason as the kingdom itself moves toward collapse.

In Malory's version of this episode, the figure of Guenevere, not Lancelot, most compellingly evinces the contradictions and conflicts that permeate the foundational ideology of the Arthurian chivalric community.[23] As queen, Guenevere's function is far from merely symbolic. As we saw in the "Tale of King Arthur," Guenevere serves as an authority on proper knightly behavior, with the power to exact punishment from a knight who has behaved in a less than satisfactory manner, particularly toward ladies. She is, in the words of Bors shortly after the poisoned apple incident, "a maynteyner of good knyghtes." This assertion is supported by the opening scene of the episode of the "Knight of the Cart," in which the queen and ten of her knights set out to go a-Maying:

> And that tyme was such a custom that the quene rode never wythoute a grete felyship of men of armys aboute her. And they were many good knyghtes, and the moste party were yonge men that wolde have worshyp, and they were called the Quenys Knyghtes. And never in no batayle, turnement nother justys they bare none of hem no maner of knowlecchynge of their owne armys but playne whyght shyldis, and thereby they were called the Quenys Knyghtes. (1121.14–18)

Malory goes on to explain that it is through proper knightly behavior in the service of the queen that young knights may move up to full fellowship with the rest of the Round Table community. Guenevere, then, not only "maynteyns" knights, but she is in fact entrusted with the crucial early stages of their chivalric training.

Yet, even as she supports the Arthurian chivalric project in that she reinforces and encourages proper knightly behavior, she also paradoxically becomes a source of disunity when the knightly desire to serve a lady becomes perverted into desire to *possess* the lady, as is the case with Meleagant: "And thys knyght sir Mellyagaunce loved passyngly well quene Gwenyver, and so had he done longe and many yerys. And the booke seyth he had lay in awayte for to stele away the quene. . ." (1121.7–10). Malory has altered his source, making Meleagant, who is an outsider to the Arthurian community in the French text, a Round Table knight in the

Morte d'Arthur. Thus, his transgression becomes all the more monstrous, and all the more significant, when considered in the light of the compulsory heterosexuality the homosocial subcommunity of knights has participated in, in a strident affirmation of "hypermasculinity"; for Meleagant, the masculinizing devotion to ladies has here crossed the line into obsession. Even more troubling, it soon becomes clear that a similar transformation has taken place in the relationship of Lancelot and Guenevere; Lancelot's devotion to the queen also crosses a line, as here in the "Knight of the Cart" Malory gives us the first and last explicit account of the act of adultery between Arthur's queen and his greatest knight. When Guenevere rebukes Meleagant for his actions in abducting her, reminding him to "Bethynke the how thou arte a kyngis sonne and a knyght of the Table Rounde, and thou thus to be aboute to dishonoure the noble kyng that made the knyght. . . . I had levir kut myne owne throte in twayne rather than thou sholde dishonoure me!" (1122.9–15), her righteous indignation loses much of its force when one realizes that her words are equally applicable to Lancelot.[24]

Malory has drastically condensed Lancelot's journey to recover Guenevere from the version recounted in his source. Gone are the numerous adventures or tests he encounters in the French, and the symbolic value of the cart has largely been lost—here, it is only a means to arrive at Meleagant's castle quickly. Having dispensed with the ignominy of cart-riding, Malory is compelled to find an alternate motivation for Lancelot and Guenevere's strained relationship when they finally encounter one another again. Upon hearing that Lancelot has arrived to reclaim the queen, Meleagant immediately falls to his knees before Guenevere and asks for mercy. "Mercy, madame, for now I putte me holé in your good grace" (1128.1–2). Guenevere is understandably disdainful of Meleagant's plea, but accepts the opportunity to take matters into her "owne handys, and . . . rule my lorde sir Launcelot" (1128.11–12). After agreeing to settle the dispute, Guenevere goes out to the courtyard to inform the newly arrived Lancelot of the change in circumstances. She finds him shouting battle challenges and derogatory epithets up at Meleagant's castle. "Sir Launcelot, why be ye so amoved?" (1128.23) asks the queen of the man who has swum the river Thames, had his horse shot out from under him, and suffered the indignity of riding in a wood cart, all for the sake of her rescue. "Madam," he says, "and I had wyste that ye wolde have bene so lyghtly accorded with hym I wolde nat a made such haste unto you" (1129.4–6). What is significant about this moment in the "Knight of the

Cart" is the clear position of power that Guenevere occupies in relationship to both Lancelot and Meleagant. In their eagerness to serve and possess her, respectively, these two knights demonstrate the fictitiousness of the ideal of masculine dominance and independent agency upon which the social structure is predicated.[25] So dependent is the chivalric community upon a subjugated feminine presence for support, its agents risk enslaving themselves to these figures.

This idea is further supported by the scene that immediately follows later that evening at Guenevere's chamber window, where Lancelot has come to converse with the queen. "'Wyte you well,' seyde the quene, 'I wolde as fayne as ye that ye myght com in to me.' 'Wolde ye so, madame,' seyde sir Launcelot, 'wyth youre harte that I were with you?' 'Ye, truly,' seyde the quene. 'Then shall I prove my myght,' seyde sir Launcelot, 'for youre love'" (1131.14–20). In Lancelot's statement lies the crux of the problem—all that he does is for the love of the queen. While such knightly devotion to one's lady is essential to the construction of a knightly masculine identity, it also constrains the knightly agents of the text. Service to the feminine becomes an obligation that dictates a knight's actions, a service from which he can never be free.

Lancelot proceeds to pull the bars from the window and enters the queen's bedchamber, where Malory tells us that "sir Launcelot wente to bedde with the quene and . . . toke hys plesaunce and hys lykynge untyll hit was the dawnyng of the day" (1131.28–31). Guenevere's earlier speech to Meleagant, in which she had threatened to cut her own throat rather than be "dishonoured," now rings hollow. Lancelot does not notice that he has injured his hand in removing the iron bars and he bleeds on Guenevere's sheets. Meleagant discovers this in the morning and immediately takes this as evidence that Guenevere has been unfaithful to Arthur with one of the wounded knights who were lodged in her chamber on the previous night: "A ha, madame! . . . now have I founde you a false traytouras unto my lorde Arthur. . . . Therefore I calle you of tresoun afore my lorde kynge Arthure" (1132.15–19).

The devotion to ladies that has made his reputation—and indeed, his devotion to this particular lady, his queen—compels Lancelot to defend Guenevere's honor in man-to-man combat with Meleagant, even though in so doing, Lancelot violates one of the articles of the Pentecostal Oath that he has sworn to uphold—never to engage in a "wrongful quarrel." For Meleagant's assertion that Guenevere has been unfaithful to Arthur is indeed true. Lancelot attempts to justify his defense of the queen by promising to prove through battle that Guenevere has not been unfaithful to Arthur with any of the knights who were lodged in her chamber on the night in question. In other words, Lancelot attempts to excuse his transgression against the rules of knighthood through a technicality: "I say nay playnly, that thys nyght there lay *none of thes ten knyghtes wounded* with my lady, quene Gwenyver, and that woll I prove with myne hondys that ye say untrewly in that" (1133.30–33; emphasis mine).

In the events of the battle between Lancelot and Meleagant, Malory proffers perhaps his strongest critique of Lancelot yet, suggestively portraying him as uncomfortably similar to the coward Meleagant. From the outset, this fight is a clear example of "wrongful quarrel," that which is expressly prohibited in the Pentecostal Oath. When Lancelot has bested Meleagant, the other begs for mercy, and according to the Oath, which Meleagant invokes, Lancelot is bound to accede to his request: "For I yelde me unto you, and I requyre you, as ye be a knyght and felow of the Table Rounde, sle me nat, for I yelde me as overcomyn, and whethir I shall lyve or dey, I put me in the kynges honde and youres" (1138.22–26). Malory then tells us that "sir Lancelot wyst nat what to do, for he had lever than all the good in the worlde that he myght be revenged uppon hym" (1138.27–29), a remarkable admission, in that according to the rules of knighthood, there should be no doubt in Lancelot's mind as to what the proper course of action should be: mercy should be granted immediately. Lancelot's hesitation further reveals that this is indeed a "wrongful quarrel"; he is not fighting in the interests of justice or honor, but rather for personal vengeance. Tellingly, he looks to the *queen*, not the king, as would be proper, for guidance on how to proceed, and she gives him a clear signal: "And anone the quene wagged hir hede uppon sir Launcelot, as to seyth 'sle hym'" (1138.31, 1139.1).

Reluctant to engage in so blatant a transgression against the rule of knightly conduct, Lancelot suggests a compromise, offering to fight Meleagant again, this time with his head and side unprotected and one arm bound to his body. Even with this handicap, Lancelot still manages to overcome and kill his opponent. This ridiculous image of Lancelot—trussed, unprotected, and still managing to handily defeat his rival—is indicative of the impossibility of sustaining the knightly subcommunity as a center of power within the larger social order that dictates a compulsory heterosexuality. The necessity of devotion to ladies as the key to establishing and maintaining masculine knightly identity complicates—or indeed, renders impossible—devotion to the other rules of knighthood. When Meleagant is finally killed, the resolution is not celebrated by the community as was the case with the trial of "The Poisoned Apple." In that instance, the accusation against Guenevere was not only revealed to be false, but the true culprit was duly identified and punished.

In the "Knight of the Cart," the outcome of the trial by combat is the death of one of the Round Table knights, and while Meleagant is indeed guilty of the dishonorable act of abducting his queen, his death does not ensure that a satisfactory resolution to the dispute is publicly achieved. Lancelot may have defeated Meleagant, and thus the truth of Lancelot's claim—that Guenevere did not commit adultery with any one of the knights lodged in her chamber—may have been technically established, but the question remains: where *did* the blood on Guenevere's sheets come from?[26] Lancelot's defeat of Meleagant cannot satisfactorily kill the rumor and innuendo that now circulate even more strongly among those who are suspicious and "opynne-mowthed," such as Mordred and Aggravain.

The episodes of "The Poisoned Apple" and the "Knight of the Cart" thus reveal Lancelot and Guenevere's relationship as the potential source of social instability and a threat to the cohesive unity of the Round Table. We see this threat further amplified in "Slander and Strife." In this episode, the figure of Guenevere and her relationship with Lancelot literally divide the community and destroy many of the knights whom she had earlier "mayntayned." Legitimately designated as the queen's champion, Lancelot has hitherto managed to successfully negotiate a balance between the queen's feelings and desires and the suspicions of the court by declaring his intention to be a "knyght wyveles" who is the particular champion of ladies everywhere. These three elements of his character—devotion to ladies in general, devotion to the queen in particular, and devotion to the unmarried state—have successfully worked to compensate for and offset one another up to this point; however, this balancing act proves increasingly difficult to maintain. The collapse of this particular balance in the last tale of the *Morte d'Arthur* corresponds with and signals other, similar collapses occurring simultaneously throughout the Arthurian community, collapses that lead ultimately to the final, definitive breakdown of the chivalric social order.

"Slander and Strife" opens with Malory's description of Sir Aggravain and his half-brother, Sir Mordred, expressing their desire to confront Lancelot and Guenevere with the charge of adultery. Malory tells us that "thys sir Aggravayne and sir Mordred had ever a privy hate unto the quene, dame Gwenyver, and to sir Launcelot; and dayly and nyghtly they

ever wacched upon sir Launcelot" (1161.11–14). Gawain, foreseeing that
such an accusation threatens to disrupt and divide the chivalric community, advises his brothers to "stynte your stryff," but they refuse. Aggravain informs Arthur of his suspicions, and he does so in significant terms:
"We know all that sir Launcelot holdith your quene, and hath done longe,
and we be your syster sunnes, we may suffir hit no lenger. And all we wote
that ye shulde be above sir Launcelot, and ye ar the kynge that made hym
knyght, and therefore we woll prove hit that he is a traytoure to youre
person" (1163.6–11; emphasis mine). Aggravain emphasizes the blood relationship, and interestingly, it is not on his own behalf that he seems af-
fronted; rather, he expresses indignation for Arthur's position. Aggravain's
speech seems to indicate that, as kinsman to the king, he takes personally
any perceived insult to his uncle: in this instance, that Lancelot seems to be
"above" Arthur in status.

What Aggravain's indignation suggests is that women in the chivalric
society function primarily as the conduits for status and prestige. As Gayle
Rubin has so cogently explained in discussing patriarchal systems of gender and exchange, "as long as the relations specify that men exchange
women, it is men who are the beneficiaries of such exchanges."[27] Here,
what Aggravain seems to be calling attention to is an "improper"—because not consented to by both parties—exchange between men. That
Lancelot is now seemingly "above" Arthur would seem to be due to his
appropriation of Guenevere. For, as I argued in chapter 1, Guenevere provides much of Arthur's status and power in that the dowry she brings to
their marriage includes the Round Table and its knights.

Heng has pointed out that "by receiving a knight's dedication and being
ascribed his motivations, resources, and accomplishments, a woman is at
once immanent in his deeds, her place and influence permanently in-
scribed in the record of his gestures."[28] While this may have been true of
Arthur at the beginning of the *Morte d'Arthur*, he has long since ceased to
actively participate in the project of chivalry. In his position and behavior
as king, one can no longer see the presence of Guenevere's influence "in-
scribed in the record of his gestures." Rather, Arthur has been surpassed by
Lancelot, he who *has* taken the queen as the source of his knightly prowess, ascribing to her "his motivations, resources, and accomplishments."
Arthur's inability as king to defend and protect his wife according to the
code of chivalry effects a *de facto* exchange of the queen with Lancelot, and
it is this that has placed Lancelot "above" Arthur.[29] The work of Eve Sedgwick on homosocial relations and adultery has relevance here: "the bond of

cuckoldry [is] . . . *necessarily* hierarchical in structure, with an 'active' participant who is clearly in ascendancy over the 'passive' one. Most characteristically, the difference of power occurs in the form of a difference of knowledge: the cuckold is not even supposed to know that he is in such a relationship."[30] That Lancelot, as the "active" participant in the relationship, is "in ascendancy" is clear; however, what does not seem clear is whether or not this hierarchy is the result of Arthur's ignorance as to the relationship between his queen and greatest knight. Malory has told us that Arthur has "a demyng" of Lancelot and Guenevere's relationship; if this is the case, why does the king seem uninterested in bringing their clandestine romance to an end?

Interestingly, Arthur apparently feels that he has benefitted from this "exchange" with Lancelot. In response to Aggravain's accusation, Malory tells us that "the kynge was full lothe that such a noyse shulde be uppon sir Launcelot and his quene; for the king had a demyng of hit, but he wold nat here thereoff, for sir Launcelot had done so much for hym and for the . quene so many tymes that wyte you well the kynge loved hym passyngly well" (1163.20–25). In essence, Guenevere's particular status as needy, vulnerable, *and* queen has brought Arthur into alliance with the greatest of all earthly knights: Sir Lancelot, the "floure of al chyvalry." For purposes of forming social bonds within the system of patriarchy, one could say that Arthur has in all but name "married" Guenevere to Lancelot, accruing a reward similar to that which a brother or father receives upon marrying off a sister or daughter: an alliance with another man.[31] Arthur and Lancelot form a homosocial bond through the masculine heterosexual desire for Guenevere.

The Arthurian justice system, then, seems to be flawed in that a king who "muste be a ryghtful juge" and "may nat do batayle for [his] wyff" must allow his wife a champion, in whose deeds she will be "immanent." As the example of Lancelot and Guenevere demonstrates, such a devoted relationship cannot be chastely maintained—neither in reality nor in terms of gossip and public opinion.[32] Rumor alone, however, seems sufficient to cause the king's fall in stature in the eyes of the chivalric community; Arthur's loyal kinsmen, who derive a large portion of their own status from their relationship to the king, demand that the situation be rectified. Arthur's reluctant acquiescence to Aggravain and Mordred's request to confront Lancelot with the charge of treason demonstrates that blood is a powerful force in the ideology of the community. In agreeing to his nephews' proposal to confront Lancelot concerning his relationship with the queen, Arthur specifically indicates that "hit be sothe as ye say, I wolde that he were takyn with the dede" (1163.18–19), possibly hoping that his greatest knight and queen would be clever enough to avoid being caught *in flagrante delicto*.

But when Aggravain, Mordred, and their company of twelve knights surround Lancelot and Guenevere in the queen's chamber, the two suspects are not actually "takyn with the dede." Whereas the French *Mort Artu* makes it perfectly plain that Lancelot and Guenevere are in bed together—"[Lancelot] se deschauça et despoilla et se coucha avec la reine" [Lancelot removed his shoes, disrobed, and went to bed with the queen][33]—Malory hedges: "For as the Freynshhe booke seyth, the quene and sir Launcelot were togydirs. And whether they were abed other at other maner of disportis, me lyste nat thereof make no mencion, for love that tyme was not as love ys nowadayes" (1165.10–13).[34]

Although unarmed when he is taken with the queen, Lancelot manages to fight his way free, killing all except Mordred, and escapes back to his nephew, Bors. If Guenevere has acted as the object of exchange that brought Lancelot and his kin into alliance with Arthur, she now serves the inverse function, severing Lancelot from Arthur, thereby dividing and bringing into opposition the knights of the community along kin lines. As Lancelot says "I am sure there nys but warre unto me and to myne. . . . I have slayne thys nyght sir Aggravayne, sir Gawaynes brothir . . . and for thys cause now I am sure of mortal warre" (1171.9–13). In kind, when King Arthur hears the news, he remarks that "now I am sure the noble felyship of the Rounde Table ys brokyn for ever, for wyth [Lancelot] woll many a noble knyght holde" (1174.14–16). Lancelot, correctly assuming that Arthur will in "thys hete and malice jouge the quene unto brennyng" (1171.15), indicates that he is compelled to rescue Guenevere for the third time, but on this occasion, there is no recourse to trial by duel. Bors, a Grail Quest knight no less, tells Lancelot that he *has* to save the queen:

> "And also I woll counceyle you, my lorde, that my lady quene Gwenyver, and she be in ony distres, insomuch as she ys in payne for youre sake, that ye knightly rescow here; for and ye ded ony other wyse all the worlde wolde speke you shame to the worldis ende. Insomuch as ye were taken with her, whether ye ded ryght othir wronge, hit ys now youre parte to holde wyth the quene, that she be nat slayne and put to a myschevous deth. For and she so dye, the shame shall be evermore youres." (1171.26–33)

Lancelot *must* defend Guenevere, regardless of whether or not it is "ryght othir wrong" because it is through his actions that she will be brought to the stake;[35] his predicament here stridently problematizes the relationship between force and justice. Although Gawain pleads with Arthur to allow Lancelot to prove Guenevere's innocence through combat, Arthur's response to this suggestion openly acknowledges the unreliability of the chivalric justice system: "I woll nat that way worke with sir Launcelot, for he trustyth so much uppon hys hondis and hys myght that he doutyth no man. And therefore for my quene he shall never more fyght, for she shall have the law" (1175.19–23).[36]

Critics have long puzzled over what Arthur means when he invokes "the law." As in "The Poisoned Apple," Malory calls attention to the law which, "in tho dayes"[37] was such that

> whatsomever they were, of what astate or degré, if they were
> founden gylty of treson there shuld be none other remedy but deth,
> and othir the menour other the takynge of the dede shulde be causer
> of their hasty jougement. And ryght so it was ordayned for quene
> Gwenyver: bycause sir Mordred was ascaped sore wounded, and the
> dethe of thirtene knyghtes of the Round Table, thes previs and
> experyenses caused kynge Arthur to commaunde the quene to the
> fyre and there to be brente. (1174.21–29)

She receives "jougement," it seems, not because of her adultery (or the appearance of adultery) but rather because of the death of the Round Table knights. But clearly, it is Lancelot, not Guenevere who is directly responsible for the deaths of the thirteen knights. As E. Kay Harris points out, "Malory's application of the law does not explain how Mordred's wounds or the dead knights signify treason by way of adultery. . . . If Aggravain's original charge of treason, adultery, is no longer in effect, what act of treason sends Guinevere to the stake?"[38]

The answer seems to lie in what is a belated recognition of the power and influence of the feminine within the masculine chivalric enterprise: Lancelot's behavior and knightly activities have their source in *Guenevere's* wants and desires. What Arthur seems to understand at long last is that the masculine project of chivalry is really nothing more than knights acting in accordance with the wishes of ladies. Thus, it is Guenevere who should be held responsible. For indeed, within the value system of the community, Lancelot has no choice but to rescue the queen from burning; he cannot abandon the lady whose devotion and favor has made him the greatest of all "erthly knyghtes," even though to do so will ensure that he incurs the enmity of some of those men whom he once held in close homosocial alliance: "I must do much harme or I rescow her, and peradventure I shall there destroy som of my beste fryndis, and that shold moche repente me" (1172.27–29).

Indeed, in the process of saving Guenevere, not only does Lancelot kill some of his "beste fryndis," but the man that he loves most in the world: Arthur's nephew, Gareth, along with Gareth's brother, Gaheris. This final act seals the inevitability of "evermore warre" between Lancelot and Arthur, for as Arthur says upon learning the news: "the deth of them woll cause the grettist mortall warre that ever was, for I am sure that whan sir Gawayne knowyth hereoff that sir Gareth ys slayne, I shall never have reste of hym tyll I have destroyed sir Launcelottys kynne and hymself bothe, othir ellis he to destroy me" (1183.27–31).[39] It is a "mortall warre" that has been in the making since the moment Arthur created the male homosocial order of the Round Table, affording it a central position of power within the larger heteronormative chivalric community. With Lancelot's third rescue of Guenevere, the final conflict and collapse can no longer be deferred.

The Day of Destiny: Incest, Kinship, and Fertility

After rescuing Guenevere for the third and final time, Lancelot departs with her to Joyous Gard. In response, Malory tells us that Arthur, his kin, and all those men loyal to them make ready "to passe over the see, to warre uppon sir Launcelot and uppon hys londis" (1211.5–6). However, someone must remain behind to oversee the kingdom: "And there kynge Arthur made sir Mordred chyeff ruler of all Ingelonde, and also he put the quene undir hys governaunce: bycause sir Mordred was kynge Arthurs son, he gaff hym the rule of hys londe and off hys wyff" (1211.8–11). Thus, the stage is set for the "day of destiny" wherein the Arthurian romance will come full circle to its tragic conclusion. While Arthur is away, his son, incestuously conceived in the first pages of the *Morte d'Arthur*, will seek to knowingly reproduce his father's sin in the last moments of the narrative. Having falsely convinced the barons that Arthur has died in battle with Lancelot, Mordred contrives to have himself crowned king, whereupon "he drew hym unto Wynchester, and there he toke quene Gwenyvere, and seyde playnly that he wolde wedde her (which was hys unclys wyff and his fadirs wyff)" (1227.8–10).

The intertwined themes that have produced the narrative of this chivalric community—homosocial bonding, heteronormativity, and kinship loyalty—here become so tightly interwoven that the threads snap. The focal point for this destruction is Guenevere, the still point around which has swirled the conflict between the houses of Arthur and Lancelot, and now, the contest between Arthur and his son, Mordred. As the wife of the king, she has fulfilled the role of the feminine in chivalric terms by serving as an object of devotion for Lancelot and other knights, inspiring them to perform knightly deeds that affirm the social order which has licensed them as its agents. As I argued above, she has, in terms of the theorization of patriarchy most famously put forth by Lévi-Strauss and modified by scholars such as Rubin and Irigaray, been commodified and exchanged among men, linking Leodegran and Arthur, and later, Arthur and Lancelot. In those instances, the benefit derived from such an exchange is clear. In the first case, Leodegran receives an increase in status and security, while Arthur receives the means by which he will rule; in the second case, Lancelot receives the love of a lady, while Arthur receives the loyalty of the greatest knight of the world.

Guenevere, as the object over which Arthur and Mordred contest, complicates romance categorizations of the feminine. Although married to Arthur, she is in fact not wholly removed from the "patriarchal marketplace"; after her exchange in marriage, she is exchanged once more by Arthur for Lancelot's loyalty. But what, at this stage exactly, is her value? Her sterility, never explicitly spoken of, haunts the final pages of Malory's text; there is no heir to Arthur's kingdom. As the father of Mordred and Borre (who is here curiously absent), Arthur's fertility is never in question. It is Guenevere who is apparently incapable of reproducing. What might be termed her pure exchange value as a virgin disappeared with her marriage to Arthur and transference of her dowry of the Round Table with its attendant knights from her father to her husband. Her relationship with Lancelot seems to be an inevitable function of her status as queen, and Arthur does not, for example, offer his wife's body to each and every nobleman with whom he desires an alliance. In this light, Mordred's desire to wed her seems all the more puzzling. Guenevere's original dowry is already technically Mordred's possession when the barons acknowledge him as king, so she can bring him no material benefit. She has produced no royal heir for her first husband, and it thus seems unlikely that she would do so for her second. And in proclaiming his intent to wed her, Mordred makes no mention of romantic love or desire, as Meleagant did when he abducted the queen and her knights whilst they were a-Maying.

Although Guenevere is not Mordred's biological mother, in medieval canon law to marry the wife of one's father or uncle constitutes incest.[40] That Mordred is himself the product of incestuous relations between Arthur and his half-sister Morgause, wife of King Lot, is apparently common knowledge by this point of the narrative: "Than cam the Bysshop of Caunterbyry, whych was a noble clerk and an holy man, and thus he seyde unto sir Mordred: 'Sir, what woll ye do? Woll ye firste displease God and sytthyn shame yourselff and all knyghthode? For ys nat kynge Arthure youre uncle, and no farther but youre modirs brothir, and uppon her he hymselffe begate you, uppon hys owne syster? Therefore how may ye wed youre owne fadirs wyff?'" (1227.31, 1228.1–5).

Despite the specific focus of the Archbishop of Canterbury on Mordred's sinful desire to commit incest, it soon becomes clear that the usurper's desire to wed Guenevere has little to do with sex and everything to do with power.[41] Even more significantly, Mordred's attempt to wed Guenevere violates the ideal of kin loyalty in addition to the incest taboo. Although in romance literature the "sovereignty theme identifies the land with the lady and makes marriage to the queen a necessary condition for assumption of kingship,"[42] such does not seem to be the case with Mordred's usurpation of the throne. Rather, Guenevere has become the contested site of a masculine struggle for dominance, symbolic now not in terms of reproduction—the primary means by which medieval romance women are classified as "feminine"—but as the mark of power for the man who possesses her. As Sedgwick has pointed out in her discussion of Girard's theorization of erotic triangles, frequently "the beloved is determined in the first place, not by the qualities of the beloved, but by the beloved's already being the choice of the person who has been chosen as a rival."[43] In effect, Mordred is here engaged in a rivalrous struggle with *two* men for possession of Guenevere—Arthur and Lancelot—seeking, as Victoria Guerin has put it, "to usurp his father's throne and the woman who belongs equally to both of his enemies."[44]

While king and knight are themselves no longer linked in homosocial alliance through Guenevere, the silent, absent figure of the queen haunts the battlefield of Benwick: although the conflict in which Arthur and

Lancelot are now engaged is specifically characterized as a kin-based blood-feud, it was in the saving of the queen that Lancelot accidentally struck down Arthur's nephews, incurring the wrathful Gawain's unrelenting quest for vengeance. Thus, the rivalries in the last section of the *Morte d'Arthur* arise from a series of overlapping erotic triangles, with Guenevere always at the point and Lancelot, Arthur, and Mordred variously occupying the other positions in a series of different relationships, both to Guenevere and to one another. The homosocial order has fractured into multiple conflicts; the queen who previously functioned to form alliances, serving as the site of homosocial bonding, now shatters not only connections between individual men, but divides kin groups as well.[45] When word reaches Arthur overseas of Mordred's treacherous activity, he immediately departs for home, leaving Lancelot and his loyal retinue—no longer members of the Arthurian order—safe at Benwick. Arthur lands at Dover to discover many of his former barons have turned against him, as there had been "voyce amonge them that with kynge Arthur was never othir lyff but warre and stryff, and with sir Mordrede was grete joy and blysse" (1228.35; 1229.1–2).

As a concession to ensure the peace of the realm, Arthur goes to parley with Mordred, having been warned in a dream by the spirit of Gawain to delay battle with the usurper at all costs, for "within a moneth shall com sir Launcelot with all hys noble knyghtes, and rescow you worshypfully, and sle sir Mordred and all that ever wyll holde wyth hym" (1234.17–19). To temporarily appease Mordred, Arthur offers him Kent and Cornwall during his lifetime and the rule of England after his death, and for a moment, it looks as if a semblance of the old order may be restored: the warring is over, and Lancelot is en route to exact vengeance from the man who has caused both his king and his lady great dishonor.

Of course, it is not to be: during the meeting an adder strikes the foot of a knight in attendance, who then draws his sword to dispatch the snake. At the sight of the drawn blade, both sides presume they have been the victims of an ambush, and "both ostis dressed hem togydirs" (1235.27). The ensuing battle decimates both armies, and the father and son at last meet face to face late on the day of battle on the corpse-strewn field. Spying Mordred still standing, Arthur commands sir Lucan, "now, gyff me my speare . . . for yondir I have aspyed the traytoure that all thys woo hath wrought" (1236.25–27). Lucan rightly reminds him of Gawain's warning, but Arthur is not to be deterred: "Now tyde me dethe, tyde me lyff . . . now

I se hym yondir alone, he shall never ascape myne hondes!" (1237.5–6).
Malory then adds a moment not to be found in either the *Mort Artu* or the
English *Stanzaic Morte Arthur:* Arthur directly addresses his nephew/
son/enemy, proclaiming "Traytoure, now ys thy dethe-day com!" (1237.11).
And indeed, Mordred is a traitor in every sense of the word: he has committed treason in the political sense in endeavoring to usurp the throne,
but of more significance, his attempt to claim both the throne and Guenevere is a violation of the blood-bond, the primary organizing principle of
the chivalric social order. At this moment he embodies multiple threats
to the chivalric community. In gruesome detail, Malory then relates how
Arthur and his son meet their ends:

> there kyng Arthur smote sir Mordred undir the shylde, with a foyne
> of hys speare, thorowoute the body more than a fadom. And whan sir
> Mordred felte that he had hys dethys wounde he threste hymselff
> with the myght he had upp to the burre of kyng Arthurs speare, and
> ryght so he smote his fadir, kynge Arthur, with hys swerde holdynge
> in both hys hondys, uppon the syde of the hede, that the swerde
> perced the helmet and tay of the brayne. And therewith Mordred
> daysshed downe starke dede to the erthe. (1237.13–22)

In the masculine arena of combat, Arthur has simultaneously slain both
his enemy and his heir, literally impaling Mordred on the spear of his status as father and king. In destroying the greatest threat to his kingdom,
however, Arthur also paradoxically puts the chivalric community in peril,
as he has destroyed any possibility of effecting the patrilineal transfer-
rence of wealth, status, and name so essential to the functioning of the kin-
based patriarchy over which he rules.[46] It is both fitting and ironic that the
end of Arthur's reign comes about through an act of violence, an extreme
and grotesque enactment of the one-to-one combat that has earlier served
as a constructive social force. In the words of Martin Shichtman and Laurie
Finke:

> The foundation of a social order on the exchange of violence creates
> the very chaos it is designed to hold at bay. Whatever its immediate
> cause, Malory's *Morte* represents violence not only as a centripetal
> force encouraging order, hierarchy, and centralization, but also as a
> centrifugal force that creates disorder, contention, and sometimes
> unbearable chaos. It recognizes both violence's potential for carnival-

esque disruption as well as the possibility that this potential may be co-opted and used to foster social control.[47]

Mortally wounded, his son and heir dead, Arthur realizes that the sword Excalibur—the violent symbol of his power and authority—has lost any meaning, and asks Bedivere to throw it back into the water from whence he received it. The most masculine of signifying objects has ceased to signify.

But there remains one final scene in Arthur's departure from the land over which he has ruled; when Bedivere returns with word that he has indeed thrown the sword into the water, Arthur asks to be carried down to the shore, where stands a barge full of wailing women attendant upon three queens, all dressed in black. Arthur asks Bedivere to place him in the barge, "And so he ded sofftely, and there resceyved hym three ladyes with grete mournyng. And so they sette hem downe, and in one of their lappis kyng Arthure layde hys hede. And than the quene sayde, 'A, my dere brothir! Why have ye taryed so longe frome me? Alas, thys wounde on youre hede hath caught over-much coulde!'" (1240.19–25). It is something of a shock to discover that the queen who speaks so tenderly to her "dere brothir" is none other than Morgan le Fay, she who had expressed nothing but hatred for her brother throughout the narrative, and who attempted on numerous occasions to destroy Arthur. Indeed, with her arrival at the king's last appearance in the text, the reader is reminded that his death is due in part to Morgan's theft and destruction of Excalibur's magic scabbard; had the scabbard been in Arthur's possession during the final battle, it would have protected him from his fatal wound.

While Malory's disclosure that this is Morgan le Fay may come as a surprise to his readers, it does not seem to surprise Arthur in the least. The king seems to willingly and knowingly seek comfort in the lap of the woman against whom he had once threatened to enact such revenge that "al chrystendom shal speke of hit." Indeed, it is Arthur who directs Bedivere to transport him to the water's edge, as if he knows and expects the barge to meet him there, come to take him away to the Isle of Avalon where his wounds may be healed. In her analysis of this scene, Geraldine Heng points out that: "The tones are the gentle, chiding ones of a protectrice and healer, not those of a mortal enemy, and in them may be discerned a suggestion of the final instability and impermanence of all constructed identity. An affinity between them is at once suggested: the bond perhaps of two actors finally away from the pageant, who need no longer play their temporarily assigned roles."[48] For indeed, the heternormative chivalric community has insisted on role-playing, providing in its idealized courtliness scripts for masculine and feminine behavior. Morgan, who has in so many ways offered a deliberate and stylized counterperformance to the script of feminine behavior, no longer plays her part. With the death of the king and the end of Camelot, those two courtly role-models of masculinity and femininity—Lancelot and Guenevere—end their chivalric gender performances as well.

Guenevere Among the Nuns: The Collapse of the Chivalric Enterprise

Arthur thus makes his last appearance in the *Morte d'Arthur* in the tender embrace of his sister and former enemy, Morgan le Fay, departing over the sea to seek healing for his wounds. Later, we learn that Arthur's corpse has been brought by a group of ladies to the Bishop of Canterbury, now a hermit, for interment, and that Bedivere, himself now also a hermit, has caused this story of Arthur's death to be recorded. Malory then tells us that

> whan quene Gwenyver undirstood that kynge Arthure was dede and all the noble knyghtes, sir Mordred and all the remanaunte, than she stale away with fyve ladyes with her, and so she wente to Amysbyry. And there she lete make herselff a nunne, and wered whyght clothys and blak, and grete penaunce she toke uppon her, as ever ded synfull woman in thys londe. And never creature coude make her myry, but ever she lyved in fastynge, prayers, and almes-dedis that all maner of people mervayled how vertuously she was chaunged. (1243.1–10)

While the tone of this passage suggests that the curtain has been rung down on the narrative of the *Morte d'Arthur*, this, however, is not the end of Malory's text. In what many critics have called the "anticlimactic" episodes, we learn the ultimate fates of Lancelot and Guenevere.[49] Although these final scenes may seem in some sense unnecessary or extraneous to the main matter of the *Morte d'Arthur*, they are in fact deeply significant in terms of understanding the masculine knightly chivalric enterprise that has driven the narrative to this point. As I have argued repeatedly above, the particular structure of the Arthurian chivalric community that locates a masculine homosocial elite as the center of power within a heteronormative social paradigm produces a continuous and strident performance of heterosexual masculine identities on the part of those knights as a necessary means of legitimizing the knightly subcommunity. The simplest means by which a knight may effect such a performance is to identify ladies—or a particular lady—as the object of devotion and the catalyst that spurs him on to perform deeds of valor.

Such is the case with Lancelot—the greatest of knights and role model for proper knightly behavior—and his chosen object of affection, Queen Guenevere. His devotion to Guenevere has so inspired Lancelot in his knightly endeavors that she may rightly be identified as the main force that has made him the paragon of knighthood. In turn, his prowess and reputation has enhanced the status of the community he represents. Those knights who choose Lancelot's side in the final conflict assert that this is the case, noting, "by the noble felyshyp of the Rounde Table was kynge Arthur upborne, and by their nobeles the kynge and all the realme was ever in quyet and reste. And a grete parte . . . was because of youre most nobeles, sir Launcelot" (1203.32–34, 1204.1–2). The source of Lancelot's "nobeles," as both he and many others have asserted throughout the *Morte d'Arthur*, has been his devotion to the feminine generally and to Guenevere in particular.

Thus, although by its title this section would seem to be about Guenevere, what quickly becomes clear is that maintaining Guenevere as the center of focus proves to be a constant struggle; the most visible and significant aspects of her character manifest themselves in terms of her effects on the other players in Malory's narrative.[50] In order to talk about Guenevere, one must of necessity spend a considerable amount of time talking about Lancelot and his actions and reactions for and to her. The impossibility of interrogating Guenevere without invoking Lancelot reveals how imbricated and interdependent courtly relationships operate as both the cause and effect of the project of chivalry in the *Morte d'Arthur*; the tensions produced by these relationships ultimately lead to the collapse of the chivalric enterprise. This is nowhere more clearly expressed than in Lancelot and Guenevere's last conversation, which takes place in the convent at Amesbury where Guenevere has taken up residence as a nun. As Lancelot prepares to take his leave of her, he asks, "I pray you, kysse me, and never no more," to which she responds, "Nay . . . that shal I never do, but absteyne you from such werkes" (1253.26–28).

When the homosocial project of chivalry has apparently collapsed with the death of Arthur, we find that in fact, this is not the case. As long as Guenevere is alive, it seems Lancelot will seek to serve her and to construct

a homosocial male community whose existence is facilitated and legitimized by his heterosexual desire for the queen. Sometime after advancing
to the position of abbess at Amesbury, Lancelot comes to visit Guenevere
there, and upon seeing him, the queen swoons. When she recovers, she
tells the assembled ladies that "Thorow thys same man and me hath all
thys warre be wrought, and the deth of the moste nobeleste knyghtes of
the worlde; for thorow oure love that we have loved togydir ys my moste
noble lorde slayne" (1252.7–11). Expressing her desire to do penance—
"for as synfull as ever I was, now ar seyntes in hevyn"—she orders
Lancelot to forsake her company, return to his own land, and take a wife.

Lancelot's response is that he will do no such thing; instead, he will
become a monk, just as she has become a nun: "therfore, lady, sythen ye
have taken you to perfeccion, I must nedys take me to perfection, of ryght"
(1253.17–19). He goes on to say in a line original to Malory that if she
were willing, he would gladly take Guenevere back to his own kingdom—
"yf I had founden you now so dysposed, I had caste me to have had you
into myn owne royame" (1253.20–22)—but as she refuses the possibility
of establishing another courtly society with Lancelot, Lancelot opts to follow her example and leave the courtly secular world for the spiritual.
Malorian critics have long noted that Lancelot's decision to enter into religious orders is influenced more by his past desire for—and service to—
Guenevere than any new-found longing to serve God; Karen Cherewatuk,
for example, refers to Lancelot's decision as "vocation by thwarted desire,
or at best, imitation."[51] What critics have not clearly articulated are the
implications Lancelot's entrance into—and subsequent career within—the
monastery has in terms of understanding the social model operating in
Malory's text, implications that become clear when Lancelot's career as a
religious is compared with Guenevere's.

Guenevere's entrance into the nunnery seems to have its motivation in
an honest desire to atone for what she perceives to be her past sinfulness.
Malory's account differs from that found in the *Mort Artu*, in which
Guenevere flees to the nunnery out of fear rather than contrition:[52] "En tel
maniere demora la reïne leanz avec les nonnains et s'i mist por la poor
qu'ele avoit del roi Artu et de Mordret" [Thus the queen stayed there
with the nuns, taking refuge because of her fear of both King Arthur and
Mordred].[53] The queen's speech to the other nuns upon Lancelot's arrival
clearly indicates that she holds herself and Lancelot responsible for the war
that has destroyed her husband and his kingdom, claiming that "I am sette
in such a plyght to gete my soule hele" (1252.12–13). Lancelot has had no

positive influence on her decision to forsake the secular world for the spiritual; if anything, her decision to become a nun is an attempt to compensate for, overcome, or distance herself from her former relationship with Lancelot. That it is a conversion prompted by an honest desire to do penance is further signified by her refusal of Lancelot's kiss. Although in creating this scene Malory has more or less faithfully followed the moment as he found it in the English *Stanzaic Morte Arthur* (itself based on the French *Mort Artu*)[54] the kiss takes on a resonance more significant than that to be found in Malory's sources due to additions and revisions Malory has made elsewhere in the closing pages of the *Morte d'Arthur*. Twice before in the "Most Piteous Tale of the Morte Arthur Saunz Gwerdon," Guenevere and Lancelot kiss at the moment of their parting, kisses that appear to be wholly Malory's own invention.

The first occurrence of the parting kiss occurs in Guenevere's chamber, when Lancelot promises to return and rescue her from the stake after he escapes from the knights who have entrapped them: "'for have ye no doute, whyle I am a man lyvyng I shall rescow you.' And than he kyste her, and ayther of hem gaff othir a rynge" (1168.34–35, 1169.1–2).[55] This is not a kiss of passion, but a pledge-kiss, and a sign of his devotion to her; it is this devotion that has made possible his reputation as the greatest of earthly knights. Regardless of whether or not they are engaged in any adulterous activity when they are surrounded (and Malory deliberately leaves this open to question), on the basis of their prior relationship it is Lancelot's duty to rescue her, or his reputation as the "flower of chivalry" will be tarnished. His kiss here represents his recognition of that obligation.

The second time he kisses Guenevere, it too is a kiss devoid of passion; rather, it is a demonstration of fealty and respect that affirms the heteronormativity which orders the chivalric community. Having saved Guenevere from execution at the stake, Lancelot ensconces her in Joyous Gard for her own protection, asserting constantly and vehemently that she is true to her lord, and asking Arthur to take her back. A reconciliation between Arthur and Guenevere is finally effected by the Bishop of Rochester, acting under order of the pope, and Lancelot delivers her to the king. In the hearing of the assembled court, Lancelot takes his leave of the woman who has been the catalyst behind his stellar knightly career, and with a kiss, pledges to come to her aid in the future, should she ever require service of him: "'Madame, now I must departe from you and thys noble felyshyp for ever. And sytthen hit ys so, I besech you to pray for me, and I shall pray for you. And telle ye me, and if ye be harde bestad by ony false tunges, but lyghtly, my good lady, sende me worde; and if ony knyghtes hondys undir the hevyn may delyver you by batayle, I shall delyer you.' And therewithal sir Launcelot kyssed the quene"(1202.11–17).[56] Lancelot's kiss at this moment is an affirmation of his relationship with Guenevere—not specifically as adulterous lovers, but more generally as knight and lady. As such, the kiss is an acknowledgment and affirmation of the foundational and organizational chivalric ideal of the devoted courtly relationship. It is a last desperate effort to rescue and maintain the threatened social order. Lancelot's kiss and pledge to Guenevere—a symbol of heterosexual desire, yet as an act, itself devoid of romantic passion—assert the relationship between knight and lady as the legitimizing force that has allowed the homosocial Round Table community to exist within the compulsory heteronormative social order of chivalry.

That the tension between homosocial bonding and heterosexual desire has ceased to have any functional meaning is demonstrated by Guenevere's refusal to kiss Lancelot when they part for the third and final time at the end of the *Morte d'Arthur*. She recognizes that the chivalric enterprise—and the homosocial subcommunity that has been its center—has failed. Guenevere has entered into her own homosocial community, one markedly different from the masculine Round Table society in the lack of manifest anxiety over the border between homosociality and homosexuality. The distinction of *this* homosocial community from the masculine homosocial order of the Round Table reveals the striking incongruity of anxiety over masculine and feminine gender identities. It is the pressing need to distinguish the homosocial from the homosexual that has driven much of the masculine chivalric activity of the narrative of the *Morte d'Arthur* forward; within the feminine homosocial world of the convent, there is no parallel manifestation of anxiety. When they meet for the last time at Amesbury, Lancelot and Guenevere's relationship has lost the significant meaning it had in helping to define knighthood and gender identity in the secular, chivalric world. The kiss, symbolic of knightly heterosexuality, no longer has any relevance, a fact that Guenevere realizes, but Lancelot, clearly, does not.

Inspired by Guenevere, just as he was in his secular life, Lancelot seeks out the Bishop of Canterbury for admittance into religious orders. Indeed, as Larry Benson has pointed out, "Lancelot enters the religious life not because he forsakes his earthly love but because he remains true to it."[57] In a moment that recalls the ceremony of knighthood, Lancelot kneels before the bishop, who "confers" his new status upon him by clothing him in a monk's habit, just as a new-made knight would be girt with a sword: "And than [Lancelot] knelyd doun on his knee and prayed the Bysshop to shryve hym and assoyle hym. . . . Than the Bysshop . . . put an habyte upon syr Launcelot. And there he servyd God day and nyght with prayers and fastynges" (1254.13–18). As Lancelot was the role model for knightly behavior in the Round Table community, so too does he play that part here— within half a year, Malory tells us, Sir Bedivere, Sir Bors, and seven more of Lancelot's fellows-in-arms become his fellows in Christ. Malory tells us that "whan they sawe syr Launcelot had taken hym to suche perfeccion they had no lust to departe but toke such an habyte as he had" (1254.39, 1255.1–2). In an often commented upon moment original to the *Morte d'Arthur,* Malory informs the reader that the new-made monks have forsaken the accoutrements of knightly life, specifically that "soo their horses wente where they wolde, for they toke no regarde of no worldly rychesses" (1255.8–9).

This new subcommunity of knights, however, maintains itself as distinct from the larger monastic community, and maintains also the principles by which the Round Table society was ordered. And as Benson points out, "[t]he result is not so much a true spiritual community so much as a recreation of the Arthurian fellowship."[58] Homosocial bonding balanced with heterosexual desire created and legitimized the knightly subcommunity, and the knightly monastic subcommunity organizes itself in the same terms. The heterosexualized knightly urge to serve one's lady (in this case, Lancelot's imitation of Guenevere) intersects with the homosocial desire to emulate and bond with one's fellows—here demonstrated by those knights who forsake the world *specifically* to follow the example of Sir Lancelot. And just as Lancelot surpassed his comrades in all things knightly within the homosocial subcommunity of the Round Table, he again exceeds his fellows within the monastic community by becoming a priest and setting the standard for penance. As members of the Round Table elite, they marveled at and were inspired by Lancelot's knightly deeds; as members of the monastic community, they marvel at and are inspired by his fasting and prayers: "they toke no force what payne they endured, for to see the nobleste knyght of the world take such abstynaunce that he waxed ful lene" (1255.11–13). This subcommunity within the monastic community refuses to forsake the model of homosocial bonding made licit by heterosexual desire, the organizational scheme by which Arthur's realm was both maintained and destroyed. Even though this social model has proved demonstrably unfeasible, they appear compelled to attempt to recreate it, seemingly unable to function and exist outside this social model, as Lancelot's reaction to Guenevere's death compellingly demonstrates.[59]

After six years as a monk and one as a priest, Lancelot has a vision telling him of Guenevere's impending death, and he and his companions set off for Amesbury. He arrives half an hour after the queen has passed away, and the nuns in attendance tell him that Guenevere had been aware of his approach and that for the last two days of her life, she had prayed, loudly and often, that she might never see Lancelot with her "worldly" eyes again. Guenevere's fervent prayer—and its affirmative answer—indicate that she understands clearly the destructive potential of the social model that the knights still follow, and that she has freed herself from the chivalric code which "is contradictory, demanding of Guenevere that she play the roles both of rewarder and reward."[60]

Lancelot buries her beside Arthur, and the devoted servant even in death, performs the funerary offices himself. When her coffin is lowered into the earth, Lancelot swoons, for which he is rebuked by a hermit. When he has recovered, Lancelot assures the holy man that his reaction was not a "rejoysing" of his former sin, but rather due to the realization that it is his own error and pride that were responsible for the downfall of Arthur's realm: "For whan I remembre of hir beaulté and of hir noblesse, that was bothe wyth hyr kyng and wyth hyr, so whan I sawe his corps and hir corps so lye togyders, truly myn herte wold not serve to susteyne my careful body" (1256.29–32). Although some scholars have argued for an interpretation of Lancelot's expression of sorrow at this moment and his subsequent mourning as a demonstration of his devotion to *both* Arthur and Guenevere[61] (and thus a response to the destruction of the social order and not simply the end of his relationship with the queen) the focus of his lament suggests that although a priest, Lancelot's sensibilities and values remain primarily secular. And while it is possible to take his speech as a response to the deaths of both his king and queen, it is the death of Guenevere, and Guenevere alone, that precipitates the final crisis for Lancelot.

Thus, if an examination of Lancelot's reaction to Guenevere's *life* among the nuns at Amesbury makes plain the significant position women occupy within the chivalric enterprise as facilitators of male homosocial bonding and chivalric social order, then Lancelot's behavior on the occasion of her *death* underscores the impossibility of sustaining the Arthurian social model without Guenevere's presence. Although Lancelot's decision to enter into religious life is a direct effect of his secular relationship with Guenevere, Malory's description of his behavior within the monastery seems at first to indicate that he truly has become a religious penitent, achieving the status of priest through his spiritual action, just as Guenevere becomes the abbess of Amesbury through her exemplary behavior in fasting, prayer, and good deeds. Malory relates that those knights who join Lancelot in the monastery are amazed at how he has changed in both appearance and temperament, just as people similarly marvel at the great change in Guenevere.

Yet, just as the homosocial Round Table subcommunity collapsed when the secular relationship between the greatest knight and the highest ranking lady of the land collapsed, so too does the new homosocial monastic subcommunity—also headed by Lancelot—fail when the relationship Lancelot has tenuously reestablished with Guenevere in spiritual terms ceases to exist. After her death, Lancelot is unable to fulfill his priestly duties:

> Thenne syr Launcelot never after ete but lytel mete, nor dranke, tyl he was ded, for than he seekened more and more and dryed and dwyned awaye … that he was waxen by a kybbet shorter than he was, that the peple coude not knowe hym. For evermore, day and nyght, he prayed, but som-tyme he slombred a broken slepe. Ever he was lyeng grovelyng on the tombe of kyng Arthur and quene Guenever, and there was no comforte that the Bysshop, nor syr Bors, nor none of his felowes coude make hym, it avaylled not. (1257.1–11)

Lancelot's dramatic reaction to Guenevere's death clearly indicates that he has hardly managed to put away the feelings of knightly devotion and attachment that he previously felt for Guenevere in the secular courtly world of Arthur's kingdom;[62] nor has he achieved the spiritual peace that the former queen, by contrast, has attained within the walls of the nunnery at Amesbury. Although he has been exemplary as a priest, inspiring his fellow knight-monks to perform acts of fasting and penance just as Guenevere has inspired him, his inability to fulfill his priestly duties as a direct result of Guenevere's death ultimately complicates the fact of his religious conversion. Indeed, Lancelot's behavior on the occasion of Guenevere's death seems to resemble medieval lovesickness more than grief, recalling Uther's condition when denied access to Igrayne rather than, for example, Arthur's sorrow for the dead Gawain.[63] Kay Harris has suggested that "by having Lancelot prostrate himself at the king's tomb rather than the altar of Christ, Malory subjects Lancelot to the law of the Round Table."[64] Yet, it is not so much that Malory subjects Lancelot to the law of the Round Table, but rather that Malory depicts Lancelot's inability to function outside the arena of the courtly and chivalric. The code meant to create a stable and ordered society has rendered its agents prisoners of the chivalric courtly ideal. Even after the death of the queen, Lancelot is unable to escape it and thus takes the only other option available to him.

When his relationship with Guenevere is finally and absolutely ended, Lancelot is unable to sustain himself and dies within six weeks of the queen. In his secular life as the prime exemplar of the Round Table, his devoted relationship to Guenevere provided the foundation upon which he constructed his knightly identity. When the chivalric enterprise fails and Guenevere finally extricates herself from the constraints placed upon her as a support of the Arthurian social order, Lancelot still manages to use her as the basis upon which he fashions his identity. Although Guenevere refuses to maintain any contact with him, in the abstract she still provides the inspiration for his deeds: for her, he excels as both knight and priest. With her death, Lancelot has indeed lost the very source of his identity as constructed within both the secular and spiritual realms.

Yet, like much in Malory, the events surrounding Lancelot's death are contradictory, suggesting that Lancelot's conversion is itself a more complex, nuanced act than might at first seem to be the case; it cannot be unequivocally judged as either success or failure. Although Lancelot has been unable to wholly forsake the secular, chivalric social order and is thus in some sense a failure in his new vocation of monk and priest, the sanctified aura surrounding his death ameliorates this perception. A month and a half after Guenevere's death, those knights who have followed Lancelot into the monastery are awakened in the night by the sound of the bishop, laughing in his sleep, and rouse him. The bishop's reaction recalls Lancelot's lament upon being awoken from his twenty-four-day coma in the quest for the grail: "'A, Jesu mercy!' sayd the Bysshop, 'why dyd ye awake me? I was never in al my lyf so mery and so wel at ease.' 'Wherfore?' sayd syr Bors. 'Truly,' sayd the Bysshop, 'here was syr Launcelot with me, with mo angellis than ever I sawe men in one day. And I sawe the angellys heve up syr Launcelot unto heven, and the yates of heven opened ayenst hym'" (1258.4–10). When the knights seek out Lancelot, they "founde hym starke dede; and he laye as he had smyled, and the swettest savour about hym that ever they felte" (1258.15–17).[65] Strikingly, although he dies a holy death, in a passage completely original to

Malory Lancelot is eulogized by Ector in *secular* terms. Although a lengthy passage, I here give it in its entirety, as it demonstrates more aptly than any paraphrase that I could offer that members of the knightly order are judged in terms of chivalric and courtly values, even when those values have been demonstrably critiqued in their ultimate failure as social ideals.

> "A, Launcelot!" he sayd, "thou were hede of al Crysten knyghtes! And now I dare say," sayd sir Ector, "thou sir Launcelot, there thou lyest, that thou were never matched of erthely knyghtes hande. And thou were the curtest knyght that ever bare shelde! And thou were the truest frende to thy lovar that ever bestrade hors, and thou were the trewest lover of a synful man that ever loved woman, and thou were the kyndest man that ever strake with swerde. And thou were the godelyest persone that ever cam emonge prees of knyghtes, and thou was the mekest man and the jentyllest that ever ete in halle emonge laydes, and thou were the sternest knyght to they mortal foo that ever put spere in the reeste." (1259.9–21)

Ector's eulogy beautifully distills the requirements for membership in the masculine homosocial world of the Round Table; the language with which he describes alternately Lancelot's behavior toward ladies and toward his fellow knights seems interestingly—perhaps even dangerously—interchangeable. A "trew frende" to his lover and a "curtes knyght" on the battlefield: the inextricability of Lancelot's identities as both valiant warrior and courteous gentleman is compellingly represented in Ector's assertion that "thou were the truest frende to thy lovar that ever bestrade hors," a statement that seamlessly links the concerns of the feminine with the activity of the battlefield. Ector's eulogy for his kinsman laments only the passing of the Round Table's greatest knight and the secular world in which he found glory, refusing to recognize any of the obvious flaws and contradictions that have brought Lancelot to this end. His praise of Lancelot as a paragon of chivalry seems straightforward, lacking any hint of irony.

Ector's inability to see that the values he lauds in Arthur's greatest knight are the same factors that contributed to the chivalric community's decline offers perhaps the strongest evidence yet that the destruction of the Arthurian society has been an inevitability from the opening pages of the book. Benson has suggested that "Malory's Lancelot remains essentially a chivalric knight, and he thus has a good end,"[66] and it seems quite clear that for Ector, at least, it is not possible to believe anything else. That the lessons of the *Morte d'Arthur* are so insistently ignored by the prime players in the narrative, and that the result of such stubborn narrowness of vision is seemingly not punished, emphasizes the complexity and ambiguity of Malory's text. Although Lancelot has failed to sustain and support the Arthurian chivalric community, he has paradoxically been a resounding success at adhering to the knightly ideals of that same community. It is the cruelest irony that the goals of communal order and knightly performance, thought to be inextricable at the beginning of the text, are in fact revealed to be mutually exclusive at the end.

These final scenes of the *Morte d'Arthur* underscore the absolute centrality of the twinned values of devotion and emulation to the organization and maintenance of the courtly chivalric community. As Lancelot cannot exist without Guenevere, so too the homosocial subcommunity of former knights cannot maintain its coherence within the larger monastic community without the Guenevere-inspired Lancelot as its central defining figure. Rather than remain with the other monks, Malory tells the reader that the former knights part company and separate one from another, each returning to his homeland: "al these knyghtes drewe them to theyr contreyes. . . . And there they al lyved in their cuntreyes as holy men" (1260.1–4). With Lancelot gone, these monk-knights can no longer live in a community, be it courtly or spiritual. The order of the Round Table is finally and irrevocably broken.

However, Malory defers the ultimate conclusion of his text one more time, offering his readers the possibility of an alternate ending on the final leaf of the manuscript:

> And somme Englysshe bookes maken mencyon that they wente never oute of Englond after the deth of syr Launcelot—but that was but favour of makers!—For as the Frensshe book maketh mencyon— and is auctorysed—that syr Bors, syr Ector, syr Blamour and syr Bleoberis wente into the Holy Lande, thereas Jesu Cryst was quycke and deed. And anone as they had stablysshed theyr londes, for, the book saith, so syr Launcelot commaunded them for to do or ever he passyd oute of thys world, there these foure knyghtes dyd many bataylles upon the myscreantes, or Turkes. And there they dyed upon a Good Fryday for Goddes sake. (1260.5–15)

Malory's treatment of this alternate ending is curious. Having just assured his readers that after Lancelot's death the remaining monk-knights depart for their home countries where they live out their lives as holy men, he quickly takes issue with those "Englysshe bookes" that assert instead that the remaining knights stayed in England as subjects of Constantine of Cornwall, Arthur's cousin and the new king of the realm. To support his position, he points to the "auctorysed" French text, which contradicts not only this "Englysshe" ending, but *also* refutes the conclusion in which the knights return singly to their homelands, the ending that Malory has, just a few lines before, assured us is correct. While the contention of some "Frensshe" books that the monk-knights embarked on a second career fighting Turks in the Holy Land certainly provides a moving and solemn conclusion to the *Morte d'Arthur,* Malory's only incidental mention of it suggests his recognition that it does not quite "fit" the story he has just finished telling.

Although he dies in an aura of sanctity, Malory's Lancelot is tellingly eulogized and remembered as the greatest of secular, chivalric heroes; as his failures in the Grail Quest remind us, earthly and spiritual chivalry are incompatible. Malory's *Morte d'Arthur* is a text that explores the limits of *secular* chivalry, that which has at its core the gendered interactions of knight and lady. Glorious as the alternative-ending exploits of the monks in the Holy Land may be, the world of the court plays no real role in producing this finale. Malory, ultimately, is testing how a code of chivalry may function when deployed in the world of the courtly romance, not the realm of the spiritual treatise. Even though this alternative ending does not "fit," however, it seems as if Malory cannot bear to leave it unsaid; what seems to be his longing for a golden age of chivalry, his desire to characterize the order of knighthood as the solution to so many social problems, shines through more strongly here than at any other moment in the text.

An examination of the *Morte d'Arthur* in the terms of these concluding scenes I have here discussed has significant implications for understanding how the chivalric community is constructed—and why the chivalric enterprise fails. For most of Malory's text, it seems that women are looked to as a means of legitimizing an already existing all-male community; in other words, the desire for homosocial bonding is arguably anterior to, and necessitates, a display of heterosexual masculinity. By contrast, in the final scenes of the *Morte d'Arthur,* Guenevere as the object of masculine heterosexual desire produces another homosocial society. Homosociality is no longer the impetus behind the social and visible formation of heterosexual relationships, but rather, Lancelot's performance of heterosexuality through his devotion to Guenevere causes the re-creation of the homosocial subcommunity of knights within the larger homosocial monastic community. That this new Round Table elite still models itself in terms of the secular, courtly social ideal becomes clear when the knights choose to leave for their own homes after Lancelot's death, rather than stay within the monastery. Monastic homosociality does not employ heterosexual desire as a legitimizing force in the same way that the knightly homosocial community does, and the Round Table knights are unable to function within any other paradigm.

An analysis of the figure of Guenevere in her role as penitent abbess among the nuns of Amesbury emphatically demonstrates the impossibility of sustaining the Arthurian chivalric enterprise and the social order that supports it. Within the homosocial feminine community of the nunnery, the queen is free from the constrained position that the chivalric society needs her—and all ladies—to occupy as a means of legitimizing itself. By contrast, masculine identity within this community—supposedly defined as free and independent—is revealed, in its utter and absolute dependence upon a feminine presence to be anything but free and independent. Lancelot and his fellow knights are enslaved to the social model they have fabricated. Unable to operate within any other idiom than that of homosocial bonding made licit by heterosexual performance, the Arthurian chivalric project has essentially collapsed under its own weight.

Yet, although the *Morte d'Arthur* ends as many tragedies do, with bodies strewn about the stage, its collapse is not wholly tragic; in the final chapter of Malory's massive Arthurian narrative—those episodes designated "anticlimatic" and "extraneous" by some—there is redemption for those characters who have in part been responsible for the community's downfall. That Lancelot and Guenevere leave the earthly realm and ascend into heaven shifts the tone of the *Morte d'Arthur*'s conclusion from despair to hope, just as Malory himself, in his explicit to the "hoole book" seems to seek such a transformation:

I PRAYE YOU ALL JENTYLMEN AND JENTYLWYMMEN THAT REDETH THIS BOOK OF ARTHUR AND HIS KNYGHTES FROM THE BEGYNNING TO THE ENDYNGE, PRAYE FOR ME WHYLE I AM ON LYVE THAT GOD SENDE ME GOOD DELYVERAUNCE. AND WHAN I AM DEED, I PRAYE YOU ALL PRAYE FOR MY SOULE. FOR THIS BOOK WAS ENDED THE NINTH YERE OF THE REYNE OF KING EDWARD THE FOURTH, BY SYR THOMAS MALEORE, KNYGHT, AS JESU HELPE HYM FOR HYS GRETE MYGHT, AS HE IS THE SERVAUNT OF JESU BOTHE DAY AND NYGHT. (1260.20–29)

At the end of his massive work, Sir Thomas Malory and his characters have both seemingly arrived at a complex and complicated understanding of chivalry. It is an understanding in which the idealized values that supposedly produce and support chivalry are in fact revealed as themselves *products* of the knightly enterprise. In Malory's text, violence and heteronormative gender identity construction concurrently function as both strengths and weaknesses of the courtly social order. The *Morte d'Arthur* offers a compelling depiction of the chivalric community, a rendition of the Arthurian legend in which it is possible to celebrate the values of chivalry while simultaneously mourning their self-destructiveness. What is most important—both for Malory and for the courtly chivalric community of his text—is that redemption is seemingly possible in the end. Lancelot goes to heaven not because he recognizes the error of his ways and repents, but because he does his "uttirmost" to adhere to the ideals of the chivalric community. That the ideals themselves are self-destructive, producing chaos instead of order, is less important than the fact that Lancelot—enthusiastically, impressively, successfully—performs them. At the end of his massive work, Malory seems to recognize this contradiction, but in his nostalgia and mourning for an idealized chivalric past, he simultaneously registers a desire that things might be otherwise. In its conflicted nature, it is a sentiment singularly appropriate for a knight prisoner, writing of King Arthur and his knights, in the last half of the fifteenth century.

Notes

Introduction

1. See, for example, Cox, *Gender and Language in Chaucer;* Crane, *Gender and Romance in the Canterbury Tales;* Dinshaw, *Chaucer's Sexual Poetics;* Hansen, *Chaucer and the Fictions of Gender;* Sturges, *Chaucer's Pardoner and Gender Theory.*

2. McCarthy, "Malory and His Sources," 91.

3. Regarding gender in Malory see Lynch, "Gesture and Gender in Malory's *Le Morte Darthur.*" The quotation is from Lynch, *Malory's Book of Arms,* xix.

4. LaFarge, "Hand of the Huntress," 264.

5. While it is not possible to give an exhaustive list of the important articles and chapters on gender and Malory that have appeared in the last few years, in addition to works already cited above, some of the most significant contributions to the field include: Batt, "Malory and Rape"; Edwards, "Place of Women in the *Morte Darthur*"; Finke and Shichtman, "No Pain, No Gain"; Fries, "Female Heroes, Heroines and Counter-Heroes"; and Heng, "Enchanted Ground" and "A Map of Her Desire."

6. Batt's book *Malory's Morte Darthur: Remaking Arthurian Tradition* is a long-awaited and welcome addition to the field; I regret that its very recent publication made it impossible for me to engage it in this study.

7. The French Lancelot-Grail Cycle (also known as the Vulgate, the Prose *Lancelot,* or the Pseudo-Map Cycle), while certainly much longer and more detailed in its elaboration of the Arthurian legend than Malory's text, does not seem to have been the work of a single author. While twelfth-century French court figure Walter Map is named as author of the *Lancelot, Queste,* and *Mort* sections of the cycle, it seems clear that he in fact died some years before the composition of the first of the romances. Similarly, while one Robert de Boron is identified as the author of the *Estoire del Saint Graal* and the *Merlin* romances, his authorship is also considered suspect. It seems most likely that the *Lancelot-Grail* was the work of several different authors. Hence, the common practice of referring to the various "branches" of

the Vulgate and Post-Vulgate. See Burns, introduction to *Lancelot-Grail*, ed. Lacy, 1:xv–xxxiii.

8. While there is evidence that some of the sections of the *Morte d'Arthur* were composed "out of sequence," the presentation of the tales seems to suggest an overarching plan of narrative coherence. McCarthy notes that "subconsciously at least [Malory] would almost seem to have had something of a *vue d'ensemble*" ("Sequence of Malory's Tales," 123). For a discussion of the debate as to whether or not Vinaver's Tale II was the first composed by Malory, see E. D. Kennedy, "Malory and His English Sources."

9. See Pickford, *L'Évolution du roman arthurien.*

10. All citations are to Vinaver, ed., *Works of Sir Thomas Malory,* revised by Field. Field has done the most extensive and exhaustive work on Malory's sources. His most important essays on the topic, revised and updated, have recently been published as *Malory: Texts and Sources.*

11. Although see Field's discussion of the "Gareth" and its possible sources in "Source of Malory's 'Tale of Gareth'"; see *Malory: Texts and Sources,* 246–60.

12. Vinaver, ed., *Works of Malory,* vol. 3, 1534.

13. McCarthy, "Malory and His Sources," 78.

14. McCarthy and others have pointed out that the "positive" Morgan comes from a different source—the Vulgate Cycle—than does the evil, villainous Morgan, who comes from the Post-Vulgate *Suite du Merlin.* Notes McCarthy: "Malory has failed to reconcile the contradiction inherent in his sources, but would the 'deep suggestiveness' not have disappeared if he had?" ("Malory and His Sources," 86). Lynch similarly notes that "in adapting his sources, Malory effectively permitted the co-existence of many narrative effects which are problematical but fascinating when taken together" (*Malory's Book of Arms,* xix).

15. Field has done the best work in summing up previous attempts to read the *Morte d'Arthur* as a sort of fifteenth-century *roman à clef* and pointing to moments that might be said to "resonate" with real historical events; see "Fifteenth-Century History in Malory's *Morte Darthur*" (*Malory: Texts and Sources,* 47–71).

16. The best recent studies that seek to situate Malory and his work in a fifteenth-century sociohistorical context include: Kim, *Knight Without the Sword;* Lynch, *Malory's Book of Arms;* Hanks, ed., *Social and Literary Contexts of Malory's Morte Darthur.*

17. There are a number of excellent studies on the "historical" Malory. The definitive work has been done by Field, *Life and Times of Sir Thomas Malory.* See also Riddy, *Sir Thomas Malory.*

18. While three Thomas Malorys have been identified as possible authors of the *Morte d'Arthur,* Thomas Malory of Newbold Revel is the most likely candidate. For the most important contributions to the century-old debate over the authorship question, see the bibliography to Field's article, "Malory Life Records."

19. Although for convenience usually described as a conflict between the royal houses of York and Lancaster, modern historians seem to agree that the political

turmoil during the Wars of the Roses was due to opposition between three or four groups on a national level, and on a more local level, the conflict was strongly marked by family interests. See, among others: Bellamy, *Bastard Feudalism and the Law;* Kaeuper, *War, Justice and Public Order;* Lander, *Conflict and Stability in Fifteenth Century England* and *Wars of the Roses;* Payling, *Political Society in Lancastrian England;* M. Vale, *War and Chivalry.*

20. For more on the medieval English economy, see Bolton, *Medieval English Economy 1150–1500;* Britnell, *Commercialisation of English Society;* Day, *Medieval Market Economy.*

21. I am referring here to the medieval social model that identified three orders, or estates. In the words of Keen, "it was traditional wisdom that society was composed of three orders, functionarily defined in their relation to one another: the clergy whose business was with prayer and spiritual well-being; the warriors who defended the land and people with their arms; and the laborers whose toil supported the other two 'orders' or estates" (*English Society in the Later Middle Ages,* 1). Although by the later Middle Ages the three estates model was no longer an intact, functioning social system, the ideal of a tripartite social order maintained its popularity and appeal. The seminal work on this question of medieval social order is Duby, *Three Orders.*

22. For more on the Paston family, see Richmond's, *Paston Family in the Fifteenth Century,* vols. 1 and 2, and *Paston Family in the Fifteenth Century: Endings.*

23. Riddy, *Sir Thomas Malory,* 82.

24. Barber notes that knighthood was meant to function on two levels: "The first was practical and economic, the payment of a warrior by his lord, and worked at a political level. The second was idealistic, the chivalric aspect of the institution. The secular ideal of a knight as brave, generous, and courteous . . . is what we might call the chivalric aspect of knighthood" ("Chivalry and the *Morte Darthur,*" 23).

25. McFarlane has compellingly demonstrated that knights occupied a particular social stratum—distinct from the nobles yet above the bourgeoisie and commons—and thus had a particular experience of this period that differed from that of the general aristocracy. See *Nobility of Later Medieval England.*

26. For more on the violent nature of late medieval English aristocratic society and private war, see, among others, Keen, *English Society,* esp. chap. 8, "Aristocratic Violence"; Kaeuper, *War, Justice and Public Order,* esp. chap. 3, sec. 3, "Private War."

27. Kaeuper, *War, Justice and Public Order,* 185. James argues that the concept of honor that undergirded constructions of noble identity and definition frequently led to violence as a means of defending that honor (*English Politics and the Concept of Honor*); on this topic see also Knight, *Arthurian Literature and Society.*

28. Henry V succeeded Henry IV in 1413 and died just nine years later, leaving his infant son Henry VI to succeed him. In 1453, Henry VI lost his sanity for the first time during his reign, causing York to be named protector of the realm; his protectorate was revoked and then reestablished in 1455, then subsequently revoked again in 1456. This situation eventually ended in warfare, and Henry VI fled to Scotland in

1461 after Edward of York took London; Edward was proclaimed king. Henry VI was briefly restored in 1470, but was ousted by Edward IV the following year, ending his days in the Tower of London. Edward V succeeded to the throne in 1483, but was promptly imprisoned—along with his brother Richard—in the Tower by his uncle Richard of Gloucester, who claimed the throne for himself as Richard III. Two years later, Henry Tudor defeated Richard III at the battle of Bosworth and ascended to the throne. As Henry VII, the king was threatened by the pretender Warbeck during his reign.

29. McFarlane has noted that knights in England at this time "turned their coats as often and with the same chequered success as their betters. Since many of them were wise or greedy enough to have more coats than one to turn, they may well have been more dexterous than the lords at changing them to suit the demands of survival" (234); see "Wars of the Roses," in *England in the Fifteenth Century,* 231–68.

30. Pochoda, *Arthurian Propaganda,* 26.

31. Field has outlined the debate over the two versions in "Caxton's Roman War"; see *Malory: Texts and Sources,* 126–61.

32. McCarthy, "Malory and His Sources," 75.

33. The *Alliterative Morte Arthure* exists today in a single manuscript—the Thornton manuscript—but it seems clear that the source Malory used is slightly different from the unique surviving copy. The Thornton MS dates to about 1440, but there is ample evidence to suggest that the poem itself was composed somewhat earlier. L. D. Benson has identified allusions to the deposition of Richard II in 1399 in his analysis of the poem; see "Date of the *Alliterative Morte Arthure.*" Field offers a discussion of Malory's story of Arthur's continental campaign and a stemma suggesting the descent of Malory's text and Thornton from a mutual origin in "Empire of Lucius Iberius"; see *Malory: Texts and Sources,* 162–86. For the relationship of the Winchester continental campaign to Caxton's version, see Field, "Caxton's Roman War."

34. Lewis, "English Prose *Morte,*" 26.

35. McCarthy, "Malory and the Alliterative Tradition," 65. Elsewhere, McCarthy has noted that "The Roman War episode is so obviously unlike the rest of the *Morte Darthur* that it is usually dismissed over-hastily, and I believe that the full depth of the poem's influence (on Tale II and on the 'hoole book') has been underestimated" ("Malory and His Sources," 84).

36. For an argument supporting the later date, see N. Wright, ed., *Historia Regum Brittanie of Geoffrey of Monmouth I: Bern, Burgerbibliothek, MS. 568,* 1:xvi. For more in general on Geoffrey of Monmouth, including a summation of the debate over the date of the text, see *Arthuriana* 8.4 (1998), "Special Issue on Theoretical Approaches to Geoffrey of Monmouth," guest ed. Tolhurst.

37. Geoffrey of Monmouth's *Historia Regum Brittaniae* has been the subject of extensive debate among scholars, as it is a text with seemingly multiple and often contradictory goals; these would seem to include the affirmation of pre-Saxon Celtic dominance in Britain, the flattering of the Norman conquerors, and a desire to ob-

tain prestigious patronage for its author. For a concise account of Geoffrey's apparent motives, see Ashe's discussion of the *Historia* in *New Arthurian Encyclopedia*, ed. Lacy. See also Flint, "The *Historia Regum Brittaniae* of Geoffrey of Monmouth"; Moorman, "Literature of Defeat and of Conquest." The competing theories concerning Geoffrey's motives are also succinctly mapped out in Martin, "Hoel-Hearted Loyalty." Wace's *Roman de Brut* is more clearly meant to appeal to and flatter the Norman inheritors of the English throne, while Laȝamon's translation of Wace (the first account of Arthur's reign in English) has often been understood as a negative reaction to the Norman presence, but like Geoffrey's text, seems rife with ambivalences and contradictions. Schmolke-Hasselmann goes so far as to suggest that Wace deliberately attempted to align Henry II with the figure of Arthur; see "Round Table." Le Saux points out that Laȝamon's text is often interpreted as "glorifying the Celtic past of Britain to the detriment of Laȝamon's own Anglo-Saxon forebears" (*Text and Tradition of Laȝamon's Brut*, viii). Scholars such as Lee Patterson have noted that while details of the Roman War in the *Alliterative Morte Arthure* are such that "Arthur's campaign can be followed on both map and calendar" (*Negotiating the Past*, 212), the poem simultaneously locates itself in a timeless Arthurian past. All of these texts seem intent on deliberately affirming, confronting, or—at the very least—engaging with the claims of dynasty and monarchy, both in the terms of a contemporary sociohistorical context, and in a fictionalized account of the distant past.

38. Geoffrey's text deliberately identifies itself as a chronicle, and Wace and Laȝamon, while both incorporating and expanding the romantic elements in the text, similarly should be understood as operating primarily within the chronicle tradition. The *Alliterative Morte Arthure* has been notoriously difficult to classify, as Göller has pointed out, noting that "If it could be called a romance, it is one with a very peculiar twist to it. The [*Alliterative Morte Arthure*] has outgrown its genre historically. While still clinging to its traditional framework, stock characters and themes, it has become its own opposite" ("Reality versus Romance," 15). Patterson has famously called attention to the way in which the *Alliterative Morte Arthure* "recognizes that there are two streams of Arthurian writing, 'romaunce' . . . and 'croncycle' . . . but located itself at the source of both by designating them as later developments and calling itself a history" (*Negotiating the Past*, 213).

39. Sklar has argued that "What we have in the *Morte Darthur* is the stuff of romance . . . embedded in a matrix that mutates from history to religious vision to tragedy, forcing a continual readjustment of generic expectation" ("Undoing of Romance in Malory's *Morte Darthur*," 311). See also Morse's argument on Malory's genres, in which she contends that Malory may have "turned romance motifs to historical significance. But it would be equally plausible to reverse the terms and say that he turned historical significance to romance motifs" ("Back to the Future," 113). Barber has put it most succinctly, stating that: "*Le Morte Darthur* is, first and foremost, a chivalric romance" ("Chivalry," 19). McCarthy accurately points out that while "it is important to see how Malory has changed the temper of his romance

material . . . a change of temper does not imply a change of genre" ("*Le Morte Darthur* and Romance," 174).

40. In some sense, the *Morte d'Arthur's* status as a romance that incorporates some elements of history, tragedy, and epic while maintaining a primary romance "mode" marks it as a true descendent of Geoffrey's text. Although the *Historia* seems to understand itself as belonging to the tradition of history and chronicle, it undoubtedly "sets the stage" for vernacular versions of his text that are arguably members of the genre of medieval romance in its infancy. It is Geoffrey's text that first links the idea of knightly prowess to the service of ladies, stating that in Arthur's kingdom, "[women] scorned to give their love to any man who had not proved himself three times in battle. In this way the womenfolk became more chaste and more virtuous and for their love the knights were ever more daring" (*History of the Kings of Britain*, 229). The works of Wace and Laȝamon, while incorporating additional elements of romance, maintain an organization that is primarily that of chronicle. The *Alliterative Morte Arthure* similarly incorporates romantic elements, but they are so at odds with the overall tenor of the poem as to create a jarring effect. See Patterson, *Negotiating the Past*, 224.

41. For more on this, see E. D. Kennedy, "Malory's Use of Hardyng's *Chronicle*." See also L. D. Benson's discussion of Malory's Roman War and his use of Hardyng in *Malory's Morte Darthur*, esp. 39–64.

42. See Riddy, "Contextualizing the *Morte Darthur*"; see also Ingham, *Sovereign Fantasies*, esp. chap. 7, "'Necessary' Losses."

43. Gravdal, *Ravishing Maidens*, 43. Although I have been arguing for the status of the *Historia Regum Brittaniae*, the *Roman de Brut*, the *Brut*, and the *Alliterative Morte Arthure*, as generically "not romance," this episode can itself be fruitfully interrogated as a romance "moment" within a chronicle text using Gravdal's discussion of rape in medieval romance.

44. Finke and Shichtman, "Mont St. Michel Giant," 68. In her recent study *History on the Edge*, Michelle R. Warren similarly reads the rape scene (in Geoffrey, Wace, and Laȝamon) in terms of dynastic and territorial concerns: "The danger of colonial sexual compromise invades Brittany during Arthur's reign when a giant abducts the duke's niece. . . . The giant's sexual desire for the woman represents the menace of heterosexual rape to genealogical integrity, and thus to expansionist settlement" (45).

45. Cohen, *Of Giants*, xii.

46. Ibid., 84.

47. Finke and Shichtman, "Mont St. Michel Giant," 68.

48. Cohen, *Of Giants*, 69.

49. Žižek, *Sublime Object of Ideology*, 87.

50. N. Wright, ed., *Historia Regum Brittaniae of Geoffrey of Monmouth*, 117–18. The translation is from Geoffrey of Monmouth, *History of the Kings of Britain*, trans. Thorpe, 238–39.

51. All quotations from Wace are taken from Arnold, ed., *Le Roman de Brut de*

Wace. All translations from Wace are my own, although I have consulted Mason, *Wace and Layamon*.

52. The quotation from Laȝamon is taken from *Brut*, ed. Brook and Leslie, 676. Translations of Laȝamon are from Allen, trans., *Lawman: Brut*.

53. All citations to the *Alliterative Morte Arthure* are from Krishna's edition.

54. *History of the Kings of Britain*, trans. Thorpe, 237–38.

55. Bartlett has recently pointed out that in the *Alliterative Morte Arthure* "the threat to the Arthurian patriarchal code is doubly underscored by the Duchess's blood relationship to Arthur (she is both a relative and a subject) and by the Giant's slaughter of all of the male children in the region, which threatens the stability of the community's patrilineal social organization" ("Cracking the Penile Code," 63).

56. Similarly, Malory enhances the giant's general danger to the social order by slightly altering the duchess's relationship to Arthur. In Geoffrey and Wace, she is the niece of Arthur's kinsman Hoel; in Laȝamon she is Hoel's daughter. In the *Alliterative Morte Arthure*, the duchess is identified as "thy wyfes cosyn" (864), but in Malory she is significantly described as "thy cousyns wyff, sir Howell the Hende, a man that we calle nyghe of thy bloode" (199.1–2). She, like Guenevere, is a wife who helps to define her husband's heteronormative masculine identity through her marriage to him.

57. Dichmann was one of the first scholars to argue persuasively that Malory's additions, revisions, and alterations to his source text, the *Alliterative Morte Arthure*, demonstrate that Malory had a clear idea as to the overall "plan" for the *Morte d'Arthur* and the place of the Roman War within the movement of the text; see "'Tale of King Arthur and the Emperor Lucius': The Rise of Lancelot."

58. As Edwards has noted: "The queen and the table are constantly linked. . . . Arthur has his patrimony and his bride at the same time. . . . The institution of a chivalric and non-hierarchical social order among men . . . is curiously dependent upon marriage" ("Place of Women," 44).

59. Shichtman and Finke make a similar argument in "No Pain, No Gain."

60. Batt, "Malory and Rape," 85–86.

61. As Cohen notes, "The ogre of Mont Saint Michel . . . [is] grossly male, embodying in gigantic form everything masculinity cannot be in order to delimit the constricted space of heroic manhood" (*Of Giants*, 50).

62. Field has suggested that this moment "may have been prompted by events leading up to the accession of the first Yorkist king. . . . Although the Yorkist leaders needed no threats to make them proceed with electing King Edward, the unusual part the commons played in that process might have caused Malory to introduce them into the election of King Arthur" ("Fifteenth-Century History," 54).

63. See Vinaver, ed., *Works of Malory*, 1:xxix–xl. Brewer offered the earliest critique of Vinaver's assertion that Malory had in fact composed eight separate romances in his article "'the hoole book.'" See also Clough, "Malory's *Morte Darthur*: The 'Hoole Book.'" For a more recent discussion of the issues and positions in the debate over the *Morte d'Arthur*'s thematic unity, see Meale, "'The Hoole Book':

Editing and the Creation of Meaning in Malory's Text." The most recent work on the debate over form of the *Morte d'Arthur* has been collected in Wheeler, Kindrick, and Salda, eds., *Malory Debate: Essays on the Texts of Le Morte Darthur*.

64. I am thinking particularly of Malory's revision of the French Prose *Lancelot*—his primary source for what Vinaver calls Tale III, "A Noble Tale of Sir Launcelot du Lake"—in order to deliberately suppress any clear evidence of an adulterous affair between Lancelot and Guenevere. Rather than include the episode of the "Knight of the Cart" in this early tale (as is the case in the source), Malory moves this episode and its scene of adultery between Lancelot and Guenevere to the end of the *Morte d'Arthur*, when the social order has already begun to seriously decay.

65. For more on the links between sections of the *Morte d'Arthur*, see Evans, "*Ordinatio* and Narrative Links."

66. Lumiansky, ed., *Malory's Originality*. It is curious that even though Lumiansky and the other contributors to this now-classic study claim to reject Vinaver's organizational scheme for the *Morte d'Arthur*, the essays in this volume are eight, each an analysis of one of Vinaver's designated Tales.

67. See Ker, ed., *Winchester Malory: A Facsimile*.

68. Knight argues that Malory's vision for his text changed from episodic to more unified as he wrote; see *Structure of Sir Thomas Malory's Morte d'Arthur*. He addresses this same issue later in *Arthurian Literature and Society*, 105.

Chapter 1. Gender and the Chivalric Community: The Rise of Arthur's Kingdom

Portions of this chapter have been published, in substantially different form, as "Gender and the Chivalric Community: The Pentecostal Oath in Malory's 'Tale of King Arthur,'" *Bibliographical Bulletin of the International Arthurian Society* 51 (1999): 293–312, and "Malory's Morgause," in *On Arthurian Women: Essays in Honor of Maureen Fries*, ed. Wheeler and Tolhurst (Dallas: Scriptorium Press, 2001), 149–60. Both reprinted by kind permission of the publishers.

1. While it is the section of the Post-Vulgate referred to as the *Suite du Merlin* from which Malory drew most of what Vinaver has described as the "Tale of King Arthur," most medieval MSS of the *Suite* also include the Vulgate *Merlin*, and it seems likely that Malory would have experienced the two linked texts as one whole continuous narrative; the distinction between the *Merlin* proper and the *Suite* is primarily a modern one. See Lacy, gen. ed., *Lancelot-Grail*, 4:xi, 4:163–66.

2. See T. L. Wright, "'Tale of King Arthur,'" 15–16.

3. Ibid., 37–40.

4. The *Suite du Merlin* is known primarily in two manuscript versions. The most well known is that referred to as the Huth *Merlin* (British Museum Add. 38117), published as *Merlin, roman en prose du XIIIe siècle*, ed. Paris and Ulrich. The discovery of another MS of the *Suite*—referred to as the Cambridge MS—in 1947 helped to fill in several lacunae in the Huth *Merlin* (British Museum Add. 7071, fols. 159–342). A portion of the Cambridge MS has been edited by Smith as *Les Enchante-*

menz de Bretaigne. The new standard English edition of the *Suite* is in the 5–volume *Lancelot-Grail,* ed. Lacy, vols. 4 and 5.

5. Vinaver, ed., *Works of Malory,* vol.3, 1330.

6. See, among others, Barber, "Chivalry"; Knight, *Arthurian Literature and Society,* esp. chap. 4, "'A grete angur and unhappe': Sir Thomas Malory's *Arthuriad*"; and Riddy, *Sir Thomas Malory.*

7. My thanks to the anonymous reader at *Arthuriana* who suggested this descriptor.

8. Lynch, *Malory's Book of Arms,* xvi.

9. Edwards, *Genesis of Narrative in Malory's Morte Darthur,* 72.

10. For example, Lancelot's defense of Guenevere from Meleagant's charge of adultery in the "Knight of the Cart" is a carefully worded technicality; Aggravain and Mordred's attempt to catch Lancelot and Guenevere together through subterfuge is cast as a desire to avenge the honor of their uncle, Arthur, although the king himself wishes nothing to do with such a plot, even if the charges are true.

11. T. L. Wright, "'Tale of King Arthur,'" 62.

12. See my discussion of this scene in chapter 5.

13. Lancelot later makes a similar decision—to help the weaker party—while in pursuit of the Holy Grail for "incresyng of hys shevalry" (931.25) and discovers he has made the wrong choice. See my discussion of this moment in chapter 4.

14. Field, *Romance and Chronicle,* 135.

15. Lambert has gone even farther than Field, suggesting that not only do all knights speak the same, but that the voices of the characters and *the narrator* are similarly indistinguishable. Lambert describes this as a "collective" effect, which creates a "singleness of vision" in the *Morte d'Arthur.* See *Malory: Style and Vision in Le Morte Darthur,* 122.

16. As Lynch notes, "The frequency of disguise and incognito in tournaments and knight errantry always permits new combats, even between established Round Table knights; though they have sworn to avoid fighting each other, the text can avail itself of a handy exception: 'but yf hit were that ony knught at his owne rekeyste wolde fyght disgysed and unknowyn'" (377.17–18); see *Malory's Book of Arms,* 86.

17. Pochoda, *Arthurian Propaganda,* 84.

18. My position here is indebted to Heng's reading of Malory (and Arthurian romance in general), in which she posits that "because the female is read as adjunctive (though necessary), a specifically feminine point of view in the work is never fully recovered" and then seeks to discover for the reader a "subtext of feminine presences" operating within the text ("Enchanted Ground," 97, 108).

19. Interestingly, Caxton's printed version of Malory's text omits the "never to enforce" subclause; see Spisak, ed., *Caxton's Malory.* B. Kennedy has suggested that Caxton removed the rape clause "perhaps because he objected to the implication that Round Table knights could be capable of such ungentle behavior" (*Knighthood in the Morte Darthur,* 39).

20. Gravdal, *Ravishing Maidens,* 43.

21. See Foucault's first volume of *History of Sexuality,* esp. the final chapter, "Right of Death and Power over Life."

22. Butler, *Gender Trouble,* 135.

23. Edwards, "Place of Women," 38.

24. Finke and Shichtman, "No Pain, No Gain," 119.

25. Butler, *Gender Trouble,* 25, 140.

26. The phrase is borrowed from de Lauretis: "The construction of gender is both the product and the process of its representation" (*Technologies of Gender,* 5).

27. B. Kennedy has identified the triple-quests in the "Tale of King Arthur" as manifesting a three-tiered "typology of knighthood," a display of the varying degrees of "moral worth" of each knight. My purpose here is not to analyze "which knight is better," but rather to argue that a demonstration of knightly prowess is impossible without the presence of the subjugated feminine. See *Knighthood,* esp. chap. 2: "A Typology of Knighthood."

28. Heng, "Map of Her Desire," 250.

29. Edwards notes that the interesting thing about the "wedding quests" is that they have "no point in either Malory or his source but to establish questing as the project of chivalry" (*Genesis of Narrative,* 2).

30. Irigaray, *This Sex Which Is Not One,* 76.

31. T. L. Wright, "'Tale of King Arthur,'" 21.

32. Pochoda similarly notes of the Torre-Pellinor-Gawain adventure that "the admonitions in the code at the end of the story have their sources in the adventures of these knights. As extensions of the king's justice, the limbs of the political body of which Arthur is the head" (*Arthurian Propaganda,* 82–83). Archibald also notes this link between the wedding triple-quest and the oath that immediately follows; see "Beginnings," 141ff.

33. Echoing Heng's discussion of gender and romance in Arthurian literature, Edwards notes that the "women who roam the landscape are not usually the object of the quest, but the means to the achievement of it" ("Place of Women," 38).

34. T. L. Wright, "'Tale of King Arthur,'" 21.

35. The passage in French from *Merlin* is taken from Sommer, ed., *Vulgate Version of the Arthurian Romances,* 2:58. The English translation is from Lacy, gen. ed., *Lancelot-Grail,* 1:199.

36. Dollimore, *Sexual Dissidence,* 33.

37. Sedgwick, *Between Men,* 21.

38. This "mirroring" of Other/Same, Good/Evil, is one of the distinguishing features of romance, as Jameson has noted: "Romance in its original strong form may then be understood as an imaginary 'solution' to this real contradiction, a symbolic answer to the perplexing question of how my enemy can be thought of as being *evil* (that is, other than myself and marked by some absolute difference), when what is responsible for his being so characterized is quite simply the *identity* of his own conduct with mine, the which—points of honor, challenges, tests of strength—he reflects as a mirror image" (*Political Unconscious,* 118).

39. In medieval canon law, such a union would constitute incest. See Brundage, *Law, Sex, and Christian Society*, esp. 140–41, 190–91, 355–56.

40. The French is from Frappier, ed., *La Mort le Roi Artu*, 212. The English translation is from Lacy, gen. ed., *Lancelot-Grail*, 4:146.

41. See Asher's introduction to the critical edition and translation of Malory's source for this scene, the thirteenth-century *Suite du Merlin* in Lacy, gen. ed., *Lancelot-Grail*, 4:163–65.

42. Wilson-Okamura, "Adultery and the Fall of Logres," 18.

43. B. Kennedy, "Adultery in Malory's *Morte Darthur*," 67.

44. V. Guerin, "King's Sin," 23.

45. See Archibald, "Arthur and Mordred: Variations on an Incest Theme." In this article, Archibald argues that the insertion of Mordred's incestuous conception into the Arthurian legend reflects "a contemporary vogue for incest stories," tracing the development of this theme through the well-known incest legends of Judas, Gregorious, Roland, and Charlemagne. Although this revision of the Arthurian legend could be said in some sense to reflect the popularity of incest stories in medieval Europe, the double-incest theme played out in the *Morte d'Arthur* departs from the traditional tale, in which an incestuously conceived child returns from exile and unknowingly duplicates his parents' sin by innocently marrying a woman who turns out to be his sister or mother. In Malory's text, the tale is turned on its head—the product of unwitting incest, Mordred deliberately and perversely seeks to marry his father's wife and thereby secure his claim to the throne. The best known example of the incest story is, of course, the myth of Oedipus. Archibald points out that the two major innovations in medieval incest stories were "the double incest theme . . . and the Christian elements of contrition, penance, and a spiritually happy ending. The Arthurian legend borrowed from the first innovation, the double incest, but not the second" (11).

46. In claiming that the significance of the adultery of Arthur with Morgause has been overshadowed by the sin of incest in Malory's source, the *Suite du Merlin*, Wilson-Okamura traces the figure of the adulterous hero-king back to the biblical figure of David, arguing that Arthur's status as adulterer and ruler is best understood in light of this tradition; see his "Adultery and the Fall of Logres." V. Guerin also calls attention to this parallel in "King's Sin." For a critical response to Wilson-Okamura's contention that adultery, not incest, is the more significant of the two sins committed by Arthur and Morgause, see Fries's "Commentary," in *Arthuriana* 7.4 (1997): 92–96.

47. Morris argues that Malory "establishes a parallel between Uther's conscious sin of lust, from which comes good (Arthur's birth) and Arthur's unconscious sin of incest, from which comes evil (Mordred's birth)"; see "Uther and Igerne: A Study in Uncourtly Love," 87. While Morris and other critics have pointed to the similarities between these acts of sinful lust, no one has yet fully appreciated the significance of the differences between them.

48. The French is taken from Paris and Ulrich, eds., *Merlin, roman en prose du*

XIIIe siècle, 1:147. The English translation is from Lacy, gen. ed., *Lancelot-Grail,* 4:167.

49. Lévi-Strauss, *Elementary Structures of Kinship,* 115.

50. Ibid., 51.

51. G. Rubin, "Traffic in Women," 37.

52. For the term "use value" see Irigaray, *This Sex Which Is Not One,* 170. The quote is taken from page 185.

53. G. Rubin, "Traffic in Women," 38.

54. For more on medieval concepts of adultery, see Bullough and Brundage, eds., *Sexual Practices and the Medieval Church;* Bullough, *Sexual Variance in Society and History.* In a recent article Bullough has pointed out that "obviously, a man who had sexual relations with someone else's wife violated *another man's property*" (emphasis mine); see "Medieval Concepts of Adultery," 8.

55. This episode will be paralleled later in Lancelot's conception of Galahad on the virgin, unwedded Elaine, who sacrifices her virginity at her father's command in order to bear the child of the best knight of the world.

56. Fradenburg, "Love of Thy Neighbor," 141.

57. Heng has noted of this episode that it is "exemplary in function, for it lays down the structures of appropriate behavior toward the feminine . . . even as it instills the right of the queen to arbitrate and judge knightly conduct" ("Enchanted Ground," 97–98).

58. Later on, the figure of Guenevere and her authority is diminished by her relationship with Lancelot and the continuing unspoken problem of her sterility: pregnancy and childbirth mark the women of the chivalric community *as* women (and thus as authority figures in those matters concerning women) in a way that marriage alone—even to a king—cannot. In her book *Meanings of Sex Difference in the Middle Ages,* Cadden observes that the "final cause of sexual differentiation is reproduction," and that the feminine, for obvious reasons, is more strongly marked than the masculine. Unlike the male, stages of the passage of the female from sterile to fertile and back again are readily discernible and bounded. The feminine is either premother, mother *in potentia,* or postmother (189). On this see also McCracken, *Romance of Adultery.*

59. For a fuller discussion of queenly behavior in Malory, see McCracken, *Romance of Adultery,* and also Dobyns, *Voices of Romance,* esp. chap. 2. On Guenevere's sterility and its implications for her status as object of knightly devotion, see Morse, "Sterile Queens and Questing Orphans."

60. As Edwards observes, to discuss the place of women in Arthurian romance, and particularly Malory's text, is to examine more than simply the social or textual position of these women: "The queens in their castles seem to have a different ontological status than the damsels who inhabit the forests of adventure" ("Place of Women," 37).

61. Pochoda, *Arthurian Propaganda,* 66.

62. Irigaray argues that "Woman 'touches herself' all the time . . . for her genitals

are formed of two lips in continuous contact. Thus, within herself, she is already two—but not divisible into one(s)—that caress each other" (*This Sex Which Is Not One*, 24).

63. Moi offers a cogent analysis of Irigaray's feminist theory in her *Sexual/ Textual Politics;* see esp. chap. 7, "Patriarchal reflections: Luce Irigaray's looking-glass."

64. McCarthy has rightly noted that "It is *her* passions that are in control; those of Accolon are irrelevant. It is because Morgan loves him that she copies the scabbard, not because he loves her" ("Did Morgan le Fay Have a Lover?," 285). McCarthy has also called attention to a discrepancy between the Winchester MS and Caxton's version of the text, pointing to Vinaver's emendation of "gaf the scawberd Excaliber to her love" to "to her *lover*," which has a strikingly different significance in terms of Accolon's willing complicity in the plot to kill Arthur. "To her love" suggests only that Accolon is the object of Morgan's affections and that he does not necessarily return the sentiment; "to her lover" implies that the feelings between them are mutual, which thus more fully implicates Accolon in Morgan's plot.

65. Holbrook has observed that Malory altered his sources to "create a deliberate balance of Morgan and Nymue [Nyneve]," an act that emphasizes the significance of a feminine presence at this moment ("Nymue, the Chief Lady of the Lake," 187).

66. The battle between Arthur and Accolon becomes what Weigand has termed "*Gesta dominarum per milites*" (the exploits of ladies through the medium of knights) (quoted in Heng, "Map of Her Desire," 254).

67. Heng has argued that the sword, while critically important in the establishment of masculine identity in Arthurian romance (and in the *Morte d'Arthur* in particular), further demonstrates the necessity of the feminine in the chivalric project, in that swords (like Excalibur) are often the gifts of women to men, and men only have use of them temporarily; see "Enchanted Ground," 98–99. The point I wish to make about Morgan's behavior here is that, while women may *give* swords to men, we never see another woman make use of the sword in the masculine idiom of combat, as Morgan does. The closest parallel would be those women who throw themselves on the swords of their dead paramours/husbands (Pellinor's daughter being one example), and that situation is not comparable to the appropriation of masculine activity that Morgan demonstrates.

Chapter 2. Chivalric Performance: Malory's Sir Lancelot

Portions of this chapter have appeared in substantially different form as "Gender and Fear: Malory's Lancelot and Knightly Identity," in *Arizona Studies in the Middle Ages and the Renaissance, 6: Fear and Its Representations in the Middle Ages and the Renaissance*, ed. Scott and Kosso (Turnhout, Belgium: Brepols, 2002), 255–73. Reprinted by kind permission of the publisher.

1. See Finke and Shichtman, "Introduction," *Arthuriana* 8.2 (1998): 3–10, and "No Pain, No Gain."

2. Connell, *Masculinities,* 37.

3. See Butler, *Gender Trouble*, esp. 16–25.

4. Butler, *Bodies That Matter*, 232.

5. Ibid., 12.

6. See LaFarge's important article "Hand of the Huntress."

7. Finke and Shichtman have argued that Arthur is necessarily excluded from the main action of the narrative in that he must detach himself from the economy of masculine violence that the Pentecostal Oath institutes: "this oath attempts to bring violence under the control of official institutions, not to eliminate it. . . . Arthur cannot himself be involved in the pursuit of value, but must be excluded. . . . Just as the image of gold, not gold itself, gives value to commodities in the economic sphere, so the image of the king, not necessarily the king himself gives value to his subjects" ("No Pain, No Gain," 120).

8. The "Tale of King Arthur," while it includes questing, incorporates this particular knightly activity into a series of events concerning the establishment of Arthur's kingdom, and is thus not predominantly concerned with an in-depth treatment of the quest. Likewise, the account of the Roman War (Vinaver's Tale II), while itself may be considered a story about a quest, is not typical of the *Morte d'Arthur* in the sense that quest participation is here collective, not individual, and there do not occur the *series* of quests, undertaken by a single individual, that distinguishes Lancelot's questing activity in "A Noble Tale of Sir Launcelot du Lake."

9. Mahoney notes that the "oath is deceptively generalized," producing problems for knights attempting to adhere to it; see "Malory's *Morte Darthur* and the *Alliterative Morte Arthure*," 531.

10. It seems clear that Malory drew from two different French sources when composing this section of the *Morte d'Arthur*—both from the "Agravain" section of the French Prose *Lancelot* and from the *Perlesvaus*. For a detailed analysis of corresponding passages in Malory and his sources, see Field, "Malory and the French Prose *Lancelot*."

11. The French is from Micha, ed., *Lancelot: Roman en prose du XIIIe siècle*, 5:39. The translated English is from Lacy, gen. ed., *Lancelot-Grail*, 3:215.

12. Brewer, "Malory's 'Preving' of Sir Launcelot," 125.

13. When I speak of chivalry here, it is in terms of a secular, not religious ideal, in keeping with Barber's definition: "The secular ideal of a knight as brave, generous, and courteous . . . is what what we might call the chivalric aspect of knighthood" ("Chivalry," 23). Although his important book *Chivalry* is in large measure concerned with the religious aspect of chivalry, Keen similarly identifies the five key components of chivalric knighthood as the "primarily secular values of *prouesse, loyaute, largesse, courtoisie*, and *franchise*" (3). This is also the definition of chivalry that Jesmok understands to be operating in Malory's text; see "'A Knyght Wyveles,'" esp. 315.

14. Butler, *Gender Trouble*, 25.

15. Knight, *Arthurian Literature and Society*, 112.

16. Reynolds is just one of many scholars who has offered a challenge to the

standard conception of feudalism, arguing that the concepts of the fief and vassalage are largely constructions of modern historians, and occlude much of the realities of medieval social structure; see *Fiefs and Vassals.* I do not propose here to engage with the current debate on "feudalism," but I use the term as a matter of convenience to describe a social structure in which bonds of loyalty and service functioned as communal supports.

17. For a comprehensive discussion on the concept of chivalry as a viable, functional model or code, see, among others: Coss, *Knight in Medieval England,* esp. chaps. 6–7; Kaeuper, *War, Justice and Public Order* and *Chivalry and Violence in Medieval Europe,* and also his edited work *Violence in Medieval Society;* J. Vale, *Edward III and Chivalry;* M. Vale, *War and Chivalry.*

18. For more on this see Göller, "Arthurian Chivalry in the Fourteenth and Fifteenth Centuries."

19. It is estimated that the outbreak of plague in 1348 and the subsequent plagues of the 1360s and 1370s reduced England's population between 40 and 50 percent. See Miller and Hatcher, *Medieval England,* 29. For more on the economic situation of the peasantry in this period, see Bolton, *Medieval English Economy,* esp. chaps. 2–6; Britnell, *Growth and Decline in Colchester,* esp. 148ff.; Dyer, *Lords and Peasants in a Changing Society;* Postan, *Medieval Economy and Society,* esp. 142–50, 157–58; M. Rubin, *Charity and Community in Medieval Cambridge,* esp. 15–33, 49–53.

20. See Dobson, *Peasants' Revolt of 1381;* and also Keen, *English Society,* esp. chap. 2: "Plague, Depopulation, and Labour Shortage."

21. Keen has noted "there were fewer people living on the land, and their holdings of land were larger, in some cases appreciably so. . . . All were better off than they had been" (*English Society,* 66).

22. McFarlane most famously used the term as "a label to describe the society which was emerging from feudalism in the early part of the fourteenth century, when most if not all its ancient features survived, even though in many cases as weak shadows of themselves, but when the tenurial bond between lord and vassal had been superseded as the primary social tie by the contract between master and man" (24); see "Bastard Feudalism," in *England in the Fifteenth Century,* 23–43. Coss has challenged McFarlane's understanding of "bastard feudalism" as a phenomenon produced by the replacement of the tenurial relationship by a cash economy, arguing that contracts and payment for service had been in use long before the period in which McFarlane understood bastard feudalism to have originated. To understand this phenomenon and indeed, to retain it as a meaningful concept in relationship to the developments of the fourteenth and fifteenth centuries, Coss suggests that we must look back into the late twelfth and early thirteenth centuries and the changes in economy and the office of knighthood taking place in that period. Coss points out that "we would seem to have two choices: either we abandon bastard feudalism altogether or, if we are to retain it as a meaningful concept, then both its constitution and its inception have to be understood differently" ("Bastard Feudalism Revised," 39). Coss goes on to argue the concept of bastard feudalism may be

usefully retained, but only if reformulated so as to function more generally; he points to "the changing meaning of knighthood" as providing key insight into understanding the shifting of relationships between crown and local society, lord and vassal during the medieval period. He suggests that "out of the social and economic changes of the thirteenth century there thus emerged a new knightly class which was ultimately to constitute the first gradation of the English gentry. It was in this context that the ethos which we may broadly term chivalric came to predominate" ("Bastard Feudalism Revised," 47, 49). See also Bellamy, *Bastard Feudalism and the Law;* Carpenter, "Beauchamp affinity"; Ferguson, *Indian Summer of English Chivalry;* McFarlane, *Nobility of Later Medieval England* and "Parliament and 'Bastard Feudalism'"; Saul, *Knights and Esquires.*

23. Crane, *Insular Romance*, 177.

24. As Knight has noted, Malory's text is by no means unusual in this period, when "a great amount of material on the theory and practice of chivalry was produced, at a time when the mounted knight was no longer a force on the battlefield, when feudalism had been transmuted into the financial and contractual arrangements of bastard feudalism, and when the incomes of the great were increasingly derived from the sale of wool and cloth" (*Arthurian Literature and Society*, 107). James has argued that this heightened interest in chivalry and its transformation, from a code of conduct directed primarily toward the knightly classes into an ideology that was appropriated by all strata of society, continued to function meaningfully well into the seventeenth century; see *English Politics*. The standard work on Malory's social and historical context is, of course, Field, *Life and Times*. On this, see also Hanks, ed., *Social and Literary Contexts* and Kim, *Knight Without the Sword.*

25. Ingham, *Sovereign Fantasies*, 193.

26. For more on this, see Dyer, *Standards of Living in the Later Middle Ages.*

27. Riddy, "Contextualizing," 71.

28. Ingham points out that the *Morte d'Arthur* enjoyed remarkable popularity well into the Tudor period and was reprinted five times between 1489 and 1634 (*Sovereign Fantasies*, 197). See also Pochoda, *Arthurian Propaganda*, appendix A, 141–45.

29. Goodman has pointed out that Malory's text is one of four in what she terms "Caxton's chivalric series," noting that these four works—the *Morte d'Arthur, Godefroy of Boloyne*, the *Book of the Ordre of Chyualry*, and *Charles the Grete*—offer "a unified political solution to the problems besetting fifteenth-century England"; see "Malory and Caxton's Chivalric Series, 1481–85," 257.

30. For more on the connection between these genres of writing, see Keen, *Chivalry*, 15–21; see also Ferster, *Fictions of Advice.*

31. Cherewatuk, "Sir Thomas Malory's 'Grete Booke,'" 43. See also her "'Gentyl' Audiences and 'Grete Bookes.'"

32. Cherewatuk, "Sir Thomas Malory's 'Grete Booke,'" 50, 47.

33. Caxton, *Book of the Ordre of Chyualry*, ed. Byles, 122.

34. Keen identifies the *Ordene* and the texts of Charny and Lull as the three most important works that offer crucial insight into the concept of chivalry as it was understood in the Middle Ages; see *Chivalry*, 6–17. I am most interested in examining these texts in terms of their translation for, and reception by, an English public, and how Malory's work functions alongside these texts in terms of the fifteenth-century chivalric revival in England.

35. Three of these texts were translated into Middle English and enjoyed wide circulation in the fifteenth century; Charny's French text is an exception, but I include it in my analysis as it is a work deeply concerned with, and representative of, anxieties of late medieval order and governance. Significantly, the *Livre* was written (at least in part) in response to a deliberate revival of the concept of chivalric orders in England, and as such both challenges and affirms the model of knightly behavior that institutions such as the Order of the Garter sought to strengthen. Hence, while most likely known only in France to those figures connected to French King Jean II's Company of the Star, Charny's text reflects chivalric concerns in both England and France: "Far from purveying a conventional topos of the past glories of an imagined golden age, Charny feels an urgent need to respond to a clear and present danger" (Kaeuper and Kennedy, eds., *Book of Chivalry of Geoffroi de Charny*, 48). For an analysis of these texts in relationship to the knighting ceremony in *Sir Gawain and the Green Knight*, see Cherewatuk, "Echoes of the Knighting Ceremony."

36. See Keen, *Chivalry*, 8–11, and Kaeuper and Kennedy, eds., *Book of Chivalry*, 25–27.

37. Caxton, *Book of the Ordre of Chyualry*, 24.

38. Ibid., 38.

39. The French is from Micha, *Lancelot*, 7:249–50. The English translation is from Lacy, gen. ed., *Lancelot-Grail*, 2:59.

40. Micha, *Lancelot*, 7:250 and Lacy, gen. ed., *Lancelot-Grail*, 2:59.

41. Kaeuper and Kennedy, eds., *Book of Chivalry*, 184–85.

42. Ibid., 198–99. See also Keen, *Chivalry*, 14.

43. The Grail Quest, the subject of chapter 4, dramatically criticizes this social model; the figure of Galahad radically undermines the conceptions of gender and chivalry upon which the Arthurian community is founded.

44. House, ed., *L'Ordene de Chevalerie*, 50–51. The English translation is mine.

45. Caxton, *Book of Fayttes of Armes and of Chyualrye*, ed. Byles, 12.

46. Kaeuper and Kennedy, eds., *Book of Chivalry*, 31.

47. Ibid., 94–95.

48. Ibid., 122–23.

49. As Riddy has observed, "When Lancelot sets out to prove himself he is both demonstrating and discovering who and what he is; the direction of the tale is both inward and outward" (*Sir Thomas Malory*, 47). Riddy also notes the ambiguity of the word "preve" in this instance: "it can mean both 'show' and 'put to the test' and is used in both senses elsewhere in the tale" (48).

50. K. C. Kelly, "Malory's Body Chivalric," 54.

51. Riviere, "Womanliness as Masquerade," 213.

52. See Butler, *Gender Trouble*, 141, and Irigaray, *This Sex Which Is Not One*, 76.

53. Irigaray, *This Sex Which Is Not One*, 133–34.

54. Burns offers an interesting treatment of the question of masculinity in medi-eval courtly romance in "Refashioning Courtly Love." In discussing the debate over whether the seal of Simon de Mondragon represents a knight doing homage to his lord or to his lady, Burns notes that while the question of the sex of the robed figure on the seal can never be finally resolved, the depiction of the armored knight will always be interpreted as masculine. Yet, "This sartorial marker of medieval maleness effectively occludes any clear determination of anatomical difference. . . . the very fact that armor so thoroughly hides the body assumed to be protected beneath it makes this specifically 'male' medieval costume the perfect mode of cross-dressing for women wishing to switch genders in the social sphere" (114).

55. As Drewes has observed of knights and names in the *Morte d'Arthur*: "In-deed, the name is the knight" ("Sense of Hidden Identity," 20).

56. See Lacan, "Meaning of the Phallus," 83–85.

57. Butler, *Gender Trouble*, 136.

58. The "knight-in-disguise" is a variation of the Fair Unknown theme, cropping up repeatedly as an episodic unit in Malory's *Morte d'Arthur*. Like the Fair Un-known romance subplot, the knight's exemplary performance is confirmed as a product of his noble blood when his identity is revealed at the end of the episode.

59. The French is from Micha, *Lancelot*, 5:44. The English translation is from Lacy, gen. ed., *Lancelot-Grail*, 3:217.

60. Micha, *Lancelot*, 5:285, and Lacy, gen. ed., *Lancelot-Grail*, 3:275.

61. Jaeger, *Ennobling Love*, esp. 36–53.

62. As Brewer has observed, "The proving of Sir Launcelot is always recognition, not discovery" ("Malory's 'Preving,'" 127).

63. Grosz, *Volatile Bodies*, 142.

64. The French is from Micha, *Lancelot*, 4:183. The English translation is from Lacy, gen. ed., *Lancelot-Grail*, 3:158.

65. Micha, *Lancelot*, 4:184, and Lacy, gen. ed., *Lancelot-Grail*, 3:158.

66. As K. C. Kelly has explained, "The removal of armor, an outward sign of masculinity, is significant. Launcelot leaves himself open, as it were, for a different interpretation" ("Malory's Body Chivalric," 60). Burns, in her work on the French Prose *Lancelot*, seems to concur with Kelly's assessment, noting that "the courtly knight's masculinity and social status derive from the fact that his specific body parts are encased and literally unseen. He is gendered masculine precisely to the extent that his anatomical sex is concealed and unverified. He is a knight and a man, curi-ously, to the degree that he has no clearly sexed body" ("Refashioning Courtly Love," 119).

67. The French is from Micha, *Lancelot*, 4:183–4. The English translation is from Lacy, gen. ed., *Lancelot-Grail*, 3:158.

68. Interestingly, Batt explicitly excludes this scene of potential male rape from analysis in her article "Malory and Rape," characterizing it as "an extraordinary threat to Lancelot's physical person" but one that does not "involve intentionality on the part of the agents" ("Malory and Rape," 95 n. 15). It is my contention that it is not intentionality that is important here, but rather, what is significant is that Lancelot *perceives* the threat as rape, and his fearful reaction is indicative of the anxiety surrounding the maintenance of masculine identity in Malory's text.

69. See Irigaray, *This Sex Which Is Not One*, 75–77.

70. See Kaeuper and Kennedy, eds., *Book of Chivalry*, 122–23.

71. Kaplan, "Is the Gaze Male?" 319. See also K. C. Kelly, "Malory's Body Chivalric."

72. The French is from Micha, *Lancelot*, 4:174. The translated English is from Lacy, gen. ed., *Lancelot-Grail*, 3:155.

73. At this point in the narrative, it seems that Malory is taking great pains to rewrite his sources in an effort to allow the Lancelot-Guenevere relationship to exist legitimately and be characterized as chaste. Several scholars have pointed out Malory's deliberate ambiguity in this regard; the nature of the affection and devotion that exists between the queen and the greatest knight becomes a particularly pressing issue later, in the quest for the Holy Grail. See, for example, S.C.B. Atkinson, "Malory's Lancelot and the Quest of the Grail," in which the author notes that Malory "contrives to leave stubbornly unanswerable the question of whether the adultery has begun" (130). See also, among others, Evans, "*Ordinatio* and Narrative Links," and Brewer, "Image of Lancelot."

74. The suppression of evidence of adultery is suggestive of the deliberate narrative progression that Malory is attempting to effect, tracing the degeneration of Lancelot and Guenevere's relationship from a supportive element of the Arthurian chivalric enterprise to a component in its destruction. Brewer notes that in "A Noble Tale of Sir Launcelot du Lake" "we are carefully shown the pre-adulterous phase of the relationship, and . . . this is part of a long chain of cause and effect tracing the development of Lancelot's character" ("Presentation of the Character of Lancelot," 18).

75. See Jesmok's discussion of this moment in "'A Knyght Wyveles,'" esp. 322.

76. Heng, "Enchanted Ground," 103. Similarly, Brewer has noted that "Lancelot's relationship to ladies in general is an intrinsic part of the moral structure of honour which underlies the whole of *le Morte Darthur* but the heart of it lies in his relationship with Queen Gwenyvere, which is also part of the implicit social structure of the tale, constantly and timelessly linking it with Arthur and his court" ("Malory's 'Preving,'" 130).

77. Riddy, *Sir Thomas Malory*, 56–57.

78. Chrétien de Troyes, *Arthurian Romances*, ed. Kibler, trans. Carroll, 67.

79. Jesmok, "'A Knyght Wyveles,'" 323.

80. L. D. Benson has argued that Gareth's marriage "symbolizes a lower order of knighthood than that of Lancelot" (*Malory's Morte Darthur*, 107). Fries, concurring

with Benson, notes that "Malory is unable to use marriage as a continuing impetus for knightly worship. . . . he . . . seems unable to imagine postmarital martial reputations even remotely analogous to Lancelot's" ("How Many Roads to Camelot?," 199–200).

81. This episode, in its clearly realized conflict between competing loyalties and proper manners, evokes *Sir Gawain and the Green Knight*, and the awkward position in which Gawain, the paragon of courtesy and good conduct, finds himself. Beholden to both his host, Bertilak, and Bertilak's wife, Gawain finds himself compelled to render a kiss to both each day of his stay at Haut Desert. See Heng, "A Woman Wants."

82. Lynch, *Malory's Book of Arms*, 18.

83. See Nitze and Jenkins, eds., *Le Haut Livre du Graal Perlesvaus*, vol. 1, branch 10, 303–57; see also Bryant, trans., *High Book of the Grail*, branch 10, 194–229.

84. See also L.D. Benson, *Malory's Morte Darthur*, 88–89, and Nolan, "*The Tale of Sir Gareth* and *The Tale of Sir Launcelot*," 175–76. B. Kennedy suggests that rather than devotion to Guenevere, Lancelot's refusal to kiss Hallewes is a consequence of his devotion to *chastity* (*Knighthood*, 115).

85. Edwards, *Genesis of Narrative*, 87.

86. See Burns, "Refashioning Courtly Love."

87. While there is always the potential possibility that Malory was drawing from a source which is now lost, my analysis of this section so far reveals a significant concern on Malory's part with adapting his source material in order to emphasize gender relations and the tensions they produce; this scene and its inclusion is key in recognizing the potential threat that women in the text may pose.

88. Brewer, "Malory's 'Preving,'" 130.

89. Edwards, *Genesis of Narrative*, 88.

90. Pochoda offers an astute assessment of Malory's understanding of the chivalric community and its function as depicted in the *Morte:* "Malory's attempt to use the Arthurian legend as an historical ideal of life leads him to uncover the fact that Arthurian society actually provided itself with a means by which all of the conflicts which were eventually to destroy it could continue to operate unacknowledged by the members of the society" (*Arthurian Propaganda*, 29).

Chapter 3. Forecast and Recall: Gareth and Tristram

1. Mahoney does the best job of summing up the scholarly positions in the debate concerning "Gareth's" sources; see "Malory's *Tale of Sir Gareth*." See also Ackerman, "'Tale of Gareth'"; Field, "Source of Malory's 'Tale of Gareth'" in *Malory: Texts and Sources*, 246–60; W. W. Guerin, "'Tale of Gareth'"; Wilson, "The 'Fair Unknown' in Malory"; T. L. Wright, "On the Genesis of Malory's 'Gareth.'"

2. Cherewatuk has recently discussed the structure of the "Gareth" and its relationship to fifteenth-century marriage practice; see "Pledging Troth in Malory's 'Tale of Sir Gareth.'" Other scholars (in addition to those listed above, n. 1) who have

recently engaged the "Gareth" include Fries, "How Many Roads"; Lynch, *Malory's Book of Arms*; Riddy, *Sir Thomas Malory*; Wheeler, "'Prowess of Hands.'"

3. As almost all recent critics who write about the "Tristram" do so with the intent to recuperate it and redress this long neglect, nearly every article or chapter on the massive middle portion of Malory's text begins by taking exception to early negative critical assessments of Malory's redaction of the French Prose *Tristan*. Those early critical responses variously describe the "Book of Sir Tristram de Lyones" as "mutilated and hybrid" (Schofield, *English Literature from the Norman Conquest to Chaucer*, 211); "tardive et corrumpue" (Vinaver, *Le Roman de Tristan et Iseut dans l'oeuvre de Thomas Malory*, 91); "largely irrelevant" (Chambers, *English Literature at the Close of the Middle Ages*, 191); and the "least attractive" of all Malory's tales (Chambers, *Sir Thomas Malory*, 5). Beginning with Rumble's study in 1964, scholarly opinion of Malory's "Tristram" has tended to align itself in direct opposition to these early negative assessments, particularly that of Malory's most famous editor, Vinaver, who pronounced Malory's version of the Tristan story "substantially the same" as that of the French Prose *Tristan* (Vinaver, ed., *Works of Malory*, vol. 3, 1444, 1446) and further argued that "there is not a line, not a word, in the whole of Malory's 'Book of Sir Tristram'" that suggests it should be viewed as an integral part of a "textually unified" *Morte Darthur*. In contrast to Vinaver's opinion, Mahoney contends that "far from being 'irrelevant' [the "Tristram"] is the center of the *Morte d'Arthur*, the heart of the work" ("Malory's 'Tale of Sir Tristram,'" 224). Similarly, E. D. Kennedy argues that the use of the *Tristan* material "contributed markedly to Malory's greater independence in the use of sources by influencing his conception of Arthur in these final tales" ("Malory's King Mark and King Arthur," 165), while L. D. Benson goes so far as to claim that he sees in the "Tristram" "a solidly coherent, even elegant thematic structure" (*Malory's Morte Darthur*, 109).

4. The exact form of the French Prose *Tristan* that served as Malory's source probably no longer exists. While the other surviving *Tristan* MSS contain many of the same episodes and themes with which Malory deals, none of them is close enough in terms of structure and plot to be a candidate for the version used by Malory. Vinaver has attempted to reconstruct what Malory's *Tristan* might have looked like through careful analysis of the surviving manuscripts. The most important of these are MSS Paris, Bibliothèque Nationale f. fr. 103, 334, and 99. He also makes use of Chantilly 646, Pierpont Morgan MS fr. 41 and MS F.V. XV. 2 of the Leningrad Public Library. For a fuller explanation of Vinaver's reconstruction of Malory's *Tristan*, see *Works*, vol. 3, 1448–60. Mahoney has suggested that Vinaver's approach is too focused, and that "a wider base of comparison must be employed." See Mahoney's important discussion of the problem of source study and Malory's "Tristram" in "Malory's 'Tale of Sir Tristram,'" esp. 225–26 n. 7. The most important recent work on the French Prose *Tristran* is that of Renée Curtis, who has edited a 3–volume edition of the first part of the text, based on MS Carpentras 404. Cooper

points out that Curtis's edition of the Prose *Tristan* does not make use of the *Tristan* manuscripts that are most likely closest to Malory's source text; see "Book of Sir Tristram de Lyones," esp. 184 n. 2. See also Löseth, *Le Roman en Prose de Tristan, Le roman de Palamède et la compilation de Rusticien de Pise*. Another edition of the Prose *Tristan* currently in progress is Philippe Ménard, ed., *Le Roman de Tristan en Prose*. Michael N. Salda has recently begun work on an edition of the *Tristan* that is "based on closely related fifteenth-century texts which will come nearer to Malory's source for much of the 'Tristram' than the edition based on thirteenth-century manuscripts being published by Ménard and company" ("Reconsidering Vinaver's Sources for Malory's 'Tristram,'" 373 n. 6).

5. For more on the links that Malory makes between the "Tristram" and the rest of the *Morte* see in particular L. D. Benson, *Malory's Morte Darthur*, esp. 109; Evans, "*Ordinatio* and Narrative Links"; Hanks, "Malory's *Book of Sir Tristram*," esp. 14; E. D. Kennedy, "Malory's King Mark and King Arthur," esp. 165; Mahoney, "Malory's 'Tale of Sir Tristram'"; Rumble, "'Tale of Tristram'"; Schueler, "Tristram Section of Malory's *Morte Darthur*." Hanks neatly lists the issues developed in the "Tristram" that are significant to the *Morte* as a whole: "[Malory] establishes the context of gentility and valor which shapes the remainder of the *Morte*'s action; develops the theme of the anti-knight; forecasts the fall of Arthur and of his Round Table; prepares the reader for the Grail Quest; paves the way for 'The Knight of the Cart'; and, in the love affair of Tristram and Isode, subtly comments upon the affair of Lancelot and Guinevere" ("Malory's *Book of Sir Tristram*," 14–15).

6. Rumble perhaps lists these most succinctly in his treatment of the "Tristram"; see "'Tale of Tristram,'" 163, 168, 171–73. Mahoney asserts that Malory's most significant change is to end the "Tristram" on "a happy note" ("Malory's 'Tale of Sir Tristram,'" 226).

7. Fries, "Tristram as Counter-Hero to the *Morte Darthur*," 612.

8. As Rumble has pointed out: "to portray the real tragedy of the fall of Arthur's realm, [Malory] had to make clearer than ever before the *causes* of that tragedy. It is just this sense of causality that is missing in the French cyclic *Arthuriad*—no matter in what combination we put together a *Merlin*, a *Quest*, and a *Lancelot*. And it is just this sense of causality that is underscored, though implicitly rather than explicitly, by the addition of the 'Tristram' material" ("'Tale of Tristram,'" 145).

9. In the words of Pochoda, the events of the "Tristram" occur in a timeless "aevum" that manifests "an endless sempiternity with past and future" (*Arthuriana Propaganda*, 38). Something similar occurs in the "Gareth"—even though Gareth moves ever closer to the object of his desire, the adventures he has on the way tend to blur together in their sameness.

10. The phrase is borrowed from Hanks, "Malory's Anti-Knights," 99.

11. This is, of course, due in part to the fact that one of Malory's primary sources for the *Morte d'Arthur*, the Prose *Lancelot*, was greatly influenced by some of the early Tristan poems. See Rumble, "'Tale of Tristram,'" esp. 124 n. 25.

12. Malory has altered this episode as he found it in his source, making Marhalt a Round Table knight when the Prose *Tristan* makes no mention of this affiliation.

13. As L. D. Benson points out, "In the first stage of Tristram's career . . . the main thematic pattern is the proof-of-knighthood theme that we examined in *Gareth*, and in its broadest outline Tristram's early career is quite similar to Gareth's. . . . The sympathetic reader can hardly miss this, since he comes to *Sir Tristram* immediately after reading *Gareth* (and the intercalated story of "La Cote Mal Tayle" serves as a further reminder of this thematic pattern)" (*Malory's Morte Darthur*, 118–19).

14. See Drewes, "Sense of Hidden Identity."

15. In an important article on the Gareth episode, Wheeler has argued that Gareth's transformation from an "unformed, unknighted . . . inexperienced youth" into a knight of prowess is best understood in terms of the alchemical process; see "'Prowess of Hands,'" esp. 183.

16. L. D. Benson has made a similar observation, noting that "All the characters in [the 'Book of Sir Tristram de Lyones'] . . . supply varying perspectives on the code of chivalry, which had been abstractly stated in *The Tale of King Arthur* and exemplified in *A Noble Tale of Sir Lancelot* but is here shown to be not one but a copious variety of 'worshipful ways'" (*Malory's Morte Darthur*, 134).

17. Lynch, *Malory's Book of Arms*, 64. See also his full discussion of blood and nobility as represented in the Gareth episode, 62–68.

18. As Lynch notes, unless the Green Knight accepts the fact that "victory 'proves' nobility of blood . . . he must confess himself guilty of begging mercy from a churl. Beawmaynes *must* become Gareth, or ruin the economy of honour" (ibid., 65).

19. As Hoffman has noted of Gareth, "[I]t is the rebukes of the dismal damsel that form his character"; see "Malory's 'Cinderella Knights,'" 146.

20. This Red Knight is different from the one Gareth defeated earlier in his tale.

21. Hoffman, "Malory's 'Cinderella Knights,'" 152.

22. See Vinaver's extensive discussion of the sources of the Alexander story and this moment in his *Works*, vol.3, 1496 ff. Vinaver points out that in MS B.N. fr. 99 the character of Alexander states "Itant vueil-je que vous sacheiz . . . que ainçois que je me couchasse avec Morgain soufferay je beau cop de male" (vol.3, 1501).

23. Hoffman has argued that Gareth, La Cote Male Tayle, and Alexander—along with Balin—are "Cinderella knights," by means of which "Malory investigates the relationship of plot and adventure" ("Malory's 'Cinderella Knights,'" 145).

24. Butler, *Gender Trouble*, 25.

25. Ibid., 112.

26. K. C. Kelly notes that "the armored body . . . both exaggerates and obscures the lineaments of the male body enclosed within it. Armor both covers the body and draws attention to its function as a cover and the *need* for a cover" ("Malory's Body Chivalric," 54). Burns has argued that "What lies beneath the knight's armor in courtly romance, then, is not sexual difference but the sexual ambiguity of a social

body that can move quite readily between genders and social stations" ("Refashioning Courtly Love," 124).

27. K. C. Kelly, "Malory's Body Chivalric," 60.

28. Butler, *Gender Trouble*, 131.

29. Garber, *Vested Interests*, 161.

30. Mahoney, "Malory's 'Tale of Sir Tristram,'" 228.

31. See Garber, *Vested Interests*, 35.

32. Keen, *Chivalry*, 202.

33. For more on tournaments and their injuries see, among others, Coss, *Knight in Medieval England;* Kaueper, *Chivalry and Violence in Medieval Europe,* esp. 161–64, and *War, Justice and Public Order,* as well as his edited work, *Violence in Medieval Society;* Keen, *Nobles, Knights, and Men at Arms in the Middle Ages;* Lander, *Conflict and Stability;* McFarlane, *Nobility of Later Medieval England;* J. Vale, *Edward the III and Chivalry;* M. Vale, *War and Chivalry.*

34. Keen, *Chivalry*, 205.

35. See, for example, Nickel's discussion of the medieval tournament, in which he notes that "in the second half of the fifteenth century the differentiation between battle and tournament armor increased to such a degree that their elements became mutually exclusive" ("Tournament," 220).

36. See, for example, L. D. Benson, *Malory's Morte Darthur,* esp. 165–84; Loomis, "Arthurian Literature on Sport and Spectacle," 553–59; Keen, *Chivalry,* esp. 93–94. Nickel notes that "Arthurian literature had a fundamental influence on tournaments and the ceremonies surrounding them" ("Tournament," 231). See also Lynch's discussion of the famous tournament meeting of the Bastard of Burgundy and Lord Scales in 1461 in *Malory's Book of Arms,* xi–xx.

37. L. D. Benson, *Malory's Morte Darthur,* 183.

38. As Putter notes, "The transvestite's power to unsettle assumptions, status, and hierarchies readily explains part of the history of the transvestite in the Middle Ages, namely the official persecution and repudiation of the transvestite, but it also prompts questions when we face the surprising fact that cross-dressing was a regular occurrence in the world of medieval chivalry and particularly in the Arthurian tournaments and romances of the later Middle Ages, where real or fictional knights frequently cross-dressed" ("Tranvestite Knights," 280). Fradenburg has perhaps most famously discussed this phenomenon in *City, Marriage, Tournament.*

39. Putter, "Transvestite Knights," 286.

40. Butler, *Gender Trouble*, 137.

41. Putter, "Transvestite Knights," 280–81.

42. Ibid., 296–97.

43. For example Kindrick notes that "Malory has transformed the vicious and bitter Dynadan of the *Tristram* into a good humored joker" ("Dynadan and the Code of Chivalry," 232). Hanks argues that "Malory condenses, deletes, and smooths; his Dinadan is considerably less abrasive, considerably less sardonic, than the Dinadan

he found in the French book" ("Foil and Forecast," 156). Vinaver has suggested that Malory tried and failed to make Dinadan "innocuous" (*Works*, vol.3, 1447–48).

44. Cooper, "Book of Sir Tristram," 194.

45. For a discussion of Dinadan in the French Prose *Tristan*, see Busby, "The Likes of Dinadan."

46. See Mahoney's discussion of Dinadan in the context of the "chivalry topos" in "'Ar ye a knyght and ar no lovear?.'"

47. Hanks, "Malory's Anti-Knights," 99.

Chapter 4. Gender, Kinship, and Community: The Quest for the Holy Grail

1. Vinaver, ed., *Works*, vol. 3, 1521–22.

2. Part of the significance of Malory's use of the *Queste del Saint Graal* is the very fact that he chose *this* particular text as his source. Scholars such as Mahoney and Riddy have pointed out that Malory could have used the more secular version of the story contained in the Prose *Tristan* or that contained in Hardyng's *Chronicle*; see Mahoney, "Truest and Holiest Tale," 112, and Riddy, *Sir Thomas Malory*, 113–15.

3. S.C.B. Atkinson notes that "The *Queste* is doubtless its author's sole contribution to Arthurian literature, an essentially self-contained work, while Malory's Grail narrative is part of a complete history of Arthur's kingdom. Thus Malory's 'Tale of the Sankgreal' cannot be isolated from its context in the *Morte Darthur* as the *Queste* can be from the other branches of the Vulgate cycle" ("Malory's Lancelot," 129).

4. Moorman, "'Tale of the Sankgreall,'" 185–86.

5. See, among others, S.C.B. Atkinson, "Malory's Lancelot," 129–52; Ihle, *Malory's Grail Quest*; Mahoney, "Truest and Holiest Tale," 109–28. Hynes-Berry has argued that while Malory did make significant alterations to his source, in fact he "did not understand the full patterns of meaning" deployed in the *Queste* ("A Tale 'Breffly Drawyne Oute of Freynshe,'" 95). Arguing against Hynes-Berry, Shichtman has theorized that what seems to be a "misunderstanding" is in fact a deliberate subversion of the "intricate network of analogues" in the *Queste* ("Politicizing the Ineffable," 174).

6. See Pochoda, *Arthurian Propaganda*, 115.

7. Vinaver notes that "[Malory's] one desire seems to be to secularize the Grail theme as much as the story will allow" (*Works*, vol.3, 1522). For many years, scholarly critics of the French *Queste* concurred with Pauphilet's contention that the text was authored by a Cistercian monk; see *Études sur la Queste del Saint Graal*. Most critics now agree with Frappier's famous assertion that "les Cisterciens n'écrivaient pas des romans" ("Le Graal et la chevalerie," 195). In *Redemption of Chivalry*, Matarasso concurs with Frappier's assessment, but maintains that a "Cistercian bias" is clearly present, and argues that the French *Queste* may have been the work of a "Cistercian seconded from his abbey to some lay or ecclesiastical dignitary" (224–

28, 241). Mann discusses the Cistercian debate at length in "Malory and the Grail Legend," noting that "the parallels with Cistercian writings and practice . . . are . . . weak and unconvincing" (207).

8. As Mahoney contends, Malory "faithfully transmits the central dichotomy of the *Queste* between worldly and spiritual chivalry, whereby the traditional chivalric standards are reinterpreted in the light of spiritual values" ("Truest and Holiest Tale," 110). See also Moorman, "'Tale of the Sankgreall,'" 185–86.

9. Edwards, *Genesis of Narrative*, 111.

10. Riddy, *Sir Thomas Malory*, 123.

11. As Riddy notes, "it is entirely fitting that [Lancelot] should be Galahad's father, since the active life is anterior to the contemplative" (ibid., 125).

12. See Thornton and May, "Malory as Feminist?," who have pointed out that Malory has augmented the presence of Perceval's sister when compared to the *Queste.* They see this as indication that Malory has a more positive attitude toward feminine characters than does his source. Hoffman has challenged Thornton and May's conclusion, arguing that the figure of Perceval's sister is less a validation of the feminine than she is "a rebuke to men" ("Perceval's Sister," 73). Both of these articles argue quite rightly that Perceval's sister plays an important role in the Grail Quest, but while *female* she does not quite fit any of the categories of the *feminine* as has been demonstrated by the chivalric project of Malory's text. She is most important because of her status as a virgin, and her value as such demands that she die with her virginity intact; her femininity is thus ultimately and completely deferred and denied.

13. Galahad later reveals that this particular sword is in fact that of Balyn le Sauvage, who in the "Tale of King Arthur" slew his brother Balan and struck the Dolorous Stroke that wounded King Pelles. The explanation of the history of the sword is not to be found in Malory's source, and this deliberate link with an earlier episode offers further evidence that Malory's intent was to produce a coherent, progressive narrative. Mann notes that Malory's addition here "makes the coming of Galahad into the completion of a history; the wound opened up by Balin is to be healed by Galahad . . . who brings the unfinished narrative to fulfillment" ("Malory and the Grail Legend," 211–12). For more on the narrative coherence of Malory's *Morte d'Arthur* and the significance of this scene in particular, see also Evans, "*Ordinatio* and Narrative Links."

14. The French is from Pauphilet, ed., *La Queste del Saint Graal*, 6. The English is translated by Burns from "Quest for the Holy Grail," in Lacy, gen. ed., *Lancelot-Grail*, 4:4.

15. Pauphilet, ed., *La Queste del Saint Graal*, 6, and Burns, "Quest," 4:4. While throughout this chapter I will primarily use Burns's translation of the *Queste*, I will also periodically cite the earlier work of Matarasso, whose translation is occasionally more direct than that of Burns. For example, Matarasso translates this line as "I was only obeying *my lord's* command" (emphasis mine); see Matarasso, ed. and trans., *Quest of the Holy Grail*, 36.

16. Ihle, *Malory's Grail Quest*, 127.

17. Morton, "Matter of Britain, " 19.

18. E. D. Kennedy, "Malory and the Marriage of Edward IV," 160.

19. Pauphilet, *La Queste del Saint Graal*, 15.

20. Ibid., 61.

21. As Ihle has observed of the French *Queste:* "the mystical nature of this quest, the object of which is to understand the Grail's meaning, separates it from traditional quests, whose primary object is to attain a physical goal" (*Malory's Grail Quest*, 69).

22. See, for example, Ihle, *Malory's Grail Quest*, esp. 84–90 and 141–59; Hynes-Berry, "A Tale 'Breffly Drawyne Oute of Freynshe,'" 93–106; Pochoda, *Arthurian Propaganda*, 114–23.

23. See Mahoney's discussion of the idea of "stabylité" in Malory's day in "Truest and Holiest Tale," esp. 121–22.

24. Mahoney notes that in both the French and English, Lancelot is the key figure: "Though he is not the hero, he is the doctrinal pivot, for it is in his partial success or partial failure that the Quest is defined" ("Truest and Holiest Tale," 118).

25. K. C. Kelly has rightly noted that "Galahad exists outside the homosocial bond, and, in fact, prevents the homosocial from becoming fully realized, even before he comes to Camelot: the Syege Perelous is an incipient rupture, a site that predicts the final destruction of the Round Table" ("Malory's Body Chivalric," 64).

26. Mann, "Malory and the Grail Legend," 210.

27. Hoffman rightly points out that the problem with Galahad as a viable model for knightly behavior is that he is in essence "a unique chivalric messiah, like whom no other knight can *choose* to be. But while valueless as a model, he remains viable as a critique. No one particularly wants to be like Galahad, but everyone thinks he ought to be" ("Perceval's Sister," 77).

28. The fact that this passage is sourceless, and that it looks forward to the end of the *Morte d'Arthur* when Lancelot will die "an holy man" again indicates Malory's intent to craft a progressive coherent narrative; the reference to Lancelot's death in this context is further evidence of the centrality of the "Tale of the Sankgreal" in the progressive degeneration of a functional chivalric ideology. See also Evans, "*Ordinatio* and Narrative Links," 38–39.

29. Ihle, *Malory's Grail Quest*, 86.

30. See Hynes-Berry, "A Tale 'Breffly Drawyne Oute of Freynshe,'" 99–102.

31. S.C.B. Atkinson, "Malory's Lancelot," 138.

32. Thus, as S.C.B. Atkinson notes, "forbidden to enter but not ordered to leave, he is left occupying a middle ground between departure from the sacred precinct . . . and approach" (ibid., 145).

33. The French is from Pauphilet, *La Queste del Saint Graal*, 278. The translated English is from Burns, "Quest," 4:87.

34. "The consuming obsessions of Malory's 'Tale of the Sankgreal' . . . are (apart from salvation) genealogy and virginity"; see Shichtman, "Percival's Sister," 12.

35. Cherewatuk, "Born-Again Virgins and Holy Bastards," 53.

36. Hynes-Berry, "A Tale 'Breffly Drawyne Oute of Freynshe,'" 95–96, 102.

37. Hoffman, "Perceval's Sister," 77.

38. Cherewatuk has recently made a similar observation: "Galahad is so perfect that he bores readers" ("Born-Again Virgins," 56).

39. Indeed, Hynes-Berry argues that Malory's alterations to his source deliberately shift the focus of the Grail Quest from Galahad to Lancelot ("A Tale 'Breffly Drawyne Oute of Freynshe,'" 96). See also L. D. Benson, who points out that Malory uses Lancelot, not Galahad, to "bracket" the Grail Quest (*Malory's Morte Darthur*, 217).

40. Looper has discussed the importance of genealogy in identifying Galahad as a "Grail hero," noting the striking absence of women in the genealogies that are cited throughout the Grail Quest as evidence of a knight's worth or prowess. Looper sees the high praise accorded Galahad due to his virginity as evidence of the text's "misogynistic program, characterized by the construction of a reformed society from which women are excluded," a program that is partially resisted by the actions of Perceval's sister ("Gender, Genealogy, and the 'Story of the Three Spindles,'" 49).

41. L'Hermite-Leclercq details the reasons for the increased emphasis on virginity: "fear of the end of time; the spiritual influence of the monasteries and of clerical reform; and the flourishing of the cult of Mary" ("Feudal Order," 212).

42. The writings of the patristic fathers demonstrate a concern with virginity, particularly as it relates to women. Such writings include Jerome's *Adversus Jovinianum*, John Crysostom's *De virginite*, Saint Cyprian's *De Habitu virginum*, Ambrose's *De Virginitate* and *De institutione virginis*, and *Hali Meidenhad*. On this topic see also Bynum, *Holy Feast and Holy Fast*, esp. 20, 24; McNamara, "Sexual Equality and the Cult of Virginity," 145–48. Newman notes that "the perception of virginity as the quintessence of female holiness had momentous consequences for the spiritual life. . . . Male chastity, while seen as an important virtue, never evoked either the same rapturous praise for its preservation or the same dire warnings about its loss" (*From Virile Woman to WomanChrist*, 28).

43. On this see C. Atkinson, "'Precious Balsam in a Fragile Glass.'"

44. Newman, *From Virile Woman to WomanChrist*, 31 and 257 n. 56.

45. The phrase is borrowed from Shichtman, "Percival's Sister," 13.

46. Fries has pointed out that in Malory's Grail Quest there is a "collision" between the "exaltation of virginity" and the "values of courtly love" ("Gender and the Grail," 61). Fries cites Duby, who asserted that chivalric romance literature "was based on the exaltation of profane love, masculine desire, and the pleasure afforded by women" ("Courtly Model," 254).

47. Plummer observes that "it is precisely such 'disinherited gentlewomen,' as the lady quite accurately points out, that Perceval as a Round Table knight has sworn an oath to protect" ("Quest for Significance," 114).

48. K. C. Kelly has recently argued that even this symbolic castration is problematic for knightly order, as it comes dangerously close to calling into question

knightly masculinity in the same way a *real* castration would; see "Menaced Masculinity and Imperiled Virginity in Malory's *Morte Darthur.*"

49. Burns, in an important article on the parallel Bors and Perceval episodes in the *Queste del Saint Graal*, has argued that the casting of the devil as a feminine figure "disrupts rigid social and linguistic categories of masculinity and femininity, subverting the regulatory, heterosexual norms that typically govern both ecclesiastical and courtly cultures" ("Devilish Ways," 11).

50. Mann has rightly noted that "the claims of virginity here over-ride the claims of blood; bodily wholeness entails separation, albeit accompanied by great emotional distress, from the bonds created by fellowship and kinship" ("Malory and the Grail Legend," 216).

51. Mahoney points out that "by traditional chivalric standards, [Bors's] first duty should be to his brother, but . . . brotherly love has no place in the *Queste*. Its doctrine demands total absorption, total detachment from worldly ties" ("Truest and Holiest Tale," 115).

52. As I have noted above, Gravdal has compellingly demonstrated that rape "constitutes one of the episodic units used in the construction of a romance [and that] sexual violence is built into the very premise of Arthurian romance. It is a genre that by its definition must *create* the threat of rape" (*Ravishing Maidens*, 43). In the "Tale of the Sankgreal" the concerns of rape are tellingly sublimated to the concerns of virginity; Bors's lament makes plain that he is not so concerned with saving the woman from the horror of rape as he is with preserving her maidenhead.

53. Lévi-Strauss, *Elementary Structures of Kinship*, 51.

54. Irigaray, *This Sex*, 171.

55. Butler, *Gender Trouble*, 17.

56. Ibid., 22.

57. Mann points out that "Galahad's superiority is not a result of his trying harder. . . . His pre-eminence consists in his wholeness, which is his from the beginning, and which the events of the narrative are designed to express" ("Malory and the Grail Legend," 210).

58. Butler, *Bodies That Matter*, 99.

59. Fries has called attention to this moment, pointing out that "the shearing of a woman's hair, a secondary but important gender sign, signifies here the abandonment of earthly for spiritual chivalry" ("Gender and the Grail," 75). For more on women's virginity and bodily disfigurement in the medieval period, see Bynum, *Holy Feast and Holy Fast*. The story of St. Cecilia, told in Chaucer's "Second Nun's Tale," has also been understood to indicate a denial of femininity through a "fanatical devotion to virginity and a punishing of the female flesh"; see Cox, *Gender and Language in Chaucer*, 65. On Chaucer's "Second Nun's Tale" see also Dinshaw, *Chaucer's Sexual Poetics*, and Hansen, *Fictions of Gender*.

60. Shichtman, "Percival's Sister," 15.

61. Ibid.

62. Thornton and May have demonstrated that Malory significantly altered his

source to depict Perceval's sister as taking a more active role in this decision. See "Malory as Femininist?," esp. 43–48.

63. Hoffman, "Perceval's Sister," 73.

64. K. C. Kelly, "Malory's Body Chivalric," 63.

65. Hoffman, "Perceval's Sister," 77.

66. Ibid., 79.

67. Butler, *Gender Trouble*, 22.

68. K. C. Kelly, "Malory's Body Chivalric," 64.

Chapter 5. Lancelot, Guenevere, and the Death of Arthur: The Decline and Fall of the Chivalric Community

1. Indeed, Meale points out that Vinaver's last two "Tales" are found together in the fourth and final section of the Winchester MS and argues that while Vinaver relied "on the manuscript evidence for the textual divisions he adopted, he was not consistent in the way he interpreted it" ("'The Hoole Book,'" 15 n. 38). As C. David Benson notes, the last two tales of the *Morte d'Arthur* "are often read in isolation from the rest of the work and have been edited separately" ("Ending of the *Morte Darthur*," 221). Brewer has edited such an edition; see *Morte Darthur: Parts Seven and Eight*.

2. I do not propose to engage at any great length with the debate surrounding whether or not so-called courtly love existed as a real phenomenon, either historically or in romance literature, but my point here is that the *Morte d'Arthur* repeatedly models knightly devotion to noble women as a means of legitimizing the existence of the homosocial Round Table at the center of the larger chivalric community, and that such relationships are accurately described as "courtly." Fries has argued that "in spite of the claims of proponents of the so-called and recently identified 'demise' of even literary courtly love, as a system it served Malory and his knights very well, as long as it maintained the social approval and personal moderation which led to worship" ("How Many Roads," 203). Jaeger has suggested that medieval romance literature offers a distorted reflection of a "cult of refined love" (*Origins of Courtliness*, 267). On this see also Boase, *Origin and Meaning of Courtly Love*; Lazar, *Amour courtois et "Fin Amours" dans la littérature du XIIe siècle.*

3. Butler, *Gender Trouble*, 25.

4. Fries, "How Many Roads," 203.

5. Finke and Shichtman have called attention to Arthur's lament as indicative of the fact that "the hypermasculine world of the Arthurian court operates within a sexual economy of homosocial desire which attributes far greater value to relationships between men than it does even to the marriage of the king and queen"; see introduction to *Arthuriana* 8.2, 3.

6. Joynt has observed that Lancelot rescues Guenevere "the first time when she is innocent, the second technically innocent, and the third guilty, each one escalating the tragedy" ("Vengeance and Love," 92). While there is some question as to whether or not Lancelot and Guenevere are engaged in any sort of misconduct in the

third episode, they are certainly *perceived* by multiple knights to be so engaged, and it is this widespread perception that is detrimental to the cohesion of the social order.

7. For Malory's sources for this section see Frappier, ed., *La Mort le Roi Artu*, and Bruce, ed., *Le Morte Arthur*.

8. Heng, "Enchanted Ground," 103.

9. While Gawain is present at the dinner in the *Mort Artu* and is indeed revealed to be the intended poisoning victim in the English *Stanzaic Morte Arthur*, only Malory, as B. Kennedy notes, "develops an explicit link between the murder of Patryse and the ongoing blood feud between Gawain's family and the house of Pellinor" (*Knighthood*, 278).

10. The use of the word "treason" here to refer to "murder" is distinct from its common usage in Malory's day, when it referred specifically to the betrayal or death of one's feudal lord. York notes that this particular use of "treason" reflects French feudal law of the twelfth century; see "Legal Punishment in Malory's *Morte Darthur*."

11. The French is from Frappier, *Mort Artu*, 86. The English translation is my own.

12. Squibb, in *High Court of Chivalry*, dates the origin of the Court of Chivalry to 1347, a finding that Keen contests, arguing that the Court of Chivalry has its origins in a military court of the late thirteenth century, out of which developed "a gradual extension of the lieutenancies that the Constable and Marshal of England traditionally exercised in royal hosts" ("Jurisdiction and Origins of the Constable's Court," 168).

13. III Edward 25, stat. 5, c. 2 (*Statutes of the Realm*, 11 vols. 1:319–20). While I do not intend to offer a comprehensive discussion of the 1352 Statute of Treasons, I feel it is important to note that the enactment of this statute, even as it declared the king to be the unique representative of the realm, benefitted his subjects in that it limited the definition of "treason." This restricted the monarch's ability to threaten his enemies by leveling the blanket charge of "treason" upon them. See Bellamy's discussion of this in *Law of Treason in England in the Later Middle Ages*, esp. 11–14.

14. Squibb notes that by 1384 the Court of Chivalry's "encroachment on the common-law courts had become so serious that it had to be arrested by Parliament" (*High Court of Chivalry*, 17–18).

15. See, for example, M. Vale, "Aristocratic Violence."

16. Maitland has pointed out that trial by combat was not officially abolished until one Abraham Thornton, in 1818, "declared himself ready to defend his innocence by his body and threw down in Westminster Hill, as his gage of battle, an antique gauntlet." When his accuser refused to respond in kind, the court had no choice but to acquit Thornton of the charges brought against him. The following year trial by battle was formally abolished by an act of Parliament (59 Geo. III, c. 46). See Maitland and Montague, *A Sketch of English Legal History*, 61–63.

17. Arthur's excuse here is curious, as according to Bracton, the king was only disallowed from acting as judge in cases of *lèse-majesté*. Because English legal pro-

cedure required three parties—plaintiff, defendant, and judge—in cases of treason as defined by the Statute of 1352 the king would effectively be *both* plaintiff and judge: "it cannot be the king himself in his own suit, for he would thus be both actor and judge in a cause involving life and members and disherison"; see Henri de Bracton, *On the Laws and Customs of England,* 2:337. This is clearly not the circumstance here, as an attempt on the life of the king has not been made.

18. R. L. Kelly points out that although Guenevere is innocent, "Lancelot's motivation is called into question" by his statement that he would serve the queen "in ryght other in wronge" which implies that "he had defended Guenevere without regard to the justice of her cause" ("Wounds, Healing, and Knighthood," 184–85). As Holichek notes, "Lancelot articulates a sense of obligation to Gwenevere that is predicated on her conduct; in fact, Gwenevere's finding his sword and giving it to him when he needed it parallels Arthur's bestowing knighthood upon him" ("Malory's Gwenevere," 117).

19. Lynch has noted this problem in the *Morte d'Arthur* more generally in terms of a split along gender lines: "In the case of men, the story provides a multitude of combats which serve as a public 'pageant' of the self and a display of noble blood. . . . Malory's women, denied the field except as spectators, must reveal their moral and emotional alignment almost solely through the expressive opportunities of speech, body language and affective reactions" ("Gesture and Gender," 285–86).

20. However, in *Law of Treason,* Bellamy cites a case of treason tried under Henry IV and recorded in the *Eulogium Historiarum,* in which a Cambridge woman accused a Franciscan friar of treason. "The judge who presided over the case ordered that the dispute be settled by combat and that the friar fight the woman with one hand tied behind his back," 145.

21. See, in particular, Knight, *Arthurian Literature and Society,* esp. chap. 4; see also Pochoda, *Arthurian Propaganda,* chap. 2.

22. For a discussion of Malory's alteration of his source material, see Walsh, "Malory's 'Very Mater of La Cheualer du Charyot.'"

23. As Hill observes: "Malory's Guenevere is a complex and pivotal character whose position in the social and political structure of the Arthurian court exposes, to a greater extent than the primary male characters, the brutality and self-destructiveness that lie beneath the veneer of Christian morality and the chivalric code of the knights" ("Recovering Malory's Guenevere," 267).

24. See Joynt, "Vengeance and Love," 106; C. David Benson, "Ending of the *Morte Darthur,*" 226.

25. Walsh argues that in Meleagant's appeal, Guenevere "realizes that her preventing the fight that she had been looking forward to with evident satisfaction a moment ago will constitute a manifestation of her power over Lancelot . . . [and] is immediately attracted to the idea" (Malory's 'Very Mater of La Cheualer du Charyot,'" 207).

26. Interestingly, neither in Malory nor any of his sources does anyone attempt

to defend the queen by claiming that this is her menstrual blood; in Chrétien de Troyes's version of "Knight of the Cart," Guenevere claims to have suffered a nosebleed in the night.

27. G. Rubin, "Traffic in Women," 37.

28. Heng, "Enchanted Ground," 102.

29. Pochoda notes that Lancelot's relationship with the queen has "upset the natural hierarchy of things" and "by sinning against the private person of the king . . . endangered the safety of Arthur's kingship as an office; this threat, of course, implies chaos for the entire realm" (*Arthurian Propaganda*, 132).

30. Sedgwick, *Between Men*, 50.

31. Marchello-Nizia has offered a similar reading of the figure of Guenevere in the Prose *Lancelot*, arguing that Guenevere is representative of homosocial ties between men, as opposed to heterosexual bonds, and that it is through her that Lancelot seeks to achieve a homosocial alliance with the king; see "Amour courtois, société masculine et figures du pouvoir."

32. Harris has pointed out that all Aggravain *has* is the "noyse" of rumor as support for his claim against the queen and Lancelot: "Aggravain integrates common knowledge or common report into his accusation. In fact, common knowledge or report is the basis of his charge" ("Evidence Against Lancelot and Guinevere," 196).

33. Frappier, *Mort Artu*, 110–11. The English translation is my own.

34. B. Kennedy has argued (often and vociferously) that Lancelot and Guenevere commit adultery only once, in the "Knight of the Cart" and that afterward both are deeply repentant: "Lancelot does not lose his virginity until he begets Galahad and actually commits adultery with Guenever only once" ("Adultery in Malory's *Morte Darthur*," 65). Thus, in Kennedy's reading, Lancelot and the queen are engaged in nothing more illicit than private conversation at the time of Mordred and Aggravain's ambush. See also her *Knighthood*, chap. 6, as well as "Malory's Lancelot: 'Trewest Lover, of a Synful Man.'" Fries has offered a scathing critique of Kennedy's reading of Lancelot and Guenevere's relationship, arguing instead that what Malory has done is create a "rich ambivalence" surrounding Lancelot and Guenevere "which requires our moral assessment of his adulterous lovers always to be deferred rather than crushed into or stretched out upon a procrustean bed" ("Commentary: A Response to the *Arthuriana* Issue on Adultery," 96). I concur with Fries's contention that Lancelot and Guenevere have begun an adulterous affair long before the one scene of *explicit* adultery that we see in the "Knight of the Cart." Although Malory has suppressed other mentions of adultery between the queen and the knight found in his sources, his intent does not seem to have been to suggest that no adultery was taking place until the fateful evening at Meleagant's castle. By the time Malory composed his *Morte d'Arthur*, it was a commonplace that Lancelot and Guenevere were lovers; every contemporary reader coming to the *Morte d'Arthur* would know from the beginning the shape and outcome of the narrative. Thus, if Malory truly were attempting to rewrite his material such that Lancelot and Guenevere commit

adultery only once, he would certainly have needed to use much more forceful and explicit language than he does here in order to "correct" the traditional perception that the two characters were long-time lovers.

35. See C. David Benson, "Gawain's Defense of Lancelot in Malory's 'Death of Arthur,'" 270; see also Holichek, "Malory's Gwenevere," 118.

36. R. L. Kelly has argued that Arthur's actions here do not reflect any fifteenth-century understanding of English common law: "Malory's contemporaries might have been troubled by Arthur's sentencing of Guinevere on three grounds: a king should not assume jurisdiction over anyone accused of lese-majesty against himself, a person accused of treason should not be condemned without a trial by her peers, and 'haste' in judicial proceedings is not wise" ("Malory and the Common Law," 119).

37. The use of this phrase here and in "The Poisoned Apple" would have puzzled readers of the *Morte d'Arthur*, in that no less a jurist than Fortescue held that, despite myriad invasions, from the time of the first Celtic inhabitants of Britain "the realm has been continuously ruled by the same customs as it is now"; see Chrimes, ed. and trans., *De Laudibus Legum Angliae*, 39.

38. Harris, "Evidence Against Lancelot and Guinevere," 204.

39. In the *Mort Artu*, Arthur's main reason for waging war on Lancelot is his affair with the queen; Malory has altered his sources to emphasize the king's love for his nephew Gawain as his prime motivation. In his *Characterization in Malory* Wilson was one of the first scholars to point out Malory's revision of his source material to demonstrate a particularly close and devoted relationship between Arthur and Gawain; see esp. 106–9.

40. See, among others, Brundage, *Law, Sex, and Christian Society;* Goody, *Development of the Family and Marriage in Europe;* Duby, *The Knight, the Lady and the Priest,* esp. 35–37; and Archibald, "Incest in Medieval Literature and Society."

41. Archibald points out that "Mordred's story is not about a son's emotional relationship with his mother, but rather about his political relationship with his father" ("Arthur and Mordred," 22).

42. M. V. Guerin, *Fall of Kings and Princes,* 71.

43. Sedgwick, *Between Men,* 21.

44. M. V. Guerin, *Fall of Kings and Princes,* 65.

45. Morse points out that "The final tragedy in the whole book is usually, and rightly, read as the collapse of Arthurian society because of and precisely through those overt values that made it what it was. Loyalties conflict" ("Sterile Queens and Questing Orphans," 42).

46. As I have noted above (and as many other scholars have noted) Sir Borre, Arthur's son by Lionors, seems to have completely disappeared.

47. Finke and Shichtman, "No Pain, No Gain," 119.

48. Heng, "Enchanted Ground," 108.

49. Moorman, Larry Benson, and Lambert are among the critics who feel that the conclusion of the *Morte d'Arthur* is in some way "unsatisfactory"; see Moorman,

Book of Kyng Arthur, esp. 101–5; Benson, *Malory's Morte Darthur*, esp. 248; and Lambert, *Malory: Style and Vision*, 145–80. More recently Morgan has called particular attention to "the ending of the ending"—the section with which I am concerned here—as particularly anticlimatic; see "Malory's Double Ending." To be fair, the *Morte d'Arthur*'s "anticlimactic" ending is not unique to Malory's version of the Arthurian story; Lacy has noted that Malory's source, the *Mort Artu* ends "not with a bang but a whimper" ("The *Mort Artu* and Cyclic Closure," 85).

50. Indeed, Lynch has pointed out that in the *Morte d'Arthur* Guenevere "draws her textual value from her relations with men" ("Gesture and Gender," 286).

51. Cherewatuk, "Saint's Life of Sir Launcelot," 67.

52. See L. D. Benson, *Malory's Morte Darthur*, 242; Frappier, *Etude sur "La Mort le roi Artu*," 226; M. V. Guerin, *Fall of Kings and Princes*, 75.

53. *Mort Artu*, 219. C. David Benson questions the sincerity of Guenevere's transformation in Malory; see "Ending of the *Morte Darthur*," 236. The English translation is from Lacy, gen. ed., *Lancelot-Grail*, 4:147.

54. Only one extant manuscript of the *Mort Artu* (Palatinus Latinus 1967) contains this final meeting between Lancelot and Guenevere; Frappier includes this scene in an appendix to his edition (264–66). This would seem to be the version of the *Mort Artu* that the author of the English *Stanzaic Morte Arthur* used as *his* source. In the *Mort Artu*, Guenevere kisses Lancelot in farewell when he leaves the nunnery; Malory apparently took the English *Stanzaic Morte Arthur* as his main source for the refusal of the kiss: "'kysse me, and I shall wend as-tyte' / 'Nay,' said the quene, 'that wyll I not / launcelot, thynke on that no more; / To Absteyne vs we muste haue thought / For suche we haue delyted in ore'" (3713–17); see Bruce, ed., *Le Morte Arthur*, 113.

55. Lancelot's farewell pledge to Guenevere in the *Morte d'Arthur* has no correspondence in either the English *Stanzaic Morte Arthur* or the *Mort Artu*. See *Le Morte Arthur*, ll. 1848–71 (Bruce, 54–55), and Frappier, 116–17.

56. In the *Mort Artu* and the English *Stanzaic Morte Arthur*, Lancelot returns Guenevere to Arthur without a farewell speech and kiss; see Frappier, 157–58, and *Le Morte Arthur*, ll. 2380–2403 (Bruce, 71–72).

57. C. David Benson, "Ending of the *Morte Darthur*," 244.

58. Ibid., 237.

59. It is significant that the knights do not choose to create a new subcommunity devoted to the Virgin Mary; in maintaining the model of knightly devotion to the feminine—importantly, to an earthly rather than spiritual representation of femininity—they demonstrate their inability to break free from the courtly chivalric social order that has now been destroyed.

60. Hill, "Recovering Malory's Gwenevere," 275.

61. Cherewatuk, for example, takes issue with an interpretation of this scene that sees the insincerity of Lancelot's priestly vows made manifest in his lament over Guenevere's body: "This claim, it seems to me, is based on a faulty grammatical reading. In the phrase 'Whan I remember of hir beaulte and of hir noblesse that was

bothe wyth hyr kyng and wyth hyr' . . . 'hir' equates not with modern English 'her,' signifying Guenevere alone, but with 'their' referring to both queen and king" ("Saint's Life of Sir Launcelot," 68). Whether or not Lancelot is explicitly articulating sorrow for both king and queen, Arthur's death has not had nearly the impact on him that Guenevere's does.

62. See B. Kennedy, *Knighthood*, 345.

63. See Wack, *Lovesickness in the Middle Ages*.

64. Harris, "Lancelot's Vocation," 233.

65. Cherewatuk points out that Malory has altered his sources slightly to emphasize the hagiographic elements of Lancelot's death; see "Saint's Life of Sir Launcelot," 63.

66. L. D. Benson, *Malory's Morte Darthur*, 245.

Bibliography

Ackerman, Robert W. "'The Tale of Gareth' and the Unity of *Le Morte D'Arthur*." In *Philological Essays: Studies in Old and Middle English Language and Literature in Honor of Herbert Dean Merritt*, edited by James L. Rosier, 196–203. The Hague: Mouton, 1970.

Adams, Jeremy duQuesnay. "Modern Views of Medieval Chivalry." In *The Study of Chivalry: Resources and Approaches*, edited by Howell Chickering and Thomas H. Seiler, 41–90. Kalamazoo, Mich.: Medieval Institute Publications, 1988.

Allen, Rosamund, trans. *Lawman: Brut*. New York: St. Martin's Press, 1992.

Archibald, Elizabeth. "Arthur and Mordred: Variations on an Incest Theme." In *Arthurian Literature VIII*, edited by Richard Barber, 1–28. Cambridge, England: D. S. Brewer, 1989.

———. "Beginnings: *The Tale of King Arthur* and *King Arthur and the Emperor Lucius*." In *A Companion to Malory*, edited by Elizabeth Archibald and A.S.G. Edwards, 133–52. Cambridge, England: D. S. Brewer, 1996.

———. "Incest in Medieval Literature and Society." *Forum for Modern Language Studies* 25 (1989): 1–15.

Archibald, Elizabeth, and A.S.G. Edwards, eds. *A Companion to Malory*. Cambridge, England: D. S. Brewer, 1996.

Armstrong, Dorsey. "Gender and the Chivalric Community: The Pentecostal Oath in Malory's 'Tale of King Arthur.'" *Bibliographical Bulletin of the International Arthurian Society* 51 (1999): 293–312.

———. "Gender and Fear: Malory's Lancelot and Knightly Identity." In *Arizona Studies in the Middle Ages and the Renaissance, 6: Fear and its Representations in the Middle Ages and the Renaissance*, edited by Anne Scott and Cynthia Kosso, 255–73. Turnhout, Belgium: Brepols, 2002.

———. "Malory's Morgause." In *On Arthurian Women: Essays in Honor of Maureen Fries*, edited by Bonnie Wheeler and Fiona Tolhurst, 149–60. Dallas: Scriptorium Press, 2001.

Arnold, Ivor, ed. *Le Roman de Brut de Wace*. 2 vols. Paris: Société des Anciens Textes Français, 1938–40.

Asher, Martha. Introduction to the *Suite du Merlin*. In *Lancelot-Grail: The Old French Arthurian Vulgate and Post-Vulgate in Translation*, edited by Norris J. Lacy, 4:163–65. New York: Garland, 1995.

Atkinson, Clarissa. "'Precious Balsam in a Fragile Glass': The Ideology of Virginity in the Later Middle Ages." *Journal of Family History* 8 (1983): 131–43.

Atkinson, Stephen C. B. "Malory's Lancelot and the Quest of the Grail." In *Studies in Malory*, edited by James W. Spisak, 129–52. Kalamazoo, Mich.: Medieval Institute Publications, 1985.

Barber, Richard. "Chivalry and the *Morte Darthur*." In *A Companion to Malory*, edited by Elizabeth Archibald and A.S.G. Edwards, 19–36. Cambridge, England: D. S. Brewer, 1996.

———, ed. *The Pastons: A Family in the Wars of the Roses*. Woodbridge, England: Boydell Press, 1991.

Barron, W.R.J. *English Medieval Romance*. London and New York: Longman, 1987.

Bartlett, Anne Clark. "Cracking the Penile Code: Reading Gender and Conquest in the Alliterative *Morte Arthure*." *Arthuriana* 8.2 (1998): 56–76.

Batt, Catherine. "Malory and Rape." *Arthuriana* 7.3 (1997): 78–99.

———. *Malory's "Morte Darthur": Remaking Arthurian Tradition*. New York: Palgrave, 2002.

Bellamy, J. G. *Bastard Feudalism and the Law*. London: Routledge, 1989.

———. *The Law of Treason in England in the Later Middle Ages*. Cambridge: Cambridge University Press, 1970.

Bennett, J.A.W., ed. *Essays on Malory*. Oxford: Clarendon Press, 1963.

Benson, C. David. "The Ending of the *Morte Darthur*." In *A Companion to Malory*, edited by Elizabeth Archibald and A.S.G. Edwards, 221–40. Cambridge, England: D. S. Brewer, 1996.

———. "Gawain's Defense of Lancelot in Malory's 'Death of Arthur.'" *Modern Language Review* 72.2 (1983): 267–72.

Benson, Larry D. "The Date of the Alliterative *Morte Arthure*." In *Medieval Studies in Honor of Lillian Herlands Hornstein*, edited by Jess B. Bessinger, Jr., and Robert K. Raymo, 19–40. New York: New York University Press, 1976.

———. *Malory's Morte Darthur*. Cambridge: Harvard University Press, 1976.

Boase, Roger. *The Origin and Meaning of Courtly Love: A Critical Study of European Scholarship*. Manchester: Manchester University Press; Totowa, N.J.: Rowman and Littlefield, 1977.

Bolton, J. L. *The Medieval English Economy 1150–1500*. London: J. M. Dent and Sons, 1980.

Boswell, John. *Christianity, Social Tolerance and Homosexuality: Gay People in Western Europe from the Beginning of the Christian Era to the Fourteenth Century*. Chicago: University of Chicago Press, 1980.

Bracton, Henri de. *On the Laws and Customs of England*. Edited and translated by Woodbine, revised by Samuel E. Thorne. 4 vols. Cambridge, Mass.: Harvard University Press, 1968.

Brewer, Derek. "'the hoole book.'" In *Essays in Malory*, edited by J.A.W. Bennett, 41–63. Oxford: Clarendon Press, 1963.

———. "The Image of Lancelot: Chrétien and Malory." In *Spätmittelalterliche Artusliteratur*, edited by Karl Heinz Göller, 105–18. Paderborn, Germany: Ferdinand Schöningh, 1984.

———. "Malory's 'Preving' of Sir Launcelot." In *The Changing Face of Arthurian Romance: Essays on Arthurian Prose Romances in Memory of Cedric E. Pickford*, edited by Alison Adams et al., 123–36. Cambridge, England: D. S. Brewer, 1986.

———. "The Presentation of the Character of Lancelot: Chrétien to Malory." In *Arthurian Literature III*, edited by Richard Barber, 26–52. Totowa, N.J.: Barnes and Noble, 1983. Reprinted in *Lancelot and Guinevere: A Casebook*, edited by Lori J. Walters, 3–28. New York: Garland, 1996.

———, ed. *The Morte Darthur: Parts Seven and Eight*. London: D. S. Brewer, 1968.

Britnell, Richard H. *The Commercialisation of English Society: 1000–1500*. Manchester: Manchester University Press, 1996.

———. *Growth and Decline in Colchester*. Cambridge: Cambridge University Press, 1986.

Bruce, J. Douglas, ed. *Le Morte Arthur*. EETS E.S. 88. London: Oxford University Press, 1959.

Brundage, James A. *Law, Sex, and Christian Society in Medieval Europe*. Chicago: University of Chicago Press, 1987.

Bryant, Nigel, trans. *The High Book of the Grail: A Translation of the Thirteenth Century "Romance of Perlesvaus."* Cambridge, England: D. S. Brewer, 1978.

Bullough, Vern L. "Medieval Concepts of Adultery." *Arthuriana* 7.4 (1997): 5–15.

———. *Sexual Variance in Society and History*. New York: Wiley, 1976.

Bullough, Vern L., and James A. Brundage, eds. *Sexual Practices and the Medieval Church*. Buffalo: Prometheus Books, 1982.

Burns, E. Jane. "Devilish Ways: Sexing the Subject in the *Queste del Saint Graal.*" *Arthuriana* 8.2 (1998): 11–32.

———. Introduction to *Lancelot-Grail: The Old French Arthurian Vulgate and Post-Vulgate in Translation*, edited by Norris J. Lacy, 1:xv–xxxiii. New York: Garland, 1993.

———. "Refashioning Courtly Love: Lancelot as Ladies' Man or Lady/Man?" In *Constructing Medieval Sexuality*, edited by Karma Lochrie et al., 111–34. Minneapolis: University of Minnesota Press, 1997.

Burns, E. Jane, trans. "The Quest for the Holy Grail." In vol. 4 of *Lancelot-Grail: The Old French Arthurian Vulgate and Post-Vulgate in Translation*, edited by Norris J. Lacy. New York: Garland, 1995.

Busby, Keith. "The Likes of Dinadan: The Role of the Misfit in Arthurian Literature." *Neophilologus* 67 (1983): 161–74.

Butler, Judith. *Bodies That Matter: On the Discursive Limits of Sex*. New York: Routledge, 1993.

————. *Gender Trouble: Feminism and the Subversion of Identity.* New York: Routledge, 1990.

Bynum, Caroline Walker. *Holy Feast and Holy Fast: The Religious Significance of Food to Medieval Women.* Berkeley and Los Angeles: University of California Press, 1987.

Cadden, Joan. *Meanings of Sex Difference in the Middle Ages: Medicine, Science, and Culture.* Cambridge: Cambridge University Press, 1993.

Carpenter, Christine. "The Beauchamp affinity: a study of bastard feudalism at work." *English Historical Review* 95 (1980): 514–32.

Caxton, William. *The Book of Fayttes of Armes and of Chyualrye.* Edited by A.T.P. Byles. London: EETS, no. 189, 1932.

————. *Book of the Ordre of Chyualry.* Edited by A. T. P. Byles. London: EETS 168, 1926.

Chambers, E. K. *English Literature at the Close of the Middle Ages.* Oxford: Clarendon Press, 1945.

————. *Sir Thomas Malory.* Oxford: Oxford University Press, 1922.

Cherewatuk, Karen. "Born-Again Virgins and Holy Bastards: Bors and Elyne and Lancelot and Galahad." *Arthuriana* 11.2 (2001): 52–63.

————. "Echoes of the Knighting Ceremony in *Sir Gawain and the Green Knight.*" *Neophilologus* 77 (1993): 135–47.

————. "'Gentyl' Audiences and 'Grete Bookes': Chivalric Manuals and the *Morte Darthur.*" In *Arthurian Literature XV,* edited by James P. Carley and Felicity Riddy, 205–16. Cambridge, England: D. S. Brewer, 1997.

————. "Pledging Troth in Malory's 'Tale of Sir Gareth.'" *Journal of English and Germanic Philology* (2002): 19–40.

————. "The Saint's Life of Sir Launcelot: Hagiography and the Conclusion of Malory's *Morte Darthur.*" *Arthuriana* 5.1 (1995): 62–78.

————. "Sir Thomas Malory's 'Grete Booke.'" In *The Social and Literary Contexts of Malory's Morte Darthur,* edited by D. Thomas Hanks, Jr., 42–67. Cambridge, England: D. S. Brewer, 2000.

Chickering, Howell, and Thomas H. Seiler, eds. *The Study of Chivalry: Resources and Approaches.* Kalamazoo, Mich.: Medieval Institute Publications, 1988.

Chrimes, S. B., ed. and trans. *John Fortescue: De Laudibus Legum Angliae.* Cambridge: Cambridge University Press, 1942.

Clough, Andrea. "Malory's *Morte Darthur:* The 'Hoole Book.'" *Medievalia et Humanistica,* n.s., 14 (1986): 139–56.

Cohen, Jeffrey Jerome. *Of Giants: Sex, Monsters, and the Middle Ages.* Minneapolis: University of Minnesota Press, 1999.

Connell, R. W. *Masculinities.* Berkeley and Los Angeles: University of California Press, 1995.

Cooper, Helen. "The Book of Sir Tristram de Lyones." In *A Companion to Malory,* edited by Elizabeth Archibald and A.S.G. Edwards, 183–202. Cambridge, England: D. S. Brewer, 1996.

Coss, Peter. "Bastard Feudalism Revised." *Past and Present* 125 (1989): 33–49.

————. *The Knight in Medieval England: 1000–1400*. Gloucestershire: Alan Sutton Publishing, 1993.

Cox, Catherine S. *Gender and Language in Chaucer*. Gainesville: University Press of Florida, 1997.

Crane, Susan. *Gender and Romance in the "Canterbury Tales."* Princeton: Princeton University Press, 1994.

————. *Insular Romance: Politics, Faith and Culture in Anglo-Norman and Middle English Literature*. Berkeley and Los Angeles: University of California Press, 1986.

Curtis, Renée. *Le Roman de Tristan*. 3 volumes. Cambridge, England: D. S. Brewer, 1985. (Vol. 1 originally published Munich: Max Hueber Verlag, 1963; vol. 2 originally published Leiden: E. J. Brill, 1976).

Day, John. *The Medieval Market Economy*. Oxford: Basil Blackwell, 1988.

de Lauretis, Teresa. *Technologies of Gender: Essays on Theory, Film and Fiction*. Bloomington and Indianapolis: Indiana University Press, 1987.

Dichmann, Mary E. "'The Tale of King Arthur and the Emperor Lucius': The Rise of Lancelot." In *Malory's Originality: A Critical Study of Le Morte Darthur*, edited by R. M. Lumiansky, 67–90. Baltimore: Johns Hopkins Press, 1964.

Dinshaw, Carolyn. *Chaucer's Sexual Poetics*. Madison: University of Wisconsin Press, 1989.

Dobson, R. B. *The Peasants' Revolt of 1381*. London: Macmillan, 1970.

Dobyns, Ann. *The Voices of Romance: Studies in Dialogue and Character*. Newark: University of Delaware Press, 1989.

Dollimore, Jonathan. *Sexual Dissidence: Augustine to Wilde, Freud to Foucault*. Oxford: Clarendon Press, 1991.

Drewes, Jeanne. "The Sense of Hidden Identity in Malory's *Morte Darthur*." In *Sir Thomas Malory: Views and Reviews*, edited by D. Thomas Hanks, Jr., 7–25. New York: AMS Press, 1992.

Duby, Georges. *The Chivalrous Society*. Translated by Cynthia Postan. Berkeley and Los Angeles: University of California Press, 1977.

————. "The Courtly Model." In *A History of Women in the West, II: Silences of the Middle Ages*, edited by Christiane Klapisch-Zuber, 250–66. Cambridge: Harvard University Press, 1992.

————. *The Knight, the Lady and the Priest: The Making of Modern Marriage in Medieval France*. Translated by Barbara Bray. New York: Pantheon Books, 1983.

————. *The Three Orders: Feudal Society Imagined*. Translated by Arthur Goldhammer. Chicago: University of Chicago Press, 1980.

Dyer, C. C. *Lords and Peasants in a Changing Society*. Cambridge: Cambridge University Press, 1980.

Dyer, Christopher. *Standards of Living in the Later Middle Ages: Social Change in England c. 1200–1520*. Cambridge, England: D. S. Brewer, 1989.

Edwards, Elizabeth. *The Genesis of Narrative in Malory's Morte Darthur*. Cambridge, England: D. S. Brewer, 2001.

————. "The Place of Women in the *Morte Darthur*." In *A Companion to Malory*, edited by Elizabeth Archibald and A.S.G. Edwards, 37–54. Cambridge, England: D. S. Brewer, 1996.

Ellis, Henry, ed. *The Chronicle of John Hardyng.* London: 1812.

Evans, Murray J. "*Ordinatio* and Narrative Links: The Impact of Malory's Tales as a 'hoole book.'" In *Studies in Malory,* edited by James W. Spisak, 29–52. Kalamazoo, Mich.: Medieval Institute Publications, 1985.

Ferguson, Arthur B. *The Indian Summer of English Chivalry: Studies in the Decline and Transformation of Chivalric Idealism.* Durham: Duke University Press, 1960.

Ferster, Judith. *Fictions of Advice: The Literature and Politics of Counsel in Late Medieval England.* Philadelphia: University of Pennsylvania Press, 1996.

Field, P.J.C. *The Life and Times of Sir Thomas Malory.* Cambridge, England: D. S. Brewer, 1993.

———. "Malory and the French prose *Lancelot.*" *Bulletin of the John Rylands University Library of Manchester* 75.1 (1993): 79–102.

———. "The Malory Life Records." In *A Companion to Malory,* edited by Elizabeth Archibald and A.S.G. Edwards, 115–32. Cambridge, England: D. S. Brewer, 1996.

———. *Malory: Texts and Sources.* Cambridge, England: D. S. Brewer, 1998.

———. *Romance and Chronicle: A Study of Malory's Prose Style.* London: Barrie and Jenkins, 1971.

Finke, Laurie A., and Martin B. Shichtman. Introduction to *Arthuriana* 8.2 (1998): 3–10.

———. "The Mont St. Michel Giant: Sexual Violence and Imperialism in the Chronicles of Wace and Laȝamon." In *Violence Against Women in Medieval Texts,* edited by Anna Roberts, 56–74. Gainesville: University Press of Florida, 1998.

———. "No Pain, No Gain: Violence as Symbolic Capital in Malory's *Morte Darthur.*" *Arthuriana* 8.2 (1998): 115–33.

Flint, Valerie I.J. "The *Historia Regum Brittaniae* of Geoffrey of Monmouth: Parody and Its Purpose. A Suggestion." *Speculum* 54 (1979): 447–68.

Foucault, Michel. *History of Sexuality. Volume One: An Introduction.* New York: Vintage, 1980.

Fradenburg, Louise O. *City, Marriage, Tournament: Arts of Rule in Late Medieval Scotland.* Madison: University of Wisconsin Press, 1991.

———. "The Love of Thy Neighbor." In *Constructing Medieval Sexuality,* edited by Karma Lochrie et al., 135–57. Minneapolis: University of Minnesota Press, 1997.

Frappier, Jean. *Etude sur "La Mort le roi Artu."* (Study on *La Mort le roi Artu.*) Geneva: Droz, 1968.

———. "Le Graal et la chevalerie." (The Grail and chivalry.) *Romania* 75 (1954): 165–210.

———, ed. *La Mort le Roi Artu.* Geneva: Droz, 1964.

Fries, Maureen. "Commentary." *Arthuriana* 7.4 (1997): 92–96.

———. "Female Heroes, Heroines and Counter-Heroes: Images of Women in the Arthurian Tradition." In *Arthurian Women: A Casebook,* edited by Thelma S. Fenster, 59–76. New York: Garland, 1996.

———. "Gender and the Grail." *Arthuriana* 8.1 (1998): 67–79.

———. "How Many Roads to Camelot?: The Married Knight in Malory." In *Culture and the King: The Social Implications of the Arthurian Legend,* edited by Martin B. Shichtman and James P. Carley, 196–210. Albany: State University of New York Press, 1994.

———. "Indiscreet Objects of Desire: Malory's 'Tristram' and the Necessity of Deceit." In *Studies in Malory,* edited by James W. Spisak, 87–108. Kalamazoo, Mich.: Medieval Institute Publications, 1985.

———. "Tristram as Counter-Hero to the *Morte Darthur.*" *Neuphilologische Mitteilungen* 76 (1975): 605–13.

Garber, Marjorie. *Vested Interests: Cross-Dressing and Cultural Anxiety.* New York and London: Routledge, 1992.

Geoffrey of Monmouth. *History of the Kings of Britain.* Translated by Lewis Thorpe. London: Penguin, 1966.

Göller, Karl Heinz. "Arthurian Chivalry in the Fourteenth and Fifteenth Centuries: History and Fiction." In *Spätmittelalterliche Artusliteratur,* edited by Göller, 53–104. Paderborn, Germany: Ferdinand Schöningh, 1984.

———. "Reality versus Romance: A Reassessment of the *Alliterative Morte Arthure.*" In *The Alliterative Morte Arthure: A Reassessment of the Poem,* edited by Göller, 15–29. Cambridge, England: D. S. Brewer, 1981.

Goodman, J. R. "Malory and Caxton's Chivalric Series, 1481–85." In *Studies in Malory,* edited by James W. Spisak, 257–74. Kalamazoo, Mich.: Medieval Institute Publications, 1985.

Goody, Jack. *The Development of the Family and Marriage in Europe.* Cambridge: Cambridge University Press, 1983.

Gravdal, Kathryn. *Ravishing Maidens: Writing Rape in Medieval French Literature and Law.* Philadelphia: University of Pennsylvania Press, 1991.

Green, Monica. "Female Sexuality in the Medieval West." *Trends in History* 4 (1990): 127–58.

Grimm, Kevin. "Fellowship and Envy: Structuring the Narrative of Malory's *Tale of Sir Tristram.*" *Fifteenth Century Studies* 20 (1993): 77–98.

Grosz, Elizabeth. *Volatile Bodies: Toward a Corporeal Feminism.* Bloomington and Indianapolis: Indiana University Press, 1994.

Guerin, M. Victoria. *The Fall of Kings and Princes: Structure and Destruction in Arthurian Tragedy.* Stanford: Stanford University Press, 1995.

———. "The King's Sin: The Origins of the David-Arthur Parallel." In *The Passing of Arthur: New Essays in Arthurian Tradition,* edited by Christopher Baswell and William Sharpe, 15–30. New York: Garland, 1988.

Guerin, Wilfred W. "'The Tale of Gareth': The Chivalric Flowering." In *Malory's Originality,* edited by R. M. Lumiansky, 99–117. Baltimore: Johns Hopkins Press, 1964.

Hanks, D. Thomas, Jr. "Foil and Forecast: Dynadan in *The Book of Sir Tristram.*" *Arthurian Yearbook* I (1991): 149–65.

———. "Malory's Anti-Knights: Balin and Breunys." In *The Social and Literary Contexts of Malory's Morte Darthur,* edited by D. Thomas Hanks, Jr., and Jessica G. Brogdon, 94–110. Cambridge, England: D. S. Brewer, 2000.

———. "Malory's *Book of Sir Tristram:* Focusing *Le Morte Darthur.*" *Quondam et Futurus* 3.1 (1993): 14–31.

———, ed. *Sir Thomas Malory: Views and Reviews.* New York: AMS Press, 1992.

———, ed. *The Social and Literary Contexts of Malory's Morte Darthur.* Cambridge, England: D. S. Brewer, 2001.

Hanning, Robert W. "The Criticism of Chivalric Epic and Romance." In *The Study of Chivalry: Resources and Approaches,* edited by Howell Chickering and Thomas H. Seiler, 91–114. Kalamazoo, Mich.: Medieval Institute Publications, 1988.

Hansen, Elaine Tuttle. *Chaucer and the Fictions of Gender.* Berkeley and Los Angeles: University of California Press, 1992.

Harris, E. Kay. "Evidence Against Lancelot and Guinevere in Malory's *Morte Darthur:* Treason by Imagination." *Exemplaria* 7.1 (1995): 180–205.

———. "Lancelot's Vocation: Traitor Saint." In *The Lancelot-Grail Cycle: Text and Transformations,* edited by William Kibler, 219–37. Austin: Univ. of Texas Press, 1994.

Heng, Geraldine. "Enchanted Ground: The Feminine Subtext in Malory." In *Courtly Literature: Culture and Context,* edited by Keith Busby and Erik Kooper, 283–300. Amsterdam: John Benjamins, 1990. Reprinted in *Arthurian Women: A Casebook,* edited by Thelma S. Fenster, 97–115. New York: Garland, 1996.

———. "A Map of Her Desire: Reading the Feminism in Arthurian Romance." In *Perceiving Other Worlds,* edited by Edwin Thumboo, 250–60. Singapore: Times Academic Press, 1991.

———. "A Woman Wants: The Lady, *Gawain,* and the Forms of Seduction." *Yale Journal of Criticism* 5:3 (1992): 101–33.

Hill, Sarah J. "Recovering Malory's Guenevere." In *Lancelot and Guenevere: A Casebook,* edited by Lori J. Walters, 267–77. New York: Garland, 1996.

Hoffman, Donald L. "Malory's 'Cinderella Knights' and the Notion of Adventure." *Philological Quarterly* 67.2 (1988): 145–56.

———. "Perceval's Sister: Malory's 'Rejected' Masculinities." *Arthuriana* 6.4 (1996): 72–83.

Holbrook, Sue Ellen. "Nymue, the Chief Lady of the Lake in Malory's *Le Morte Darthur.*" *Speculum* 53 (1978): 761–77. Reprinted in *Arthurian Women: A Casebook,* edited by Thelma S. Fenster, 171–90. New York: Garland, 1996.

Holichek, Lindsay. "Malory's Gwenevere: After Long Silence." *Annuale Mediævale* 22 (1982): 112–26.

House, Roy Temple, ed. *L'Ordene de Chevalerie: An Old French Poem*. Norman: University of Oklahoma Bulletin, 1919.

Hynes-Berry, Mary. "A Tale 'Breffly Drawyne Oute of Freynshe.'" In *Aspects of Malory*, edited by Toshiyuki Takamiya and Derek Brewer, 93–106. Cambridge, England: D. S. Brewer, 1981.

Ihle, Sandra Ness. *Malory's Grail Quest: Invention and Adaptation in Medieval Prose Romance*. Madison: University of Wisconsin Press, 1983.

Ingham, Patricia Clare. *Sovereign Fantasies: Arthurian Romance and the Making of Britain*. Philadelphia: University of Pennsylvania Press, 2001.

Irigaray, Luce. *This Sex Which Is Not One*. Translated by Catherine Porter with Carolyn Burke. Ithaca: Cornell University Press, 1985.

Jaeger, C. Stephen. *Ennobling Love: In Search of a Lost Sensibility*. Philadelphia: University of Pennsylvania Press, 1999.

———. *The Origins of Courtliness: Civilizing Trends and the Formation of Courtly Ideals, 939–1210*. Philadelphia: University of Pennsylvania Press, 1985.

James, Mervyn. *English Politics and the Concept of Honor: 1485–1642*. Oxford: Oxford University Press, 1978.

Jameson, Frederic. *The Political Unconscious: Narrative as a Socially Symbolic Act*. Ithaca: Cornell University Press, 1981.

Jesmok, Janet. "'A Knyght Wyveles': The Young Sir Lancelot in Malory's *Morte Darthur*." *Modern Language Quarterly* 42.4 (1981): 315–30.

Johnson, Lesley. "Reading the Past in Laȝamon's *Brut*." In *The Text and Tradition of Laȝamon's Brut*, edited by Françoise Le Saux, 141–60. Cambridge, England: D. S. Brewer, 1994.

Joynt, Irene. "Vengeance and Love in 'The Book of Sir Launcelot and Queen Guinevere.'" In *Arthurian Literature III*, edited by Richard Barber, 91–112. Cambridge, England: D. S. Brewer, 1984.

Kaeuper, Richard. *Chivalry and Violence in Medieval Europe*. Oxford: Oxford University Press, 2001.

———. *War, Justice and Public Order: England and France in the Later Middle Ages*. Oxford: Clarendon Press, 1988.

———, ed. *Violence in Medieval Society*. Woodbridge, England: Boydell Press, 2000.

Kaeuper, Richard, and Elspeth Kennedy, eds. and trans. *The Book of Chivalry of Geoffroi de Charny: Text, Context, and Translation*. Philadelphia: University of Pennsylvania Press, 1996.

Kaplan, E. Ann. "Is the Gaze Male?" In *Powers of Desire: The Politics of Sexuality*, edited by Ann Snitow et al., 309–27. New York: Monthly Review Press, 1983.

Kay, Sarah. "The Contradictions of Courtly Love and the Origins of Courtly Poetry: The Evidence of the *Lauzengiers*." *Journal of Medieval and Early Modern Studies* 26.2 (1996): 209–53.

Keen, Maurice. *Chivalry*. New Haven: Yale University Press, 1984.

———. *English Society in the Later Middle Ages: 1348–1500*. London: Penguin, 1990.

———. "The Jurisdiction and Origins of the Constable's Court." In *War and Government in the Middle Ages*, edited by J. Gillingham and J.C. Holt, 159–69. Cambridge: Harvard University Press, 1984.

———. *Nobles, Knights, and Men at Arms in the Middle Ages*. London: Hambledon Press, 1996.

Kelly, Kathleen Coyne. "Malory's Body Chivalric." *Arthuriana* 6.4 (1996): 52–71.

———. "Menaced Masculinity and Imperiled Virginity in Malory's *Morte Darthur*." In *Menacing Virgins: Representing Virginity in the Middle Ages and the Renaissance*, edited by Kathleen Coyne Kelly and Marina Leslie, 97–114. Newark: University of Delaware Press, 1999.

Kelly, Robert L. "Malory and the Common Law: *Hasty jougement* in the "Tale of the Death of King Arthur." *Medievalia et Humanistica*, n.s., 22 (1995): 111–40.

———. "Wounds, Healing, and Knighthood in Malory's 'Tale of Lancelot and Guenevere.'" In *Studies in Malory*, edited by James W. Spisak, 173–98. Kalamazoo, Mich.: Medieval Institute Publications, 1985.

Kennedy, Beverly. "Adultery in Malory's *Morte Darthur*." *Arthuriana* 7.4 (1997): 63–91.

———. *Knighthood in the Morte Darthur*. 2nd edition. Cambridge, England: D. S. Brewer, 1992.

———. "Malory's Lancelot: 'Trewest Lover, of a Synful Man.'" *Viator* 12 (1981): 409–56.

Kennedy, Edward D. "Malory and His English Sources." In *Aspects of Malory*, edited by Toshiyuki Takamiya and Derek Brewer, 27–55. Cambridge, England: D. S. Brewer, 1981.

———. "Malory's King Mark and King Arthur." *Medieval Studies* 37 (1975): 190–234. Reprinted in *King Arthur: A Casebook*, edited by E. D. Kennedy, 139–72. New York: Garland, 1996.

———. "Malory and the Marriage of Edward IV." *Texas Studies in Literature and Language* 12.2 (1970): 155–62.

———. "Malory's Use of Hardyng's *Chronicle*." *Notes and Queries* 16 (1969): 169–70.

Ker, N. R., ed. *The Winchester Malory: A Facsimile*. EETS SS 4. London: Oxford University Press, 1976.

Kibler, William W., ed. *Chrétien de Troyes: Arthurian Romances*. Translated by Carleton W. Carroll. London: Penguin, 1991.

Kim, Hyonjin. *The Knight Without the Sword: The Social Landscape of Malorian Chivalry*. Cambridge, England: D. S. Brewer, 2000.

Kindrick, Robert L. "Dynadan and the Code of Chivalry." *Bibliographical Bulletin of the International Arthurian Society* 27 (1975): 232–33.

Kinney, Clare R. "The (Dis)Embodied Hero and the Signs of Manhood in *Sir*

Gawain and the Green Knight." In *Medieval Masculinities: Regarding Men in the Middle Ages,* edited by Clare A. Lees et al., 47–60. Minneapolis: University of Minnesota Press, 1994.

Knight, Stephen. *Arthurian Literature and Society.* New York: St. Martin's Press, 1983.

———. *The Structure of Sir Thomas Malory's Morte d'Arthur.* Sydney: Sydney University Press, 1969.

Krishna, Valerie, ed. *The Alliterative Morte Arthure.* New York: Burt Franklin and Company Publishers, 1976.

Lacan, Jacques. *Feminine Sexuality: Jacques Lacan and the École Freudienne.* Edited by Juliet Mitchell. Translated by Jacqueline Rose. New York: Norton, 1985.

Lacy, Norris J. "The *Mort Artu* and Cyclic Closure." In *The Lancelot-Grail Cycle: Text and Transformations,* edited by William W. Kibler. Austin: University of Texas Press, 1994.

———, gen. ed. *Lancelot-Grail: The Old French Arthurian Vulgate and Post-Vulgate in Translation.* 5 vols. New York: Garland, 1993–1996.

LaFarge, Catherine. "The Hand of the Huntress." In *New Feminist Discourses: Critical Theories on Essays and Texts,* edited by Isobel Armstrong, 263–79. New York: Routledge, 1992.

———. *The Wars of the Roses: History in the Making.* London: Secker and Warburg, 1965.

Lambert, Mark. *Malory: Style and Vision in Le Morte Darthur.* New Haven: Yale University Press, 1975.

Lander, J. R. *Conflict and Stability in Fifteenth Century England.* London: Hutchinson University Library, 1969.

Laȝamon. *Brut.* Edited by G. L Brook and R. F. Leslie. 2 vols. Oxford: Oxford University Press, 1963.

Lazar, Moshe. *Amour courtois et "Fin Amours" dans la littérature du XIIe siècle* (Courtly love and "Fin Amours" in the literature of the twelfth century). Paris: Klincksieck, 1964.

Le Saux, Françoise, ed. *The Text and Tradition of Laȝamon's Brut.* Cambridge, England: D. S. Brewer, 1994.

Lévi-Strauss, Claude. *The Elementary Structures of Kinship.* Boston: Beacon Press, 1969.

Lewis, C. S. "The English Prose *Morte.*" In *Essays on Malory,* edited by J.A.W. Bennett, 7–28. Oxford: Clarendon Press, 1963.

L'Hermite-Leclercq, Pauline. "The Feudal Order." In *A History of Women II: Silences of the Middle Ages,* edited by Christiane Klapisch-Zuber, 202–49. Cambridge: Harvard University Press, 1992.

Loomis, Roger Sherman. "Arthurian Literature on Sport and Spectacle." In *Arthurian Literature in the Middle Ages,* edited by Loomis, 553–59. Oxford: Clarendon Press, 1959.

Looper, Jennifer. "Gender, Genealogy, and the 'Story of the Three Spindles' in the *Queste del Saint Graal.*" *Arthuriana* 8.1 (1998): 49–66.

Löseth, Eilert. *Le Roman en Prose de Tristan, Le roman de Palamède et la compilation de Rusticien de Pise: Analyse critique d'après les manuscrits de Paris.* (The Romance of Tristan in Prose, the Romance of Palomides and the compilation of the hermit of Pisa: Critical analysis based on the Paris manuscripts). Geneva: Slatkine Reprints, 1974.

Love, Nicholas. *The Mirrour of the Blessed Lyf of Jesu Christ: A Critical Edition.* Edited by M. G. Sargent. New York: Garland, 1992.

Lumiansky, R. M., ed. *Malory's Originality: A Critical Study of Le Morte Darthur.* Baltimore: Johns Hopkins Press, 1964.

Lynch, Andrew. "Gesture and Gender in Malory's *Le Morte Darthur.*" In *Arthurian Romance and Gender/Masculin/Feminin dans le roman arthurien médiéval/ Geschlechterrollen in mittelalterlichen Artusroman,* edited by Friedrich Wolfzettel, 285–95. Amsterdam and Atlanta: Rodopi, 1995.

———. *Malory's Book of Arms: The Narrative of Combat in the Morte Darthur.* Cambridge, England: D. S. Brewer, 1997.

Mahoney, Dhira. "'Ar ye a knyght and ar no lovear?': The Chivalry Topos in Malory's *Book of Sir Tristram.*" In *Conjunctures: Medieval Studies in Honor of Douglas Kelly,* edited by Keith Busby and Norris J. Lacy, 311–24. Amsterdam: Rodopi, 1994.

———. "Malory's *Morte Darthur* and the *Alliterative Morte Arthure.*" In *The Study of Chivalry: Resources and Approaches,* edited by Howell Chickering and Thomas H. Seiler, 529–56. Kalamazoo, Mich.: Medieval Institute Publications, 1988.

———. "Malory's *Tale of Sir Gareth* and the Comedy of Class." *Arthurian Yearbook* 1 (1991): 165–81.

———. "Malory's 'Tale of Sir Tristram': Source and Setting Reconsidered." *Medievalia et Humanistica,* n.s., 9 (1979): 175–98. Reprinted in *Tristan and Isolde: A Casebook,* edited by Joan Tasker Grimbert, 223–53. New York: Garland, 1995.

———. "The Truest and Holiest Tale: Malory's transformation of La Queste del Saint Graal." In *Studies in Malory,* edited by James W. Spisak, 109–28. Kalamazoo, Mich.: Medieval Institute Publications, 1985.

Maitland, F. W., and Francis C. Montague. *A Sketch of English Legal History.* New York: G. P. Putnam's Sons, 1915.

Mann, Jill. "Malory and the Grail Legend." In *A Companion to Malory,* edited by Elizabeth Archibald and A.S.G. Edwards, 203–20. Cambridge, England: D. S. Brewer, 1996.

Marchello-Nizia, Christiane. "Amour courtois, société masculine et figures du pouvoir." (Courtly love, masculine society, and figures of power.) *Annales E.S.C.* 36 (1981): 969–82.

Martin, Carol A. N. "Hoel-Hearted Loyalty and the Ironization of Arthur in

Geoffrey of Monmouth's *Historia Regum Brittaniae.*" *Arthuriana* 11.3 (2001): 21–48.

Mason, Eugene. *Wace and Layamon: Arthurian Chronicles.* London: J. M. Dent and Sons, 1912; rep. 1966.

Matarasso, Pauline. *The Redemption of Chivalry: A Study of the Queste del Saint Graal.* Geneva: Droz, 1979.

———, ed. and trans. *The Quest of the Holy Grail.* London: Penguin Books, 1969.

McCarthy, Terence. "Did Morgan le Fay Have a Lover?" *Medium Ævum* 60.2 (1991): 284–89.

———. "*Le Morte Darthur* and Romance." In *Studies in Medieval English Romances*, edited by Derek Brewer, 148–75. Cambridge, England: D. S. Brewer, 1988.

———. "Malory and the Alliterative Tradition." In *Studies in Malory*, edited by James W. Spisak, 53–85. Kalamazoo, Mich.: Medieval Institute Publications, 1985.

———. "Malory and His Sources." In *A Companion to Malory*, edited by Elizabeth Archibald and A.S.G. Edwards, 75–95. Cambridge, England: D. S. Brewer, 1996.

———. "The Sequence of Malory's Tales." In *Aspects of Malory*, edited by Toshiyuki Takamiya and Derek Brewer, 107–24. Cambridge, England: D. S. Brewer, 1981.

McCracken, Peggy. *The Romance of Adultery: Queenship and Sexual Transgression in Old French Literature.* Philadelphia: University of Pennsylvania Press, 1998.

McFarlane, K. B. *England in the Fifteenth Century: Collected Essays of K. B. McFarlane.* London: Duckworth, 1981.

———. *The Nobility of Later Medieval England.* Oxford: Clarendon Press, 1973.

———. "Parliament and 'Bastard Feudalism.'" *Transactions of the Royal Historical Society* 4th series, 26 (1944): 53–73.

McNamara, Jo Ann. "Sexual Equality and the Cult of Virginity in Early Christian Thought." *Feminist Studies* 3 (1976): 145–48.

Meale, Carol. "'The Hoole Book': Editing and the Creation of Meaning in Malory's Text." In *A Companion to Malory*, edited by Elizabeth Archibald and A.S.G. Edwards, 3–18. Cambridge, England: D. S. Brewer, 1996.

Ménard, Philippe, ed. *Le Roman de Tristan en Prose.* (The romance of Tristan in prose.) Geneva: Droz/Textes littéraires français, 1987–.

Micha, Alexandre, ed. *Lancelot: Roman en prose du XIIIe siècle.* (Lancelot: romance in prose from the thirteenth century.) 9 vols. Geneva: Droz, 1980.

Miller, E., and J. Hatcher. *Medieval England: Rural Society and Economic Change.* London: Longman, 1978.

Moi, Toril. *Sexual/Textual Politics: Feminist Literary Theory.* London: Methuen and Company, 1985.

Moorman, Charles. *The Book of Kyng Arthur: The Unity of Malory's Morte Darthur.* Lexington: University of Kentucky Press, 1965.

———. "'The Tale of the Sankgreall': Human Frailty." In *Malory's Originality: A*

Critical Study of the Morte Darthur, edited by R. M. Lumiansky, 184–204. Baltimore: Johns Hopkins Press, 1964.

———. "Literature of Defeat and of Conquest: The Arthurian Revival of the Twelfth Century." In *King Arthur Through the Ages*, edited by Valerie M. Lagorio and Mildred Leake Day, 1:22–43. New York: Garland, 1990.

Morgan, Jeffery L. "Malory's Double Ending: The Duplicitous Death and Departing." In *Sir Thomas Malory: Views and Reviews*, edited by D. Thomas Hanks, Jr., 91–106. New York: AMS Press, 1992.

Morris, Rosemary. "Uther and Igerne: A Study in Uncourtly Love." In *Arthurian Literature IV*, edited by Richard Barber, 70–92. Woodbridge, England: D. S. Brewer, 1985.

Morse, Ruth. "Back to the Future: Malory's Genres." *Arthuriana* 7.3 (1997): 100–123.

———. "Sterile Queens and Questing Orphans." *Quondam et Futurus*. 2.2 (1991): 41–53.

Morton, A. L. "The Matter of Britain: The Arthurian Cycle and the Development of Feudal Society." *Zeitschrift für Anglistik und Amerikanistik* 8 (1960): 5–28.

Newman, Barabara. *From Virile Woman to WomanChrist: Studies in Medieval Religion and Literature*. Philadelphia: University of Pennsylvania Press, 1995.

Nickel, Helmut. "The Tournament: An Historical Sketch." In *The Study of Chivalry: Resources and Approaches*, edited by Howell Chickering and Thomas H. Seiler, 213–62. Kalamazoo, Mich.: Medieval Institute Publications, 1988.

Nitze, William A., and T. Atkinson Jenkins, eds. *Le Haut Livre du Graal Perlesvaus.* (The High Book of Perceval and the Grail.) Chicago: University of Chicago Press, 1932.

Noble, James. "Laʒamon's 'Ambivalence' Reconsidered." In *The Text and Tradition of Laʒamon's Brut*, edited by Françoise Le Saux, 171–82. Cambridge, England: D. S. Brewer, 1994.

Nolan, Barbara. "*The Tale of Sir Gareth* and *The Tale of Sir Launcelot*." In *A Companion to Malory*, edited by Elizabeth Archibald and A.S.G. Edwards, 153–82. Cambridge, England: D. S. Brewer, 1996.

Paris, Gaston, and Jacob Ulrich, eds. *Merlin, roman en prose du XIIIeme siècle.* (Merlin: romance in prose from the thirteenth century.) Paris: Société des Anciens Textes Français, 1886.

Patterson, Lee. *Negotiating the Past: The Historical Understanding of Medieval Literature*. Madison: University of Wisconsin Press, 1987.

Pauphilet, Albert. *Études sur la Queste del Saint Graal.* (Studies on the *Queste del Saint Graal.*) 1921; Paris: H. Champion, 1980.

———, ed. *La Queste del Saint Graal: Roman du XIIIeme Siècle.* (*La Queste del Saint Graal:* a thirteenth-century romance.) Paris: Editions Champion, 1984.

Payling, Simon. *Political Society in Lancastrian England: The Greater Gentry of Nottinghamshire*. Oxford: Clarendon Press, 1991.

Pickens, Rupert T. "Arthur's Channel Crossing: Courtesy and the Demonic in Geoffrey of Monmouth and Wace's *Brut.*" *Arthuriana* 7.3 (1997): 3–19.

Pickford, Cedric. *L'Évolution du roman arthurien en prose vers la fin du moyen âge d'après le manuscrit 112 du fonds français de la Bibliothèque Nationale.* (The evolution of the Arthurian romance in prose from the end of the Middle Ages, as recorded in manuscript 112 of the French Bibliothèque Nationale.) Paris: Nizet, 1960.

Plummer, John. "The Quest for Significance in *La Queste del Saint Graal* and Malory's *Tale of the Sankgreal.*" In *Continuations: Essays on Medieval French Literature and Language in Honor of John L. Grigsby,* edited by Norris J. Lacy and Gloria Torrini-Roblin, 107–20. Birmingham, Ala.: Summa Publications, 1989.

Pochoda, Elizabeth. *Arthurian Propaganda: Le Morte Darthur as an Historical Ideal of Life.* Chapel Hill: University of North Carolina Press, 1971.

Postan, M. M. *The Medieval Economy and Society.* London: Pelican, 1986.

Putter, Ad. "Tranvestite Knights in Medieval Life and Literature." In *Becoming Male in the Middle Ages,* edited by Jeffrey Jerome Cohen and Bonnie Wheeler, 279–302. New York: Garland, 2000.

Reynolds, Susan. *Fiefs and Vassals: The Medieval Evidence Reinterpreted.* Oxford: Clarendon Press, 1994.

Richmond, Colin. *The Paston Family in the Fifteenth Century: Volume 1, The First Phase.* Cambridge: Cambridge University Press, 1990.

———. *The Paston Family in the Fifteenth Century: Volume 2, Fastolf's Will.* Cambridge: Cambridge University Press, 1996.

———. *The Paston Family in the Fifteenth Century: Endings.* Manchester, U.K.: Manchester University Press, 2001.

Riddy, Felicity. "Contextualizing the *Morte Darthur:* Empire and Civil War." In *A Companion to Malory,* edited by Elizabeth Archibald and A.S.G. Edwards, 55–74. Cambridge, England: D. S. Brewer, 1996.

———. *Sir Thomas Malory.* Leiden, Holland: Brill, 1987.

Riviere, Joan. "Womanliness as Masquerade." *International Journal of Psycho-analysis* 10 (1929): 201–20.

Rubin, Gayle. "The Traffic in Women: Notes on the 'Political Economy' of Sex." In *Toward an Anthology of Women,* edited by Rayna Reiter, 157–210. New York: Monthly Review Press, 1975. Reprinted in *The Second Wave: A Reader in Feminist Theory,* edited by Linda Nicholson, 27–62. New York and London: Routledge, 1997.

Rubin, Miri. *Charity and Community in Medieval Cambridge.* Cambridge: Cambridge University Press, 1987.

Rumble, Thomas C. "'The Tale of Tristram': Development by Analogy." In *Malory's Originality: A Critical Study of "Le Morte Darthur,"* edited by R. M. Lumiansky, 118–83. Baltimore: Johns Hopkins Press, 1964.

Salda, Michael N. "Reconsidering Vinaver's Sources for Malory's 'Tristram.'" *Modern Philology* (1991): 373–81.

Saul, Nigel. *Knights and Esquires: The Gloucestershire Gentre in the Fourteenth Century.* Oxford: Oxford University Press, 1981.

Saunders, Corinne. "Malory's *Book of Huntynge:* The Tristram Section of the *Morte Darthur.*" *Medium Ævum* 62.2 (1993): 270–84.

Schmolke-Hasselmann, Beate. "The Round Table: Ideal, Fiction, Reality." In *Arthurian Literature II,* edited by Richard Barber, 41–75. Cambridge, England: D. S. Brewer, 1983.

Schofield, William Henry. *English Literature from the Norman Conquest to Chaucer.* New York: The Macmillan Company, 1906.

Schueler, Donald G. "The Tristram Section of Malory's *Morte Darthur.*" *Studies in Philology* 65 (1968): 51–66.

Sedgwick, Eve Kosofsky. *Between Men: English Literature and Homosocial Desire.* New York: Columbia University Press, 1985.

Shichtman, Martin B. "Percival's Sister: Genealogy, Virginity, and Blood." *Arthuriana* 9.2 (1999): 11–20.

———. "Politicizing the Ineffable: The *Queste del Saint Graal* and Malory's 'Tale of the Sankgreal.'" In *Culture and the King: The Social Implications of the Arthurian Legend,* edited by Martin B. Shichtman and James P. Carley, 163–79. Albany: State University of New York Press, 1994.

Shichtman, Martin B., and James P. Carley, eds. *Culture and the King: The Social Implications of the Arthurian Legend.* Albany: State University of New York Press, 1994.

Sklar, Elizabeth. "The Undoing of Romance in Malory's *Morte Darthur.*" *Fifteenth Century Studies* 20 (1993): 309–27.

Smith, Patrick Coogan, ed. *Les Enchantemenz de Bretaigne: An Extract from a Thirteenth Century Prose Romance La Suite du Merlin.* Chapel Hill: University of North Carolina Department of Romance Languages, 1977.

Sommer, H. Oskar, ed. *The Vulgate Version of the Arthurian Romances.* 7 vols. Washington, D.C.: The Carnegie Institute, 1908–16.

Spisak, James W., ed. *Caxton's Malory: A New Edition of Sir Thomas Malory's Le Morte Darthur Based on the Pierpont Morgan Copy of William Caxton's Edition of 1485.* Berkeley and Los Angeles: University of California Press, 1983.

———. *Studies in Malory.* Kalamazoo, Mich.: Medieval Institute Publications, 1985

Squibb, G. D. *The High Court of Chivalry: A Study of the Civil Law in England.* Oxford: Clarendon Press, 1959.

Sturges, Robert S. *Chaucer's Pardoner and Gender Theory.* New York: Palgrave, 2000.

Takamiya, Toshiyuki, and Derek Brewer, eds. *Aspects of Malory.* Cambridge, England: D. S. Brewer, 1981.

Thornton, Ginger, and Krista May. "Malory as Feminist? The Role of Percival's Sister in the Grail Quest." In *Sir Thomas Malory: Views and Reviews*, edited by D. Thomas Hanks, Jr., 43–53. New York: AMS Press, 1992.

Vale, Juliet. *Edward III and Chivalry: Chivalric Society and Its Context, 1270–1350.* Woodbridge, England: Boydell Press, 1982.

Vale, Malcolm. "Aristocratic Violence: Trial by Battle in the Later Middle Ages." In *Violence in Medieval Society*, edited by Richard W. Kaueper, 159–82. Woodbridge, England: Boydell Press, 2000.

———. *War and Chivalry: Warfare and Aristocratic Culture in England, France, and Burgundy at the End of the Middle Ages.* London: Duckworth, 1981.

Vinaver, Eugène. *Le Roman de Tristan et Iseut dans l'oeuvre de Thomas Malory.* (The Romance of Tristan and Iseult in the works of Thomas Malory.) Paris: H. Champion, 1925.

———, ed. *The Works of Sir Thomas Malory.* 3 vols. 3rd edition. Revised P.J.C. Field. Oxford: Clarendon Press, 1990.

Wack, Mary. *Lovesickness in the Middle Ages: The "Viaticum" and Its Commentaries.* Philadelphia: University of Pennsylvania Press, 1990.

Walsh, John Michael. "Malory's 'Very Mater of La Cheualer du Charyot': Characterization and Structure." In *Studies in Malory*, edited by James W. Spisak, 199–226. Kalamazoo, Mich.: Medieval Institute Publications, 1985.

Warren, Michelle R. *History on the Edge: Excalibur and the Borders of Britain 1100–1300.* Minneapolis: University of Minnesota Press, 2000.

Wheeler, Bonnie. "'The Prowess of Hands': The Psychology of Alchemy in Malory's 'Tale of Sir Gareth.'" In *Culture and the King: The Social Implications of the Arthurian Legend*, edited by Martin B. Shichtman and James P. Carley, 180–95. Albany: State University of New York Press, 1994.

Wheeler, Bonnie, Robert L. Kindrick, and Michael N. Salda, eds. *The Malory Debate: Essays on the Texts of Le Morte Darthur.* Cambridge, England: D. S. Brewer, 2000.

Wiethaus, Ulrike. "In Search of Medieval Women's Friendships: Hildegard of Bingen's Letters to her Female Contemporaries." In *Maps of Flesh and Light: The Religious Experience of Medieval Women Mystics*, edited by Wiethaus, 93–111. Syracuse: Syracuse University Press, 1993.

Wilson, R.H. *Characterization in Malory: A Comparison with His Sources.* Chicago: University of Chicago Libraries, 1934.

———. "The 'Fair Unknown' in Malory." *PMLA* 58 (1943): 1–21.

Wilson-Okamura, David Scott. "Adultery and the Fall of Logres in the Post-Vulgate *Suite du Merlin*." *Arthuriana* 7.4 (1997): 16–46.

Wright, Neil. "Angles and Saxons in Laȝamon's *Brut*: A Reassessment." In *The Text and Tradition of Laȝamon's Brut*, edited by Françoise Le Saux, 161–70. Cambridge, England: D. S. Brewer, 1994.

———, ed. *Historia Regum Brittaniae of Geoffrey of Monmouth I: Bern, Burgerbibliothek, MS. 568.* Cambridge, England: D. S. Brewer, 1984.

Wright, Thomas L. "On the Genesis of Malory's 'Gareth.'" *Speculum* 57 (1982): 569–82.

———. "'The Tale of King Arthur': Beginnings and Foreshadowings." In *Malory's Originality: A Critical Study of Le Morte Darthur,* edited by R. M. Lumiansky, 9–66. Baltimore: Johns Hopkins Press, 1964.

York, Ernest C. "Legal Punishment in Malory's *Morte Darthur.*" *English Language Notes* 11 (1973): 14–21.

Žižek, Slavoj. *The Sublime Object of Ideology.* London: Verso, 1989.

Index

Dorsey Armstrong is assistant professor of medieval literature at Purdue University. She is currently working on a book about William Caxton and late medieval English society.